W9-BCL-336

MILTON STUDIES
# XVIII

EDITORIAL BOARD

Mario Di Cesare  Barbara Lewalski
Stanley Fish  William G. Madsen
Michael Fixler  Louis L. Martz
O. B. Hardison, Jr.  John M. Steadman
Robert B. Hinman  Arnold Stein
Thomas Kranidas  Kathleen M. Swaim
Marcia Landy  Philip K. Wion
Joseph A. Wittreich, Jr.

GRACE LIBRARY, CARLOW COLLEGE
PITTSBURGH, Pa. 15213

# MILTON STUDIES

# XVIII ❦ Edited by

# James D. Simmonds

UNIVERSITY OF PITTSBURGH PRESS

PR
3579
M5
v. 18

CATALOGUED

# MILTON STUDIES

is published annually by the University of Pittsburgh Press as a forum for Milton scholarship and criticism. Articles submitted for publication may be biographical; they may interpret some aspect of Milton's writings; or they may define literary, intellectual, or historical contexts — by studying the work of his contemporaries, the traditions which affected his thought and art, contemporary political and religious movements, his influence on other writers, or the history of critical response to his work.

Manuscripts should be upwards of 3,000 words in length and should conform to the MLA *Style Sheet.* Manuscripts and editorial correspondence should be addressed to James D. Simmonds. Department of English. University of Pittsburgh, Pa. 15260.

*Milton Studies* does not review books.

Within the United States, *Milton Studies* may be ordered from the University of Pittsburgh Press, Pittsburgh, Pa. 15260.

Overseas orders should be addressed to Feffer and Simons, Inc., 100 Park Avenue, New York, N.Y. 10017, U.S.A.

Library of Congress Catalog Card Number 69-12335

ISBN 0-8229-3484-1

US ISSN 0076-8820

Published by the University of Pittsburgh Press, Pittsburgh, Pa. 15260

Copyright © 1983, University of Pittsburgh Press

All rights reserved

Feffer & Simons, Inc., London

Manufactured in the United States of America

# CONTENTS

vi                              *Contents*

MILTON STUDIES
# XVIII

# "AND BY OCCASION FORETELLS":
# THE PROPHETIC VOICE IN *LYCIDAS*

## *John C. Ulreich, Jr.*

In this monody the author bewails a learned friend. . . . And by occasion foretells the ruin of our corrupted clergy then in their height.

I N  T H E  epigraph which Milton added to the 1645 edition of *Lycidas*,
when events had fulfilled his dire foreboding, the poet seems to echo
the Revelation to St. John, "which God gave him, to show unto his servants things which must shortly come to pass" (i, 1).[1] As Joseph Wittreich
observes, "Through its references to drowning at sea and to the corrupt
clergy, [the] epigraph points to the Book of Revelation, establishing it
as *Lycidas*'s primary context."[2] Milton's claim to prophetic inspiration
further serves to emphasize the way in which his pastoral elegy transforms the historical occasion of Edward King's death into a prophetic
moment—"that critical juncture when the prophetic order of history is
revealed."[3] Indeed, the epigraph identifies the moment of transformation itself, St. Peter's ecclesiastical satire. The present ruin of the clergy,
*then* in the height of spiritual corruption, ironically foreshadows the resurrection of Lycidas, *then* "sunk low," but *now* "mounted high" (172).[4]
Irradiated by St. Peter's vision of judgment, the death and rebirth of Edward King becomes a figure for the Resurrection of Christ, by which all
of history is prophetically redeemed.

In the light of Milton's epigraph, the historical occasion of *Lycidas*
would appear to be (at least) threefold: the death of King, the ruin of
the clergy, and the monody itself, in which those other occasions are
memorialized. Each of these occasions implies a radical transformation:
from death to eternal life, from corruption to incorruption, from the scenic
"shade[s] and rill[s]" (24) of pastoral to the "other groves, and other
streams" (174) of prophetic vision. Each of these transformations invites
investigation; on this occasion, however, I wish to direct attention primarily to St. Peter's dirge, as the occasion, or downfall, which most fully
and immediately reflects the transformation of history into prophecy. For
it is here, I believe, in the harsh accents of Peter's ecclesiastical satire,

3

that the specifically prophetic development of *Lycidas* is most fully articulated, as a typological progress in which shadowy pagan types of judgment are clarified by the sure word of Hebrew prophecy and finally fulfilled in the antitype of Revelation.[5]

When we seek to explore the visionary implications of St. Peter's satire, as a transformation of history *then* into prophecy *now*, it seems appropriate to consider the scriptural sources of that vision — not only in Revelation itself, whose bearing on *Lycidas* has been rather thoroughly examined, but in the letters of St. Peter, which have been largely neglected.[6] Indeed, given Milton's explicit reference to "The Pilot of the *Galilean* lake" (104), it seems not unreasonable to wonder whether a number of scriptural allusions in *Lycidas* might not be traced to the two "pastoral" epistles of St. Peter.[7] As it happens, *Lycidas* contains a number of probable allusions to Peter's letters, all of which contribute materially to our understanding of Milton's elegy. And this confirmation invites the further speculation that Milton may have known, and made use of, certain apocryphal traditions associated with the figure of Peter, especially the pseudepigraphical *Acts of Peter*.[8]

The question of sources, however, is only preliminary to the more fundamental question of context. As Wittreich has shown, "The Book of Revelation . . . is both *a* context and *the* model, a generic analogue, for *Lycidas*."[9] In the same way, I believe, the letters of Peter are both *a* context and *the* model for St. Peter's "prophetic invective." As a context for St. Peter's ecclesiastical satire, the Petrine epistles share with it, and with *Lycidas* as a whole, the crucial theme of Christian vocation, which they also embody in a pastoral metaphor: "When the chief shepherd shall appear, ye shall receive a crown of glory that fadeth not away" (1 Pet. v, 4). Peter's letters also share with *Lycidas* a common prophetic vision of the end, of the dread engine of the Apocalypse "that is ready to judge the quick and the dead" (1, iv, 5). That being the case, the prophecy of 1 Peter, that "the *end* of all things is at hand" (iv, 7), together with its reinterpretation in 2 Peter, as the *beginning* of "new heavens and a new earth, wherein dwelleth righteousness" (iii, 13), constitutes an essential context for interpreting the prophetic moment of *Lycidas*. Milton uses the New Testament text, not only as a source of specific verbal allusions throughout the elegy, but as a basis for its prophetic structure, and by this means he articulates the transformation of pagan into Christian pastoral, which, as Wittreich observes, is also "the transformation of pastoral into prophecy."[10] St. Peter's invective against the clergy makes this transformation explicit: it redefines the conventional imagery of pastoral by infusing that imagery, typologically, with the prophetic spirit of the Old Testament.

As a consequence, not only the Petrine epistles, but the figure of Peter himself, as he appears in the Gospels and in Acts, becomes a crucial context for *Lycidas*. For as Milton suggests in *The Christian Doctrine*, the Apostle Peter is a type of "particular repentance," whose fall from grace and subsequent redemption testifies that "eternal salvation was through Christ alone." As this testimony is focused by Peter's prophetic oracle, the "apostle of the circumcised" becomes both a type of judgment under the Old Law and, as circumcision foreshadows the sacrament of baptism, a type of salvation in Christ.[11]

## I

The new Testament text most often cited as a source for St. Peter's speech is of course St. John's parable of Christ as "the good shepherd" (John x, 14). John's "He that entereth not by the door into the sheepfold, but climbeth up some other way" (x, 1) is the obvious source for Milton's corrupt clergy, who "Creep and intrude, and climb into the fold" (115). John's condemnation of the hireling shepherd, who "seeth the wolf coming, and leaveth the sheep, and fleeth: and the wolf catcheth them, and scattereth the sheep" (x, 12), obviously stands behind Milton's image of "the grim wolf with privy paw" who "Daily devours apace" (128–29). And John's vision of Christ as "the door of the sheep" (x, 7) bears directly on Milton's vision of that dread "engine at the door" (130).

As it happens, however, the epistles of Peter contain a number of similar echoes, generally overlooked by previous scholarship, some of which may contribute significantly to our understanding of *Lycidas*. And because their influence has been largely overlooked, I wish now to concentrate on them, to suggest, if possible, some of their hitherto unapprehended relationships to Milton's elegy. Though not obviously pastoral in the fashion of John's gospel, the letters of Peter are nonetheless deeply imbued with the pastoral spirit. In 1 Peter, the salvation of the elect is adumbrated in a parable: "ye were as sheep going astray; but are now returned unto the Shepherd and Bishop of your souls" (ii, 25). The redemptive implications of this figure are sharply focused by the image of Christ as "a lamb without blemish and without spot" (i, 19). It is essentially through this pastoral (and paschal) metaphor that Christians become "partakers of Christ's sufferings" (iv, 13), rejoicing in the affliction which they endure for his sake. The primary theme of 1 Peter is the nature of Christian vocation — the moral and spiritual obligation of those who are called to belief in Christ. The crucial metaphor for that vocation is again pastoral: "Feed the flock of God" (v, 2). This image of the pastoral office (which is barely hinted in John's parable) is obviously crucial to the most scathing ironies of Milton's satire, Peter's contempt for those "Blind mouths" (119) who care only "for their bellies" (114), and his compassion for "the hungry sheep" who "are not fed" (125).

The bestial depravity of those who deny spiritual nourishment to the flock, who pervert wholesome doctrine to satisfy their own corrupt appetites, is made explicit in 2 Peter. Those who deliberately falsify truth, who "walk after the flesh in the lust of uncleanness" (2, ii, 10) are "as natural brute beasts, made to be taken and destroyed"; they "speak evil of the things that they understand not; and [so they] shall utterly perish in their own corruption" (ii, 12). "What recks it them? What need they? They are sped" (122). They are indeed "satisfied" because their "swift destruction" (ii, 1) is properly and inevitably "the reward of [their] unrighteousness" (ii, 13). "And many shall follow their pernicious ways" (ii, 2). So, like the hungry sheep whom they have betrayed, the faithless shepherds "Rot inwardly, and foul contagion spread" (127).

The general thematic affinity between *Lycidas* and the epistles of Peter is reinforced by a network of specific verbal allusions, both within Peter's speech and elsewhere in the elegy. Milton's image of those who "scramble at the shearer's feast" (117), for example, with its oblique reference to Communion, echoes 2 Peter's condemnation of those "false teachers" (ii, 1) who are "*sporting* themselves with their own deceivings while they *feast* with you" (ii, 13). Those faithless shepherds who "shove away the worthy bidden guest," Milton explains in *An Apology for Smectymnuus*, are false prophets, who "chase away all the faithful Shepheards of the flocke" (YP I, 952). "Daring, self-willed, they tremble not to rail at dignities" (2 Pet. ii, 10). And Milton's "grim wolf with privy paw" recalls those same "false teachers . . . who *privily* . . . bring in damnable heresies" (ii, 1).[12] The voracity of Milton's wolf, who "Daily *devours* apace" (129), may also recall 1 Peter's image of the devil "as a roaring lion," who "walketh about, seeking whom he may *devour*" (v, 8). This allusion is rendered still more probable by a passage in the *Acts of Peter* which simultaneously identifies the ravenous beast as a wolf (rather than a lion) and associates it explicitly not only with the devil but with his emissary, Simon Magus, whom Peter calls "the ravening wolf, the devourer and scatterer of eternal life."[13]

The identification of the ravening wolf with false prophets, who are "like brute beasts" (2 Pet. ii, 12), is confirmed by frequent passages in Milton's prose. In *Animadversions* he weaves together the themes of simony and false prophecy, of self-serving lust which ravishes those whom it ought to nurture: faithless shepherds "have fed themselves, and not their flocks. . . . They have fed his sheep (contrary to that which Saint *Peter* writes) . . . not of a ready mind, but for filthy lucre, not as examples to the flock, but as being Lords over Gods heritage" (YP I, 726–27).[14] *The History of Britain* enlarges upon this twofold theme: "subtle Prowlers, Pastors in Name, but indeed Wolves; intent upon all occasions, not to feed the Flock, but to pamper and well line themselves: not call'd, but seising on the Ministry as a Trade [simony], not as a Spiritual Charge: teaching the people, not by sound Doctrine, but by evil example [Simony]: usurping the Chair of *Peter* . . . they stumble upon the Seat of *Judas*" (YP V, i, 175).

In *Lycidas* Milton weaves an even more complex pattern of scriptural allusion, fusing the themes of false prophecy and spiritual hunger into a single apocalyptic image of corruption: "The hungry sheep look up, and are not fed" (125).[15] Behind the parable, of course, stands not only Peter's condemnation of "false prophets," who are "insatiable for sin" (2 Pet. ii, 1, 14),[16] but Paul's warning to the Ephesians: "I know that after my departing grievous wolves shall enter in among you, not sparing the flock" (Acts xx, 29). And behind Peter and Paul stands the Word himself: "Beware of false prophets, who come to you in sheep's clothing, but *inwardly* are ravening wolves" (Matt. vii, 15; emphasis added). Such false prophets, Milton argues in *Defensio Secunda*, should be called "Sheep, rather than shepherds," for "they are fed more than they feed" (YP IV, i, 650). They are, in fact, "grievous Wolves" (*PL* XII, 508), who supplant truth with falsehood, "hireling wolves whose Gospel is their maw" (Son. XVI, 14). In *Of Reformation* they are identified as "*Wolves*, that wait and thinke long till they devoure thy tender Flock" (I, 614). Being pastured on lies, "the hungry Sheep . . . not fed . . . Rot *inwardly*" (125–27).

The theme of false prophecy is further elaborated by images of vanity and blindness, and these images, too, are drawn from 2 Peter's apocalyptic vision. Milton's image of sheep "*swoll'n* with wind, and . . . rank *mist*" (126) contains a twofold echo of 2 Peter, which castigates the false teachers of heresy as "wells without water . . . to whom the *mist* of darkness is reserved for ever. For . . . they speak great *swelling* words of vanity" (ii, 17–18; emphases added).

The text of 2 Peter also illuminates the voracious blindness of Milton's shepherds. Those who add "to faith virtue: and to virtue knowledge" (i, 5), who add

> Deeds to . . . knowledge answerable, add faith,
> Add virtue, patience, temperance, add love,
> By name to come called Charity, the soul
> Of all the rest,                    (*PL* XII, 582–85)

they "*shall* neither *be* barren nor unfruitful in the knowledge of our Lord Jesus Christ. But he that lacketh these things is blind, and cannot see afar off" (i, 8–9) — cannot see past the shadow cast by his own lust.[17] And one who has been called to the pastoral office, and who has corrupted that vocation, has lost sight of the very good which he had been especially chosen to nurture; he has deliberately "forgotten that he was purged from his old sins" (i, 9). Furthermore, the catechretic voracity of that blindness is powerfully suggested by 2 Peter: "Blind mouths" (119) are those who "have eyes full of adultery, *insatiable* for sin" (RSV ii, 14). Their hunger is insatiable because they are "the servants of corruption" (ii, 19); their blindness is perpetual because they "cannot cease from sin" (ii, 14). Peter assures us that such false prophets "shall receive the reward of [their] unrighteousness" because they "shall utterly perish in their own corruption" (ii, 13, 12). "Through the blindness of their own worldly lusts," Milton affirms in *The History of Britain*, those who "have preach't thir own bellies, rather then the gospel," shall be led "to a fearful condemnation doutless by thir owne mouthes" (YP V, i, 175, 449, 447). Like the sheep upon whom they feed, these false pastors will rot *inwardly*.

## II

Taken individually, of course, none of the foregoing allusions is either sufficiently close in its form of words or sufficiently distinctive in its imagery to constitute unambiguous evidence that the letters of Peter are an explicit source for Peter's speech in *Lycidas*. Taken collectively, however, these allusions strongly suggest that the New Testament texts are a vital context for Milton's elegy, an essential source of its imaginative life. At the same time, as Wittreich has shown, "What the Old Testament is to the Apocalypse the pastoral tradition is to *Lycidas*," so that "the Book of Revelation" becomes also a "model, a generic analogue, for *Lycidas*." In the same way, I would suggest, the epistles of Peter are a model for St. Peter's prophetic oracle in *Lycidas*, which reinterprets scripture "in the light of a new prophetic moment," the ruin of *our* corrupted clergy. St. Peter's speech is "a perfect judgment oracle, beginning with an indictment and concluding with a sentence": Those who "Creep and intrude and climb into the fold" and "shove away the worthy bidden guest" will be met with judgment: "that two-handed engine at the door / Stands ready to smite once, and smite no more" (115, 118, 130–31), "For the time *is come* that judgment must begin at the house of God" (1 Pet. iv, 17). And as a judgment oracle, St. Peter's invective against the clergy is "the prophetic center of *Lycidas*," a "prophecy within a larger prophecy, a focusing and an expression of what the poem is."[18] Just as 2 Peter reinterprets 1 Peter's vision of judgment—"the end of all things . . . at hand" (iv, 7)—in the light of a new prophetic moment, "new heavens and a new earth, wherein dwelleth righteousness" (iii, 13), so the resurrection of Lycidas, then "sunk low, but [now] mounted high" (172) transforms Peter's "two-handed engine" of judgment (130), which stands "ready to judge the quick and the dead" (1 Pet. iv, 5), into a parable of redemption, "according to his promise" (2, iii, 13): "So *Lycidas*, . . . Through the dear might of him that walk'd the waves," will become "the Genius of the shore" and will be "good / To all that wander in that perilous flood" (172–73, 183–85).

This suggestion is borne out by other allusions, found elsewhere at crucial points in the elegy. I shall at present concern myself with three of these. One, concerning the figure of Baptism, is general rather than specific, but it bears directly on Lycidas' crucial metamorphosis into a "Genius of the shore" (183). The second, touching on the nature of true fame, is more specific in its verbal reference and not less suggestive in its figurative relevance. The third allusion, which virtually manifests the apotheosis of Lycidas as a son of God, is both uniquely specific and absolutely comprehensive; so far as the question of source is concerned, it seems to me conclusive.

The general relevance of Baptism to a poem about death by drowning scarcely needs to be argued at length, but the precise significance of the figure may be more difficult to discern. To say that someone who has literally drowned has been figuratively, or spiritually, purified by the waters of Baptism would strike most of us as a grotesque conceit. It simply will not answer to the emotional intensity with which Milton envisages Lycidas visiting "the bottom of the monstrous world" (158). One might say, however, that one truly baptized, not merely physically, by "putting away the filth of the flesh," but spiritually, by "the answer of a good conscience toward God," and so "by the resurrection of Jesus Christ" (1 Pet. iii, 21), had actually undergone a spiritual death and rebirth. It is in these terms that Milton's *Christian Doctrine* interprets the sacrament of Baptism, wherein "the bodies of believers . . . are immersed in running water . . . to signify our union with Christ through his death, burial and resurrection" (*CD* I, xxviii; YP, VI, 544). And these are also the terms in which Peter interprets the significance of Baptism: it redeems man from sin and death, not merely by cleansing him from corruption, morally, but by uniting him, spiritually, with Christ, in his death and resurrection. By means of such suffering, Christians become "partakers of Christ's sufferings" (iv, 13). That the Apostle does indeed regard Baptism as a form of suffering becomes clear from the context: "for he that hath suffered in the flesh hath ceased from sin" (iv, 1). Peter likens the effect of Baptism to the salvation of Noah and his family "*by* water" (iii, 20). The preposition is curious, inasmuch as we should expect salvation *from* the waters of the flood. Yet the Greek is unambiguous: δι' ὕδατος means "through (the agency of) water." And that would seem to be Peter's paradoxical point: the few faithful in Noah's time were saved, not *from* the cataclysm, but *by* the waters which cleansed their world of its irremediable corruption. And it is on this account that death by drowning becomes an image of salvation.

Some of the implications of this figure are drawn out by 2 Peter. 1 Peter implicitly likens the waters of the flood to a "fiery trial" of suffering which is to purify the elect. The point at which these apparently incongruous images intersect is "the end of all things" (iv, 7). 2 Peter explicitly contrasts these images of ruin and makes their juxtaposition the basis for its vision of the end. In his condemnation of the "false teachers" (ii, 1), Peter recalls that God "spared not the old world" when he brought "in the flood upon the world of the ungodly" (ii, 5). A little later, when he turns to contemplate the end of creation itself, he juxtaposes images of flood and conflagration: "by the word of God the heavens were of old, and the earth standing out of the water and in the water: Whereby the world that then was, being overflowed with water, perished: But the heavens and the earth, which are now, by the same word are kept in store, reserved unto fire against the day of judgment and perdition of ungodly men. . . . wherein the heavens being on fire shall be dissolved, and the elements shall melt with fervent heat. Nevertheless we, according to his promise, look for new heavens and a new earth, wherein dwelleth righteousness" (iii, 5–7, 13). So also Lycidas, whose death by drowning symbolizes the death of the old world, the end of pastoral innocence, and whose fiery rebirth, flaming "in the forehead of the morning sky" (171), foreshadows a new heaven and a new earth, where he shall eternally enjoy "other groves, and other streams" (174). To those who remain in this world, bound for a time to "wander in that perilous flood" (185), Lycidas, "the Genius of the shore," has become a sign — like Baptism, a figure of possible salvation.

To enjoy the fruits of that salvation, however, fallen man must confront his own mortality, and the severe limitations which death places even upon the most spiritual of his strivings. In his anguish, the uncouth swain asks:

> Alas! What boots it with uncessant care
> . . . . . . . . .
> To scorn delights, and live laborious days [?]

[Since] the fair guerdon when we hope to find,
And think to burst out into sudden blaze,
Comes the blind Fury with th'abhorred shears,
And slits the thin-spun life.                    (64, 72–76)

The answer which the swain receives to this question is not altogether satisfactory: "in heaven expect thy meed" (84). But that is precisely the point of my second alusion.

Phoebus Apollo tells the swain that true fame

> is no plant that grows on mortal soul,
> . . . . . . . . .
> But lives and spreads aloft by those pure eyes,
> And perfect witness of all-judging Jove.        (78, 81–82)

1 Peter uses similar imagery to adumbrate the dichotomy between mortal and immortal, perishable and imperishable. Those who believe in "the resurrection of Jesus Christ" (i, 3) are "born again, not of corruptible seed, but of incorruptible. . . . For all flesh *is* as grass, and all the glory of man as the flower of grass. The grass withereth, and the flower therof falleth away: But the word of the Lord endureth for ever" (i, 23, 24–25). "As he pronounces lastly on each deed, / Of so much fame in heaven expect thy meed" (83–84). "And when the chief Shepherd shall appear, ye shall receive a crown of glory that fadeth not away" (v, 4). As Rosemond Tuve has wisely observed: "It is a perfect instance of subtle literary judgement that Milton did not phrase this [oracle], as he might have done, in the imagery of . . . 1 Peter. He saved for his second great answer the overtly Christian terms of St. Peter's speech, by which time the sudden blaze and clear light of unequivocal terms is wanted. This is not a matter of 'Christian' and 'pagan' but of direction and indirection, of a less or a more figurative functioning in the language. Both are Christian."[19]

In *Lycidas*, as in 1 Peter, the image of an incorruptible florescence is employed structurally, to incarnate the theme of resurrection. Peter repeatedly and emphatically juxtaposes the two possible spiritual conditions of mankind: those who believe in Christ, and who remain steadfast in their faith, are called "to an inheritance *in*corruptible, and *un*defiled, and that fadeth *not* away" (i, 4). Peter's fundamental opposition between life and death finds its natural expression in a highly antithetical style: "ye are a chosen generation . . . which in time past *were* not a people, but *are* now the people of God: which had not obtained mercy, but now have obtained mercy" (ii, 9). Milton's juxtaposition of frail mortality with immortal life is generally thematic rather than rhetorical, implied rather than explicit, but the dichotomy is no less emphatic, and at certain crucial points it is made explicit—as it is in Phoebus' speech, and again when Peter compares his faithful (121) swain with "such as . . . scarce themselves know how to hold / A sheep-hook" (119–20). His rhetorical question, "What recks it them?" (122), echoes the uncouth swain's earlier complaint, "What boots it?" (64), and the implied answer is even more emphatic than Apollo's explicit one. Once again the line is drawn, this time more emphatically and irrevocably, between those who seek their only good in this world, their own good, by which they are *sped*, and those who seek some good beyond themselves, who may at least hope "to burst out into sudden blaze" (74). What Apollo offers the swain, implicitly, is not the "sudden blaze" of mortal fame but the hope of true immortality.

The image which Milton uses to signify that hope embodies his final, and in my view, conclusive, allusion to Peter's epistles:

> So sinks the *day-star* in the ocean bed,
> And yet anon *repairs* his drooping head,
> And tricks his beams, and with *new spangled* ore,
> *Flames* in the forehead of the morning sky.　　　(168–71)

This culminating image of the Resurrection, this triumphant assertion that Lycidas lives, not in spite of but because of his confrontation with death, contains two crucial allusions to Peter's second epistle. The way in which Milton's metaphor associates the sun's "beams" with "new spangled ore" suggests that the sun's rays have been purified by their temporary extinction. Gold, in this context, is not merely decorative, as if set off in "glistering foil" (79); it has been newly refined from its ore, so that it flames rather than merely glistens. Accordingly, the sun does not merely return—repairing, as it were, to its wonted place—it is repaired; its renewed lustre is not merely apparent, because it is actually restored. The lineaments of this metallurgic transformation—and the paradox which distinguishes the sun's apparent from its actual radiance—are traced in 2 Peter's metaphor for the purification of faith by suffering. Although it is perishable, gold is "tried with fire" (i, 7); so much the more may faith, which is imperishable, be strengthened and purified by a "fiery trial" (iv, 12). Once again we glimpse the underlying metaphoric structure which unites believers in the body of Christ, making them "partakers of Christ's sufferings" (iv, 13).

Even more crucial to Milton's purpose, however, is the image of the newly risen sun as the day star, filling the morning sky with his radiance. By this sign Milton fully reveals his prophetic intent, and by his explicit allusion to 2 Peter he indicates the way in which the sign is to be interpreted, as a "sure word of prophecy," to which "ye do well that ye take heed, as unto a light that shineth in a dark place, until the day dawn, and the *day star* arise in your hearts" (i, 19).[20] All who wander in the "perilous flood" (185) of this world are subject to its corrruption and consequent blindness. "So much the rather" must "Celestial Light / Shine inward" (*PL* III, 51–52). In *Lycidas*, too, the day star must shine inward, for that is the only place, finally, in which the self-renewing sun of faith can arise, in the purified hearts of those who have been "called out of darkness into his marvellous light" (1 Pet. ii, 9). By this prophetic internalization, the image of the day star is transformed from an image of merely natural renewal into a symbol of the Resurrection: "Through the dear might of him that walk'd the waves" (173), the sun becomes in fact "the radiant image of His glory" (*PL* III, 63).

## III

That radiant vision of historical transcendence is mediated to us by the dread voice of Simon Peter, the rock of God's judgment, who prophesies "the end of all things" (1, iv, 7), the Apocalypse wrought by God's "two-handed engine" (130). By making the Apostle a crucial voice in his poem, Milton has indicated one source of its imaginative life in the New Testament epistles which bear Peter's name. But more is meant by this association than a mere locus of quotations, more even than a coherent focus of scriptural allusion. Peter's function in the elegy is not merely episcopal and epistolary; it is also apostolic — both pastoral and prophetic. As I suggested earlier, not only the Petrine epistles, but the figure of Peter himself, as he appears in the Gospels and in Acts, constitutes an essential context for *Lycidas*. As an "apostle of the circumcised" (*CD* I, xxix; *YP* VI, 566), St. Peter becomes both a type of judgment under the old Law and a type of salvation in Christ. As Wittreich observes, *Lycidas* embodies a "prophetical progression . . . proceeding from obscurity to clarity, from shadowy types to truth — from Orpheus, to Peter, to Michael, to Christ; from type, to type, to manifestation, to the reality — each new vision interpreting the one it supersedes."[21]

As a symbol of apostolic authority, as one who has seen and borne witness, Peter embodies the literary and scriptural traditions which *Lycidas* inherits and transforms. Peter is himself a good shepherd. According to the Gospel of St. John, the resurrected Christ asked Peter, "Simon, *son* of James, lovest thou me?" Peter replied, "Yea, Lord: thou knowest that I love thee." Christ then commanded him, "Feed my sheep" (John xxi, 16). As shepherd, caring for the spiritual nurture of his flock, Peter takes up into himself the essential themes of Milton's pastoral — its exploration of the poet's, or anyone's vocation. By expressing the Christian dimension of pastoral imagery — the "other groves, and other streams" only dimly shadowed by pagan pastoral — Peter infuses that imagery with new meaning. The renewal of pastoral, however, requires a radical transformation; the creation of a new world requires the destruction of the old: "Forasmuch as ye know that ye were not redeemed with corruptible things . . . from your vain conversation *received* by tradition from your fathers" (1 Pet. i, 18). That which has been "*received* by tradition" is precisely the pastoral vision which *Lycidas* finally transcends, not by rejecting images of shepherds feeding their flocks, but by transforming their "rural ditties" (32) into the "unexpressive nuptial Song" (176) of the Lamb.

Furthermore, the tradition which Peter inherits is not, primarily, the literary pastoral of Theocritus and Vergil. The natural world of pagan pastoral defines for us the mortal limitations, and the "false surmise" (153), of the "uncouth swain" (186). The "dread voice" (132) of St. Peter shrinks those streams because it articulates instead the pastoral vision of the Old Testament, of the twenty-third Psalm, for example, and of the prophets. In Peter's voice we hear the echo of Ezekiel's: "Woe *be* to the shepherds of Israel that do feed themselves! should not the shepherds feed the flocks? . . . *but* ye feed not the flock. The diseased have ye not strengthened, neither have ye healed that which was sick. . . . Therefore, O ye shepherds, hear the word of the LORD. . . . I will feed my flock, and I will cause them to lie down, . . . but I will destroy the fat and the strong; I will feed them with judgment" (Ezek. xxxiv, 2–4, 15, 16).[22] This judgment, and the resurrection which it foreshadows, is the "sure word of prophecy" (2 Pet. i, 19), the "salvation . . . of which . . . the prophets have inquired and searched diligently. . . . Unto whom it was revealed, that not unto themselves, but unto us, they did minister the things, which are now reported unto you by them that have preached the gospel unto you" (1 Pet. i, 10, 12). And when he thus reaffirms the judgment of the prophets against God's chosen people, the Pilot of the Galilean lake also foreshadows the judgment to come: "For the time *is come* that judgment must begin at the house of God: and if *it* first *begin* at us, what shall the end *be* of them that obey not the gospel of God?" (1, iv, 17).

Peter's attack on the corrupted clergy is doubly appropriate. In the first place, it begins "at the house of God" by asking, in effect, "if the righteous scarcely be saved, where shall the ungodly and the sinner appear?" (iv, 18). And in the second place, Peter asks this question of those who have been especially chosen to obey the gospel and whose corruption is the more deplorable on that account: "For if after they have escaped the pollutions of the world through the knowledge of the Lord and Saviour Jesus Christ, they are again entangled therein, and overcome, the latter end is worse with them than the beginning" (2 Pet. ii, 20). Paganism is, in a sense, innocent; though subject to the universal curse of mortality, it is not subject to the specific indictment of the Mosaic law. But those who have placed themselves under the law, and who have thereby received a knowledge of the Lord, incur a special obligation, for they are "a chosen generation, a royal priesthood" (1, ii, 9). For them "it had been better . . . not to have known the way of righteousness, than, after they have known *it*, to turn from the holy commandment delivered unto them" (2, ii, 21). In thus echoing Peter's condemnation of a corrupted clergy, *Lycidas* "foretells" Milton's own sustained assault on that same clergy in *Of Reformation*, when he denounces "the grossenesse, and blindnesse, of [those false] Professors, and the fraud of deceivable traditions, [which] drag so downwards, as to backslide one way into the Jewish beggery, of old cast rudiments, and stumble forward another way into the new-vomited Paganisme of sensuall Idolatry" (YP I, 520). Indeed, "it is happened unto them according to the true proverb, The dog *is* turned to his own vomit again" (2, ii, 22).

In condemning the corrupted clergy, therefore, and foretelling their ruin, Peter expresses the judgment of God against his "holy nation" (1, ii, 9), who have become, not a "chosen generation," but "an evil and adulterous" one (Matt. xii, 39). This condemnation, surely, accounts for our feeling that Peter's diatribe is oppressively, even indecorously, mortifying. Like the uncouth swain, we long for consolation and atonement, for recompense, and are met instead with judgment. "And if it first begin at us . . . (1 Pet. iv, 17)? We seek life, or at least the illusion of life, and meet only death. Small wonder that we recoil from "that dread voice," which seems to shrink the very possibility of hope. More horrible, surely, than the blind fury which spills life at random is the dreadful vigilance of "that two-handed engine at the door," which "stands ready to smite once, and smite no more" (130–31). Nothing could be more final, or more appalling—nothing, that is, except the "gory visage" (62) of Lycidas, visiting "the bottom of the monstrous world" (158). Again we hear the voice of Old Testament prophecy, echoing this time Jonah's prayer from the belly of Leviathan: "The waters compassed me about, even to the soul: the depth closed me round about" (Jon. ii, 5). In part, at least, Peter's dread voice prepares us for the greater horror to come. And so it must be, for only in this way can we come to a renewal of hope, "through the dear might of him that *walk'd* the waves" (173), but who also surrendered himself to the depths. "I went down to the bottom of the mountains . . . yet hast thou brought up my life from corruption. O LORD my God" (Jon. ii, 6). This generation of Milton's readers naturally searches the world of the pastoral for some sign of consolation, but "there shall no sign be given to it, but the sign of the prophet Jonas: For as Jonas was three days and three nights in the whale's belly; so shall the Son of man be three days and three nights in the heart of the earth" (Matt. xii, 39–40). So also Lycidas, "Sunk though he be beneath the watery floor . . . repairs his drooping head" and "Flames in the forehead of the morning sky" (167–69, 171).

So also Simon Peter: he did not walk the waves, but he nonetheless renewed his faith, by partaking "of Christ's sufferings" (1 Pet. iv, 13), and so he lived, and died, bearing witness to the "light that shineth in a dark place" (2 Pet. i, 19), even in the darkness of his own unbelief. As the archetypal bishop, shaking "his Mitred locks," and as pastor, presiding over the communion feast, Peter symbolizes the conjunction of Old with New Testament prophecy. By passing through those who have defiled the feast, he reinterprets the Passover: "Drink ye all of it; For this is my blood of the new testament, which is shed for many for the remission of sins" (Matt. xxvi, 27–28).

By articulating, and reinterpreting, the "sure word of [Old Testament] prophecy" (2, i, 19), Milton's Pilot of the Galilean lake becomes, like Jonah, a twofold sign, both of judgment and of resurrection. "The men of Nineveh shall rise in judgment with this generation, and shall condemn it." But, "behold, a greater than Jonas is here." As Jonas, "so shall the Son of man be three days and three nights in the heart of the earth," but on "the third day he shall rise again" (Matt. xii, 41, 40; xx, 19). Through "the answer of a good conscience toward God" (1 Pet. iii, 21), Peter is united with Christ "in his death, burial, and resurrection" (YP VI, 544). And as in the scriptural figure of St. Peter is unfolded in *Lycidas*, first "inwrought with figures dim" (105) and then expounded in "the unexpressive nuptial Song" (176) of the Lamb, "without blemish and without spot" (1 Pet. i, 19), the type receives a threefold definition: as (1) an apostle of circumcision, Peter shadows the sacrament of baptism, which (2) he also embodies in his failure to walk the waves; and finally, (3) both significations, typological and sacramental, are united in the conception of Peter as a parable of "particular repentance" (*CD* I, xix; YP VI, 469).

In the twenty-ninth chapter of *The Christian Doctrine*, on "The Visible Church," Milton calls Peter "the apostle of the circumcised" (YP VI, 566),[23] and this allusion to Galatians (ii, 8) becomes highly significant in the light of what Milton had previously said about circumcision in

his treatment of the sacraments — Chapter xxviii: "Of the External Seal-
ing of the Covenant of Grace." Galatians makes circumcision itself a sign
of bondage to the law, at best a burden of unnecessary obligation, "a debt
of obedience to the whole law" (v, 3), and at worst only "a fair outward
and bodily show" (vi, 12). Accordingly, Milton regards circumcision as
"a symbol for the covenant of works" (543). In discussing those "external
signs" which we call sacraments, however, Milton follows common usage
in equating circumcision "under the law" with baptism "under the gospel" (542). For "it is commonly supposed . . . that baptism has taken the
place [*successit*] of circumcision, and resembles it closely" (I, xxix; 573).[24]
Both the resemblance (*similis*) and the succession are crucial to an understanding of the figure. Circumcision is only "a sign in the flesh, and a
very obscure one at that, of the grace which was to be made known long
afterwards" (YP VI, 548). To us it has been "revealed, that not unto themselves, but unto us they did minister the things, which are now reported
unto you" (1 Pet. i, 12). "Baptism, on the other hand, is a seal of grace
already revealed, of the remission of sins, of sanctification . . . a sign of
our death and resurrection with Christ" (548). Circumcision is thus a type
of baptism, a foreshadowing of Christ's death and resurrection. But like
the sign of the prophet Jonas, the type is twofold, a sign of judgment
under the Old Covenant and a foreshadowing of salvation in the New.
As a typological fulfillment of circumcision, baptism is a sign of "Christian Liberty . . . whereby we are loosed . . . through Christ our deliverer, from the bondage of sin . . . to the intent that being made sons instead of servants . . . we may serve God in Love through the guidance
of the spirit of truth" (*CD* I, xxvii; CM XVI, 153, 155).[25]

The vision of Peter which is reported in Acts (x, 9–xi, 18) adumbrates
a similar transformation of judgment into salvation, of circumcision (x,
45) into baptism (x, 48). Being hungry, Peter "fell into a trance, And
saw . . . a certain vessel descending . . . Wherein were all manner of four-
footed beasts. . . . And there came a voice to him, Rise, Peter; kill, and
eat. But Peter said, Not so, Lord; for I have never eaten any thing that
is common or unclean. And the voice *spake* unto him again the second
time, What God hath cleansed, *that* call not thou common. This was
done thrice: and the vessel was received up again into heaven" (x, 10–16).
The purport of this vision is unfolded when Peter accepts an invitation
to dine from one Cornelius, a devout gentile: "Ye know how that it is
an unlawful thing for a man that is a Jew to keep company, or come unto
one of another nation; but God hath shewed me that I should not call
any man common or unclean" (x, 28). Then Peter prophesied, and "the
Holy Ghost fell on all them which heard the word. And they of the cir-

cumcision which believed were astonished . . . because that on the Gentiles also was poured out the gift of the Holy Ghost" (x, 44–45). And Peter commanded that the gentiles should be baptized, for God is "the Judge of quick and dead" (x, 42), and "through his name whosoever believeth in him shall receive remission of sins" (x, 43). And all who heard Peter bore witness, "saying, Then hath God also to the Gentiles granted repentance unto life" (xi, 18).

*Lycidas* enacts a similar transformation of uncircumcised paganism into baptized faith. As Wittreich observes, "*Lycidas* is about our capacity to rise out of sorrow into joy, to experience a second baptism, to be renewed through prophecy and to create in the here and now a new heaven and a new earth."[26] And *Lycidas* is also about the transformation of a pagan, pastoral consciousness into a prophetic, Christian revelation. The uncouth swain begins his song as a pagan, mourning the loss of nature and his own unripeness:

> I come to pluck your Berries harsh and crude,
> And with forc'd fingers rude,
> Shatter your leaves before the mellowing year.          (3–5)

Even in this pagan context, however, the swain's sense of "bitter constraint" (6) echoes Isaiah's professed unworthiness before God's altar: "Woe *is* me! for I am undone; because I *am* a man of unclean lips" (vi, 5). And Isaiah echoes Moses, who had confessed himself a man "of uncircumcised lips" (Exod. vi, 12). Like Isaiah, the swain must have his "iniquity taken away, and [his] sin purged" (vi, 7). Because he is a gentile, however, and is to become Christian, the means to his purification will be, not the fiery trial of circumcision, but baptism. The swain is "saved by water" (1 Pet. iii, 21) because he participates in the "death, burial, and resurrection" of Lycidas (YP VI, 544). And the agent of that resurrection is St. Peter, whose "dread voice" (132) urges the uncircumcised swain to become baptized in the spirit. Peter pronounces the judgment of circumcision against those who have not been bidden to the feast, the wolves who devour God's flock. In doing so, however, he opens the door to all those who *have* been called, even those gentiles who have been cleansed by baptism and so "by the resurrection of Jesus Christ" (1 Pet. iii, 21). Although the swain at first resists this dread revelation, as a sign of judgment, he comes finally to perceive the salvation which it foreshadows: "For *Lycidas* your sorrow is not dead"; in his "large recompense," he "lives and spreads aloft" (166, 184, 81).

So also Simon Peter, who not only mediates the resurrection of Lycidas to the swain, but who had also undergone an analogous transformation himself. In Acts we witness Peter's enlargement: from being merely an apostle of circumcision, he becomes a universal prophet, who shall "be good / To all" (185) "which heard the word," "whosoever believeth in him" (Acts x, 45, 43).

As he is presented in *Lycidas*, however, Peter is not merely a type of God's judgment (circumcision) prefiguring salvation (baptism); he is also an embodiment of God's mercy—as it were, a sacrament, a "visible sign" of "saving grace" (YP VI, 542). As the "Pilot of the *Galilean* lake," Peter undergoes a figurative baptism, by immersion "in running water" (544).

> When Peter was come down out of the ship, he walked on the water, to go to Jesus.
> But when he saw the wind boisterous, he was afraid; and beginning to sink, he cried, saying, Lord, save me.
> And immediately Jesus stretched forth *his* hand, and caught him, and said unto him, O thou of little faith, wherefore didst thou doubt? (Matt. xiv, 29–31)

Peter was saved, not by his own little faith, but by the power of "him that walk'd the waves" (173). So also Lycidas, "sunk low, but mounted high," whose large baptismal recompense may serve to mediate salvation "To all that wander in that perilous flood" (185).

Moreover, as a type of judgment transformed into a sign of grace, Peter is also a parable of "particular repentance" (YP VI, 469), for Peter's proverbial faithlessness recalls another, even more famous episode, one whose analogy with the swain's own experience presses even more closely on his consciousness. At the Last Supper, Jesus tempts Peter, saying "this night, before the cock crow, thou shalt deny me thrice" (Matt. xxvi, 34). After Christ is taken and before he is crucified, Peter denies him three times (xxvi, 69–74), saying "I know not the man. And immediately the cock crew. And Peter remembered the word of Jesus. . . . And he went out and wept bitterly" (xxvi, 74–75). Christ had said, "whosoever shall deny me before men, him will I also deny before my Father which is in heaven" (x, 33). But Peter is not finally denied because he repents. Even "one who is already converted," Milton observes, may feel "penitence for some particular sin." Of this "consciousness of sin," which "is found even in the regenerate," and of the "particular repentance" which it inspires, "we have examples in David and in Peter." And "in regenerate man repentance precedes faith" (YP VI, 468–69).

Even so does repentance operate in the regeneration of the uncouth swain, who thrice denies the dread vision and who is finally redeemed when his eye turns "homeward" (163), away from the "gory visage" (62) of Lycidas and inward upon his own "hapless youth" (164). As the swain struggles to accept the fact of Lycidas's death, the meaning of that occasion is unfolded to him through a series of revelations, which are, in fact, three answers, pagan, Judaic, and Christian, to the same question: Since it must end in death, what good is life? The answer which pagan philosophy yields to this question is suggestive but inherently unsatisfactory: Phoebus argues an immortality of fame, but it is a fame wholly unconnected with any mortal striving or achievement. "So much fame" is not enough, and so the uncouth swain naturally returns to the lower "mood" (87) of the pastoral, struggling to find within nature some consolation for his own mortal nature. Between the swain and this "false surmise" (153) of pastoral innocence, however, stands the uncompromising moral law of the Hebrews. In the world which Peter utters, no escape is possible; the "foul contagion" (127) of nature itself is condemned, so that it cannot "interpose [even] a little ease" (152). Peter implicitly answers the shepherd's question: the good of life is a good life. But that answer, too, proves unsatisfactory, and the swain continues to struggle against that searing illumination, knowing that his "frail thoughts" (158) are futile, but not knowing what to hope for instead; he sees only "through a glass, darkly" (1. Cor. xii, 13). But then, even as we confront the gory visage of Lycidas, we shall see God "face to face: for now I know in part; but then shall I know even as also I am known" (1 Cor. xiii, 12). The final, Christian reply to the swain's question is "unexpressive" (176), a revelation rather than an answer, a realization of the truth already implicit in our nature, that we may die to rise again and that only so do we live.

The swain's first impulse is to reject once more this "sure word of prophecy" (2 Pet. i, 19); he recoils from the vision of Lycidas at "the bottom of the monstrous world" (158). But that emphatic denial of the poet's "moist vows" (159) begets a final affirmation:

> Weep no more, woeful Shepherds weep no more,
> For *Lycidas* your sorrow is not dead.            (165–66)

Even as Peter wept for his sin, he was cleansed of it, and renewed in his faith. So too the uncouth swain: having "wipe[d] the tears for ever from his eyes" (181), he also shall arise and join with Lycidas in "warbling" (189) "the unexpressive nuptial Song" (176); together they shall tend their flocks amid those "other groves, and other streams" (174) which have been revealed in the prophetic moment of Lycidas's resurrection:

> At last he rose, and twitch't his Mantle blue:
> Tomorrow to fresh Woods, and Pastures new.            (192–93)

That, I believe, is the occasion of *Lycidas*: nothing less than a "lively hope," "begotten . . . by the resurrection of Jesus Christ from the dead" (1 Pet. i, 3). What Milton foretells "by occasion" is no accident of history but its cause, the incarnate Word transforming the world, as the word of the poet transforms the occasion of Edward King's death into a prophetic moment.

The University of Arizona

NOTES

1. Unless otherwise noted, scriptural quotations are taken from the Authorized Version of 1611. I have also referred, on occasion, to the Revised Standard Version, in the *New Oxford Annotated* edition (New York, 1973); to the New English Bible, in the *Oxford Study Edition* (New York, 1976); to the Geneva Bible, in a facsimile of the 1560 edition, ed. Lloyd E. Berry (Madison, Wis., 1969); to the Jerusalem Bible (Garden City, N.Y., 1971), to the Greek text of the New Testament, in the *Novum Testamentum Graece*, ed. Alexander Souter, 2nd ed. (Oxford, 1947); and to the Latin Vulgate (revised), in the *Biblia Sacra juxta vulgatam Clementinam* (Rome and Paris, 1947).

2. *Visionary Poetics: Milton's Tradition and His Legacy* (San Marino, Calif., 1979), p. 135.

3. Angus Fletcher, *The Prophetic Moment: An Essay on Spenser* (Chicago, 1971), p. 45.

4. All quotations of Milton's poetry are taken from *John Milton: Complete Poems and Major Prose*, ed. Merritt Y. Hughes (New York, 1957) and are cited parenthetically in the text.

5. Others, of course, have noted the typological transformations at work in *Lycidas*. William G. Madsen, for example, in *From Shadowy Types to Truth: Studies in Milton's Symbolism* (New Haven, 1968), argues that the symbolic structure of *Lycidas* is radically typological, that Milton "converts the pastoral tradition to Christian use" (p. 15).

6. St. Peter's speech has been examined from a number of perspectives, historical, theological, and structural; many earlier readings are summarized in the *Variorum Commentary on the Poems of John Milton*, ed. A. S. P. Woodhouse and Douglas Bush (New York, 1972), vol. II, pt. 2, pp. 672–79 et passim. The most comprehensive of these readings is by Ernest Tuveson, "The Pilot of the Galilean Lake," (*JHI*, XXVII (1966), 447–58 (summarized in the *Variorum*, p. 678). The hypothesis that Peter's epistles are a source for Peter's speech receives some inferential confirmation from allusions throughout Milton's work. The index to the Columbia Milton, *The Works of John Milton*, ed. Frank Allen Patterson et al. (New York, 1931–38) XVIII, pp. 1478–81, gives 125 references to 1 Peter, 102 of which are in *CD*, and 69 to 2 Peter, 50 in *CD*.

7. The term *pastoral* is here used descriptively, to suggest the quality and prophetic provenance of Peter's epistles. In strict canonical usage, they are numbered among the "catholic" or "general" epistles. Modern scholarship questions the attribution of 1 Peter to the Apostle and is certain that 2 Peter is the work of another, later writer. Notwithstanding their diverse authorship, however, the epistles of Peter invite consideration as a

single (albeit twofold) prophetic moment. Regarded as literature, they reveal common patterns of imagery (such as fire and flood); a unified thematic development (Christian vocation), articulated in terms of a common (pastoral) metaphor; and a coherent pattern of allusion to the Old Testament (the flood in Genesis as typological foreshadowing of the Resurrection). Considered as prophecy, they represent a twofold interpretation — a vision and a revision — of the apocalypse. For our present purpose, therefore, it seems appropriate to regard Peter's epistles collectively, as a unity, and thus as a context for the prophetic moment of *Lycidas*.

8. The Apostle Peter is associated with a number of apocryphal writings, including a *Gospel of Peter* and an *Apocalypse of Peter*, neither of which need concern us here. The *Acts of Peter*, however, suggests a number of possible echoes in *Lycidas* (as noted below). According to Montague Rhodes James, *The Apocryphal New Testament*, rev. ed. (Oxford, 1953), p. 300, the *Acts of Peter* exists (somewhat fragmentarily) in a number of early manuscripts, the most important of which is the so-called Vercelli Acts, a Latin manuscript of the seventh century. The historical question, whether Milton knew, or could have known, the *Acts of Peter*, requires further investigation. For my present purpose, however, the crucial question is not whether the *Acts* was (or could have been) a source for *Lycidas*; all that I seek to assert here is that the *Acts* can enrich our sense of Peter himself as a figural context for *Lycidas*.

9. *Visionary Poetics*, p. 136.

10. Ibid., p. 80.

11. *CD* I, xix, xxix, xxvi, xxix, xxviii; in *Complete Prose Works of John Milton*, ed. Don M. Wolfe et al., 8 vols. (New Haven, 1953–82), VI: *The Christian Doctrine*, ed. Maurice Kelley, trans. John Carey, pp. 469, 566, 519–20, 566, 542. Unless otherwise noted, Milton's prose is quoted from this edition, hereafter referred to as YP and cited parenthetically in the text.

12. Tuveson, "The Pilot of the Galilean Lake," p. 252, identifies this allusion.

13. *Acts of Peter* III, viii, trans. M. R. James, in *The Apocryphal New Testament*, p. 312.

14. "In covetousness," 2 Peter inveighs, "they with feigned words make merchandise of you" (ii, 3), and as the gloss in the Geneva Bible explains, "This is euidently sene in the Pope & his Priests which by lies & flatteries sel mens soules, so that it is certeine that he is not the successour of Simon Peter, but of Simon Magus."

15. Milton's language here may echo the parable of Marcellus as a "hungry sheep" in the *Acts of Peter* III, x, *Apocryphal New Testament*, p. 314: "We beseech thee, Lord, shepherd of the sheep that once were scattered, but now shall be gathered in one by thee. So also receive thou Marcellus as one of thy lambs and suffer him no longer to go astray (revel) in error or ignorance. Yea, Lord, receive him that with anguish and tears entreateth thee."

16. I here adopt the Revised Standard translation, "insatiable for sin," where the AV has "that cannot cease from sin."

17. Such priests as these, Milton says in *Of Reformation*, do not perceive "the heavenly brightness, and inward splendor of their more glorious *Evangelick Ministry*" (YP I, 539). As a gloss in the Geneva Bible explains, "The Greeke worde signifieth him, that naturally can not se, except he holdeth nere his eyes. So Peter calleth suche as can not se heauenlie things which are farre of, purre blinde or sandblinde."

18. *Visionary Poetics*, pp. 88, 136, 131.

19. *Images and Themes in Five Poems by Milton* (Cambridge, Mass., 1957), pp. 75–76. A similar figurative pattern informs the apocryphal *Acts of Peter*, which *Lycidas* may also seem to echo: "the Lord is able to stablish you in his faith, and will found you therein

and make you *spread abroad,* whom he himself hath planted, that ye also may plant others through him" (*New Testament Apocrypha,* p. 333; emphasis added).

20. A. W. Verity, cited in the *Variorum,* p. 726, remarks the allusion to 2 Peter.

21. *Visionary Poetics,* p. 163.

22. Ezekiel is here meant to supply a focus for pastoral themes which recur throughout the prophets; see, for example, Isaiah xliv, 11: "the LORD God . . . shall feed his flock like a shepherd," and Jeremiah l, 6 "My people hath been lost sheep: their shepherds have caused them to go astray."

23. The phrase alludes to Paul's distinction between Peter, who was charged with "the apostleship of the circumcision," and himself, to whom "the gospel of the uncircumcision was committed" (Gal. ii, 8, 7).

24. *De Doctrina Christiana* I, xxix; the Columbia Milton (hereafter CM), XVI, 246: Nam si, baptismus circumcisioni successit, ut vulgo volunt, tamque similis est. Bishop Sumner (CM XVI, 247) translates: "And if it be true that baptism has succeeded to the place of circumcision, and bears the analogy to it which is commonly supposed."

25. I here prefer Sumner's translation to Carey's.

26. *Visionary Poetics,* p. 86.

# MILTON'S *COMUS* AND
# WELSH ORAL TRADITION

## *Violet O'Valle*

CRITICS ARE generally agreed that Milton derived most of his inspiration for *Comus* from the philosophy of the Platonists. To this Platonic foundation he added a framework of allusions to classical mythology and some Christian embellishments, thus reinforcing the strong appeal to Aristotelian temperance and Pauline purity so evident in his dialogue. Although valid, this traditional view ignores a cluster of components that are highly important to the action of the play, elements which, oddly enough, seem neither to be derived from Greek sources nor to reflect Graeco-Christian values.

The Greek myth most often associated with *Comus* is, of course, the Circe story in the *Odyssey*. There can be no doubt that Milton meant to keep this myth in the foreground of his play; he goes to certain lengths to see to it that Comus is recognizable to his audience as Circe's son. But he also establishes a set of circumstances that seem thoroughly incompatible with this myth. Instead of the sunny, semitropical world of the Greeks, a world filled with divinities of a highly colorful and very palpable sort, he presents us with a dark, foggy cosmos teeming with supernatural creatures so elusive they may be only the offspring of moonlight and mist. Instead of turning the Lady into a swine, the spell figuring in the Circe incident, he simply immobilizes her in a great chair, imposing a strange, stonelike paralysis on her. And perhaps most significantly, instead of giving us characterizations we can consistently associate with Greek matters, Milton introduces a pivotal character derived from a completely different tradition, so that the Being who breaks the spell and resolves the action seems a strange and incongruous intruder. Certainly there is no one quite like Sabrina in all the Greek pantheon, nor is it possible that she is an invention.

According to Welsh tradition, Sabrina is the goddess of the Severn River, a tributary of which flows next to Ludlow Castle, located near the border of England and Wales. Blenner-Hassett is probably correct when he asserts that Milton included her in celebration of the occasion for which *Comus* was written: the appointment of the earl of Bridge-

25

water as lord president of Wales.[1] But Sabrina's presence and her over-whelming importance to the action of the play seem to trouble him and several other critics as well. However, if we examine the play closely in conjunction with the milieu in which Sabrina naturally figures, that of Welsh folklore, legend, and mythology, we see that her presence is not at all incongruous and that her importance does not represent a depar-ture from the rich tradition informing Milton's dramaturgy. In fact, much of Milton's characterization and many of his plot devices recall specific analogues in Welsh culture. Viewed in such a light, Sabrina becomes part of Welsh matter represented consistently throughout the masque and serv-ing an integral purpose. Not only is Sabrina's appearance pertinent, but many other seeming disparities are cleared up when we see this. Accord-ingly, this essay explores elements in the oral tradition of Wales which seem to bear directly on *Comus* and which, while not completely over-riding the Platonic elements, do contribute significantly to the work.

The inclusion of such elements would certainly be consistent with the genre Milton had chosen as a vehicle. Renaissance playwrights based many of their plays on folk tradition, and critics have long recognized the fact that *Comus* may have been influenced by George Peele's *The Old Wives Tale*, which is almost a montage of folk beliefs.[2] Katharine Briggs points out that the Jacobean masques, in particular, made exten-sive use of folklore. "The masque is an extreme example of the sophistica-tion of a folk tradition," she says. "It was natural that the masque writ-ers, in their search for themes, should turn to folk-lore. Artificial though the masque was in its Jacobean form, a mere flower upon the revelry of the court, it yet had its roots in folk customs."[3] Furthermore, folklorists tend to believe that those folk customs were specifically Celtic. E. K. Chambers believes that the masque developed from the musical perfor-mances of the "guisers," boys in false faces who until quite recently went from door to door in Scotland on Halloween.[4] We can see in the Celtic traditions still associated with Halloween in our own country, the elabo-rate costumes, the appeal to spirits, ghosts, witches, and hobgoblins, many of the components of the masque in general and of *Comus* in particular.

Wales was evidently much on Milton's mind as he was composing *Comus*. The attendant Spirit's opening speech refers to this "old and haughty Nation proud in Arms," that "fronts the falling Sun,"[5] and throughout the play this West-East relationship of Wales to England is emphasized through allusions. The landscape is decidedly Welsh. The three young people must pass through "a drear Wood / The nodding hor-ror of whose shady brows / Threats the forlorn and wand'ring Passen-ger" (37, 39). A "bleak unkindly Fog" (269) pervades the forest laced with green pathways, luscious valleys, and wooded streams. ("I know each lane and every alley green, / Dingle or bushy dell of this wild Wood, / And every bosky bourn," says Comus [311–13]). A rich undergrowth of flowers and vines creeps through these woods, apparently located on one of Wales's several small mountain ranges (89, 295). In short, this landscape is northern, not southern; it is the moist, luxuriant wilderness associated with fairy mischief.

Before the action of the play begins, the attendant Spirit says to his audience, "Listen . . . for I will tell ye now / What never yet was heard in Tale or Song / From old or modern Bard, in Hall or Bow'r" (43–45), a likely reference to the ancient singing poets of Wales who were the chief perpetuators of the country's oral tradition. Regarded in terms of this tradition, the rest of the play seems to abound in references to the supernaturalism which was often the substance of these tales, derived as they were from the ancient Celtic religions presided over by the druids.

This supernaturalism is especially reflected in Milton's characters. The play includes three kinds of characters: the three children, who are mortal; a large collection of spiritual "supernumaries," whose ubiquity is simply alluded to; and the three stunning figures whose magical powers control the action. These last two groups of characters are clearly linked, in one way or another, with the spiritual beings worshipped by the ancient Welsh, beings who were, in turn, closely identified with nature. Most scholars recognize that the elder faith was clearly animistic and that it degenerated into the fairy lore still current to an extent among the insular Celts. W. Y. Evans Wentz, in *The Fairy-Faith in Celtic Countries*, explains that the "Celtic Fairy-Faith" is "a specialized form of belief in a spiritual realm inhabited by spiritual beings which has existed from prehistoric times until now in Ireland, Scotland, Isle of Man, Wales, Cornwall, Brittany, or other parts of the ancient empire of the Celts."[6] These spiritual beings were thought of "as gods and as fairies of many kinds" who inhabited, epitomized, or somehow formed the essence of various natural phenomena. They entered folklore and became "daemons" and spirits of all sorts: ghosts, hags, bogies, and, as the influence of Christianity spread, even angels. Milton's slight references to dragons in the play, and to such creatures as "pert Fairies and dapper Elves" (118), are examples of general allusions to spirits of this sort.

But some of the spirits in the play can be definitely identified with more specific types descended from the Welsh fairy faith. The landscape of Wales is particularly ominous at night, and according to folklore it is teeming with strange "shadows" of many kinds whose purpose it is to prey on the solitary traveler. The Elder Brother describes the kind of mental and physical environment that propagates these creatures of the imagination as one of "grots and caverns shagg'd with horrid shades" (429). The mountainous wooded sections of Wales are supposed to be inhabited by four of these shades who are particularly frightening and who figure in a minor way in *Comus:* the will-o-the-wisp, the Mountain Hag, the unlaid ghost, and the *coblynau*.

The will-o-the-wisp is actually the phenomenon known as St. Elmo's fire, occasionally seen on misty nights in swampy areas. It looks like patches of moving flame, and the Welsh believe that it is the torches of elves who are trying to lead mortals astray. These elves are animated by souls of mortals, and they wander the earth because they are not quite welcome in the elfin world. Their torchlights will hypnotize innocent humans, who will follow them into a deadly bog, over a cliff, or into a lake, the entranceway to the Celtic Land of the Dead.[7] In most countries they are thought to be mildly mischievous, not deliberately evil, but in Wales they are sometimes thought to be demons.[8]

The Mountain Hag, who may be a witch of some kind, also inhabits the desolate reaches and comes out at night to mislead the traveler. Young people are especially to beware of her, for she eats them alive if they wander in the fens alone after dark. One of these hags, called *Canthrig Burt*, haunts Llamberis Pass; another, *yr hen wrach*, a bog called Cors Fochno near Aberystwyth. The *gwrach y rhibyn*, "hag of the dribble," thought to be the wife of a Welsh death god, emits a long, frightening keen. She appears in mountain mist, and according to a Welsh acquaintance of the U.S. consul to Cardiff in 1878, is "a horrible old woman, with long red hair, a face like chalk and great tusk-like teeth."[9] A very special Mountain Hag is the *Cailleach Bheur*, who, in spite of her Scottish name, is probably recognized in all Celtic countries. She is the personification of winter and therefore blue in color.[10]

Even if the wary traveler escapes the will-o-the-wisp and the Mountain Hag, he is still in danger from the great number of ghosts who roam the Welsh countryside. Lewis Spence explains that the Celtic concept of ghosts differs from that of most other peoples in that once a person crosses the barrier into the Land of the Dead, unless he can manage to return in the form of a bird, or tree, or some other natural manifestation, he undergoes a fundamental change which forever separates him from benevolent relationships with the living and which inevitably renders him "horrible" and "repulsive." Furthermore, a Celtic ghost is never at rest; at night, it travels miserably over all the countryside it traveled when it was alive, at least terrifying, if not actually harming, other travelers. According to some beliefs, a ghost is required to stand watch in the churchyard in which its body is buried for a period of one year or until the next burial.[11]

The last of these dreadful creatures, the *coblynau,* is a mine "knocker," a small fairy who inhabits mines and can often be heard making scary sounds. *Coblynaus* are classified as "dark elves" by folklorists and belong to the group of fairies who "make their homes in the earth and their skin reflects its colours: grey, brown, red, and black."[12] *Coblynaus* are sometimes called *coblyns,* presumably because they are often confused with the English *goblins.*[13]

The Second Brother certainly has ample reason to be concerned over the safety of his sister, lost and alone in a place inhabited by such evil spirits. The Elder Brother, in trying to reassure him, specifically alludes to each of them in turn:

> Some say no evil thing that walks by night
> In fog or fire, by lake or moorish fen,
> Blue meager Hag or stubborn unlaid ghost
> That breaks his magic chains at curfew time,
> No goblin or swart Faery of the mine,
> Hath hurtful power o'er true virginity.          (432–37)

Katharine Briggs has no doubt that Milton intends the "Blue meager Hag" to be the *Cailleach Bheur.*[14] Although this hag is most often spotted in the highlands of Scotland, she has frequently found her way into English literature.[15] It is noteworthy that elsewhere in the masque Milton makes another allusion to the special properties of Celtic ghosts when he speaks of

> those thick and gloomy shadows damp
> Oft seen in Charnel vaults and Sepulchers,
> Lingering and sitting by a new-made grave.          (470–72)

Ghosts, hags, and *coblyns* are among the most frightening of fairies, but the Welsh countryside is full of other sorts as well. The *Plant Annwn* live under the ground in order to keep the dead company; Comus must be thinking of them when he warns the Lady that should humans no longer extract diamonds from the earth "they below" will become used to the light and live on the earth's surface (735). The Celts consider it unlucky to say the word *fairies* aloud, and usually refer to them as simply *they* or *themselves.* Some Welsh fairies are actually benevolent, however. "Good neighbors" are rustic fairies possessing extensive knowledge of healing herbs which they sometimes impart to mortals. The "certain Shepherd Lad / Of small regard to see to" (619–20), who the attendant Spirit says first introduced him to *Haemony,* sounds as if he must be one of these.

The three major characters in *Comus* most intimately connected with magic — Comus, Sabrina, and the attendant Spirit — have much in common with three specific character types widely known in Welsh oral tradition. Like the myriads of less important spiritual beings inhabiting nature, these character types apparently evolved from the elder faith, which has sometimes been thought to be a synthesis of a purely Celtic religion and an aboriginal religion of Iberian origin.[16] Owen says of this religion: "We have not as yet gathered together fragments of the ancient religion of the Celts, and formed of them a consistent whole, but evidently we are to look for them in the sayings and doings of the people quite as much as in the writings of the ancients."[17] Again, he is referring to the way in which the religion first degenerated into folk belief and then became assimilated into the daily lives of the people.

In spite of his Greek name, Comus is very like a figure still more or less prominent in the lives of the Welsh people, the *cwmshurcur,* or conjurer. A man may become a conjurer in any one of three ways: by selling his soul to the devil, by obtaining knowledge of the magical arts from books, or by inheriting magical powers from a progenitor. *Conjurer* is a general term encompassing all who have magical power whether they use this power for good or ill. Those who do not purposely use their power for evil are more specifically called *magicians;* those who do are called *wizards.* Magicians and wizards are both descendants of the druids (supreme religious leaders) and bards (subordinate priests, sometimes also referred to simply as druids) who presided over rituals and provided religious instruction in song, story, and verse.[18] In order to understand the long tradition informing Comus' characterization, we must first trace the development of the druids and bards into conjurers.

The druids and their followers, supposedly believing that it was sinful to enclose the deity within a building, worshiped in forests in the open air, and because of their animistic philosophy became as closely associated with nature as were the gods they worshiped. Each of the three orders of priests carried a different tree branch; the cult, later referred to as the Secret Tradition, made much of the magical, medicinal, and perhaps hallucinogenic properties of plants, flowers, twigs, and leaves. Because they placed much emphasis on the zodiac, they were long believed to have worshiped in the moonlight in their famous stone circles and to have brewed a cauldron in the name of Keridwen (a mother goddess, representing a First Principle) around which they danced. The druids themselves were closely associated with fire, possibly because they officiated over and probably ignited the dreadful sacrificial fires, bonfires, and the flames under Keridwen's cauldron. Spence recreates the kind of incantation supposed to have been recited by the druid as part of an ancient ritual accompanying the preparation of the cauldron:

I am he who animates the fire, to the honor of the god Duvydd, in behalf of the assembly of associates qualified to treat of mysteries — a bard with the knowledge of a *Sywedydd*, when he deliberately recites the inspired song of the Western Cudd on a serene night amongst the stones.

With priests of intelligence to officiate on behalf of the moon. . . . And bards with flowers and perfect convolutions and primroses and leaves of the *Briw*, with points of the trees of purposes. . . . Hence the stream of Gwion and the reign of serenity and honey trefoil and horns flowing with mead — Meet for a sovereign is the lore of the Druids.[19]

The last paragraph refers to finished brew. According to Spence, the ingredients of Keridwen's cauldron "produced the stream of Gwion to which is ascribed the beginning of genius, the power of inspiration, and the reign of serenity."[20] Initiates evidently drank the brew in order to gain these qualities, and this tradition apparently survives in folklore in many forms. The Korrigans, for example, granddaughters of nine continental druidesses, are supposed to hold a festival each spring at which "they drink the secrets of poetry and earthly wisdom from a crystal goblet."[21]

The druids were supposed to have organized themselves into colleges devoted to instruction in arcane knowledge, and the chief druid was believed to have occupied a large stone chair that signified his superior knowledge and dominion. Taliesin, a Welsh bard who took the name of a Celtic god, sings: "Is not my chair protected by the Cauldron of Keridwen? Therefore let my tongue be free in the sanctuary of the praise of the goddess." And again, "I have presided in a toilsome Chair over the circle of *Sidin* whilst that is continually revolving between the elements."[22] *Annwn*, the Welsh underworld, was divided into many crystal castles of which *Caer Sidi* was apparently the most blessed. It contains, among other magical objects, a chair of which the bard again sings:

> Perfect is my chair in *Caer Sidi*,
> Plague and age hurt him not who's in it.[23]

Some authorities have believed that the druidic temples were recreations of the *Caer Sidi*. At any rate, there have been reports from time to time, perhaps, of course, stemming from overactive imaginations, of remains of large stone chairs spotted in various remote British forests.

All in all, the elder religion, with its strange, probably intoxicating brews, its wild round-dancing in the moonlight, its bands of initiates and priests decked with convolutions of flowers and carrying various twigs, must have been a shocking sight to the early Christian missionaries. St. Samson of Dol, in Brittany, witnessed one of these rites while visiting in Britain and called the participants "Bacchanalians."[24]

As the formal organization of the religion disintegrated, the druids became associated with simple magic, and the tree branches they carried apparently acquired the power to hypnotize. An account of the chief bard of Ulster relates that in the middle of a terrible war he "waved the peaceful branch of Sencha, and all the men of Ulster were silent, quiet."[25] By the medieval period the Welsh bard had become a magician and his branch a magic wand. Welsh magicians were known for their ability to change shapes, which they originally acquired from drinking the liquid in Keridwen's cauldron, for their ability to give magic attributes to objects, and for their ability to obtain for themselves the object or person of their desires. Their magic powers were passed down from parent to the child of the opposite sex, that is, from father to daughter and from mother to son. In due time many magicians became wizards by selling their souls to the devil. (Keridwen also acquired a reputation as a witch.) Wizards often lived as wild men in the woods, and since they had the power to change humans into animal shapes, were often surrounded by satyrlike creatures. In fact, they sometimes dressed in a grotesque satyrlike fashion themselves, with "a cap of sheepskin with a high crown, bearing a plume of pigeon feathers."[26]

Another group of exalted beings from Celtic mythology gradually blended with these conjurer types. The beautiful race of fairies, most prominent in Ireland as the *Sidhe*, but certainly not unknown to other Celts, was often associated in lore with the bards, and finally they apparently acquired some druidic attributes. Like the druids, they form enchanted circles; like the magicians, they can cast spells over persons of their desire. In this way, they kidnap people (especially fair-haired girls) and force them to become their slaves or concubines. They take their victims to their luxurious palaces, reminiscent of *Caer Sidi*, which Wentz describes: "Beautiful damsels and their lovers were the inhabitants of the palace; in it there was music and abundance of food and drink, and on its floor stood a chair of crystal."[27] Unlike the ancient religious figures, however, the *Sidhe*, both male and female, are young and beautiful.

One last character type who probably belongs in this druidic tradition is the Prince of the Palace of Iniquities. According to one hypothesis, the druidic circles were guarded by a personage known as a "Prince" or "the guardian of the gate of Godo."[28] Perhaps this is the ultimate origin of this character who still figures prominently in the Lake Legends of Wales. He has now become a mortal prince who, like the *Sidhe*, owns

an unbelievably beautiful palace, the inhabitants of which are given over
to luxury, gluttony, and revelry. He invariably angers some of the rustic
fairies, for a quality he has in common with his predecessors—bard, magician, wizard, and *Sidhe*—is his dominion over, and antipathy toward,
the shepherds and farmers of Wales. Perhaps this stems from the long-
held theory that the ancient druids, on occasions when they could not
find criminals to feed their enormous sacrificial fires, forced hundreds
of peasants to participate instead.

The qualities which Comus shares with this general character type
should be fairly obvious. The attendant Spirit tells us that Comus

> ripe and frolic of his full grown age,
> Roving the *Celtic* and *Iberian* fields
> At last betakes him to this ominous Wood,
> And in thick shelter of black shades imbow'r'd,
> Excels his Mother at her mighty Art,
> Off'ring to every Traveller
> His orient liquor in a Crystal Glass. (59–65)

His Celtic-Iberian origin perhaps makes Comus a practitioner of the ancient religion, the Secret Tradition, for he silences the Lady by warning
her that her "moral babble" is "direct / Against the canon laws of our
foundation" (807–08). In fact, his connection with the fairy faith is made
rather plain when he speaks to the Lady of having seen her brothers on
the side of the hill:

> I took it for some faery vision
> Of some gay creatures of the element
> That in the colors of the Rainbow live
> And play i' th' plighted clouds. I was awe-struck,
> And as I past, I worshipt; if those you seek,
> It were a journey like the path to Heav'n
> To help you find them. (298–304)

The Lady speaks of his "dear Wit and gay Rhetoric" (790), attributing
to him the qualities of the bard, and the "cordial julep" he offers her
"flames and dances . . . / With spirits and balms and fragrant Syrups
mixt" (673–74), as the contents of Keridwen's cauldron might be expected
to. Like the contents of the cauldron, this brew will confer some sort of
special knowledge. "Be wise, and taste," says Comus (813).

The rites which Comus presides over are obviously bacchanalian in
nature, and his description of them features a reference to himself and
his followers as somehow fiery in substance, recalling the Druid's claim
to be the animator of the fire. His followers, in fact, are "glistering," and

they carry torches, perhaps recalling the ritual torches used to light the various ceremonial fires. As part of the revels, Comus' rout, decked with convolutions of flowers, will do a round dance meant to imitate the movement of the heavens:

> Meanwhile welcome Joy and Feast,
> Midnight shout and revelry,
> Tipsy dance and Jollity.
> Braid your locks with rosy Twine
> Dropping odors, dropping Wine.
> Rigor now is gone to bed,
> And advice with scrupulous head,
> Strict Age, and sour Severity,
> With their grave Saws in slumber lie.
> We that are of purer fire
> Imitate the Starry Choir,
> Who in their nightly watchful Spheres,
> Lead in swift round the Months and Years.          (102–14)

Comus' rhetoric is full of references to plant life, and at one point the attendant Spirit speaks of "entering the very lime-twigs of his spells" (646), recalling, in addition to the subtle "bird-snare" metaphor, the twigs and branches of druidic magic.

If Comus possesses qualities of the druid, he, of course, possesses those of the magician and the wizard as well. Briggs says that he "is an airy and poetic enchanter, intellectually sinister; his home is in the wild woodland, and the sweets of nature are still sweet to him."[29] Like all Welsh magicians he has the ability to change shapes, the ability to attract the person he desires, and a magic wand with which to hypnotize others. However, his ability to change people to stone would specifically mark him as a wizard in the eyes of the Welsh, for they attribute this power to the devil. Like the Welsh wizards, he is also surrounded by beastlike creatures. The attendant Spirit refers to him as "unblest enchanter vile" (907), "that damn'd wizard" (571), and "that damn'd magician" (602). The Welsh would say that as the son of Circe he probably inherited his talent for sorcery, but may have also surrendered himself to the devil on his own. It is perhaps relevant to mention here that in later folktales about Keridwen, she has acquired a son to whom she passes her black art.

Like the *Sidhe*, Comus is probably youthful and takes his fair victim to a beautiful palace containing an "enchanted chair," apparently in the hope of enslaving her. Like the Prince of the Palace of Iniquities, he is rapacious and sensual, delighting in voluptuousness. Like bard, magician, wizard, fairy, and prince, he is at odds with the simple shepherd (really a rustic fairy) who comes to the rescue of the three ingenuous young people.

Welsh folklore recognizes a number of striking female character types who, like the male enchanters, have their origins in Welsh legend and mythology. It is from one of these general character types that Sabrina, the most overtly Welsh influence in *Comus*, is derived. The legend of Sabrina, or *Habren* in Welsh, is found in Book II of Geoffrey of Monmouth's *History of the Kings of Britain*, which Milton used as a source when he was compiling his *History of Britain*. Habren was the illegitimate daughter of Locrine, ruler of Loegria (England). Gwendolen, Locrine's wife, had Habren and her mother flung in a river and issued an edict that the river should be called the River Habren, which through gradual changes in pronunciation has become Severn to the English.[30]

Rhys suggests that Habren may have been the pre-Celtic goddess of the Severn, since the aboriginal natives of Wales are known to have venerated river goddesses.[31] If so, she belongs to a rich tradition of river goddesses (and gods) from that mythology, including Morgain la Fee, originally a river nymph, and Nudons, a water divinity whose temple was located on the western banks of the Severn. River gods and goddesses were considered rulers of the Other World, and they went about under the water in chariots drawn by beautiful horses. Morgain la Fee was known for her magnificent horse, and Nudons for his horse-drawn chariot.

Milton's Sabrina seems to combine the most pleasing qualities of two descendants of these ancient deities: the River Woman and the Lady of the Lake. Welsh lore is full of stories concerning River Women, who are either benevolent or sinister depending upon their individuality and ascend from under the water to aid or to harm mortals as they please. Magnificently beautiful, they appear dressed in blue or green and have hair the color of the sunset. Rhys recognizes that these women are somehow related to the Lady of the Lake who figures so prominently in the Lake Legends of Wales. She is one of a race of beautiful women the Welsh call the *Gwragen Annwn*.

The Lady of the Lake is a protector of livestock and is known for the unusual breed of cattle she raises. She sometimes leaves her banks to steal gently over the pastures and meadows, perhaps to see the children she produced with a mortal farmer. In spite of this marriage, she is thought of as one of the lake "maidens," a "young and beautiful woman whom neither death awaits nor old age." Sometimes it is asserted that in the land from which she comes "there are none but women and girls."[32] She knows the secrets of healing and herbal medicine, which she imparts to her male offspring, a renowned race of physicians. Her lore is connected with the legends (common to all peoples, of course) concerning the healing properties of water, and fairies are often seen dancing on the surfaces of her lakes.

Like all Welsh river goddesses, Sabrina possesses a "sliding Chariot" (892) in which she traverses the underwater world. Like the River Women, she is associated with various shades of green and blue (894–95). The attendant Spirit refers to her "amber dropping hair" (864) and her "rosy head" (885), indicating that her hair is, indeed, the color of the sunset. Like the Lady of the Lake, she "Visits the herds along the twilight meadows" (844). She sometimes leaves her banks to steal gently "O'er the Cowslips Velvet head" (898), and "she with precious vial'd liquors heals" (847). In spite of her illegitimate origin, she is strongly associated with maidenhood; she is a "Virgin pure" (826). The attendant Spirit actually calls her "Goddess of the silver lake" (865), and speaks of the "*Nymphs*" who "nightly dance / Upon thy streams with wily glance" (883–84).

As a lake maiden, Sabrina would have strong connections with the fairies; in fact, according to most stories lake maidens are fairies themselves. As a fairy she would be the same kind of spiritual being as the attendant Spirit. Although the attendant Spirit is probably the character in the play most clearly derived from Platonist philosophy, he is reminiscent of several character types in Welsh tradition as well.

Nancy Arrowsmith points out that fairies can be divided into light elves and dark elves. The light elves are "masters at shape-changing and can travel through the four dimensions. Their beauty is often evanescent, like that of a butterfly. They are among the best-natured Little People."[33] This beautiful race of fairies is usually renowned for its musical ability and, according to some Celtic traditions, lives in the land of eternal youth on floating islands beyond the western sea. Welsh lore also contains many stories of the "good neighbors," rustic fairies, like the "certain Shepherd Lad," who are somehow connected with the dead ancestors of the modern inhabitants of a village and often appear to help members of a particular family. Similarly, "familiar spirits" are demons who nevertheless sometimes attach themselves to mortals in order to protect them or do them favors.

The qualities the attendant Spirit shares with these Welsh spirits are, of course, obvious. He can not only change his shape at will, but he says "I can fly, or I can run / Quickly to the earth's end, / Where the bow'd welkin slow doth bend, / And from thence can soar as soon / To the corners of the Moon" (1013–17). His evanescent beauty is indicated by his "sky robes spun out of Iris' Woof" (83); indeed, the fact that the rainbow is somehow the substance of his being clearly marks him as a fairy from the elder faith. He has musical ability (623–25) and lives in a land of eternal youth beyond the ocean. He is as helpful as a "good neighbor" or a "familiar spirit" would be.

It may be significant that a group of Welsh legends exists in which all three of these character types appear together: Enchanter-Prince, Lady of the Lake, and a protecting Spirit. Rhys calls these stories "inundation legends."[34] The one told about Lyn Tegid, or Bala Lake, is typical.

A cruel prince once lived near the lake in a magnificent palace. Like the conjurers of old, this prince was an enemy of the rustic classes, oppressing them in every way. His palace, called by the people the Palace of Iniquities, was the scene of revels and abandonment. One night a poor harper was ordered to play at one of these entertainments. During the intermission a good fairy, in the shape of a bird, appeared to him singing "Vengeance, vengeance," all the while beckoning the harper to follow him out of the palace. The harper was so intent on following the bird that he forgot his harp. When he returned to the site of the palace the next day to fetch it, he discovered that the palace and all its inhabitants had been completely flooded by the waters of the lake. He could find no trace of any of the splendor he had seen the night before except for his harp floating on the surface of the waters.

If we strip this story down to its essential elements, we find that in general type it is similar to *Comus*. A wicked ruler, keeper of a palace that is the scene of unbridled sensuality, forces an innocent to accompany him there. But a rustic fairy, in league with a water divinity, probably the Lady of the Lake, rescues the innocent. The Lady of the Lake, by rising out of her banks, washes away the evil accomplished by the wicked ruler.

It may be especially relevant to note here that *Comus* contains several other plot devices common to Welsh folklore. The lost brother or sister sought by siblings of the opposite sex is a common fairy-tale type found in many cultures.[35] The concept of *geis* in the play is probably even more significant. According to Reinhard, the lore of all Celtic peoples depended heavily on this concept, although the word for it has been lost in all but the Gaelic language.[36] The closest equivalent we have for *geis* in English is *taboo*, but that word does not quite express what *geis* meant to the Celts. A *geis* was a kind of divine necessity to do, or more often *not* to do something. A Welsh audience might suspect that the Lady is under a *geis* not to drink the liquid Comus offers her. Finally, the notion of a good fairy coming to the rescue of the person devoted to purity is pervasive in Welsh lore and has since carried over into stories from the Christian era.

Most stories from Welsh tradition also depend heavily on magical objects. Sometimes these objects have power themselves and sometimes they confer power on others, but often they simply protect their owners from falling prey to enchantment. Milton makes use of some of the most common of these types of objects: a magic wand, some magic dust, magic potions, an enchanter's glass, and perhaps most significantly, a protective herb.

The use of a plant such as *Haemony* as protection against evil was common practice in Wales for centuries and apparently, like so much in Welsh tradition, grew out of the supernaturalism associated with the old religion. The druids recommended that *Selago*, an evergreen, should "be carried as a charm against every kind of evil."[37] Elias Owen lists several kinds of plants believed by the Welsh to protect people from being "charmed": hyssop, elder tree, snapdragon, and something the Welsh call *Meipen Fair*.[38] St. John's Wort, also known as *Hypericum*, is singled out by Katharine Briggs as "one of the most beneficent of the magic herbs, protecting equally against Fairies and the Devil."[39] Owen points out that this plant, known as *Llysiau Ifan* in Wales, is extremely prominent in Welsh lore and is hunted by young women on St. John's Eve (*Wyl Ifan*) since it has some connection with marriage.[40] Interestingly, Charlotte F. Otten, after reviewing the plant's physical properties and researching written accounts of its alleged effectiveness against sickness and ghosts in England, asserts that St. John's Wort is actually Milton's *Haemony*.[41] It is noteworthy that protective plants were not actually carried by the Welsh, but according to Jones, "their roots were powdered and worn in sachets on the chest."[42] The attendant Spirit explains that when he obtained the *Haemony*, he "purs't it up," and he adds, "if you have this about you / . . . you may / Boldly assault the necromancer's hall" (647–49), giving us the impression that the plant may be in a small container which will be worn rather than carried.

The enchanter's "Glass" that Comus enters carrying may also be more significant than it at first seems. Although it may simply be a glass in the sense of a container for the strange "syrup" Comus wishes to administer to the Lady, conjurers apparently did possess a magical object known as *Glain-nan Druidhe*, or Druid's Glass, an oval crystal ball used especially to obtain a desired person. It was supposedly formed from the foam of a number of snakes in congress.[43] Pliny includes a complicated account of the esoteric way the amulet was made, although some modern killjoys have suggested that the druids were merely practicing glassblowing. The traditional explanation for the existence of the glass, however, appropriately emphasizes the sensual nature of the druidic cults which Comus seems so well to epitomize and which were understandably so appalling to the spiritually oriented Christians. That Milton would seemingly confuse the traditional terminology with something akin to our modern meaning of the word *glass* is at least interesting, for it may indicate that he was drawing his information from oral sources already in his memory rather than methodically researching Welsh tradition.

One other technique in the play that must also be mentioned is the overt emphasis on a dualistic principle represented by light imagery, which is then set against a triadic principle governing not only much of the imagery but much of the structure as well. Although the play of light against darkness and the metaphysical significance of the number *three* are important to people of many cultures, they were especially so to the Celts and to the Welsh in particular.

The Celtic calendar was elaborately based on the alternation between light and darkness, and the ancient Welsh are sometimes said to have worshipped three-headed deities consisting of the Sun, the Night, and Keridwen, the mother of them both. The religion also supposedly featured a triune *logos* symbolized as three golden apples or three bulls.[44] Moreover, the ethical instruction administered by the druids and the bards was presented in the form of triads and tricolons. The triad thus became the basis of much symbolism in Welsh tradition, and most stories were somehow organized on a tripartite basis and depended heavily on the mystical overtones that *three* continued to have in the minds of the people. Vincent Hopper explains that "among the Welsh triads were extraordinarily popular, both narrator and audience apparently delighting in 'the 3 costly pillages,' 'the 3 ill resolutions,' 'the 3 frivolous bards,' 'the 3 inventors,' and so on. Even the letters of the Welsh alphabet were composed of 3 elements."[45] But woven throughout both overtly religious literature and the more secular folktales in which these triads appeared was the concept of life as a continuing struggle between light and darkness.

There are six speaking characters in the masque: three mortals and three immortals. The action is also divided into three scenes: "a wild wood," "a stately palace," and "Ludlow town and the President's castle." Concrete images of *threes* are scattered throughout the work. In the first scene, the attendant Spirit alludes to the "little tridents" belonging to Neptune's "tributary gods" (24–27). "*Circe* with her sirens three" is mentioned (253), as are "*Hesperus* and his daughters three" (982), and "Three fair branches of your own" (969), evidently referring to Bridgewater's three children. At one point, the Second Brother remarks that "night and shades" have combined with "hell" to make a "triple knot" against the Lady (580–85). Most significantly, in order for Sabrina to break Comus' spell, she must touch the Lady "Thrice upon thy finger's tip, / Thrice upon thy rubied lip" (914–15) with her healing waters, reminding us of the famous tricolon which is the basis of the Lady's philosophy: Faith, Hope, and Chastity (213–15).

These recurring images of *three* are set against a background of light and dark, "falling Sun" and "thievish Night," recalling the two subordinate figures in the Welsh trinity. The masque itself depicts a contest between darkness and light, between Comus' "black Art" and the power of one of Jove's "bright aerial Spirits." The dualistic image of the "sable cloud / Turn[ing] forth her silver lining on the night" (221–22) and casting a "gleam over this tufted Grove" (225) is one that would surely be appreciated by audiences of both "old and modern Bard."

It is essential to mention here E. M. W. Tillyard's interpretation of the masque, with which some critics disagree. Taking a slightly allegorical view, he believes that Milton is advocating marriage, or the reconciliation of virtue with natural pleasure which results in "married chastity."[46] Tillyard bases his interpretation on certain classical allusions in the epilogue of the text. In view of his arguments, it is at least interesting that folklorists agree that the Lady of the Lake and similar legends are, at their core, "marriage myths" symbolizing "the victory of a principle from an upper realm over the sinister powers of a lower one, a victory won on the conditions set by those powers themselves. The prize is the emancipation from the lower realm of the opposite principle and the consummate union of the two."[47]

Surely there can be no doubt that *Comus* revolves around a struggle between two opposing powers, one from an "upper realm," the other from a "lower" one. As John Arthos says, "The conflict finally is between Jove and whatever powers of nature Comus can enlist."[48] Furthermore, Comus, as a practitioner of the Secret Tradition, is an enemy of the simple, the pure, the Christian, and the English. He is the embodiment of a false system of thought and practice based on sensuality rather than spirituality. He especially represents the magnetic attraction of animism and pagan magic. The (English) Lady, on the other hand, firmly grounded in the teachings of Plato and Paul, is clearly his adversary. Her "magic" is of a different sort. In fact, the dialogue between them is strongly reminiscent of the dialogues and the "magic" contests between the druids and the Christian saints which form the heart of many stories from Celtic tradition.[49]

It is difficult for us to imagine the immediacy and seriousness with which Milton might have regarded such a struggle.[50] The religion of the druids had been rediscovered during the Renaissance with the rediscov-

ery of the classical texts. Observers such as Pliny and Caesar had emphasized the more shocking aspects of this system: huge wicker figures in
which hundreds of peasants were burned at once, cattle runs associated
with the worship of horned gods, the bizarre mistletoe ceremony. The
fact that the elder faith had never quite been extinguished in the Celtic
regions of Britain by the seventeenth century troubled some Englishmen
who, rightly or wrongly, saw this as a sign of the latent barbarity of the
Welsh, Scottish, Cornish, and Irish peoples. Long after the introduction
of Christianity to the isles, reports of brutality in connection with ancient rites were circulated among the English. Edmund Spenser remarked
that he had once seen some Irishmen drinking blood in connection with
a secret tradition. Primitive sacrifices involving sacred oxen, probably to
a horned god, occurred in Wales as late as 1538. Bulls were sacrificed
in Scotland during the seventeenth century, and this practice continued
well into the nineteenth.[51] From the attention accorded in our own day
to the Loch Ness monster, whose home is obviously the Land of the Dead,
we can perceive something of the grip the elder faith maintains over Celtic sensibilities.

The struggle in *Comus*, then, is the important one between the powers of darkness and the powers of light, between barbaric paganism and
Christianity, between "uncivilized" Wales and civilized England. That
the victory is brought about by a character who figures in the mythology
of the "lower realm" should not bother us, for this fulfills the requirement that the struggle must be won under conditions set by the sinister
powers themselves, in this case, by the kind of magic associated with the
elder faith. Furthermore, the Lady of the Lake is herself the embodiment of a pagan deity who had been superseded by a counterpart from
a higher realm, her identity having been subjugated and merged with
that of the Christian Virgin Mother. Besides embodying the triumph of
Christianity in its merger with paganism, she also epitomizes the relationship between England and Wales that Milton foresaw. Because of her
adoption into and merging with English tradition, and especially because
of her newer status as the illegitimate daughter of the king of England,
she perfectly symbolizes the triumph of English culture over that of the
subjugated Welsh and the final harmonious union of the two.

Finally, we can conclude that although the Welsh elements in *Comus*
clearly do not negate the Greek orientation of the play, they do add other
dimensions to an unusually rich text. Lewis Spence, in his attempt to determine the way in which Celtic magic differs from that of other cultures,
concludes that while Celtic magic resembles other kinds of magic in technical and external ways, it is unique in those qualities which we think

of as purely aesthetic.[52] Closely linked by traditional belief with abstract and psychic considerations, it is inseparable from poetic inspiration — and from moonlight madness. Central to the tradition growing out of it is the unforgettable figure of the Conjurer, sinister yet beautiful, poet and priest — and pagan. Milton's charming masque, with its translucent poetry, its remarkable scenery that at times becomes a projection of the human mind, and above all, its unforgettable antagonist, seems almost to belong within the colorful tradition it appears to so completely denounce. Perhaps the play itself epitomizes the happy results brought about by the synthesis of all lower systems under the final authority of Platonic Christianity.

Texas A&M University

NOTES

1. R. Blenner-Hassett, "Geoffrey of Monmouth and Milton's *Comus*," *MLN*, LXIV (1949), 315–18.

2. Sylvia Lyons-Render has isolated over ninety folk motifs in the plot of *The Old Wives Tale*. See "Folk Motifs in George Peele's *The Old Wives Tale*," *Tennessee Folklore Society Bulletin*, XXVI (1960), 62–71. For a discussion of the major motifs in *TOWT* and a review of the literature on the subject, see *The Dramatic Works of George Peele*, ed. Mark Benbow, Elmer Blistein, and Frank S. Hook (New Haven, 1970), pp. 319–41. John Arthos in *On a Mask Presented at Ludlow Castle*, Univ. of Michigan Contributions in Modern Philology, No. 20 (Ann Arbor, Mich., 1954), p. 51, mentions the possibility that Milton may have known folklore in its "plainer" forms.

3. Briggs, *The Anatomy of Puck* (1959; rpt. New York, 1977), pp. 83, 82.

4. *The Elizabethan Stage* (Oxford, 1923), I, p. 150; cited by Briggs, p. 82.

5. *John Milton: Complete Poems and Major Prose*, ed. Merritt Y. Hughes (1957; rpt. Indianapolis, 1978), 33, 30. Subsequent references appear within the text.

6. *The Fairy-Faith in Celtic Countries* (London, 1911), p. xvi.

7. Nancy Arrowsmith, *A Field Guide to the Little People* (New York, 1977), p. 34.

8. T. Gwynn Jones, *Welsh Folklore and Folk-Custom* (London, 1930), p. 32.

9. Lewis Spence, *The Magic Arts in Celtic Britain* (London, n.d.), pp. 83–84.

10. Briggs, *An Encyclopedia of Fairies, Hobgoblins, Brownies, Bogies, and Other Supernatural Creatures* (New York, 1976), pp. 58–59.

11. Spence, *Magic Arts*, pp. 79–80.

12. Arrowsmith, *Field Guide*, p. 3.

13. Jones, *Welsh Folklore*, p. 51.

14. Briggs, *Anatomy*, p. 87.

15. According to Briggs, her most famous derivative is Chaucer's Loathly Lady in *The Wife of Bath*.

16. See Lewis Spence, *The Mysteries of Britain: Secret Rites and Traditions of Ancient Britain Restored* (1928; rpt. New York, 1970), p. 158, and *Magic Arts*, p. 54. It should

be noted that much controversy still surrounds the ancient Celtic religion, and modern scholars and archaeologists do not accept some of the older, more romantic notions about it. This essay does not purport to put forth a factual, historical account of the circumstances and particulars surrounding the elder faith. Milton would be interested in evoking his audience's notions about Welsh culture; therefore, what is important for this study is not verifiable facts but popular belief about the druidic religion. For this reason, I have chosen older sources which perpetuate the popular view of the druids.

17. Elias Owen, *Welsh Folklore: A Collection of the Folk-Tales and Legends of North Wales* (1896; rpt. Norwood, Pa., 1973), p. 226.

18. Classical sources list three orders of priests among the Celts: the druids, who conducted ceremonies, interpreted sacred matters, and acted as judges; the bards, who composed hymns and instructive stories and sang and chanted them; and the *vates*, who helped with the sacrifices and studied nature. Members of all three orders are traditionally referred to simply as druids.

19. Spence, *Mysteries*, p. 194.

20. Ibid., p. 196.

21. Arrowsmith, *Field Guide*, p. 221.

22. Spence, *Mysteries*, pp. 209–10.

23. Spence, *Magic Arts*, p. 141.

24. Spence, *Mysteries*, p. 209.

25. Wentz, *Fairy-Faith*, p. 344.

26. Owen, *Welsh Folklore*, p. 262.

27. Wentz, *Fairy-Faith*, p. 293. These distinctive chairs show up again and again in Welsh fairy lore. Sometimes a fairy seated in one appears to a peasant; sometimes an empty chair is spotted in the woods that later cannot be found again. This probably reflects the later tradition that confounded druids with fairies. According to some Welsh lore, fairies are the souls of druids who cannot go to heaven because they are not Christians but are too "good" to go to hell. George Lyman Kittredge remarks that "magic" chairs occur in Greek mythology but are "common" in "Celtic and Germanic saga." See *Witchcraft in Old and New England* (New York, 1929), pp. 201–02.

28. Spence, *Mysteries*, p. 211.

29. Briggs, *Anatomy*, p. 87.

30. Geoffrey of Monmouth, *History of the Kings of Britain*, trans. Sebastian Evans, 1912; rev. Charles W. Dunn (New York, 1958), pp. 30–32.

31. John Rhys, *Celtic Folklore: Welsh and Manx* (1901; rpt. New York, 1971), II, pp. 448–49.

32. Proinsias MacCana, *Celtic Mythology* (New York, 1970), p. 90.

33. Arrowsmith, *Field Guide*, p. 13.

34. Rhys, *Celtic Folklore*, p. 415.

35. Antti Aarne, *The Types of the Folktale: A Classification and Bibliography*, trans. Stith Thompson, 2nd ed. (1928; rpt. Helsinki, 1964); see nos. 451, 451A, 452A, 312A.

36. For a thorough definition and linguistic history of *geis* and a discussion of its prevalence among the Celts, see John Revell Reinhard, *The Survival of Geis in Mediaeval Romance* (Halle an der Saale, 1933), pp. 2–8.

37. Spence, *Mysteries*, p. 196.

38. Owen, *Welsh Folklore*, p. 249.

39. Briggs, *Encyclopedia*, p. 346.

40. Owen, *Welsh Folklore*, p. 280.

41. "Milton's *Haemony*," *English Literature Renaissance*, V (1975), 81–95.

42. Jones, *Welsh Folklore*, p. 21.

43. Spence, *Magic Arts*, p. 21.

44. Spence, *Mysteries*, p. 219.

45. *Medieval Number Symbolism: Its Sources, Meaning, and Influence on Thought and Expression*, Columbia Univ. Studies in English and Comparative Literature, No. 132 (New York, 1938), p. 203.

46. *Studies in Milton* (1951; rpt. London, 1964), pp. 82–99.

47. Alwyn Rees and Brinley Rees, *Celtic Heritage: Ancient Tradition in Ireland and Wales* (New York, 1961), p. 271.

48. Arthos, *On a Mask*, p. 24.

49. The most famous of the stories growing out of this tradition are those about Ossian and St. Patrick in Irish lore. Some folklorists suspect that the legends in which the Christians win the contests and debates, sometimes even subduing and converting their pagan adversaries, are those preserved — and tampered with — by the monks. Legends in which the Celts win, or at least do not give in, were most likely preserved in oral tradition and finally by native families who had somehow learned to write. If this theory is true, it of course reveals a great deal about the true sympathies of the Celts.

50. Stuart Piggot, in ch. 4 of *The Druids* (New York, 1968), pp. 131–81, surveys English attitudes toward the druids from the sixteenth through the nineteenth centuries. He believes that Milton expressed "vague but respectful admiration" for them in *Lycidas* and some of the earlier Latin poems but admits that in later life he wrote of the Britons as "progenitors not to be glory'd in" and of the druids, "philosophers I cannot call them, men reported factious and ambitious" (p. 139).

51. Spence discusses these modern manifestations of druidism in *Magic Arts*, pp. 45–51.

52. Ibid., p. 182.

# UNBINDING "THE HIDDEN SOUL OF HARMONY": *L'ALLEGRO, IL PENSEROSO,* AND THE HERMETIC TRADITION

## Gerard H. Cox

I T I S obvious that *L'Allegro* and *Il Penseroso* are companion poems, but precisely how and why they are related remains an open question. The traditional view that these poems afford a balanced contrast has now largely yielded to the view that the two poems are in conflict, with *Il Penseroso* representing a progressive and superior advance over *L'Allegro*.[1] At the risk of seeming to discount most recent scholarship, I propose that *L'Allegro* and *Il Penseroso* are complementary, that their reconciliation is a function of harmony, and that this conception of harmony derives from a sophisticated and self-conscious hermetic tradition.[2]

This tradition might also be described as Neoplatonic — and this term admittedly has the advantage of bringing to mind Milton's well-known use of Neoplatonic notions in works and passages ranging from *De Idea Platonica* through *A Mask*, Raphael's speech to Adam in *Paradise Lost* (V, 469–505), and *Paradise Regained* (IV, 221–364). But for *L'Allegro* and *Il Penseroso, hermetic* is preferable to *Neoplatonic* not only because of the reference to "thrice great *Hermes*" in the latter poem but because, following the legend that Hermes invented a seal to make vessels airtight, *hermetic* came to mean "completely sealed" from outside influences, "closed off" or cloistered from the profane and vulgar world. Not the least of Satan's temptations by wisdom in *Paradise Regained* is his promise that Jesus will "hear and learn the secret power / Of harmony in tones and numbers hit / By voice or hand, and various-measur'd verse" (IV, 254–56).[3] Although Satan alludes to the "secret" power of harmony, he withholds any fuller revelation from the uninitiated Jesus. Leaving aside the obvious irony of the situation, this combination of allusion and secrecy is characteristic of the hermetic tradition, and by attending to a less Satanic but equally mysterious power of harmony we can discover some of the unexplored resonances of *L'Allegro* and *Il Penseroso.*

Milton's single reference to harmony in the two poems occurs when

45

the persona of *L'Allegro* longs to hear "soft *Lydian* Airs, / Married to immortal verse" that will pierce the soul, "Untwisting all the chains that
tie / The hidden soul of harmony" (136–44). The verbal construction here
is similar to the one employed in *Il Penseroso* when that persona desires
to "unsphere / The spirit of *Plato* to unfold" the location of the soul after
death (88–92). In both cases, the prefix *un-* expresses the opposite and
complementary reaction to some antecedent action, for harmony clearly
has to be chained before it can be unchained just as the spirit of Plato
has to be ensphered before it can be unsphered. As the optative mood
of these passages suggests, the preceding action is potentially reversible
by someone who has learned enough to know what he as yet does not
know: if one knows that the soul of harmony is hidden, it potentially can
be manifest; if one knows that the spirit of Plato has been ensphered,
it can be unsphered to unfold "What Worlds, or what vast Regions hold /
The immortal mind that hath forsook / Her mansion in this fleshly
nook" (90–92). In neither case, however, does Milton state what will be
revealed through this process. To all intents and purposes, harmony remains hidden; the location of the soul after death remains a mystery.
While alluding to revelation, therefore, Milton is simultaneously practicing concealment.

This mode of composition is the approved Renaissance way of com-
municating occult lore supposedly derived from antiquity. Someone in
the Renaissance who believed he had rediscovered an ancient mystery
was in a double bind: if he did not publish it, it would not be known
to exist and hence would have no authority; if he did publish it, it would
not be a mystery because it was no longer secret but profaned by the vulgar. As Edgar Wind has demonstrated, Renaissance writers and artists
solved this problem by adopting a cryptic mode of expression that they
thought was sanctioned by the practice of the very ancients they revered.
In his commentary on the *Parmenides*, for example, Ficino declares that
"it was the custom of Pythagoras, Socrates, and Plato everywhere to cover
up divine mysteries in figures and wrappings . . . to jest seriously and
to play most studiously" (*ubique divina mysteria figuris involucrisque
obtegere, . . . iocari serio, et studiosissime ludere*).[4] Here are the dual
means to resolve the double bind: first, by imitating the method of concealment used by the ancients a Renaissance writer could assist with the
rebirth of a mystery without lessening its authority; second, by imitating
the mode of serious playfulness he could prevent the vulgar from suspect-
ing that there was any hidden meaning. Only the initiated would know
how to unfold the hermetic mystery infolded beneath this playful surface. Milton demonstrates his familiarity with this method when he de-

clares in the Second Prolusion that the teaching of Pythagoras on the harmony of the spheres "seems to have followed the example of the poets — or, what is almost the same thing, of the divine oracles — by which no sacred and arcane mystery is ever revealed to vulgar ears without being somehow wrapped up and veiled" (p. 603). Both the playful wit of the Second Prolusion as a whole and his specific claim to be speaking "as it were, in jest" ("*quasi per lusum*") illustrate Milton's familiarity with the approved mode of hermetic communication.

Fortunately for our purposes, this logic of infolding allows for, and perhaps even depends on, a comparable logic of unfolding. By this I do not mean that the critic must offer a word-for-word translation. Such a procedure not only would miss entirely the spirit of the hermetic tradition itself, but would ignore the playfulness with which Milton treats this tradition in his companion poems, and such playful treatment is also a part of the hermetic tradition. Milton is playing seriously with a hermetic system of harmonious correspondences, with the result that both poems come under the category he praises in *Il Penseroso*, songs "Where more is meant than meets the ear."

## I

The opening of *L'Allegro* sets up the first of the many like-and-unlike correspondences in the two poems. "Loathed Melancholy" is obviously at odds with "heart-easing Mirth," but then so too are the "vain deluding joys" exorcised in favor of "divinest Melancholy." If the Mirth-Melancholy opposition is dominant, each of these modes is also opposed to the lesser version of itself. The significance of these separate and unequal versions of mirth for *L'Allegro* is suggested by Plato in *Timaeus* 47d: "Harmony, which has motions akin to the revolutions of our souls, is not regarded by the intelligent votary of the Muses as given by them with a view to irrational pleasure . . . but as meant to correct any discord which may have arisen in the courses of the soul, and to be our ally in bringing her into harmony and agreement with herself." "Vain deluding joys, / The brood of folly without father bred," thus can exemplify the irrational pleasure condemned by Plato. Rather than indulging in this kind of pleasure, the persona of *L'Allegro* first attends to the correction of any discord in his own soul and then, guided by Euphrosyne and her companion, "sweet Liberty," projects "unreproved pleasures free" that bring his soul into agreement with Harmony itself.

The two genealogies of Euphrosyne suggest how this conversion process is possible. Milton's first genealogy has Euphrosyne, like her two sister graces, be the daughter of Bacchus and Venus. Venus of course can represent divine beauty, as perhaps most notably in Botticelli's *Primavera*. As we know from Elegy VI, Milton associated Bacchus with wine, mirth, and poetry (13–14). Furthermore, Bacchus is often associated in the Renaissance with poetic *furor*. Alluding to Plato's description in *Phaedrus* 245 of the Muses' madness that awakens a gentle virginal soul and inspires it to song and poetry, Pico asserts in his "Oration" that we too can be inspired by these frenzies and "drink in the heavenly harmony of our ears" (pp. 13–14). This potential follows from the hermetic notion of emanation, conversion, and return. Because the elemental world reflects the celestial world, man is able to attain this higher state of being by contemplating its representation in nature. In a typically Renaissance synthesis of Plato and St. Paul (Rom. i, 20), Pico continues, "Then Bacchus the leader of the Muses, will show the invisible things of God to us as we philosophize, and will make us drunk with the abundance of the house of God" (p. 14).

Milton's second genealogy for Euphrosyne reinforces these notions of inspiration and conversion. Zephyr, the west wind "that breathes the Spring," can represent the gale of passion that has power to transform. In *Primavera*, for example, Zephyr embraces Chloris and with his breath "inspires" her Ovidian metamorphosis into Flora.[5] The mother of Euphrosyne is Aurora, the goddess of the dawn. The "friend of the Muses," to quote Milton's conventional tag in the First Prolusion, she too is linked to inspiration. As their daughter, Euphrosyne affords man the inspiration to transform himself and so reach a higher level of being. The two competing genealogies thus point to a similar hermetic process (although Milton's phrase for the second, "as some Sager sing," suggests that this is his preferred version): the figure called on earth "heart-easing Mirth" awakens man to his joyful potential. Under her guidance, the persona brings himself into harmony with his own soul. By so doing, he is able to participate in the higher significance of Mirth, "In Heav'n yclep'd *Euphrosyne*," for, according to Ficino, Euphrosyne symbolizes heavenly beauty that reaches the soul through musical sounds.[6] The movement of *L'Allegro* therefore guides the persona to an apprehension of Harmony itself.

As is appropriate for the daughter of Aurora, Euphrosyne's "unreproved pleasures free" begin by awakening man to the sounds heralding the onset of dawn and the rising of the sun:

> To hear the Lark begin his flight,
> And singing startle the dull night,
> From his watch-tow'r in the skies,
> Till the dappled dawn doth rise:

> Then to come in spite of sorrow,
> And at my window bid good-morrow,
>
> . . . . . . . .
>
> While the Cock with lively din,
> Scatters the rear of darkness thin.                              (41–50)

Much critical ingenuity has been expended on this unspecified "sorrow,"
but I take it to refer to the vague grief that Ficino and Pico believe to
be caused by the awareness while at leisure of the dissatisfaction inherent in a life that does not lead to divine things.[7] The singing of the lark,
the crowing of the rooster, and the echoing of the hounds and horn that
"Cheerly rouse the slumb'ring morn" can help to awaken the persona's
discontented mind to cheerfulness. These sounds all announce the rising
of the sun, and they appear to represent the "singings, and harmonical
sounds" that Agrippa ascribes to the sphere of the sun. The "sweet con-
sonancy" of these sounds, Agrippa declares, "drives forth of the minde
any troublesomeness therein, and chears it up."[8] The lark in *L'Allegro*
(as well as the nightingale in *Il Penseroso*) may be glossed by Milton's
declaration in the Second Prolusion, "Why, it is quite credible that the
lark herself soars up into the clouds at dawn and that the nightingale
passes the night in solitary trilling in order to harmonize their songs with
that heavenly music to which they studiously listen" (p. 603). Just as the
singing of the lark startles the night, the "lively din" of the rooster "Scat-
ters the rear of darkness thin"; and these verbs reinforce an almost buried
sense in which the persona participates in these actions: the startling and
scattering of dull night parallel the persona's waking from his sorrowful
night of the soul. As Pico observes, "At the crowing of this cock, erring
man returns to his senses. In the morning dawn this cock daily crows
in harmony with the morning stars praising God" (p. 15).[9] Even the sounds
of "the Hounds and horn . . . Through the high wood echoing shrill" contribute to this harmony, for, as Theseus and Hippolyta remind us in *A
Midsummer Night's Dream*, "the musical confusion / Of hounds and echo
in conjunction" can make "the groves, / The skies, the fountains, every
region near / Seem all one mutual cry" (IV, i, 110–17).

Led by Mirth and accompanied by her crew, the speaker goes abroad
to behold the sun, that conventional symbol of hermetic illumination:

> Some time walking not unseen
> By Hedgerow Elms, on Hillocks green,
> Right against the Eastern gate,
> Where the great Sun begins his state,
> Rob'd in flames, and Amber light,
> The clouds in thousand Liveries dight.                           (57–62)

Here, as in *Paradise Lost* V, 171, the sun may well be "of this great World both Eye and Soul." According to Pico's "Oration," the sun is the "father and leader" of man's contemplation of sacred mysteries (p. 15); its physical light reflects that celestial light that Milton in *Paradise Lost* believes can "Shine inward, and the mind through all her powers / Irradiate" (III, 52–53).

If the following passages in *L'Allegro* do not at first appear to exhibit any celestial light by telling "Of things invisible to mortal sight," the pleasures encountered on the persona's imaginative journey function like the sounds heard earlier, but they operate on a higher level of enlightenment. The speaker first sees and hears the varied activities of man in pastoral harmony with nature. Not only does the rotation of work and play drive off the tedium of satiety, as Milton comments in the Sixth Prolusion (p. 613), but pleasure results from what Giordano Bruno describes as a "definite transit, journey, and motion" from one condition to another.[10] The successive contrasts of fertile plains and barren mountains, romantic castle and country cottage, daytime dancing and nighttime tale-telling in the country are followed by the changes rung on pleasures afforded by "Tow'red Cities" and their characteristic forms of art. Even in so brief a summary, this catalog clearly illustrates the variety of pleasure available to one who follows Mirth.

In my view, however, these pleasures derive their larger importance from the relation that obtains between them. City and country, art and nature are harmoniously related through their very contrariness. As Boethius explains, "Not without cause is it said that all things, which consist of contraries, are conjoined and composed by a certain harmony. For harmony is the joining together of several things and consent of contraries."[11] Guided by "heart-easing Mirth" and illuminated by the lucid essence of the sun, the persona has experienced the pleasing satisfaction of natural harmony.

But in the hermetic tradition, this pleasure is less an end in itself than the means to realize what was called the coincidence of contraries. According to Bruno's deliberately cryptic statement, the "philosopher who has arrived at the theory of the 'coincidence of contraries' has not found out little" (p. 90). Significantly, Bruno's hermetic philosopher reaches this insight about harmonious correspondences by precisely the kind of journey that Milton catalogues in *L'Allegro*. After contrasting the recreation afforded by the country and by the city, for example, Bruno's Sophia concludes: "So mutation from one extreme to the other through its participants, and motion from one contrary to the other through its intermediate points, come to satisfy [us]; and, finally, we see such familiarity between one contrary and the other that the one agrees more with the other than like with like" (p. 90).

Having attained the knowledge of the coincidence of contraries, the persona is now prepared for hermetic revelation of a yet higher harmony. In the concluding passage of *L'Allegro*, Milton extends the possibility of pleasure from the natural to the celestial world. As these lines point to the ultimate delights afforded by Euphrosyne, I shall quote them in their entirety:

> And ever against eating Cares,
> Lap me in soft *Lydian* Airs,
> Married to immortal verse,
> Such as the meeting soul may pierce
> In notes, with many a winding bout
> Of linked sweetness long drawn out,
> With wanton heed, and giddy cunning,
> The melting voice through mazes running;
> Untwisting all the chains that tie
> The hidden soul of harmony;
> That *Orpheus'* self may heave his head
> From golden slumber on a bed
> Of heapt *Elysian* flow'rs, and hear
> Such strains as would have won the ear
> Of *Pluto*, to have quite set free
> His half-regain'd *Eurydice*.                    (135–50)

The exquisitely varying rhythms of these lines are far more complex than the earlier "Come, and trip it as ye go / On the light fantastic toe" (34–35), and the presumable reason is that this is an early example of Milton feeding "on thoughts, that voluntary move / Harmonious numbers" (*PL* III, 37–38). In any case, Milton's own "melting voice through mazes running" gives us a clue — as no argument could — to the "hidden soul of harmony." What begins as entreaty soon modulates to a series of appositive statements on the effect of this union of voice and verse: the "meeting" or welcoming soul is pierced by the Lydian mode that could be associated with Jupiter in Renaissance musical theory.[12] Earlier, we may recall, the nymph Liberty accompanies Mirth, implying that man is free, at liberty, to reach his fullest potential. Now, in this jovial mood, Liberty seemingly concludes her office by "Untwisting all the chains that tie / The hidden soul of harmony." Yet if harmony is no longer "hidden," it equally is not revealed. The reason it remains mysterious, I suggest, is that Milton is cryptically if playfully alluding to man's potential for apprehending celestial harmony, or the music of the spheres.

Conventionally, of course, man is incapable of hearing the music of the spheres. "Such harmony is in immortal souls," as Lorenzo rather academically explains to Jessica in *The Merchant of Venice;* "But whilst this muddy vesture of decay / Doth grossly close it in, we cannot hear it" (V, i, 63–65). Milton's own view appears to have been more qualified. In the Second Prolusion, "On the Music of the Spheres," he remarks that "Pythagoras alone of mortals is said to have heard this harmony" (p. 604). Yet Milton ends the prolusion by an explicit statement that man could again hear the music of the spheres if he became like Pythagoras: "If our hearts were as pure, as chaste, as snowy as Pythagoras' was, our ears would resound and be filled with that supremely lovely music of the wheeling stars" (ibid.).

The ending of *L'Allegro* appears to explore this potential. Under the guidance of Euphrosyne, the speaker's soul has become so in tune with Harmony (the subject of Pythagorean doctrines) that it can hear music that would awaken the archetypal poet/singer Orpheus to wonder, for the strains he hears so surpass his own that Pluto would "have quite set free / His half-regain'd *Eurydice.*" The haunting sense of limitation and loss in these lines suggests that Milton regards Orpheus here less as the founder of esoteric Greek religion than as the ethically influential poet and musician.[13] In this tradition, Orpheus was an allegory of savage man brought unto the rule of reason, as More explains in *Utopia*, Book II. His kind of music produces a balanced temperament in man. The marriage of verse and music described at the close of *L'Allegro* goes beyond that of Orpheus, for that only brought man into harmony with himself (or what Boethius termed *musica humana*), but this brings man into harmony with Harmony itself (what Boethius termed *musica mundana*).[14] Because the revolutions of the persona's soul have become perfectly attuned to the motions of Harmony, he can imagine hearing the harmony of the spheres that has been hidden from man since Pythagoras.

*L'Allegro* thus is self-referential, for it simultaneously unfolds, through its marriage of voice and musical numbers, Milton's attempt to harmonize his own song with that "supremely lovely music of the wheeling stars," and infolds the way for others to be guided by that "Goddess fair and free, / In Heav'n yclep'd *Euphrosyne,*" the divine beauty that reaches the soul in the form of musical sounds.

## II

In contrast to the nonintellectual approach to God through Mirth, *Il Penseroso* portrays the contemplative approach through Melancholy. If *L'Allegro* infolds a progression from earth to the spheres, *Il Penseroso* infolds a progression from earth to the ecstatic vision of heaven. The latter is clearly of a higher order than the former, but that need not mean that *L'Allegro* is merely a preparative exercise, an imaginative evocation of a mode of life that may allure but must finally be rejected for the intellectual exaltation of *Il Penseroso*. The relation of the two poems, I shall argue, is not that of inferior to superior but that of counterpoint: the two are unlike contraries that stand in harmonious relation.

As scholars have demonstrated, Milton's portrait of "divinest Melancholy" is heavily indebted to the hermetic tradition of the Renaissance.[15] The invocation of this "Goddess, sage and holy" explicitly refers to the *facies nigra* associated with melancholy in the Renaissance:

> Hail divinest Melancholy,
> Whose Saintly visage is too bright
> To hit the Sense of human sight;
> And therefore to our weaker view,
> O'erlaid with black, staid Wisdom's hue.          (12–16)

Following the Plotinian emphasis on Saturn as the Mind of the world (and hence superior to Jupiter, the Soul), Renaissance thinkers like Ficino, Pico, and Agrippa associated melancholy with contemplative genius. Those who dedicated themselves to melancholy could learn the secrets of the divine realm and excel in theology and prophecy.

The "first, and chiefest" of Melancholy's companions indicates the means by which this hermetic illumination is attained. Melancholy is accompanied by the "Cherub Contemplation" who "soars on golden wing, / Guiding the fiery-wheeled throne" (52–54). Pico's "Oration" is customarily cited to gloss this cherub,[16] but Pico's emphasis on the throne's steadfastness of judgment does not illuminate Milton's pun on the throne of Ezekiel's vision. Agrippa, on the other hand, while agreeing with Pico about the cherubim, assigns to the angelic order of thrones an office that does suggest how the Cherub Contemplation "guides" the throne: "From the Thrones, we are knit together, and being collected into our selves, we fix our memory on those eternall visions: From the Cherubins, is light of mind, power of wisdom, very high phantasies and figures, by the which we are able to contemplate even the divine Things; From the Seraphins . . . the perfect flame of love." In a metaphor that presumably derives from Genesis xxviii, 12, Agrippa concludes, "These are the degrees, these the ladders, by the which men easily ascend to all kinds of powers" (p. 468).

Il Penseroso progresses to "something like Prophetic strain" (174) by ascending the steps of this hermetic ladder. As in *L'Allegro*, the visible

things of nature can point to the invisible things of God. The persona's
movement from out-of-doors to the tower apparently represents a symbolic progression of the eyes of the soul. Il Penseroso first "beholds" the
"wand'ring Moon" often "stooping through a fleecy cloud" (72). The moon
can signify both the planet and, particularly given its association with
water ("some wide-water'd shore"), the Soul of the World that according
to Ficino is represented on earth by the changeable light of the moon
and is associated with the element of water.[17] The "high lonely Tow'r"
where the speaker "may oft outwatch the *Bear*, / With thrice great
*Hermes*" (86–88) fuses, as D. C. Allen observes, the Platonic comparison
of the mind to a tower (*Tim.* 70a; *Rep.* 560b) and the watchtower of
Isaiah xxi, 5, 8.[18] Il Penseroso's contemplation in the tower progressively
rises above space and time to the intellectual world. Just as beholding
the moon can represent the attainment of the Soul of the World, so contemplating the stars that comprise the constellation of the Great Bear
can represent the attainment of the next higher degree. According to
Ficino, for example, the firmament of the stars manifests the fullness of
ideas, or the divine Intellect.[19] By outwatching the Bear, therefore, man
can participate in the intellectual world. As "thrice great *Hermes*" declares, contemplating the course of the Great Bear (which never sets but
turns around itself and carries the entire cosmos around with it) is a means
of making the unmanifest God manifest to the intellect.[20]

The persona thus becomes able to gain knowledge that otherwise
remains hidden. Now he may

> unsphere
> The spirit of *Plato* to unfold
> What Worlds, or what vast Regions hold
> The immortal mind that hath forsook
> Her mansion in this fleshly nook:
> And of those *Daemons* that are found
> In fire, air, flood, or underground,
> Whose power hath a true consent
> With Planet, or with Element.                    (88–96)

Yet Milton once again does not reveal the substance of this mystery. It
remains mysterious, much indeed as it remains mysterious in Plato himself. Plato states in the *Timaeus* (42b) that the righteous man will return
to dwell in his native star and enjoy a blessed and congenial existence,
but the location of this star is left obscure. In the *Phaedo* (114c), Plato
observes that those who have purified themselves by philosophy will "live
thereafter without bodies, and reach habitations even more beautiful [than

the earth], which it is not easy to portray—nor is there time to do so now." In the Fourth Ennead, however, Plotinus suggests what method should be followed to "unfold" this mystery:

Souls, body-bound, are apt to body-punishment; clean souls no longer drawing to themselves at any point any vestige of body are, by their very being, outside the bodily sphere; body-free, containing nothing of body—there where Essence is, and Being, and the Divine within the Divinity, among Those, within That, such a soul must be.

If you still ask Where, you must ask where those Beings are—and in your seeking, seek otherwise than with the sight, and not as one seeking for body.[21]

By unsphering not the body but the "spirit of *Plato*," the persona is seeking otherwise than with the sight, and his act of self-intellection focuses on divine Intellect. According to the Hermetic corpus (II, 204–05), he who abandons corporal sensation comes to know that his own essence has been constituted by the divine Powers. It thus is significant that Milton next mentions "those *Daemons* that are found / In fire, air, flood, or underground," for in the Hermetic system these demons are the lofty powers that minister to the order of the cosmos, descending from heaven to earth in water and air and reascending in fire. They are above the Great Bear, and their "power" protects and embraces the universe by day and by night. According to the *Asclepius*, "familiarity with the race of demons" teaches man that he has issued from the same divine origin: there is one cosmos, one Soul, one God.[22] The question of "What Worlds, or what vast Regions hold / The immortal mind that hath forsook / Her mansion in this fleshly nook" is thus implicitly answered: such a soul must be with God.

Following the movement of *L'Allegro*, the celebration of these mysteries of nature in *Il Penseroso* is succeeded by the mysteries of art. After naming "Gorgeous Tragedy," an obvious contrast to the comedy of *L'Allegro*, Milton now emphasizes those works and figures that represent the mythical "power" of art: Musaeus and Orpheus, Chaucer's "*Cambuscan*," and whatever else "great Bards" have sung "Where more is meant than meets the ear" (120). According to the commentary of George Sandys on the tenth book of Ovid's *Metamorphoses*, the Testament of Orpheus exhorted Musaeus "to the hearing and understanding of that knowledge, which was revealed from Heaven."[23] Like Chaucer's "Squire's Tale," therefore, these symbolic narratives may represent what Milton praises in the Second Prolusion as the "example of the poets—or, what is almost the same thing, of the divine oracles—by which no sacred and arcane mystery is ever revealed to vulgar ears without being somehow wrapped up and veiled" (p. 603).

To realize this sacred and arcane mystery, Il Penseroso progresses from night to day, from enlightened darkness to darkened illumination through dreams in sleep and through the Cloister's "dim religious light" (160). Just as Melancholy's "Saintly visage is too bright / To hit the Sense of human sight," so the sun must be shadowed. Given that the speaker asks to be hidden "Where no profaner eye may look" (140), and given that when he awakes from "some strange mysterious dream" (147), music breathes "Above, about, or underneath" him, Milton is clearly representing an initiation into hermetic mysteries. Because sleep is a form of *vacatio*, a state in which the Soul withdraws from the body, Ficino explains, sleep makes the Soul accessible to divine influence.[24] If the sleeper has already risen above concerns with the merely corporeal and directed his attention toward God, his dream will not be a product of the temperament or the fantasy but rather a divine inspiration. Il Penseroso's "strange mysterious dream" can thus be a form of prophecy, a further step toward the attainment of "something like Prophetic strain."

Lest this form of prophecy seem pagan rather than Christian, the desire for an initiation by dream is followed by the desire for an explicitly Christian ecstasy:

> But let my due feet never fail
> To walk the studious Cloister's pale,
>
> . . . . . . . .
>
> There let the pealing Organ blow
> To the full voic'd Choir below,
> In Service high and Anthems clear,
> As may with sweetness, through mine ear,
> Dissolve me into ecstasies,
> And bring all Heav'n before mine eyes.          (155–66)

The mystery stated so succinctly here can be illuminated by several other passages of Milton's.[25] Here, as in "At a Solemn Music," the "Sphere-born harmonious Sisters, Voice and Verse," present to his "high-rais'd fantasy" Heaven's "undisturbed Song of pure concent." If in *L'Allegro* the speaker's soul comes into harmony with Harmony and hears the music of the spheres, in *Il Penseroso* the soul comes into harmony with the source of Harmony and attains union with God. The soul's inner journey from ear to eye, from earth to heaven, is also anticipated in "At a Vacation Exercise," a work whose title may well be punning on "*vacatio*":

> clothe my fancy in fit sound:
> Such where the deep transported mind may soar
> Above the wheeling poles, and at Heav'n's door

> Look in, and see each blissful Deity
> How he before the thunderous throne doth lie,
> Listening to what unshorn Apollo sings
> To th' touch of golden wires.                    (32–38)

Finally, it should be observed that Milton explicitly refers to the condition of ek-stasis in the phrase "Dissolve me into ecstasies," conventionally correct even to the use of *dissolve* for the disuniting of the soul from the body (we may compare 2 Cor. v, 1, "For we know that if our earthly house of this tabernacle were dissolved, we have a building of God, an house not made with hands, eternal in the heavens"). If the ecstasy projected in *Il Penseroso* is necessarily temporal rather than eternal in the heavens, it may nevertheless correspond to the condition of the soul after death. In the hermetic tradition, the goal of the contemplative life is the intuition of God. This intuition not only gives new meaning to all of human experience but is a metaphor for the future life. As Ficino declares, "It does not escape [the attention of the philosophers] of what kind the state of the pure Soul will be after death. It will be of such a kind as is always experienced at the highest peak of contemplation (*in summo contemplationis fastigio*)."[26]

The closing lines of the poem represent both a descent from this peak of contemplation and a projection of the knowledge gained into the future:

> And may at last my weary age
> Find out the peaceful hermitage,
> The Hairy Gown and Mossy Cell,
> Where I may sit and rightly spell
> Of every Star that Heav'n doth shew,
> And every Herb that sips the dew;
> Till old experience do attain
> To something like Prophetic strain.            (167–74)

The "hidden soul of harmony" in *L'Allegro* is reinvoked, but in a different mode. In the hermetic system, the structure of the whole is replicated in every part, and hence every smaller unit — every star, every herb — reflects the image of the One. The "study of the hidden virtues of stones and herbs" that Milton recommends in the Third Prolusion (p. 606) presumably leads to a more informed sense of harmonious relations. As Agrippa explains: "There is therefore a wonderful vertue, and operation in every Hearb, and Stone, but greater in a Star, beyond which, even from the governing Intelligencies every thing receiveth, and obtains many things for it self, especially from the Supream Cause, with whom all things do mutually, and exactly correspond, agreeing in an harmonious

consent, as it were in Hymnes, alwaies praising the highest Maker of all
things" (Bk. I, Ch. 13; p. 31). Yet, as Agrippa himself ruefully observes,
the diversity of things is so great that very few of these harmonious relations have become known to us. The "ancient Philosophers, & Chyroman-
cers," he continues, achieved more knowledge of these harmonies, "partly
by reason, and partly by experience" (Bk. I, Ch. 33, p. 67). Having attained the ecstatic experience of ultimate harmony, Milton's persona hopes
to discover through his own "old experience" the harmonious relations
that Agrippa states "yet ly hid in the treasury of nature."

## III

L'Allegro and Il Penseroso thus infold a plenitude of hermetic correspondences for the reader who is able to untwist "all the chains that
tie / The hidden soul of harmony." Through their mode of serio ludere,
the two poems represent opposing ways to union with the divine: L'Allegro
is the way of pleasure, Il Penseroso the way of wisdom. L'Allegro is an
encomium of Mirth altogether different from the "vain deluding joys"
exorcised in the opening of Il Penseroso, for Mirth reveals the means for
man to put himself in tune and thus add his own voice to the heavenly
harmony of God's creation. Il Penseroso is an encomium of Melancholy
altogether different from the "loathed Melancholy / of Cerberus and
blackest midnight born" castigated in L'Allegro, for Melancholy reveals
the means to attain first the ecstatic vision of Heaven and then "something
like Prophetic strain." If these latter attainments appear to be of a higher
order than the former, they are also complementary. Insofar as the achievement of prophetic strain is knowing the harmonious correspondences between all things and their supreme cause, then Il Penseroso projects yet
another analogue of discovering L'Allegro's "hidden soul of harmony."
Here, as in the familiar contrasts of night and day, darkness and light,
solitude and society, nature and art, poet-singer and poet-priest, seeming contraries can be reconciled harmoniously, for as Boethius reminds
us, "harmony is the joining together of several things and consent of
contraries." In the more paradoxical formula beloved by Renaissance
hermeticists, harmonia est discordia concors.[27] This is the conception
of harmony that informs Pico's declaration in Heptaplus that the distinct natures of all four worlds — angelic, celestial, elemental, and man
himself — are "linked together by a certain discordant concord and bound
by many kinds of interwoven chains" (p. 80). This is the conception of
harmony that Milton, speaking "as it were, in jest," describes in the Second Prolusion as "that universal interaction of all things, that lovely concord among them (conspirationem rerum universam, & consensum ama-
bilem), which Pythagoras poetically symbolized as harmony" and which

Homer "splendidly and aptly represented" by the figure of the golden chain suspended by Jove from heaven (p. 603). To untwist "all the chains that tie / The hidden soul of harmony" is thus to realize that like the worlds they describe, *L'Allegro* and *Il Penseroso* replicate this lovely concord.

In the hermetic system, however, all such unity-in-multiplicity points toward the One. Here is the reason, I suggest, why these companion poems each end on a conditional note. After we make due allowance for the difference in emphasis between "These delights if thou canst give, / Mirth with thee I mean to live" and "These pleasures *Melancholy* give, / And I with thee will choose to live," it is clear that the retention of the conditional for *Il Penseroso* indicates that neither poem is adequate to express man's highest good. Even as a harmonious pair of companion poems, *L'Allegro* and *Il Penseroso* project only a conditional good, and in this emphasis they agree with hermetic tradition. According to Ficino's summary of the *Philebus*, the highest good of the soul is a "conditional good," for the principle of all things, God, is the absolute good.[28] Because man's conditional good proceeds from the absolute good, man can become like God. Neither pleasure nor wisdom alone enables man to attain his highest good, and therefore, Ficino concludes, Plato "located man's highest good in the mixture of wisdom and pleasure" ("*in sapientiae voluptatisque conmixtione locavit*"). In these terms, the optative mood of *L'Allegro* and *Il Penseroso* suggests that Milton was attempting to represent what Ficino describes as "the enjoyment of that first good—an enjoyment which coincides with the mixing together of wisdom and pleasure through truth, proportion, and beauty" (p. 486). Rather than simply declaring that "Beauty is truth, truth beauty,—that is all / Ye know on earth, and all ye need to know," however, Milton employs the "hidden soul of harmony"—the unifying principle of truth, proportion, and beauty—to reconcile the apparent oppositions of the way of pleasure infolded in *L'Allegro* and the way of wisdom infolded in *Il Penseroso*. In their playful seriousness, *L'Allegro* and *Il Penseroso* harmoniously project the means for man to enjoy his highest good: to become one with the God who, in the famous phrase of Nicholas Cusanus, is himself the *coincidentia oppositorum*.

University of Washington

NOTES

1. The summary of criticism in *A Variorum Commentary on the Poems of John Milton*, II, *The Minor English Poems*, ed. A. S. P. Woodhouse and Douglas Bush (New York, 1972), Part I, pp. 241–69, should be supplemented by George L. Geckle, "Miltonic Ideal-

ism: *L'Allegro* and *Il Penseroso*," *TSLL*, IX (1968), 455–73; John A. Via, "The Rhythm of Regenerate Experience: *L'Allegro* and *Il Penseroso*," *Renaissance Papers 1969*, ed. George Walton Williams (Southeastern Renaissance Conference, 1970), 47–55; Ivy Dempsey, "To 'Attain to Something Like Prophetic Strain,'" in *Papers on Milton*, ed. P. M. Griffith and L.F. Zimmerman (Tulsa, Okla., 1969), p. 9–24; Gary Stringer, "The Unity of 'L'Allegro' and 'Il Penseroso,'" *TSLL*, XII (1970), 221–29; David M. Miller, "From Delusion to Illumination: A Larger Structure for *L'Allegro–Il Penseroso*," *PMLA*, LXXXVI (1971), 32–39; Leslie Brisman, "'All Before Them Where to Choose': 'L'Allegro' and 'Il Penseroso,'" *JEGP*, LXXI (1972), 226–40; John F. Huntley, "The Poet-Critic and His Poem-Culture in 'L'Allegro' and 'Il Penseroso,'" *TSLL*, XIII (1972), 541–53; Stanley Fish, "What's It Like to Read *L'Allegro* and *Il Penseroso*," in *Milton Studies*, VII, ed. Albert C. Labriola and Michael Lieb (Pittsburgh, 1975), pp. 77–79; Annabel Patterson, "*L'Allegro, Il Penseroso* and *Comus*: The Logic of Recombination," *MQ*, IX (1975), 75–79; Thomas Lavoie, "The Divine Vision of the Inward Eye: The Structural Hierarchy of the 'L'Allegro–Il Penseroso' Sequence," *Thoth*, XVI (1976), 3–17; Norman B. Council, "*L'Allegro, Il Penseroso*, and 'The Cycle of Universal Knowledge,'" in *Milton Studies*, IX, ed. James D. Simmonds (Pittsburgh, 1976), pp. 203–19; Lowell Edwin Folsom, "'L'Allegro' and 'Il Penseroso': The Poetics of Accelerando and Ritardando," *Studies in the Humanities*, V (1976), 39–41; Kathleen M. Swaim, "Cycle and Circle: Time and Structure in *L'Allegro* and *Il Penseroso*," *TSLL*, XVIII (1976), 422–32; Thomas J. Embry, "Sensuality and Chastity in *L'Allegro* and *Il Penseroso*," *JEGP*, LXXVII (1978), 504–29.

2. This approach has been anticipated by Michael Fixler, "The Orphic Technique of 'L'Allegro' and 'Il Penseroso,'" *English Literary Renaissance*, I (1971), 165–77, and, less specifically, "Plato's Four Furors and the Real Structure of *Paradise Lost*," *PMLA*, XCII (1977), 952–62. Some of the best recent studies that touch on these companion poems include S. K. Heninger, Jr., "Sidney and Milton: The Poet as Maker," in *Milton and the Line of Vision*, ed. Joseph Anthony Wittreich, Jr. (Madison, Wis., 1975) pp. 57–95; Wittreich, *Visionary Poetics: Milton's Tradition and His Legacy* (San Marino, Calif, 1979), esp. pp. 79–83; Raymond B. Waddington, "Milton Among the Carolines," in *The Age of Milton: Backgrounds to Seventeenth-Century Literature*, ed. C. A. Patrides and Raymond B. Waddington (Manchester, Eng., 1980), esp. pp. 345–52.

3. Quotations from Milton in English are taken from *John Milton: Complete Poems and Major Prose*, ed. Merritt Y. Hughes (New York, 1957); the Latin of the Prolusions is taken from Vol. XII of *The Works of John Milton*, ed. Frank Allen Patterson et al. (New York, 1931–38) (hereafter cited as CM).

4. Ficino, *In Parmenidem (Prooemium)*, my trans. of the Latin quoted by Edgar Wind, *Pagan Mysteries in the Renaissance*, rev. ed. (New York, 1968), p. 236 n. 1. Cf. Pico's "Oration on the Dignity of Man": "as was the practice of ancient theologians, Orpheus covered the mysteries of his doctrines with the wrappings of fables, and disguised them with a poetic garment, so that whoever reads his hymns may believe that there is nothing underneath but tales and the purest nonsense" (trans. Charles Glenn Wallis, [Library of Liberal Arts, Indianapolis, 1965], p. 33).

5. See Wind's analysis in *Pagan Mysteries*, pp. 115–16.

6. On Ficino's Euphrosyne and her English habitation as Laetitia, see D. J. Gordon, "The Imagery of Ben Jonson's *Masques of Blacknesse and Beautie*," in *The Renaissance Imagination*, ed. Stephen Orgel (Berkeley, 1975), p. 149.

7. Paul Oskar Kristeller, *The Philosophy of Marsilio Ficino* (New York, 1943), pp. 208–09. Pico's "On Being and the One" (trans. Paul J. W. Miller) declares that "our mind, to which even divine things are accessible, cannot be of mortal race, and will be happy

only by the possession of divine things" (Library of Liberal Arts ed., p. 61). Cf. the lines Milton cut from "At a Solemn Music" (CM I, Pt. II, p. 421):

> and whilst yo[r] equall raptures temper'd sweet
> in high misterious holie spousall meet
> snatch us from earth a while
> us of our selves & home bred woes beguile.

8. Henry Cornelius Agrippa, *Three Books of Occult Philosophy*, trans. J. F. (London, 1651), Bk. III, Ch. 46, p. 501.

9. Marilyn L. Williamson refers to Pico's use of "feed the cock" in "The Myth of Orpheus in 'L'Allegro' and 'Il Penseroso,'" *MLQ*, XXXII (1971), 383. In *The Untuning of the Sky* (Princeton, 1961), John Hollander quotes the madrigal "*Sy dolce no sono chol' lir' Orfeo*" by Landini that exalts the music of a rooster over the music of Orpheus (p. 164).

10. Bruno, *The Expulsion of the Triumphant Beast*, ed. and trans. Arthur D. Imerti (New Brunswick, N. J., 1964), p. 89. In terms of logic, these topics illustrate the diagonally adverse relation of affirming contraries, a relation that, as Wittreich has pointed out in *Visionary Poetics* (p. 83), also holds for these two poems: see Milton's *Art of Logic*, Ch. XV (CM XI, pp. 131–35).

11. Boethius, *De arithmetica*, 2.32; quoted by S. K. Heninger, Jr., *Touches of Sweet Harmony: Pythagorean Cosmology and Renaissance Poetics* (San Marino, Calif., 1974), p. 104.

12. See the frontispiece to *The Practica musicae of Franchinus Gafurius*, ed. and trans. Irwin Young (Madison, 1969), p. 1. For texts that condemn the Lydian mode, see *A Variorum Commentary*, II, Pt. I, pp. 304–05.

13. On Orpheus, see D. P. Walker, *The Ancient Theology: Studies in Christian Platonism from the Fifteenth to the Eighteenth Century* (Ithaca, N.Y.: 1972), pp. 22–41, and Michael Fixler, "The Orphic Technique of 'L'Allegro' and 'Il Penseroso,'" *ELR*, I (1971), 165–77. For the inability of Orpheus to hear the harmony of the spheres, see the discussion of the *Testament* by John B. Friedman, *Orpheus in the Middle Ages* (Cambridge, Mass., 1970), pp. 14–17.

14. Hollander gives succinct accounts of these categories in *The Untuning of the Sky*, pp. 25, 169.

15. Raymond Klibansky, Erwin Panofsky, and Fritz Saxl, *Saturn and Melancholy: Studies in the History of Natural Philosophy, Religion, and Art* (New York, 1964). See also Panofsky, *The Life and Art of Albrecht Dürer* (Princeton, 1971), esp. pp. 156–71.

16. See A. S. P. Woodhouse, "Notes on Milton's Early Development," *UTQ*, XIII (1943–44), 66–101, rpt. in Woodhouse, *The Heavenly Muse: A Preface to Milton*, ed. Hugh MacCallum (Toronto, 1972), pp. 45–46.

17. Ficino, *De sole*, quoted from *Renaissance Philosophy*, vol. I: *the Italian Philosophers*, ed. and trans. Arturo B. Fallico and Herman Shapiro (New York, 1967), p. 135. Cf. Kristeller, *Philosophy of Marsilio Ficino*, p. 384.

18. Don Cameron Allen, *The Harmonious Vision*, rev. ed. (Baltimore, 1970), pp. 17–18.

19. Ficino, *De sole*, p. 135.

20. *Corpus Hermeticum*, ed. A. D. Nock and trans. A.-J. Festugière, 4 vols. (Paris, 1945), III, p. 37; I, p. 61; cf. Allen, *Harmonious Vision*, p. 13.

21. Plotinus, *The Enneads*, trans. Stephen MacKenna, 2nd ed., rev. B. S. Page (London, 1956), IV.3.24.

22. *Corpus Hermeticum*, II, pp. 298, 302; cf. *Marsilio Ficino's Commentary on Plato's "Symposium,"* trans. Sears Reynolds Jayne, University of Missouri Studies, XIX (Colum-

bia, 1944), p. 185. On daemons, see also D. P. Walker, *Spiritual and Demonic Magic from Ficino to Campanella* (Notre Dame, 1975), pp. 46–51.

23. Sandys, *Ovid's Metamorphosis*, ed. Karl K. Hulley and Stanley T. Vandersall (Lincoln, Neb. 1970), p. 479. On Chaucer's symbolic narrative, see Allen, *Harmonious Vision*, pp. 12–13.

24. Kristeller, *Philosophy of Marsilio Ficino*, p. 313. Cf. pp. 216, 365. Agrippa observes in his chapter "Of Prophetical Dreams" that the pure soul loosed from the body receives beams and representations from the divine mind; it sees clearly in "a deifying glass" what reason is unable to discern (Bk. III, Ch. 51; pp. 511–15).

25. These passages have been adduced in differing contexts by the following: Sigmund Spaeth, *Milton's Knowledge of Music* (1913; rpt. Ann Arbor, Mich., 1963); James Hutton, "Some English Poems in Praise of Music," *English Miscellany*, II (1951), 1–63; Nan C. Carpenter, "The Place of Music in *L'Allegro* and *Il Penseroso*," *UTQ*, XXII (1952–53), 354–67; Allen, *The Harmonious Vision*, pp. 14–16; Hollander, *The Untuning of the Sky*, pp. 324–31.

26. Quoted from Kristeller, *Philosophy of Marsilio Ficino*, p. 227; cf. pp. 228–29.

27. See Wind's "Virtue Reconciled with Pleasure," in *Pagan Mysteries*, pp. 81–96.

28. *Marsilio Ficino: The "Philebus" Commentary*, ed. and trans. Michael J. B. Allen (Berkeley, Calif., 1975), Appendix 3, p. 484.

# ALCESTIS AND THE
# "PASSION FOR IMMORTALITY":
# MILTON'S *SONNET XXIII*
# AND PLATO'S *SYMPOSIUM*

## Patrick Cheney

I N *SONNET XXIII* Milton associates his "late espoused Saint" with Alcestis, the domestic heroine who had returned "from the grave" to reunite with her husband, Admetus. Most critics have followed Thomas Warton in citing Euripides' *Alcestis* as Milton's source. Yet the Euripides citation does not account for Milton's placing of Alcestis in a context that many readers since Leo Spitzer have recognized as Platonic or Neoplatonic.[1] Evidently, the first to offer another source was Dixon Fiske who, in a largely Neoplatonic reading, suggested Pico's interpretation in the *Commento sopra una canzone de amore*. Fiske, however, does not mention what John Spencer Hill reveals in his subsequent reading — that Pico is commenting on Plato's use of Alcestis in the *Symposium*.[2] Though directing us to the *Symposium* as a possible source for Milton's Alcestis, Hill's discussion has two limitations. First, it mentions only one of Plato's references to Alcestis — that in the speech of Phaedrus; thus it misses the most important one — that in the speech of Socrates. Second, Hill's discussion does not explore the significance of the new source for Milton's sonnet, especially in the light of recent Neoplatonic readings. The present essay aims to extend the commentary on the Alcestis reference by examining Milton's Alcestis in the light of Plato's Alcestis.[3] This analysis, in addition, will enable us to place Milton's last sonnet within a new literary context: English Renaissance sonnets responding to Platonism, such as those by Sidney and Spenser.

Leo Spitzer was the first to introduce the theme of Platonism into commentary on Milton's twenty-third sonnet. In his 1951 article, Spitzer argued that Milton presents himself as a "Christian Platonist" (p. 20). Though Spitzer does not consider that Milton might have had Plato himself in mind, he does argue that the sonnet focuses on a Platonic or Neoplatonic theme, "the generally human problem of the Ideal in our world"

(p. 22). For Spitzer, the sonnet uses a "tripartite *crescendo* arrangement" of similes — pagan, Hebrew, Christian (p. 21) — to illustrate the persona's "harrowing realization that, for all his craving for reunion with the Ideal, in this life there exists no intermediary realm between Earth and Heaven" (p. 20).

In a more recent Neoplatonic reading, John J. Colaccio accepts Spitzer's tripartite arrangement but adds that the sonnet has two "spiritual" movements: a linear one, derived from the tradition of Christian typology, in which man progresses to God through a life in history that parallels the life of Christ, and a vertical one, derived from the tradition of Christian Neoplatonism, in which man ascends the Platonic ladder through love of God.[4] From the perspective of Christian typology, the Alcestis-like Saint mirrors Christ's self-sacrifice: as Christ sacrificed himself for mankind, so Alcestis sacrificed herself for her husband (pp. 184–85). From the perspective of Christian Neoplatonism, the Saint descends the Neoplatonic ladder, drawing the persona up (p. 191). Taken as a whole, however, the sonnet focuses on the persona's ultimate blindness to the "richly Christlike and kerygmatic nature" of the Saint (p. 185): "The persona . . . is guilty of a kind of *Luxuria*, or excessive love of a person, which can cloud a deeper perception of that person's newly achieved spiritual status" (p. 191). It is such a "fancied sight,"Colaccio concludes, that causes the persona to "wake" to the Christian Neoplatonic dream life of mortality (p. 194).

Like Colaccio, Dixon Fiske seeks to extend and qualify Spitzer's original Neoplatonic reading. Fiske argues that the progression of the sonnet represents "not just a progression toward the general Christian ideal, as Spitzer suggests, but a progression toward the more specifically Miltonic and Puritan ideal of purifying Christian zeal. The progression dramatizes a purification of the speaker's own love" (p. 157). For Fiske, Alcestis appropriately becomes a Neoplatonic figure of purification, for "she achieved the equivalent of zeal, a divine, purifying love of God" (p. 156). He cites Pico's *Commento* as evidence that Alcestis could be adapted to Neoplatonism in this way. The Pico reference, evidently the first to go beyond the traditional citation of the Euripides play, is important, because it represents a precedent for Milton's Christianizing the myth within a Neoplatonic context. Hence, Fiske retains Spitzer's general theme of man's ultimate separation from the ideal but adjusts Colaccio's specific theme from self-sacrifice to purification: purification cannot be attained in this life, and "even in the dream [the persona] cannot enjoy the full freedom of Christian liberty" (p. 159). According to Fiske, the persona "has certainly transcended his earlier perceptions and succeeded in viewing his wife in terms of the new law of love that calls for purification of the inward man. But in this life the inward man cannot escape the limitations of the outward man and be entirely purified" (ibid.).

It was evidently Fiske's identification of the Pico source that led John Spencer Hill to mention the subject of Pico's discussion in the *Commento*: Plato's reference to Alcestis in the *Symposium*. By following Pico, Hill is left to conclude that Alcestis is a "paradigm of wifely devotion and self-abnegation" (p. 130). His main point is modest: "to notice that Pico interprets the myth of Alcestis within the context of Judaeo-Christian resurrection and of Christian mysticism" (p. 132). In arguing that the elements of the Alcestis myth are echoed in the other two parts of the poem (and thus suggesting that the pagan myth is assimilated to the Christian vision), Hill sees Alcestis principally as a figure of resurrection. He thus works from Spitzer's original tripartite structure, but shifts the specific theme from Colaccio's self-sacrifice and Fiske's purification to that of resurrection.[5]

What Spitzer, Colaccio, and Fiske (in particular) reveal is a trend in Milton criticism to read *Sonnet XXIII* in a Neoplatonic context. Taken as a whole, these Neoplatonic readings have emphasized a single idea interpreted from a variety of perspectives: man's inability to unite himself with the ideal within the confines of human mortality. The key figure in the commentary has become Alcestis, and accordingly the commentary has turned to Plato's *Symposium* — that treatise on the ideal — for an actual Alcestis reference. What has not been noticed, however, is that Plato refers to Alcestis twice, and that the one reference identified by Hill is actually the least significant. A closer look at Plato's *Symposium* can reveal another source for the central figure of Alcestis as well as the core idea of Christian Neoplatonism to which, I will argue, Milton's last sonnet is responding.

In the opening speech of the *Symposium*, Phaedrus treats Alcestis as a figure of the devoted lover (as Hill pointed out): "for she alone was ready to lay down her life for her husband."[6] It is this kind of "magnanimity," says Phaedrus, that causes the gods to grace Alcestis with immortality—"that her soul should rise from the Stygian depths" (179c). For Phaedrus, Alcestis becomes a type of the heroic lover who is willing to "offer his life for another's" (179c). Love becomes an act of self-sacrifice that the gods will ultimately grace with resurrection; Alcestis herself becomes a type of the self-sacrificing lover who experiences resurrection.

Importantly for Milton's sonnet, Phaedrus emphasizes the role of Alcestis rather than that of her savior, Hercules. Hence, it is because Al-

cestis is both a figure of self-sacrificial love and a figure of resurrection
that she becomes analogous to Christ, and thus easily adaptable to a Christian Neoplatonic context. According to Pico, "Alcestis loved perfectly; she
turned to go to the beloved through death, and in dying through love
she was restored to life by the grace of the gods — that is, regenerated into
life, not through corporal but through spiritual regeneration" (Fiske, p.
157). Fisk interprets Pico as meaning that Alcestis' love "was so divorced
from worldly things, she so loved the Idea and so wanted to unite herself
with it, that she was willing to die in order to penetrate the fleshly barrier between her spirit and the Idea" (pp. 156–57). This self-sacrificial
quest for union with the ideal, Fiske adds, allows her the power of resurrection and ultimately spiritual regeneration. Milton's Saint seems *like*
Alcestis because she has three features which, according to Pico, Phaedrus emphasizes. Hill has referred to Phaedrus in regard to the third of
these features (resurrection). I would thus extend Spitzer's emphasis on
the first (the ideal) and Colaccio's on the second (self-sacrifice) from their
context of Neoplatonism to Platonism itself.

Plato's use of Alcestis would perhaps not be so significant for Milton's last sonnet if Diotima did not use the figure in the central speech
of Socrates. Diotima is trying to convince the young Socrates that love
is the power by which "the body and all else that is temporal partakes
of the eternal" (208b). Love, she says, is a "passion for immortality" (208b).
As the first of three examples, she cites Alcestis, who "laid down her life
to save Admetus" (208d).[7] For Diotima, Alcestis' heroic action reveals her
to be "in love with the eternal" (208e). Immediately before *and* after the
Alcestis reference, Diotima distinguishes between two kinds of procreation: that of the "flesh," the physical children created when man and
woman unite physically, and that of the "spirit," the spiritual children
of "Wisdom and all her sister virtues" (209a). Diotima goes on to applaud spiritual procreation over physical procreation precisely because
it creates "something lovelier and less mortal than human seed" (209c).
This discussion prepares Diotima to introduce the famous Platonic ladder, in which the lover is led from seeing the physical beauty of a beloved
to see the beauty of the mind and, after seeing the beauty of the world
in general, to see the ideal form of beauty in the eternal kingdom of God
(210b–211e). According to Diotima, man should contemplate the ideal
form of beauty because it will allow him to participate in the divine love
that can make man immortal and beloved of God: "when he has brought
forth and reared this perfect virtue [of ideal love], he shall be called the
friend of God, and if ever it is given to man to put on immortality, it
shall be given to him" (212a).

Diotima's entire discussion, then, focuses on the idea of immortality, especially as it relates to love. To what extent, she seems to ask, can man become immortal in this life? What kinds of loving action can he perform to become immortal? She seems to offer a range of answers: physical procreation, spiritual procreation, and intellectual ascent of the Platonic ladder. The first of these is clearly the least satisfactory, because it consists of action tied to the body. The second, in which the Alcestis reference occurs, is more satisfactory, because it consists of action that transcends the corporal. Evidently, the third is the most satisfactory, because it consists of action that aims to fully elevate the soul above ordinary mortality. For our purposes, the relation between the second and third answers is crucial. Although Diotima's logic here lacks rigor, it seems that her discussion of spiritual procreation (as the proper expression of love because it confers immortality) is a foundation for her next point — that man should ascend the Platonic ladder. That is, once she has convinced Socrates that love is a passion for immortality, she can then show him the specific means by which man's passion confers immortality: by ascending the Platonic ladder. In this regard, the point she makes in the Alcestis passage proper can be seen to foreshadow the point she makes in the Platonic ladder passage; the two ideas are sequentially related. Hence, a poet with a syncretic habit of mind could see that Alcestis has performed an action like that which Diotima is discussing; thus Alcestis can become analogous to Diotima herself, and thus analogous to Socrates: a figure for the ideal lover, whose wisdom and virtue lead her to sacrifice the world of sense and physical procreation for the sake of the ideal world of forms and spiritual procreation, as the most effective way to achieve immortality. What Pico has said about Alcestis in the first of Plato's references seems even more appropriate for the second; this makes sense, since Pico would have interpreted Alcestis not in the light of Phaedrus' speech alone, but in the light of Plato's philosophy as a whole. In this regard, Alcestis could become for Milton more than merely a figure of the devoted wife, or even a figure of self-sacrifice and resurrection: she could become an incarnation of Platonic love itself, a figure for ideal love in its power to confer immortality on man in this life.

Hill was certainly right to refer to Plato's first Alcestis reference to find a Platonic source for Milton's use of Alcestis as a figure of resurrection. But by missing Plato's second reference, he misses the source most pertinent to Milton's sonnet. According to Spitzer and his followers, the sonnet's central theme is man's inability to unite himself with the ideal in this life. In the larger context in which the Alcestis reference occurs in the *Symposium*, Plato makes precisely the opposite point: man *can* succeed in his quest for union with the ideal. Colaccio has suggested that Milton's sonnet opposes the traditional view of Christian Neoplatonism (p. 195). It is possible that Milton used Alcestis, at least in part, to lead the reader back to the source of the idea to which he will ultimately respond. Milton's response to Plato consists of his portrait of the persona attempting to participate in Platonic love but then finding it of little consolation for his own circumstances. As we shall see, Milton's sonnet and Plato's second Alcestis passage have three main themes in common: love as the power of immortality; procreation as a means of achieving immortality; and the intellectual or spiritual ascent of the Platonic ladder, to union with the ideal, as the most efficacious way to achieve immortality. Suggestively, these themes occur in each of the three parts of the sonnet outlined by Spitzer.

In the first part, the persona *thinks* he sees the image or spirit of his wife returning from the grave, in a manner that reminds him of the story of Alcestis returning to her husband, Admetus.

> Methought I saw my late espoused Saint
>   Brought to me like Alcestis from the grave,
>   Whom Jove's great Son to her glad Husband gave,
>   Rescu'd from death by force though pale and faint.

Although the simile emphasizes the role of the rescuer, Hercules, the dramatic context in which the simile occurs, that of the dream vision, emphasizes the relation between husband and wife. In other words, whereas the simile leads us back to the Euripides play, in which Hercules becomes the hero, the dream vision leads us back to a version of the myth like the one in Plato's *Symposium*.[8] Evidently, the persona believes that his wife's love for him has enabled her to ovecome the laws of death and return to him immortal from the grave. The first simile, in short, uses Alcestis in part to reveal that the central relationship in the poem is that between husband and wife. Specifically, it reveals that the persona believes he is envisioning the spiritual return of his wife "from the grave." This in turn suggests that he believes she is the embodiment of a love conferring immortality.

In the second part of the *"crescendo* arrangement," the persona turns from present vision to actual past, and emphasizes his belief that the present visitation transcends the past death and foreshadows a future reunion in heaven:

> Mine as whom washt from spot of child-bed taint,
>   Purification in the old Law did save,
>   And such, as yet once more I trust to have
>   Full sight of her in Heaven without restraint.

Hinting at a difference between Alcestis and his wife that will become important later, the persona here recalls the circumstance of his wife's death: childbirth. What *saves* her, he believes, is the "old law" of Leviticus xii, which purifies a woman who has died in childbirth. This notion has led many commentators to see the wife as Katherine Woodcock, rather than Mary Powell, mainly because only Katherine died directly from childbirth.[9] Since the old law does *not* "save" his wife in the way that the new law of Christ's love ultimately will, some commentators have believed the persona remains partly deceived.[10]

In the background here may be Diotima's speech in the *Symposium*, which also focuses on the theme of procreation. Diotima's point is that the true end of love is procreation, because procreation confers immortality: "Why all this longing for propagation? Because this is the one deathless and eternal element in our mortality. . . . Love is a longing for immortality" (207a). Katherine, we will recall, has died in the kind of procreation that Diotima has found less valuable, the physical procreation that attempts to give birth to children. With that kind of procreation now denied him (through his wife's death), the persona participates in the spiritual procreation that Diotima has found more valuable. It as if he has come to see the full import of Diotima's point: that physical procreation leads only to death — a bitter embrace with man's own mortality; and that, therefore, man should participate in spiritual procreation — to transcend mortality. This reading coincides with the persona's belief that he is seeing the true ideal of his wife here; the words "once more" reveal his belief that he is having "full sight" of her *now* and that he can "trust" in seeing her *again* "in Heaven." The theme of procreation (both physical and spiritual), as it relates to the theme of mortality and immortality, which Milton's sonnet has in common with Plato's dialogue, may be further evidence for believing Katherine Woodcock the wife Milton has in mind.

Not surprisingly, in the third part of the crescendo arrangement, Milton introduces the Saint as a kind of incarnate Platonic ideal, who

> Came vested all in white, pure as her mind:
> Her face was veil'd, yet to my fancied sight,
> Love, sweetness, goodness, in her person shin'd
> So clear, as in no face with more delight.

Milton handles his poetic problem of describing the *physical appearance* of a spirit within a vision by attempting to spiritualize matter. Though he portrays the Saint coming vested all in white (that is, as having actual physical appearance), he quickly associates that appearance with the purity of the Saint's mind: in a subtle piece of Platonism, Milton converts physical appearance into spiritual reality. Similarly, though portraying the Saint as "veil'd," Milton presents the persona as seeing not so much a "face" (the word occurs in a simile) as an emanation of spiritual beauty—a kind of Neoplatonic "virtue" or power of light: "Love, sweetness, goodness, in her person *shin'd*." The full effect of Milton's Platonizing technique is to reveal his persona participating in Platonic love, in which physical beauty becomes spiritual beauty and spiritual beauty the ideal form of beauty. For, as Colaccio has observed, the unmentioned medium by which Saint and persona relate is the Platonic ladder. If the phrase "Love, sweetness, goodness" can refer to the Pauline concepts of hope, faith, and charity, as Martin Mueller has suggested in a Christian reading, then in a Neoplatonic or Platonic reading, the phrase can refer to three concepts at the center of the *Symposium*: love, virtue, and goodness.[11] The Saint becomes a type of the Platonic ideal of love that is both virtuous and good precisely because it confers immortality on the soul. The loving Saint both embodies and seems to promise the "passion for immortality"; hence, in trying to unite with her, the persona is essentially trying to participate in this passion as well.

If the first twelve lines of the sonnet have depicted the persona participating in Platonic love, revealing the persona's belief that he is having "full sight" of his beloved now, the last two lines introduce a jarring change: "But O, as to embrace me she inclin'd, / I wak'd, she fled, and day brought back my night." In these haunting lines Milton seems to be, at least in part, exposing the truth about Platonic love: rather than making man immortal and beloved of the gods, as Diotima has promised, ideal love leads man to a total sense of his own mortality and a complete separation from the ideal world. This is so not merely because Milton believes the ideal remains veiled from man until he himself enters heaven, as Spitzer and his followers have suggested, but also because Milton believes that man's attempt to unite with the ideal leads him to violate the procedure of Plato's theory of love: the persona attempts to convert the union of imagination and ideal into a physical union between two bodies: "as to *embrace* me she *inclin'd*, / I wak'd, she fled, and day brought back my night." In terms supplied to us by the *Symposium* itself, the persona attempts to convert the Socratic notion of love as man's intellectual union with the ideal form of beauty into the Aristophanic notion of love as man's physical union with the body of an actual beloved.[12]

The fundamental limitation of the "ideal" reading of Milton's sonnet postulated by Spitzer and his followers is the one noted by Anna K. Nardo: the persona "sees a real woman, not an unidentified ideal."[13] Nardo's rejection of a Neoplatonic reading is based on the assumption that a real woman cannot serve as an ideal. According to Plato, she is right: "Neither will [the lover's] vision of the beautiful [ideal] take the form of a face, or of hands, or of anything that is of the flesh" (211b). In fact, the Platonic ideal represents a complete depersonalization of a beautiful individual — a process of abstraction. If man is to fully participate in Platonic or Neoplatonic love, he must *disembody* his beloved.

I would agree with Spitzer and his followers that Milton presents himself as a "Christian Platonist" trying to participate in Platonic love, or union with the ideal — hence the persona's attempt in lines 9–12 to Platonize or depersonalize the Saint: "Came vested all in white, pure as her mind: / Her face was veil'd, yet to my fancied sight, / Love, sweetness, goodness, in her person shin'd." Yet I would disagree with the strict Neoplatonic reading, and meet the charge of the sensitive reader, like Nardo, who believes that Milton is seeing the spirit of a real woman, by suggesting that the persona sets out to participate in Platonic love only to be checked by the inner urges of the soul: in a sense, he abandons Socrates for Aristophanes, spiritual union for physical union, the abstract ideal for a real woman.[14]

Milton here is responding to what Sidney and Spenser had responded to in their earlier sonnet sequences: the haunting maxim of Plato's *Symposium*, originally articulated in a Christian or Neoplatonic form by Ficino in his commentary and subsequently echoed by Castiglione in *The Courtier*, that man should transcend his love of a personal beloved to love the abstract ideal. "Through the vertue of imagination," says Cardinal Bembo in Book IV of *The Courtier*, the lover should "take [earthly love] for a stayre (as it were) to climbe up to another farre higher than it. . . . And thus shall he beholde no more the particular beautie of one woman, but an universall, that decketh out all bodies."[15] Bembo underscores the importance of participating in this ideal love by elaborating on its benefits: "there shall wee find a most happie end for our desires, true rest for our travels, certaine remedie for miseries, a most healthfull medicine for sicknesse, a most sure haven in ye troublesome stormes of the tempestuous sea of this life."[16] Bembo joins Ficino, Pico, Benivieni, and other Neoplatonists in believing that a Christianized Platonism, in which man depersonalizes the beloved to embrace the abstract ideal by ascending the Platonic ladder, is the most efficacious means by which man transcends the limits of mortality.

It is this traditional Christian type of Neoplatonism that Sidney and Spenser were to respond to in their sonnet sequences. Together, they helped shift the age's belief from the more ascetic kind of Neoplatonism to a special kind, traceable to the philosophies of Mario Equicola and Leone Ebreo, which attempted to reconcile man's love of woman — both her spirit and her body — with his love of the divine world of God.[17] In *Sonnet V* of *Astrophil and Stella*, for example, Astrophil spends the first thirteen lines evoking the Neoplatonic love ethic. First, he suggests that the Platonic theory of the ideal is valid "(It is most true, what we call Cupid's dart, / An image is") and that the earthly beloved is "but a shade" of ideal or "true Beauty"; then he suggests the validity of the spiritual ascent of the Platonic ladder: "It is most true, that eyes are form'd to serve / The inward light"; "on earth we are but pilgrims made, / And should in soule up to our countrey [of the ideal] move." But then, in the last line, he introduces a turn: "True, and yet true that I must Stella love."[18] Astrophil recognizes the "truth" of Ficino's and Bembo's Neoplatonic code at the same time that he recognizes his own desire to unite physically with a personalized beloved. In the end, he is unable to follow Plato's and Bembo's advice of depersonalizing his beloved and contemplating the ideal form of beauty; in fact, his attempt drives him even more forcefully back to Stella herself. In *Sonnet LXXI*, Astrophil again evokes the Neoplatonic love ethic in the first thirteen lines, but this time he rejects the Platonic theory of abstraction outright, by seeing Stella as an incarnation of the ideal, in whom "true goodness show[s]" and in whose eyes "that inward sun . . . shineth so." This rejection of Plato's theory of the abstract ideal foreshadows a related rejection made in the last line: even though he tries to see the ideal *in* Stella — that is, to contemplate her spiritual essence — "desire still cries, 'Give me some food.'" The attempt to participate in even a modified Platonic love fails, and the lover, as it were, collapses back on his beloved's breast. Although Astrophil may be seen here merely as a lustful youth hotly pursuing an adulterous love affair that he will never consummate, Sidney's preoccupation with rejecting Neoplatonism is significant.

It is significant, for example, in Spenser's *Amoretti XLV* and *LXXXVIII*, which can be seen to take the fundamental Neoplatonic notions of Sidney's *Sonnets V* and *LXXI* and legitimize them — by making the love relationship between man and future wife (thus serving as forerunners to Milton's sonnet on *his* wife). As with Sidney's *Sonnet LXXI*, Spenser in *Sonnet XLV* thinks of his beloved not as an abstract ideal but as a personalized form of the ideal:

> Within my hart, though hardly it can shew
>    thing so divine to vew of earthly eye,
>    the fayre Idea of your celestiall hew,
>    and every part remaines immortally.[19]

Robert Ellrodt is certainly right in arguing that this is not true Platonism: "both the thought and the language show that Spenser either did not care for philosophical accuracy or had not yet fully grasped the theory of abstraction and idealization. The sonnet is not susceptible of a truly Platonic interpretation, for, unless Idea meant image, the conceit would be absurd."[20] But the lines are significant precisely because they represent Spenser's movement away from strict Platonism or Neoplatonism. This movement foreshadows a related movement away from the Platonic theory of love in *Sonnet LXXXVIII*. As in both of Sidney's sonnets, the first twelve lines of this sonnet concentrate on the lover's participation in Neoplatonic love, in which the lover transcends his view of the beloved by contemplating the ideal form of beauty — this time with what Ellrodt would call an actual technical Platonic reference:[21]

> beholding the Idaea playne,
> through contemplation of my purest part:
> with light thereof I doe my selfe sustayne,
> And thereon feed my love-affamisht hart.

Picking up Sidney's love-as-food metaphor, the persona here endures the trial of separation by fully participating in a real Neoplatonic love, beholding the "Idaea playne." As with Sidney, however, Spenser introduces a turn: "But with such brightnesse whylest I fill my mind, / I starve my body and mine eyes doe blynd." Introducing here within a Neoplatonic context the themes of light and darkness, sight and blindness, which look forward directly to Milton's last sonnet, Spenser suggests that mere Platonic union with the ideal is finally dissatisfying, because man has both a body and a soul: both must be "fed" in order for man to "see" clearly and thus for him to become truly happy. Both Spenser's and Sidney's personas represent precedents in the sonnet tradition for a lover attempting to participate in Platonic or ideal love and then ultimately feeling its sorrowful consequences.

Milton inherits this sonnet tradition, and in *Sonnet XXIII* he extends the familiar sonnet *topos*, a lover's separation from his beloved, to its ultimate and tragic form: death. Sidney's and Spenser's laments are not so serious in the light of Milton's: they at least had the hope of realizing their desires; he has none. For Milton, the persona's vision of the ideal through the medium of the Platonic ladder is merely the agent of mental anguish and haunting loneliness, because it leads the persona to see merely an illusion of divine union. The persona's separation is not only from his beloved Saint, but also from the comfort of a philosophy central to Western thought: Platonism, Christianized to suit the occasion of a man's relation with his wife. It is as if the persona has been testing the value of Platonic or Neoplatonic love by putting it to the greatest challenge of all: its capacity to console for the death of a beloved spouse. The appropriate subtitle for Milton's sonnet is "the agony of the *extasie.*"

What Milton feels in *Sonnet XXIII* is what any sensitive man feels when he has just lost his wife: the utter shallowness of any philosophy calling for contemplation of the ideal, the utter futility of any attempt to disembody a beloved who has been loved in the full beauty of the flesh. Importantly, Milton has portrayed his Saint as wearing a veil. Fiske has rightly referred to the veil that Moses wears in Exodus XXXIV, 29–35, together with Paul's commentary on it in 2 Corinthians iii, 7–18. According to Fiske, the veil is a symbol of the persona's blindness (p. 160). However, a closer look at Paul's commentary will reveal that the veil also symbolizes the "old Law," which becomes for Paul the law of death. Hence, in wearing the veil, the Saint is wearing a mask of mortality. From the Neoplatonic perspective that I have introduced, the veil symbolizes the inefficacy of the Platonic ideal of love as a power conferring immortality in this life: the ideal form of beauty remains veiled from man, because man remains fully a creature of this world.

In a sense, Milton in *Sonnet XXIII* can be seen to rewrite the Alcestis myth as interpreted by Plato in the *Symposium*. In using Alcestis to direct the reader back to the source of the idea that he will so powerfully respond to, Milton reveals himself to be more than just a sonneteer in the great Renaissance tradition: he becomes a Renaissance mythographer, interpreting the symbolic personages of the classical past in the light of Christianity. The fact that the Saint finally differs from Alcestis signals the difference between the persona's experience and that of the Platonic lover: unlike Admetus, the persona does not reunite with his wife. Milton uses the Alcestis myth to convert the "occasion" of his wife's death into a powerful commentary on a specific tenet of world philosophy: love as the "passion for immortality." In the end, Milton reminds us that just as the Saint must return to her own spiritual kingdom, so must man return to the world from which he himself has come.

The Pennsylvania State University

## NOTES

1. Spitzer, "Understanding Milton," *Hopkins Review*, IV (1950–51), 16–27. Spitzer is responding to the biographical reading of the sonnet by George Boas, "The Problem

of Meaning in the Arts," in *Meaning and Interpretation*, University of California Publications in Philosophy, 25 (1950), 318–19. Spitzer and Boas represent the two main approaches that critics of the sonnet have taken. Although I follow Spitzer's Neoplatonic reading at the outset, I do so in order to adjust it and, ultimately, to reconcile it with the reading that argues Milton's persona is seeing not an abstract ideal, as Spitzer argues, but his real wife. All four major annotated editions treating Milton's sonnet — the *Variorum*, Merritt Y. Hughes, John Carey, and E. A. J. Honigmann — cite only Euripides' play as Milton's source for Alcestis. For Warton's reference to Euripides, see *A Variorum Commentary on the Poems of John Milton*, ed. A. S. P. Woodhouse and Douglas Bush (New York, 1972), II, Pt. 2, 499. All quotations of Milton's *Sonnet XXIII* are from the edition of Merritt Y. Hughes, *John Milton: Complete Poems and Major Prose* (New York, 1957), pp. 170–71.

2. Fiske, "The Theme of Purification in Milton's *Sonnet XXIII*," in *Milton Studies*, VIII, ed. James D. Simmonds (Pittsburgh, 1975), pp. 156–57; and Hill, "'Alcestis from the Grave': Image and Structure in *Sonnet XXIII*," in *Milton Studies*, X, ed. Simmonds (Pittsburgh, 1977), p. 132. Both Fiske and Hill are indebted to Edgar Wind, *Pagan Mysteries in the Renaissance* (New York, 1968), pp. 156–57. For Pico's reference in the *Commento*, see *De hominis dignitate*, ed. Eugenio Garin (Florence, 1942), pp. 555, 558.

3. That Milton knew the *Symposium* is almost certain. See Harris Francis Fletcher, *The Intellectual Development of John Milton* (Urbana, Ill., 1961), II, pp. 286–87.

4. "'A Death Like Sleep': The Christology of Milton's Twenty-Third Sonnet," in *Milton Studies*, VI, ed. Simmonds (Pittsburgh, 1975), p. 183.

5. Hill does not analyze Phaedrus' reference to Alcestis. His reading is not strictly Neoplatonic, like those of Spitzer, Colaccio, and Fiske: he does not focus on the theme of the ideal, and argues for a reading in which Milton balances hope and despair (p. 136).

6. *Symposium*, 179c, trans. Michael Joyce, in *The Collected Dialogues of Plato*, ed. Edith Hamilton and Huntington Cairns (Princeton, 1961). All quotations will be from this edition.

7. The other two are Achilles/Patroclus and Codrus. Together, the three examples illustrate the love between man and woman, man and man, and man and country — or the themes of love, friendship, and patriotism.

8. In "Understanding Milton," Spitzer notes the discrepancy between Euripides' and Milton's use of Alcestis (p. 22). Because it is not directly pertinent to my argument, I will not examine how Alcestis functions within the simile itself; doing so would lead me away from Neoplatonism to Christian typology, which Colaccio has examined in detail. See also J. C. Ulreich, "Typological Symbolism in Milton's *Sonnet XXIII*," *Milton Quarterly*, VIII, (1974), 7–10.

9. The traditional view that Katherine Woodcock was the wife Milton wrote about went unchallenged until W. R. Parker suggested Mary Powell, in "Milton's Last Sonnet," *RES*, XXI (1945), 235–38. For a summary of the controversy, see the Milton *Variorum*, II, Pt. 2, 486–91.

10. See Martin Mueller, "The Theme and Imagery of Milton's Last Sonnet," *Archiv*, CCI (1964–65), 268. See also Kurt Heinzelman, "'Cold Consolation': The Art of Milton's Last Sonnet," in *Milton Studies*, X, ed. Simmonds (Pittsburgh, 1977), p. 119.

11. Mueller, "The Theme and Imagery of Milton's Last Sonnet," p. 271, n. 9. For Plato in the *Symposium*, virtue means the virtuous action of contemplating the ideal (211a–212a), while goodness is really an ideal itself, closely connected to beauty (201c–e, 204e–206b).

12. See the *Symposium*, 189d–193e. These two views of love form a central controversy in English Renaissance literature, as I go on to suggest.

13. *Milton's Sonnets and the Ideal Community* (Lincoln, Neb., 1979), p. 41. See also pp. 39–40.

14. "De Idea Platonica quemadmodum Aristoteles Intellexit" (Hughes, pp. 56–58) may express Milton's more academic, less personalized rejection of the Platonic Idea. See Harris Fletcher, *The Intellectual Development of John Milton*, II, p. 427.

15. *The Courtier*, trans. Sir Thomas Hoby, 1561 (New York, 1928), pp. 317–18. For the similar idea in Ficino's *Commentary on Plato's "Symposium,"* see the Sixth Speech, Chapter VI, trans. Sears R. Jayne (Columbia, Mo.), p. 188.

16. Castiglione, *The Courtier*, trans. Hoby, p. 321.

17. Robert Ellrodt, *Neoplatonism in the Poetry of Spenser* (Geneva, 1960), pp. 144–45. According to Ellrodt, Equicola "argued that spiritual love by itself, when disembodied, could not endure. He who loves permanently, he concluded, must needs love both the soul and the body in the beloved" (p. 144). Similarly, says Ellrodt, Leone Ebreo "argued that the union of the lovers' souls was the perfect end of perfect love but could only be fully achieved when the bodies, too, were united: the bodily union therefore made spiritual love more perfect" (p. 144). Equicola and Leone Ebreo join Louis Le Roy as the only Neoplatonists Ellrodt has found with philosophies similar to Spenser's. Where Castiglione and Ficino kept their notions of married love and Platonic love separated, Spenser fused the two: "In Italian courtly circles and in the language of fashion, married love and Platonic love indeed were usually contrasted. . . . The originality of Spenser's philosophy of love lies in the association of Platonic idealism with an acceptance of bodily union" (p. 146). As I hope to show, Ellrodt's analysis of Spenser also applies to Sidney—and Milton.

18. All quotations from *Astrophil and Stella* are taken from *The Poems of Sir Philip Sidney*, ed. William A. Ringler, Jr. (Oxford, 1962).

19. All quotations from *Amoretti* are taken from *The Poetical Works of Edmund Spenser*, ed. Ernest De Sélincourt and J. C. Smith (Oxford, 1910), I. The i–j and u–v have been modernized.

20. *Neoplatonism in the Poetry of Spenser*, p. 42.

21. See ibid., p. 44, for Ellrodt's discussion of Spenser's sonnet.

# POSTSCRIPT AND PRESCRIPT
# IN TWO MILTON SONNETS

## J. S. Lawry

I N  T W O  of Milton's most self-concerned sonnets, "How Soon Hath Time" and "When I Consider How My Light Is Spent,"[1] statement seems to proceed in a binary sequence.[2] First, a tense proposition or "assay" is presented in the octave. It is heavy with pathos and protest. It is then opposed by a second, and corrective, assertion in the sestet. The resulting pattern suggests related binary forms within a long tradition — debate; dialogue; question-and-answer; expostulation and reply; elegaic doubt and consolation; a contingent proposition, followed by an absolute or analytic conclusion; and a limited human assertion, which is also rebellious, temporal, and mortal, followed by illimitable doctrine, which is reconciliative, eternal, and immortal. Such sequences reach back to Job and Jonah, and outward to works such as Herbert's *The Collar*. With appropriate local adjustments, this form, together with the statement that it both conveys and generates, appears in much of Milton's poetry. The impression of binary sequence must therefore be taken to be just, so far as it goes, and of obvious value for reading Milton.

However, because the hinge effect between the two parts of the Italian sonnet (even in its flexible Della Casan form) is so mechanical and abrupt, the progress from one part to the other in these two sonnets by Milton may seem easy, automatic, and unearned. So may the implied emphasis produced by that movement. Although the greater length of the eight-line "protest" over that of the six-line "reply" may argue a proportionate care that the "reply" should not come in too patly, the "patience" of the sestet may nevertheless seem to revoke the "murmur" of the octave.[3] The sonnet's progress from hesitation into a "strictest measure ev'n" accordingly can seem submissive and orthodox, sacrificing the preceding pathos of whirlwind days flying in full career. Furthermore, the unbending sestet presents readers with neither the expansive complexity of Job's God speaking from just such a whirlwind, nor the extreme dramatic simplicity of Herbert's divine voice, stilling rebellious protest with the sympathetic murmur "Child." Instead, the sestets in Milton can seem at once extensive, yet curt; deliberative, yet doctrinal. Largely for such reasons, Milton can appear to have surrendered each sonnet's first text, as feeling, to its second text, as formula. If that impression were correct, Milton would again stand accused of being of the rebel's party without knowing it, or of again letting God the schoolmaster take possession of the voice of the poem.

Such objections can be countered in a number of ways, including the unsurprising observation that up to a point the form of a sonnet is prescriptive. Progress within it ultimately must needs be "in strictest measure ev'n," no matter how freely enjambment and sympathetic metrical alterations in the octave may have suggested a purely improvised response to emotion. A somewhat different answer obtains if we also consider, at a deeper reach, the effects produced even in the octave of each sonnet by occasionality; by two or more distancing removals from experience; and by conditionality. Those effects at once add self-criticism to the personal pathos and also generalize the particular protest. They thereby mitigate the impression of a temporal sequence under which the octave moves inexorably to the sestet, where it is snuffed out, or of an impassioned poetic outcry that is silenced by a somewhat flat and doctrinaire close. Thereafter, the sestet can be seen as a logical fulfillment rather than a contradiction of the octave. In given ways, the sestet is indeed virtually the predecessor. What in the sestet had seemed to be a postscript to the octave then appears instead as its "prescript."

In the sonnet on Milton's twenty-third year, the impression of hurtling speed effected by the words and rhythms in "How soon hath Time," "Stol'n on his wing my three and twentieth year," and "My hasting days fly on with full career," is similar to that of Marvell's "wingèd chariot hurrying near." However, those effects are impeded (surely deliberately) by the pause, deceleration, and thickness of diction interposed by the caesural epithet, "that subtle thief of youth." Similarly, the potential for an impression of speed that might have been gained by offering the mind's eye two fixed objects and then a swift movement between them is denied in "My late spring no bud or blossom showth": the eye is given nothing at all with which to register haste and motion. Pathos also is balked when in the next four lines of the octave time is almost literally arrested. Description turns toward analytical discourse, and metaphor toward reasoned comparisons: first, that of external to internal manhood or poetic maturity, one condition of which has already appeared even for the speaker, and within the blessing and fructiveness of time; and second, that of the speaker with a more "timely-happy" poet.[4] Even though at the given instant the comparisons occasion more despair than comfort, they nevertheless are mental and verbal acts proceeding from reason, not mere spastic cries of loss. Because of such comparisons, the character of time as threat has been altered. Time now *can* bring a poet to full manhood, promising arrival and completion rather than loss or absence. Lexically, time also now *can* compound with happy, to produce "timely-happy." More importantly still, the initial pathetic proposition of the octave has wavered. It now seems occasional rather than fixed, even as the line between "semblance" and "truth" is now indistinct. In having brought forward qualifying comparisons in order to establish a truth of protest, the speaker finds that its asserted truth has itself been qualified. We may now observe that the octave in its murmur had at first been just as doctrinaire as the sestet in its patience will appear to be.

Not only, then, was time slowed metrically and "visually" in the first four lines and then subjected to comparisons in the next four that showed it to be capable of bringing gifts as well as of stealing youth, but also the general pathos of assertion was critically disputed, and to that extent freed from the seeming certainty in its declaration. That process is assured by means of the quiet cumulative effect of the words "semblance," "deceive," "appear," and "perhaps." Each casts a shadow of doubt on the initial doubt. Its protest thereby becomes less a fixed truth than an occasional murmur.

The change that had taken place within the octave's assertion, involving a revaluation of the initial sense of time, attested the speaker's surprising yet demonstrable distance from the entire assertion. Even in the first four lines, he had looked back from a fixed point in his twenty-third year. Prior time was thereby made the product of his perception, rather than of direct, sequential, undistanced experience. Furthermore, in the twice-negating phrase "No bud or blossom," time and speed had become in one way self-denying; we see nothing because time and speed have not been *great* enough to show us anything. When we then are invited to conceive of time as an earthly season moving toward maturity, we may observe that a calendrical progress from (say) January to April of course will show no growth. Even though such a reflection is coarsely overliteral, it serves to suggest how thoroughly the poem can turn the tables on its topos. The sonnet itself has thus become a subtle thief from time. It has arrested time by means of diction, by means of occasionality (for not until the speaker was twenty-three, we may suppose, was any loss marked), and by means of observations concerning growth or the lack of growth which tend to measure time, rather than being measured by it. Such effects of distancing (which admittedly are at times vestigial) had produced a condition that invited textual self-criticism even in the first four lines. In the second set of four, that condition nears accomplished fact. By their nature, the comparisons appearing in those lines tend to analyze rather than to complain of time. They also register poets not only within a long tradition but also, at least by inference, within a considerable range of variations in maturity or maturation. Neither of those two intimations accepts the original feeling in the octave that loss within time is absolute. By our conceiving of physical and artistic progress within a time that proceeds in one way or another to literary fulfillment, and by our seeing poets in full relation to their individual historical "seasons," time is perceived not so much as a heartless measurer of loss as one of the measures — albeit often questionable, often obscure — of achievement, happiness, and fulfillment.

Such suggestive alterations within the speaker's sense of time and loss within the octave make possible a sestet that brings not so much a turn and contradiction as progress and confirmation. The binary oppositions that introduce the sestet —"soon or slow," "less or more"— are thus almost replicative; they have already been all but posed, bridged, and resolved in the octave. We are therefore ready, intellectually and even rhythmically, for the "strictest measure ev'n" into which the poem now moves. Words and rhythms are an imitative confirmation of the poem's own achieved intellectual measure. Movement is no longer that from loss into gain. Instead, it is pure, and absolute, and confirmed *measure*. Within an assured rhythm (for no longer do we meet the slips or skids of seeming haste), time now strides confidently toward that which in no way is to be measured as loss.[5] Even when the subsequent seeming opposition of "mean or high" seems to revive despair, the poem responds by accepting that seeming opposition into its steady, ongoing pulse, as another element within one assured measure. The pairing of "mean or high" also invites our recollection that in the Bible, the first is measured as last, and the last as first. The judicial and rhythmic measure thus achieved or thus demonstrated is at once strict, yet equitably even. Time is brought into the measure of eternity. Man's limited perception is brought correctively into line with the illimitable and just measuring of God's eye. And the evenhanded, reliable pulses of justice and creation are repeated in the poem's responsive rhythmic measure. Whatever opposition of time to eternity remains is now lodged not within loss or ending (as opposed to possession and achievement) but within the speaker's chosen *use* of time: that is, by his election or rejection of his authorizing measure of grace. Movement and statement here reach the last perimeter within which any seeming binary sequence, or even a language of distinctions, can still operate. Beyond rests the divine substance, "All is," which absorbs "less and more"; and a divine "ever," which resolves "soon or slow." The poem thus has found the true measure "for measure," and confirmed a whole, from seeming fractions.

Much the same process — which surely must constitute an expansion rather than a subjugation of human understanding — appears in the even more powerfully pathetic sonnet "When I Consider How My Light Is Spent." However, the initial circumstances of the earlier sonnet have been significantly altered. Whereas the earlier work had at first envisioned time and a lack of fulfillment by looking back into negation from a given point in early life, the later work — almost as if in an ironic or malevolent reply — looks forward from a given point of achievement into a future emptying into a desert of seeming loss.[6] The later sonnet suggests that it is worse to have achieved and lost than never to have achieved at all. Any movement from the one condition to the other must therefore threaten a progress only into despair.

As was the case with "How Soon Hath Time," however, in "When I Consider" two stages of distancing and counterassertion stir even within the passion of the octave. Indeed, with the third word, reasoning "consideration" rather than dramatic exclamation has now become primary in the assertion. Also, the statement in the octave is framed even more firmly in the occasional than it was in "How Soon Hath Time," as is indicated immediately by the words "when" and "consider." Even the seeming finality of "how my light is spent" is reserved for reconsideration. If on the one hand it intimates total loss, on the other it also intimates the possibly fruitful way in which, during half a lifetime, light has already been expended. The speaker thus considers *how*, not merely *that*, the light is spent. Although the terror of "this dark world and wide" is not dispelled by such a distancing, it nevertheless is potentially positioned within a hemispheric, night-and-day balance, capable even of being received as a grateful vicissitude. In much the same way, if the complaint about a talent's being lodged uselessly in man at the same instant that its use is commanded by God seems to justify a protest more rebellious than that against spent eyesight in a dark world, it also is far more general. Not only does the second passage by inference look all the way back to the terrible Alpha of a universe receding from light into chaos, and forward to the terrible Omega of a Last Judgment in which the returning Master may chide a lack of works, but it also removes the complaint partly into a reasonable "consideration" by framing it as a virtual dilemma ("Does God demand day-labor, light denied?"). The interrogative tends to create here the same deliberative distancing that comparisons had achieved in the earlier poem. Such distancing in the octave — produced both by the occasional mode of "When I Consider" and by the logical dilemma — may help readers to infer that the rebellious question had indeed been fond, even before the octave, in a conclusion suggestively extended into the sestet, suddenly asserts that general judgment.

Nevertheless, apart from the general revision of judgment within the octave that is produced by its surprising termination, the octave in the second of the two sonnets has offered fewer internal rousing motions than had the earlier. Almost no direct conversion of darkness or loss has here duplicated the implicit transformation of time and growth that occurred in "How Soon Hath Time." Nor has the later sonnet's initial assertion been extensively reperceived even before its sestet imposes a new measure of perception. Apart from the escape from finality offered by the adverb "fondly," the only equivalent opening into freedom in the later octave appears in its progress from the statement of a condition to a question about the description of that condition. Such yielding offers little comfort. Similarly, although we may avoid an error of judgment when a question is declared to be fond, we are brought no nearer to a resolution of the larger, unstated questions that had elicited that specific question.

When we take account of the major differences in the sestets of the two sonnets, however, the major reason for such differences in their octaves becomes clear. In "How Soon Hath Time," the sestet had followed the octave partly as correction, but partly also as confirmation. The pivotal word "yet," which joined sestet to octave, had at once marked but also permitted a general countering analysis. However, it also had given assurance that the time-sense of the octave was to continue in the sestet: time would remain "yet," and would be "as ever." By contrast, in "When I Consider," the seeming postscript formed by the sestet even more radically asserts a character as prescript. In "constant" time, the sestet *absolutely* precedes the octave, and is the condition for it. Its statement thereby "prevents" *all* merely conditional and occasional considerations. It certifies that the judgment in the octave had indeed been "fond." It of course suggests an act and a text of prevenient grace.

At the center of the sestet in "When I Consider" is patience, prevenient always to the octave's questioning murmur. *Whenever* we encounter the doubt posed in the octave, patience "prevents" it.[7] In that sense, the confident sestet unwrites and deasserts the doubt-filled octave. Although far less openly, something of the same "deconstruction" within the text, by the text, had also appeared, in the sestet of "How Soon Hath Time," by virtue of the words "yet," "All is," and "ever." In the later sonnet, the assertion "His state is kingly" serves to make fond and to unwrite all of the otherwise harrowing statement that precedes it. We now realize that it was the human worker, not the divine master, who had chidden, and that it was he who had demanded an accounting—and "preveniently" received it. Any residual binary distinctions between active and contemplative service,[8] as well as any divisive distinctions within the idea of service itself (such as willing service as opposed to unwilling servitude) are absorbed into the general kingly state. It intimates plenitude, "needy nothing." Rather like the issue of time and substance in the earlier sonnet, the question of light and achievement here has been altered into the opportunity of man's making graceful use of anything whatsoever, within the freedom and fullness of divine measure. It does not matter whether to human eyes the act or substance is positive or negative, full or empty. Although God may well make use of human service in whatever kind, none is needed. If it is not needed by God, it is not needed among men. Human awareness of that plenitude, which had once seemed an emptiness, can serve to still a multitude of fond questions.

In both sonnets, patience and grace thus had preveniently "written" unstated poems in which no shadow of the binary, or the sequential, or even the discursive, could finally stand. When a mortal poet in his temporal pathos engenders "murmurs" of impatience, however, and when he weighs time outside the effects of grace and the measure of eternity, he seems to write a "new" work. To him, it is born of the pressing occasion and his dark condition; it seems completely topical and personal, lacking all underlay and pentimento. His own outcry, however, generates and then records its own distancing "consideration," so that it adduces a countertext. This countertext must be mainly vertical, standing over and against the binary and "horizontal" complaint of man within time and loss. Distancing and reason now inform even the octave, which at first had seemed to be written by man "alone," in every sense. Such energies from within his own statement work against the speaker's initial single-mindedness. The way is thereby prepared for a sestet that measures, as with the eye of God, "All [that] is," for "ever."[9] At this point—a point that will recur variously in each of Milton's greatest works, and will be imaged in Blake's final great drawing for *Milton*—word and measure themselves reach into the ending that is also their beginning. Movement to that juncture guides but also terminates the poem. Yet its simultaneous origin-and-end in prescript guarantees and validates all the visible text which then follows, and which stands forth eventually as a celebrative postscript.

Purdue University

## NOTES

1. *Sonnets VII* and *XIX;* the text for quotations is that in *John Milton: Complete Poems and Major Prose,* ed. Merritt Y. Hughes (New York, 1957), pp. 76–77, and 168. The two sonnets have been studied together previously by Macon Cheek, "Of Two Sonnets of Milton," *Renaissance Papers* (Columbia, S.C., 1956), pp. 82–91; rpt. in *Milton: Modern Essays in Criticism,* ed. Arthur E. Barker (New York, 1965), pp. 125–35, and by Anna K. Nardo in a chapter entitled "Center and Circumference" in *Milton's Sonnets and the Ideal Community* (Lincoln, Neb., 1979), pp. 137–57. One of the most recent studies of these poems, Nardo's is also one of the best. The present study is in substantial agreement with it.

2. No reference is intended to the use of *binary* by Roman Jakobson and later students in linguistics. A more suitable allusion would be to the idea of the binary star.

3. Cf. John S. Smart, *The Sonnets of Milton* (Glasgow, 1921), pp. 34–35, upon the supposed necessity for a "suspense or turn" in the sonnet; Edward Tayler, *Milton's Poetry: Its Development in Time* (Pittsburgh, 1979), p. 41, upon the "Schizoid Axiom" that opposes the "Puritan Moralist" in Milton to the "Humanist Artist"; and A. S. P. Woodhouse, "Notes on Milton's Early Development," *UTQ,* XIII (1943–44), 97, upon Milton's "resolution of conflict by imposition of aesthetic pattern."

4. Cf. Allen Grossman, "Milton's Sonnet 'On the Late Massacre in Piedmont': A Note on the Vulnerability of Persons in a Revolutionary Situation," *Triquarterly,* XXIII–XXIV (1972), 283–317, upon Milton's thrust, in a comparable sonnet, toward "intelligibility of experience" and "sightedness." See in addition Paul Goodman, *The Structure of Literature* (Chicago, 1954), pp. 204–15.

5. Cf. Tayler, *Milton's Poetry,* p. 131, upon a "reconciliation of *chronos* with *kairos.*"

6. Dixon Fiske, "Milton in the Middle of Life: Sonnet XIX," *ELH,* XLI (1974), 37–49, emphasizes the "fall" involved in such an attitude.

7. Cf. Roger L. Slakey, "Milton's Sonnet 'On His Blindness,'" *ELH,* XXVII (1960), 122–30, and Joseph Pequigney, "Milton's Sonnet XIX Reconsidered," *TSLL,* VIII (1966–67), 485–98.

8. Although the premises of Harry F. Robins, "Milton's First Sonnet on His Blindness," *RES,* n.s. VII (1956), 360–66, have been widely questioned, it still is useful to consider that a waiting "Mary" may be superior to a posting "Martha," all questions of God's will aside.

9. In a reading of *Sonnet XVIII* as in three parts, Kester Svendsen, "Milton's Sonnet on the Massacre at Piedmont," *Shakespeare Association Bulletin,* XX (1945), 147–55, describes an ascent from vengeance to love. Such a view may be contrasted with a reading of the entire body of sonnets in three parts by William McCarthy, "The Continuity of Milton's Sonnets," *PMLA,* XCII (1977), 96–109; it holds that *Sonnet XIX* deals with an "inscrutable disaster." Despite the contention of Sidney Greenbaum, "The Poem, the Poet, and the Reader: An Analysis of Milton's Sonnet 19," *Language and Style,* XI (1978), 117–18, that the sonnets are initiated in a "self-reflexive mimesis" of the poet's mind, and of Stanley Fish, "Interpreting the *Variorum,*" *Critical Inquiry,* II (1976), 465–85, that indirections in the poems effect a correspondent uncertainty in readers, it seems to me that both sonnets aspire to an imitation of the double-visioned God of *Paradise Lost,* who "bent down his eye, / His own works and their works at once to view" (III, 58–59).

# MILTONIC METAPHOR AND RAMIST "INVENTION": THE IMAGERY OF THE NATIVITY ODE

## Bernard S. Adams

T HE READING of a poem in the context of another art—in the present case, the art of logic—should tell us something of the creative process. As such a reading focuses upon the function of metaphor, we should expect logical complexity, contradiction, and qualification—Ezra Pound's "intellectual and emotional complex"—rather than the more common implicit description and amplification. To view metaphor in the context of logic is to make connections, to perceive abstractions in concretions, to amalgamate disparate experience, and finally to participate with the poet in a logical act. In Rosemond Tuve's words, images derived from the forms and patterns of logic become "units in an aesthetic pattern by which one man could change another's mind."[1] The emphasis is less on sensuous and expatiating imagery and more on subtle articulation of multiple mental associations; the result is poetry mainly representative of a state of mind. Such poetry draws upon the reader's fund of imagination rather than upon his pictorial sense and becomes an implicit manifestation of idea rather than object.

The sixteenth- and seventeenth-century reader was accustomed to viewing imagery more as synecdoche than as description. Parts representative of wholes and particulars expressive of universals appeared naturally as metaphors, simply because the Renaissance mind perceived truth through the relation and interaction of part and whole. This was not the modern play of association but the assertion of a principle of verbal relationship articulated, for the Renaissance reader, by Peter Ramus in his *Dialecticae Institutiones* published in Paris in 1543. The Ramist logic was founded upon verbal interaction and interrelationship that encouraged an affinity for aptness, proportion, perspicuity, analogical force, and witty tenuousness. A Ramist poet, through trope, often would relate apparent dissimilars on the basis of single characteristics or concepts common to both. Thus, metaphor would function to force readers to make precise distinctions and to perceive connections that are implied rather than stated. Readers imbued not only with Ramist principles of relatedness but with Platonic concepts of reality must have perceived synecdochal meaning (parts manifesting their perfected or abstract wholes) almost in an instant.

The traditional explanation for the necessity of metaphor is that an explicit statement always is incomplete and that metaphor, which embodies the implicit, can articulate economically what ordinary language is powerless to express. Ramist poets conceived of images as logical "arguments" capable of relating one word, object, or idea to another, thus leading to an almost infinite progression of relationships in an unbroken, reasonable pattern. Such images often define, differentiate, or explain and thus function logically to advance an idea. The power of a metaphor, in particular, to convey an idea precisely and economically encouraged Ramist poets not to "prove something" but to examine reality, analyze cause and effect, and declare universal truths. Ramist logic insisted that an orderly disposition of axioms, without recourse to formal, syllogistic argumentation, served to delineate truth. This conviction gave great dialectical validity to metaphor, for imagery functioning as argument embodied the universal in the particular and stood as an axiom — not proving a truth but actually constituting that truth.

Rosemond Tuve's influential study *Elizabethan and Metaphysical Imagery* contains a lengthy chapter dealing with the logical function of imagery and the influence of Peter Ramus. Surprisingly, Tuve focuses her discussion on Sidney, Marlowe, and the Metaphysicals in spite of her assertion that Sidney and Milton are the two poets in English "most indisputably connected with Ramist thought."[2] In the intervening years, and in spite of increased scholarly interest in Ramus and the arts of the Scholastic trivium, no published study has dealt directly with logical "invention" as reflected in the imagery of any of Milton's shorter poems.[3]

John Milton lived toward the end of the "age of logic" and was himself the author of a textbook on the art. His *Artis Logicae Plenior Institutio* (A Fuller Institution of the Art of Logic) is an enlargement, a clarification, and an interpretation of Ramus's *Dialecticae*. Although Milton's work was not published until 1672, the available evidence suggests that it could have been written as early as 1630 or as late as 1640. The earlier date falls near the end of his studies at Cambridge where the controversy between the Ramist and Aristotelian logicians was at its height; the latter comes soon after the start of his short career as schoolmaster and suggests that the *Artis Logicae* could have been written for his pupils. For present purposes, it is important simply to note that Milton's shorter poems date from these same years when he was under the influence of the Cambridge logicians and was himself expounding the art of logic.

Ramus's *Dialecticae* is called by Perry Miller "in terms of immediate influence on the times, one of the three or four outstanding books of age."[4] Milton probably first came to know Ramus through George Downham, fellow of Christ's College, who published a commentary on the *Dialecticae* in 1610. According to Walter J. Ong, there were in the century between 1550 and 1650 eleven hundred separate printings of individual works by Ramus and his disciple Omer Talon and two hundred fifty editions of the *Dialecticae* alone.[5]

Ramus's treatise separated rigidly the classical arts of logic, rhetoric, and grammar and assimilated the first two parts of classical rhetoric, *inventio* and *dispositio*, to logic alone. *Inventio* was defined as a systematic means of "finding something to say" or "discovering" subject matter or "arguments"; *dispositio* was the systematic means by which such arguments were "disposed" or "arranged" into a composition, an oration, or some other form of discourse. The umbrella term *argument* referred to any concept or word employed in speech or reasoning which had the capacity to relate one thing to another and hence to advance an idea or develop a proposition.

The Ramist logic was essentially a classification of these arguments and specifically a classification by dichotomy. The central assertion was that any concept, art, or discourse could be divided into its component parts, divided again, and so on until the fundamental corpuscular units or most basic arguments had been set forth in their most elemental forms. Dichotomous division, therefore, became the basis of a logical approach to any and all subject matter. The binary arrangement of Ramist logic provided something very close to what we would call today an information storage and retrieval system. Father Ong speaks of such a system as a means of "racking up information so that it can be retrieved in bits as required" and calls it a "precursor" of the computer flow charts of today.[6]

"Invention" is an inaccurate, perhaps even a lazy, translation of the Latin *inventio*. As suggested above, the first part of logic consisted not so much of the creation or "invention" of knowledge as of the recollection or recovery of what was already known. The purpose of the dichotomized diagram was to present, in spatial groupings, a means of proceeding from what was observed or known to what was unobserved or unknown. This was Ramist "method"— moving, in any discourse, from the general to the particular while always relating the one to the other. Invention, then, was the art of systematic identification of self-evident truths and had little to do with the rhetorical skill of devising arguments. It included the general logic of causality (especially the efficient cause), that of inherence or relation, and that of genus or distribution. By moving all such questions of organization from rhetoric to logic, Ramus took an itemizing, highly diagrammatic approach to discourse. Developing a continuous discourse (e.g., a poem) was, therefore, a matter of arranging preexisting, corpuscular units in an organized spatial pattern.

One would expect a relationship between logical invention and the "discovery" and use of images in poetry. Jackson Cope writes that Ramism "induced man to leap the aural structure of syntactical discursion in search of an objective, 'corporeal' status for the word itself, a status in which it would not be a dependent sign but an immediate creative entity." He becomes even more precise when he remarks that, even in our day, we have a literature in which "time and space coalesce creatively in metaphor and in that extension of metaphor, myth."[7] But again it is Father Ong who relates Ramism most directly to poetic imagery. "In particular," he writes, "Ramism stressed the use of 'specials' or individual examples to prove 'generals' or universal propositions, and it emphasized the use of disjunction. . . . Thus Ramism assimilated logic to imagery and imagery to logic by reducing intelligence itself, more or less unconsciously, in terms of rather exclusively visual, spatial analogies."[8] The diagrammatic structure of logical invention especially invited a "one-for-one" correspondence between words and things. It encouraged the perception of reality in terms of metaphor.

Before considering exactly how the spatially oriented units of discourse embodied in Ramist logic were reflected in the visual and spatial analogies of the Miltonic poetic, it is necessary to identify more precisely some of the logical forms embraced by invention. Milton's *Artis Logicae*, following the Ramist model, classified the individual "topics" of invention by dichotomy. The topics, then, were those fundamental, corpuscular units by which compositions, sermons, orations, or discourses (including poems) could be organized, amplified, and varied. Thus, any subject could be considered according to its source (the topic "cause") and the results of its reaction with forces around it (the topic "effect"). The subject's "adjuncts" (characteristics extrinsic to its essence) could be established. Its precise character could be noted ("definition"). It could be divided into its component parts ("distribution"). It could be compared with others of its own species and shown to be "greater," "lesser," "equal," or "unequal" (all distributions of the topic "quantity"). Or it could be compared with *different* species to show "likes" or "unlikes" (distributions from "quality"). The subject could be contrasted with its "opposite" or merely with its "disparate," its "contrary" or its "privative" (all topics resulting from distribution of the topic "dissentany"). It could be derived from its verbal root (its "conjugates") or simply named ("notation," the topic from which the terms *denotation* and *connotation* derive). A self-conscious logician, as John Milton surely was, found himself almost "programmed" to draw his subject matter through the topics of invention as part of the process of composition.

Renaissance composition, of course, required much more than "inventing" subject matter and "disposing" it into enunciations and propositions. It was necessary as well to give attention to that major part of the art of rhetoric, *elocutio* or style. Especially in poetic composition, a concern for rhetorical style meant a concern for figures. And the great majority of the hundreds of figures appearing in the Renaissance poetic, including almost all of the important ones, were derived from the topics of invention.

The rhetorical figure most relevant to poets steeped in Ramism was trope — a figure that turned the significance of a word or sentence from its ordinary, "proper" meaning to another perhaps not proper yet near enough in meaning to increase its force. Renaissance rhetoricians recognized dozens of tropes but the Ramists only four — all of them directly related to the topics of invention. Sister Miriam Joseph identifies the four as *metonymy* (of logical cause, effect, subject, adjunct), *synechdoche* (resulting from distribution into genus, species, parts, and wholes), *irony* (drawn from the dissentany topics disparates, contraries, relatives, adverses), and *metaphor* (drawn from the comparative topic quality).[9] The relationships between tropical and logical forms become apparent as they are considered in poetic contexts. Indeed, in the work of a poet-logician like Milton, the schematic practice of developing tropes out of the topics of invention must have resulted virtually from a mental habit.

A brief essay on Ramist invention as a wellspring of Miltonic imagery does not permit detailed analysis of the *Artis Logicae*, even one limited to the topics of logic utilized in the creation of a single poem. It would seem important, however, to select from the *Logic* passages dealing directly with metaphorical constructions and to exemplify therein the relationship between logical concepts and poetic forms. This single sample from Milton's treatise should enrich the reading of the Nativity ode and should afford some insight into Milton's creative processes.

In the *Artis Logicae*, Milton locates his discussion of the various forms of logical similitude under the topic "comparatives," which he sets in dichotomized opposition to "simples." Comparative arguments are distributed into the modes "quantity" and "quality." Quantity is broken further into "equals" and "unequals" and unequals into "greaters" and "lessers." Quality, in turn, is divided into the topics "likes" and "unlikes." Milton declares the "extraordinary usefulness" of comparatives to derive from their capacity to transfer knowledge from one term which is understood to another which is less understood and, thereby, to illuminate or "make plain" rather than to persuade.[10] To "transfer knowledge" in order to "illuminate" is one of the obvious functions of metaphor.

In the important chapters on logical quality, Milton takes care to distinguish likes and unlikes from those other comparative arguments that articulate relationships in purely quantitative terms. He points out that "equals do not admit superiority or inferiority, but likes admit it, for even the things most alike can be greater or less but equals cannot."[11] He introduces the term *similitude*, defined from Aristotle and Boethius as unity of quality, proportion, or analogy. And he distinguishes metaphor as "the short form of similitude," specifically as a similitude "contracted to one word without the signs which, however, are understood."[12]

It is interesting that Milton (as poet as well as logician) did not explain and illustrate the function and effect of logical quality in defining relationships, framing arguments, drawing logical distinctions, analyzing cause and effect. Christopher Grose points out a passage in Milton's chapter dealing with "likes" that does not appear in the *Dialecticae* of Ramus and, therefore, represents a departure from Milton's main source:[13]

Warning, however, should be given that likes whether of short or full form are not to be urged beyond that quality which the man making the comparison intended to show as the same in both. Thus a magistrate is likened to a dog, yet merely in the fidelity of his guardianship, whence came the saying of the schools: "Nothing similar is identical; likeness does not run on four feet; every likeness hobbles."[14]

Milton is reminding the logical inventor (or poet?), the person making the comparison, about the Ramist tendency to expand boldly the province of similitude. He expresses, near the end of the chapter, disapproval of "similars opportunely compared for display" and, by implication, the use of extreme and indiscriminate comparisons. The main function of comparative arguments is simply to "make plain," and hence Milton counsels moderation in the use of analogies.

"Unlikes," the last of the arguments from comparison, are "comparatives, the quality of which is diverse."[15] Unlike arguments set forth differences that arise out of comparison and not out of the intrinsic nature of the subject or subjects. From unlikes are drawn figures of dissimilitude, one of the most familiar of the tropes drawn from the arguments of quality. Catachresis probably is the best example of a figure which may employ first a similitude and then a dissimilitude in the same argument. An implied metaphor, catachresis removes a word from its usual application (which nevertheless remains in the reader's mind as a similitude) and transfers it to another not so usual (on the surface, at least, a dissimilitude). Such a figure, more than a simple and direct metaphor or simile, can forge a sudden concentration of meaning and secure compression, energy, and intensity. Comparisons from quality which move in both directions between the two modes of likes and unlikes are among the most vital and creative instruments of poetic expression.

If space permitted, it would be well to set forth, in diagrammatic summary, the full distribution of Ramist invention, topic by topic and dichotomy by dichotomy. This would demonstrate rather conclusively that the Ramist *tabula generali* of logical invention was, indeed, a spatial model for conceiving both mental and communicational processes. This corpuscular epistemology, as much a guide to effective composition as an instrument for the perfection of reason, provided a methodology for the poet as well as for the schoolmaster. For John Milton, the arts of logic and poetic occupied almost identical positions — that is, the spatially oriented units of discourse in Ramist logic closely paralleled the visual and spatial patterns operative in poetic intelligence. To perceive the interworking of logical invention and metaphorical structure, even in a single poem, is to enrich our understanding of the essential unity of Renaissance thought.

We know from Milton's sixth elegy, to Charles Diodati, that *On the Morning of Christ's Nativity* was composed "for the birthday of Christ" in the same year in which the poet attained the age of twenty-one. We know also that, shortly before, Milton had bought a copy of Pindar, the volume (now in the Harvard library) dated and closely annotated in Milton's hand. The Nativity ode is more on the Horatian model than the Pindaric, but it reflects the influence of his Cambridge years more than his study of either of the classical poets. Milton was to proceed B.A. only three months after the composition of the Nativity ode, and one would expect to find evidence of his training in logic here as, perhaps, in no other of his works.

The fact that the Nativity ode celebrates a mystery (the Incarnation) rather than an event (the Nativity) governs the form as well as the function of the imagery. Balachandra Rajan points out that the ode is "activist," is less concerned with what the Incarnation *is* than with what it *does*. It is the transforming event in history, an "intervention" linking

Creation and the Last Judgment and also the first and final paradises.[16] Tuve asserts that the full impact of mystery is achieved by "a kind of orchestrated interweaving of themes carried by great symbols traditionally used to present such meanings."[17] Thus, the central theme of perpetual and universal peace is manifested through metaphors of darkness lightened, harmony retuned, and nature transcended. These and other images in the ode will be seen to function in a logical context and to derive from the Ramist topics of invention.

The poem begins, as is customary in the odic tradition, with an announcement of theme and occasion. In stark, denotative plainness, the first stanza moves in time from prophetic song to the Incarnation and Crucifixion to Judgment Day to the "perpetual peace" of universal concord. Not until the paradoxical reference to "wedded Maid and Virgin Mother" is there relief from direct and unmetaphorical expression.

The "maid and mother" figure is, of course, chiasmus — the "crossing" of two adjectives with the nouns they modify. The crossing results in a second figure, oxymoron, a form of paradox in which there is an apparent contradiction that, in fact, argues a fundamental truth. The figures derive from "contradictories," one of the "dissentany" topics of invention.

The dissentany topics were those disagreeing with, denying, or dissenting from the essence of the thing argued. In addition to "contradictories," the *Artis Logicae* also defines the dissentany topics "diverse," "opposite," "disparate," "contrary," "relative," "adverse," and "privative"— the various modes representing degrees of unlikeness or dissension. Rhetorical figures derived from the dissentany topics function to particularize and to unify seemingly dissimilar ideas. By employing figures apparently self-contradictory, a poet could amplify meaning by indirection. Paradox, the most famous dissenting figure, would modify one part of a metaphorical structure (the tenor) through unlikeness rather than likeness to the other part (the vehicle). Functioning metaphorically, paradox was the supreme agent by which apparently unconnected ideas could be brought together. It demonstrated the Ramist axiom that matter often is more clearly understood when viewed in relation to its opposite or its contrary.

From the largely denotative first stanza, the second brings a sudden shift to metaphor. Christ is "That glorious *Form*, that *Light* unsufferable, / And that far-beaming *blaze* of Majesty" (8-9).[18] Here is a series of metonymies drawn from the main distribution of logical quality "likes." In the ode, light, along with harmony, is to become the main symbol of God's reconcilement of all things to himself. Light is to be viewed not only as brightness but, connotatively, as power, love, and truth — and it is not to conflict with darkness but to make of darkness a means of salvation. Thus, heaven and earth are opposed metaphorically in the image of Christ, who "Forsook the Courts of everlasting *Day,* / And chose with us a *darksom* House of mortal Clay" (13–14). Note the shift from a metaphor derived from the topic "likes" to one derived from "contraries." "Day" and "darksom," as logical contraries, merge paradoxically as participants in the same act of salvation, thus arguing the principle of concord among opposites.

Light imagery continues in the third stanza, where the approach both of dawn and of Christ is symbolized in sun and star imagery: the heavens still "by the Suns team untrod" (i.e., in darkness) and the "spangled hosts" keeping watch in "squadrons bright." Again, the merging of logical contraries (darkness and light) suggests concord among opposites. But the figures also derive from "quality" as a logical comparative (Christ as heavenly light but also as the lights of nature that herald his birth). Thus, as the proem ends, the ode gives concrete definition to the mystery of the Incarnation, and metaphor functions logically in support of theme.

Stanza I of the hymn introduces the symbolic narrative of the sun which is to culminate in Stanza VII. The sun is presented not as the lifegiver, the pagan Sol, but as the symbolic efficient cause of nature's blemishes. Nature, conceived as the sun's mistress, finally recognizes her true love as that other "Son" who is about to appear. What some might decry as a pathetic fallacy (nature removing her gay attire) or brand a conceit (the sun a "lusty paramour") becomes functional through the thematic implications and the logical tension of the figures.

As dissentany topics denied or dissented from the essence of things argued, consentany topics affirmed or consented with what was argued. First among the consentany topics was "cause," declared to be "this first place of invention . . . the fount of all knowledge"; and chief among the causes was the "efficient," shown in Milton's treatise to be the means "*by* which things happen."[19] The treatise then defines "effect" as that produced by or resulting from the operation of all the causes. Some metonymies developed out of the reciprocal relations of these two topics of logic, with cause substituted for effect or effect for cause. Death, for example, may be the cause of paleness, but paleness, the effect, may also stand for death. "Death is pale" is a metonymy in which the effect is developed out of the efficient cause.

"Subject" and "adjunct" also are consentany topics. The subject is defined as an active form or force, fully constituted by its causes, to which something extrinsic to its essence (the adjunct) is adjoined. Again, some metonymies are derived from these topics — for example, in the substitution of adjunct for subject or subject for adjunct. To return to the figures in the first stanza of the hymn, note that an insignificant logical adjunct of nature is "doff't" as a result of the important change in efficient cause that is taking place. The new controlling power is represented in that greater "Son" whose logical effect is to force the lesser "sun" into hiding and to require that nature acknowledge her own insufficiences. The several "sun-Son" images are derived from the "nominal" topic, notation — defined as "an argument elicited from the power of a name."[20] And the "great Son — lesser sun" comparisons obviously are drawn from the topic "quantity."

The startling comparisons and witty conceits continue through Stanzas II and III, providing a baroque effect of homeliness combined with sublimity and quaintness merged with extravagance. The images of polluted earth hiding her "naked shame" and "foul deformities" under a veil of snow and of personified Peace sliding down to earth, olive-crowned and equipped with turtle wing and myrtle wand, each comprise whole stanzas. Both images are complete with logical adjuncts which function to provide the baroque texture — deformities capped by the veil of white to describe nature, pagan symbolism in Christian context to portray peace. More important, each image is a metaphorical representation of the incarnate Christ with the metaphors drawn from logical quality. Nature purified is a logical effect of Christ's birth but can also be viewed as a manifestation of Christ from the topic "likes." Peace, too, is a logical effect of Christ's birth but can also be understood as the Son himself — sent "meek-ey'd" by God to strike "a universal Peace through Sea and Land." It seems apparent that Milton found in the topic "quality" the kinds of particulars that would best show forth his intended universal — Christ as cause incarnate and cause as procreant of universal effect.

Stanzas IV and V present the immediate effects of "universal Peace" in images of halted hostility and whispering calm. It is the adjuncts of war that are laid aside — the spear, shield, chariot, and trumpet — and those of peace that are invoked. Again Christ becomes manifest as "Prince of light" (the metaphor from quality) and again there is juxtaposition with "night." This time the image of darkness is not metaphorical, but its direct logical disparity (with light) reminds the reader of the quite literal darkness which the light of Christ will illumine. The sense of ambiguity is further heightened by a final image from the topic "effect"— the halcyon birds "brooding on the charmed wave." Connotations both of meditative calm and of impending birth are obvious enough. The logical topic, of course, is "notation," and its function is to provide both a change of mood (from the noise of war to the quietness of peace) and a double illumination of meaning.

The burden of the imagery in Stanzas VI and VII is to negate time, to assert the utter timelessness of the Nativity by portraying sun and stars transfixed in universal atemporality. The stars are a type of unswerving steadfastness, phenomena that will not fade from sight "Until their Lord himself bespake, and bid them go." Lucifer, another figure from the topic "notation," is both the morning star (the last to fade) and the rebel angel who tries to distract the stars (as well as men) from the fact of the Nativity. Whereas the images of wandering winds and smooth seas in Stanza V are personifications, the stars of Stanza VI are metaphors. Specifically, the stars are synecdochic representations of the orderly concord of the universe. Arrested motion, a symbolic foretaste of eternity, is repeated in the image of "The Sun himself" who withholds "his wonted speed" to hide his head for fear and shame. The images of fixed stars and stopped sun, figures quite distinct from one another, are fused to give the impression of halted time. A normal adjunct (movement) of both subjects (stars and sun) is denied in order to provide the desired mood of atemporality. The image is grounded in the dissentany topic "privative"— a negating contrary in which the thing denied (in this case the movement of the stars) normally is present as an inherent adjunct. The privative argument thus functions to show the logical effect of Christ's birth operative in time as well as space.

From the indirect, metaphorical representations of the fixed stars and the greater and lesser "suns," the scene suddenly shifts in Stanza VIII to the uncomplicated, direct icon of the shepherds "simply chatting in a rustic row." Pan, then, is introduced as a type of Christ appropriate to the pastoral scene — the Greek god presented not only as a divine shepherd but as a symbol of the universal life of nature. That Pan/Christ "Was *kindly* come" suggests his appearance on earth both as "kin" (to mankind) and "with kindness." The basic Pan/Christ figure is grounded in logical analogy (from "quality"), while the adjunct "kindly" embodies a double meaning derived from the topic "conjugates."

Conjugates, as Milton defines them in the *Artis Logicae*, are "words variously derived from the same root."[21] His example: "Justice is the cause why anyone is just and, since he is just, therefore he does justly."[22] Here an abstraction, "justice," is the cause of a concretion, "just," which, in turn, is the cause of an adverb, "justly." In Stanza VIII, the adjunct "kindly" embodies metaphorically the abstract in the concrete, giving expression to a cause-and-effect relationship similar to that in the "justice" example. The general term is the cause of the particular which, in turn, reflects the general; the metaphor, accordingly, functions as a logical argument.

The real logical significance of this passage, however, lies in the overall tension developed between pagan and Christian images. To view Christ in pastoral terms is to assert not so much a reconcilement of opposites or disunities as a negation of difference in a new and higher unity. As Milton asserted in the *Artis Logicae* (the chapter on diverse arguments), dissentany arguments "by their dissent . . . more evidently appear."[23] The Pan/Christ metaphor, by contrast of pagan and Christian opposites, argues the perfection of an all-embracing, atemporal unity.

In Stanzas IX through XIII, the same perfect unity is expressed in images of harmony. Here, there is a juxtaposition of dissentanies to symbolize concord — pagan harmony (of the spheres) merging with Christian harmony (of the angelic song). Stanza IX describes, in conventional terms, the logical effect of the heavenly music upon the shepherds—"as all their souls in blissful rapture took." Stanza X records the effect of the music upon nature, for "She knew such harmony alone / Could hold all Heav'n and Earth in happier union" (107–08). Nature, it seems, saw in the angelic song a more powerful efficient cause than that exerted by the music of the spheres and rejoiced in the logical effect — the entire cosmos "in tune" for the first time. Stanza XI adds visual to auditory imagery with its representation of the angelic host as a "*Globe* of circular *light*"— the globe, like the circle, a symbol of perfection. Then, juxtaposed with the light metaphor, is "shame-fac'd night," the image of darkness a metonymy of nature's fallen state. The beams of heavenly glory are to clothe ("array") the nakedness of night in the same fashion as, in Stanza II, the snow was to veil the "naked shame" of nature. The metaphorical "clothing" of darkness by light, a visual image, parallels the reestablishment of perfect harmony expressed earlier in the auditory image.

Music appears again as the central metaphor of Stanzas XII and XIII, this time to symbolize the atemporality of the Nativity and the expansiveness of history. The music of the Nativity had been heard only once before —"when of old the sons of morning sung"— that is, at the Creation. The implicit assertion is almost syllogistic in its logic: if music of such character had not been repeated since the Creation, it followed that the Nativity was of equal significance with the Creation. Adding the metaphors of pagan harmony — the "silver chime" and "ninefold harmony" of the "Crystal spheres"— includes all the natural universe and all of time in a single, all-embracing metaphor of universal concord.

Here, Milton employs several species of the genus "harmony" as specials to make manifest the generals of his theme — a procedure quite pointedly recommended in the *Artis Logicae*'s discussion of logical distribution. To begin, there is the definition: "There is distribution when the whole is divided into parts."[24] The division, we learn, can be from cause, from effect, from subject, or from adjunct — all the consentany arguments. When genera are divided into species, as in the "harmony" metaphors, the distribution is from effect; portrayal of universals in particulars embodied in a cause-and-effect relationship between genus and species. The result of such metaphoric interaction of part with whole is an organic union of special with general, concrete with abstract, image with idea — and accordingly, in these stanzas, establishes that all-embracing metaphor of universal concord.

Stanzas XIV and XV conclude the first section of the hymn. The central figure remains the "holy song" which again negates time by bringing back the Age of Gold, when "speckl'd vanity" and "leprous sin" were no part of man's earthly lot. One effect, then, of the Nativity is to return Truth and Justice to the world of men — especially as Christ's birth anticipates, ultimately, the day of judgment. Milton is linking the sinless Age of Gold to the bliss of the second coming by employing a metonymy derived from an inherent adjunct (justice as part of the essence of two subjects, the Age of Gold and Judgment Day). Mercy, then, is introduced as mediating between Truth and Justice in order to bring reconciliation between apparently opposing forces.

In the images of the Age of Gold and the second coming are representations of the "general" effects of the "holy song." The baroque conceits — vanity dying, sin melting away, hell itself withdrawing before the light of Christ — are "special" effects, the *particular* kinds of things produced by the "holy song" as efficient cause. The image of hell leaving "her *dolorous mansions* to the peering *day*" doubtless was intended to parallel the earlier figure of Christ leaving the "Courts of everlasting *Day*" to join man in his "*darksom House* of mortal Clay." Both of these are metaphors from logical contraries, and the function of such parallel figures is to demonstrate actual unity in apparent disunity.

With the second section of the hymn, Milton turns from his treatment of the redemption of Nature — its restored participation in the divine harmony and its final union with divine light — to consider man's fatal proneness to idolatry and the consequences of the Incarnation upon the various manifestations of evil. Stanza XVI, beginning with its blunt "no," suggests that man cannot perfectly hear the divine music or fully join the universal concord delineated in the first section. The return of the Age of Gold is only apparent, not actual, because, as truth and justice are inherent adjuncts of man's state on earth, so also is evil — and as much after the birth of Christ as before. Only when Christ's sacrifice "redeem(s) our loss" and when the terror of the "world's last session" (Judgment Day) is past, will man's bliss "Full and perfect" be.

The central image of the second section of the hymn is, of course, that of the pagan gods, first constrained by Christ's birth and then put to flight. The figure of the abdicating gods parallels that of night in the first section. Both are metaphors of the natural failings to which man and nature are heir, and both represent external forces with which humankind always will struggle. The abdicating gods, like the undefined powers of darkness, are embodied in images of constraint and confinement — contrasting vividly with the display of radiance and openness in the manifestations of Christ and the effects of his coming. The figures function, of course, to portray Christ as classical hero rather than divine sufferer. The end of the hymn will see the symbolic joining of the abdicating gods and the powers of darkness — as the pagan spirits troop away on their "nightsteeds" into the darkness of their "Several grave(s)."

Stanza XVIII presents the first of the metaphorical manifestations of evil, the "old Dragon" himself. Here, Milton employs the reciprocal relations of logical cause to logical effect — the coming of Christ (the efficient cause) restricting Satan's activities (the subject) within "straiter limits" (the effect). These constraints (the secondary efficient cause) result ultimately in the failure of "his Kingdom" (the secondary effect). The metaphorical portrayal of Satan is further amplified by the circumstantial adjunct of his "usurped sway" (which is denied) and by the containing adjunct of his "folded tail." The "old Dragon" as metaphor is, of course, drawn from the topic "likes."

The continuing logical effect of the Nativity is the gradual driving away of all forms of error. The Oracles of Stanza XIX are "dumb" because only Christ can bring the final revelation; the Genius must depart and the Nymphs mourn because partial truth, no matter how lovely and how innocent, cannot bring perfect peace and harmony. Cataloging the many species of error and describing the effect of the Nativity on them is to suggest, almost allegorically, the deception that has been wrought upon mankind through the ages. Mere pagan loveliness, for example, has been mistaken for sacredness and must now be repudiated. The image of the "*chill* Marble" (of statues dedicated to the pagan gods) seeming "to *sweat*" is a paradoxical figure developed out of "contradictories." (To "sweat" ordinarily is the result of heat, not "chill.") But here is a further effect of truth driving away falsehood.

The more demanding gods — Baal, Dagon, Ammon, Moloch, Osiris, and others who required actual worship — are treated less gently. Their departure is marked by images of burning, battering, blindness, and "dismal dance." Viewed in their several logical qualities, the abdicating gods may be considered allegorical representations of various kinds of human error. These representations resulted from application of the topic "notation" to attributes derived from the comparative "likes," and the poetic effect is a vivid manifestation of natural and human fallacy. Nature especially is given a metaphorical dimension through an allegorical presentation of her false gods.

With Stanzas XXV and XXVI, the controlling imagery again settles on the infant Christ. There appears first the synecdochal metaphor of the "dreaded Infant's hand," the substitution of part (hand) for whole marking the subfigure "merismus" formulated by distribution from adjuncts. A light metaphor follows—Christ manifested in "The rays of Bethlehem" which blind the "dusky Eyn" of Osiris. The image is from "likes," but the argument itself is grounded in the rays as efficient cause and the blindness as logical effect. Finally, there is the image of the "snaky" Typhon who was vanquished by Hercules, now forced to flee by the infant Christ. The implied metaphor argues, from logical comparatives, the strength of an incarnate Christ who, even as "Our Babe . . . in his swaddling bands," is the very antithesis of "meek majesty" or "gentle shepherd"—briefly, a classical hero.

The image of Christ in his cradle is juxtaposed immediately with that of the "Sun in bed" which introduces the next stanza. In this much-criticized conceit is found the culmination of the "sun-Son" comparisons developed throughout the hymn, for the sunrise is an explicit analogy both of the birth of Christ and of his resurrection. The parallel, from "likes," is between Christ and the sun as light-bringers, and its logical extension is the image of Christ dismissing the false gods even as the sun disperses shadows. Thus, as the sun (and Christ) rises, "The flocking shadows pale / Troop to th' infernal jail" (232–33), and the dawn of Christmas Day has broken. Supporting the basic image is the submerged metaphor "flocking," suggesting the sheeplike character of the pagan spirits whom the all-powerful shepherd is herding into confinement. The exact, logical precision of this metaphor stems from the specificity of the analogy from "likes" and the tight cause-and-effect relationship between the sun and dispersed shadows, the Son and dismissed gods.

With Stanza XXVII, the Nativity ode concludes in images of degree, order, and stability. "Heav'n's youngest-teemed Star," the star of the Wise Men, is a lesser light subordinate and attentive to the Prince of Light. "Teemed," of course, carries the connotations of fertility and overabundance as well as of newborn, its ambiguity derived from logical "notation" grounded in effect. The "*Handmaid* Lamp" with which the star attends "Her sleeping Lord" emphasizes her lesser degree and marks the metaphor as derived from comparative "quantity." The paradoxical image of the "Courtly Stable" and the portrayal of "Bright-harness'd Angels" also suggest the deference of degree. The angels sitting "in order serviceable" symbolize an active purpose, the energy of light mobilized, ordered, and held ready for a creative role in human history. The significant concluding word, *serviceable*, is a diminishing figure from the topic "quality" and is intended to translate greatness into humility. It provides a final contrast with the celestial glory and the infernal creations which have gone before.

The "serviceable" image also reminds the reader that the entire poem has been a tissue of contrasts from which Milton has drawn a pattern of reconciliations more splendid than the conflicting parts. Nature abandoned is opposed to nature redeemed, and the result is nature untarnished and immutable. In the temporal dimension, past is opposed to present and future (literally from Creation through the Nativity to the Last Judgment), and the reconciliation is in timelessness. Pagan harmony is opposed to Christian harmony, and from that is derived the eternal concord of heaven. Each of these reconciliations is presented in metaphors which function to resolve the great paradox of the existential and to symbolize the universal harmony of a Creation ordered by an all-powerful God.

Much of the imagery in the Nativity ode supports H. V. S. Ogden's contention that late Renaissance rhetorical theorists (including poets) were turning away from "exuberant variety" and adopting contrast as a means of revealing nature's "*discordia concors.*"[25] The *Artis Logicae* advanced the proposition that the contrast of two dissenting objects or ideas produces tension, often resulting in their consolidation in a third object or idea representative of the unity in the original two.[26] In the ode, pagan and Christian images merged to produce the symbolic motif of universal harmony. The pastoral form, itself a metaphor, brought together the paradoxical combination of the heroic, the courtly, and the rustic. In addition to these great tropes, there were the smaller ones grounded in the same principle of contrast — light and darkness, temporality and atemporality, freedom and constraint. Such imagery functions, in part, to develop an atmosphere of diffuseness, expansiveness, and timelessness. More importantly, the particulars of such images argue their universals and the images themselves become axiomatic truth.

What, finally, was the effect of Ramist logic upon the Miltonic poetic and especially upon the use of metaphor? First, we have seen that images based on logical concepts are more than vehicles for description and amplification. They are operative units in a poem's aesthetic structure, pointing out differences as well as similarities, and showing depth, range, and subtlety of concept. Many function to provide a metaphorical delineation of cause and effect, thus imparting to the poem a logical base. Such images range in complexity from bare similitudes based on common properties or common topics of invention, to intensifying comparisons built simultaneously on several logical bases, to complex and tenuously implied associations designed to establish a mood and influence an attitude.

What Ramus did was virtually to identify poetry with dialectic, suggesting that pointed, economical, and intellectually subtle imagery was a kind of ideal toward which poets of his age should strive. Furthermore, the Ramist proclamation of the unity of all learning prohibited the separation of poetic forms that made men "feel" from conceptual statements that made them "think." Imagery, as an organic part of this ordered pattern of composition, functioned to define, to contrast, and to argue a point of view with compression and precision. It contributed dialectical subtlety and profound suggestiveness rather than sensuous richness to the poetic context. Such presentation of intellectual conflict through imagery was a manifestation of actual logical complexity in much of the poetry of John Milton. Tuve writes that a poem possesses logical unity when it is "a reasoned and reasonable whole, manifesting its 'cause' through a judicious and formal expression of its matter."[27] What better characterization of the imagery out of which Milton built his Nativity ode?"

Ripon College

## NOTES

1. *Elizabethan and Metaphysical Imagery* (Chicago, 1974), p. 286.
2. Ibid., p. 332.
3. See, in addition to the citations in the present text, the following studies of logical forms in the major poems and in Milton's prose works: Don C. Allen, *The Harmonious Vision: Studies in Milton's Poetry* (Baltimore, 1970); Jackson I. Cope, *The Metaphoric Structure of "Paradise Lost"* (Baltimore, 1962); Peter F. Fisher, "Milton's Logic," *JHI*, XXIII (1962), 37–60; Harry P. Frissell, "Milton's Art of Logic and Ramist Logic in the Major Poems" (Ph.D. diss., Vanderbilt, 1951); Franklin Irvin, "Ramistic Logic in Milton's Prose Works" (Ph.D. diss., Princeton, 1941); John M. Major, "Milton's View of Rhetoric," *SP*, LXIV (1967), 685–711; Isabel G. MacCaffrey, *"Paradise Lost" as "Myth"* (Cambridge, Mass., 1959); Father Walter J. Ong, *Rhetoric, Romance and Technology* (Ithaca, N.Y., 1971); William J. Roscelli, "The Metaphysical Milton," *TSLL*, VIII (1967), 463–84.
4. *The New England Mind: The Seventeenth Century* (New York, 1939), p. 116.
5. *Ramus, Method, and Decay of Dialogue* (Cambridge, 1958), p. 24.

6. "Logic and the Epic Muse: Reflections on Noetic Structure in Milton's Milieu," in *Achievements of the Left Hand*, ed. Michael Lieb and John T. Shawcross (Amherst, 1974), p. 248.

7. *The Metaphoric Structure of "Paradise Lost"* (Baltimore, 1961), pp. 178–79.

8. *Ramus, Method, and Decay of Dialogue*, p. 286.

9. *Shakespeare's Use of the Arts of Language* (New York, 1947), p. 36.

10. *The Works of John Milton*, ed. Frank Allen Patterson et al. (New York, 1931–38), XI, p. 153; hereafter cited as CM.

11. Ibid., p. 193.

12. Ibid., p. 197.

13. "Milton on Ramist Similitude," in *Seventeenth Century Imagery*, ed. Earl Miner (Berkeley, 1971), p. 109.

14. CM XI, p. 195.

15. Ibid., p. 205.

16. "In Order Serviceable," *MLR*, LXIII (1968), 16.

17. *Images and Themes in Five Poems by Milton* (Cambridge, Mass., 1957), p. 62.

18. *John Milton: Complete Poems and Major Prose*, ed. Merritt Y. Hughes (New York, 1957). All citations that follow are to this edition.

19. CM XI, p. 31.

20. Ibid., p. 219.

21. Ibid., p. 215.

22. Ibid., p. 217.

23. Ibid., p. 99.

24. Ibid., p. 227.

25. "The Principles of Variety and Contrast in Seventeenth-Century Aesthetics," *JHI*, X (1949), 159–82.

26. CM XI, p. 215.

27. *Elizabethan and Metaphysical Imagery* (Chicago, 1974), p. 336.

# THE LANGUAGES OF ACCOMMODATION
# AND THE STYLES OF *PARADISE LOST*

## *Walter R. Davis*

---

I N   T H I S   essay, I wish first to characterize the styles or uses of language in *Paradise Lost* generally, and then in that context of styles
to offer a specific interpretation of the language of the war in Heaven
in Books V and VI.

### I

Joan Mallory Webber recently reminded us that Milton was a key
figure in inaugurating "the inward turn of the epic" that Wordsworth
later claimed to have completed in creating an "epic of the mind."[1]
*Paradise Lost* takes action of an epic scope and shows it happening to
Adam, Eve, Satan, and other distant characters; but it also takes care
to show us readers that the same spiritual combat is occurring within
each of us today. It is "Man's" disobedience and his "first" one that the
poem records, and it leads us as readers to experience in the reading of
the poem (as a heightening of our own experience) the cycle of sin, fall,
death, and regeneration.[2] This effect is produced, as the invocation to
Book IX makes explicit, by focusing on mental or psychological action,
by displacing wars, battles, races, games, and feasts from the center of
attention and replacing them by such subjects as

> the better fortitude
> Of Patience and Heroic Martyrdom
> Unsung.[3]                                                    (IX, 31–33)

Furthermore, not only is this a poem about the mind, but it is also a poem
that manages to evoke in the mind of the reader various states of consciousness, so that Hell, Heaven, Paradise, and the postlapsarian Earth
come to the fore primarily as states of mind.

One primary element in placing the reader in *Paradise Lost* in a
position to experience the movement of its plot as successive states of mind
is its style, the means by which events are conveyed to us. And the changes
which style goes through actually form a major element of its action or

plot; they direct the actions which the reader moves through in his mind, and they heighten the attention given to such mental actions.

"*Paradise Lost* has not one style but several, as Pope was among the first to recognize," writes Balachandra Rajan. "There is at the simplest level of discrimination, an infernal style, a celestial style, and styles for Paradise before and after the fall."[4] In what follows I should like to break this general statement down a bit in a brief sketch of the changes in style of *Paradise Lost*, book by book.

Book I is visual in its orientation, and heavily imagistic. When Satan first casts his eyes—"baleful eyes" that "witnessed" (both showed and saw) "huge affliction" (I, 56–57) — around Hell, he first sees mental qualities that may be said to project his mind upon the scene, "Regions of sorrow, doleful shades, where peace / And rest can never dwell, hope never comes" (65–66). Only gradually do distinct images of "a fiery Deluge" and such come into ken. Fittingly, Hell first appears as privation of good and of being, and then such privation starts to assume definition and shape, or intelligibility. Hell gradually arises as a state of mind by what we may term "lyric definition," or a series of gradual and indirect processes, from the vague to the relatively clear, from the chaotic to the formed, from the drab to the speciously gorgeous (marked by the rash of similes that introduces the catalogue of demons [283–310]), and from the low to the high (marked by the continual surpassing in the raising of the standard [531–49]). Thus a state of mind gradually assumes visual shape. These processes come to completion in the raising of Pandemonium, which stands at the end of Book I as a visual monument to Satan's reiterated claim that "The mind is its own place, and in itself / Can make a Heav'n of Hell, a Hell of Heav'n" (254–55).

While Book I is lyric in its development, Book II is dramatic, and works by conflicts and contrasts. It is itself divided into two parts with high contrast between them (like Milton's earlier two-panel composition, *L'Allegro* and *Il Penseroso*), the parliamentary scene of the infernal consult, conveyed to us almost entirely in direct dialogue, and the narration of Satan's adventures through Hell-mouth to the edge of the cosmos. Within each half we have conflict. In the consult we hear not only conflicting and mutually critical plans, but also gradual redefinition of what the being of these rebel angels is in the program of each of them, and a sense of what the mind of Hell is in the style of each: to Moloch they are still angels, their minds filled with pain and cruelty, to Belial they are slaves of God who shrink from pain, to Mammon they are an independent people greedy for material gain.[5] Thus the conflict promotes in the reader a greater degree of differentiation and conscious definition, as does

Satan's conflict with Sin and Death, which yields (partly by means of explicit allegory, now) a full sense of what Sin is, how she developed, and what her wages are.

Book III reaches a high point of conscious definition. In their dialogue the Father and the Son lay out the entire Providential plan, relating with the utmost clarity contrasting though related concepts such as justice and mercy. And they do so in a purely auditory style almost devoid of images, highly schematic rather than troped, which repeats and rings the changes on individual words (such as "fall" [III, 95–102], or "will" and "grace" [167–216]) to such an extent that concepts seem to acquire body. This is the style of the Word of God, of light and pure being. In it the reader senses what Heaven is as a state of mind. With the completion of God's plan by the Atonement, we realize that this scene between Father and Son has been the reality of which the infernal consult was a parody, images start to flow in once more (350–71),[6] and the rest of the book is dominated by what are now seen as deceptive *visibilia*, the paradise of fools.

The auditory and the visual, words themselves and their referents, *logos* and *mythos*, achieve different adjustments of emphasis as Milton's style moves through its changes.[7] Book IV is primarily descriptive as Book I was. But the description is clearer, ceremonial, and more orderly (as in Satan's two views of Eden, IV, 131–72 emphasizing hierarchy, 205–323 emphasizing harmony and fruitfulness). More importantly, it is symbolic, for every myth or analogue cited in description is shown to be expressive of the truth while not literally true (as the Hesperides [250–51], or Amara [281]), and almost every visual detail is followed by an indication of its significance (for one instance among many, "His fair large Front and Eye sublime declar'd / Absolute rule" [300–01]). This is the style of Paradise, of "Heaven on Earth" (208) or truth in images; it argues a state of mind in which all things seen bespeak their true meaning directly and immediately. Here even Satan sees the sun and tells the truth about himself.

The language of accommodation governs Books V and VI. In them the image, instead of being a visible object pointing to the truth, becomes a multifaceted analogue of the truth, and the angel's use of corporal things to express incorporeal truths makes the image transcendent. As Raphael says:

> what surmounts the reach
> Of human sense, I shall delineate so,
> By lik'ning spiritual to corporal forms,
> As may express them best.                    (V, 571–74)

Thus Raphael will uncover the system of the cosmos in a plant (V, 468–90), will redefine time and the stars symbolically (V, 579–82 and 618–25), and will recount the events in Heaven before Adam's birth as if they constituted a kind of strife to be known later to Adam, and all too well known already by us. The angel's effort is to make difficult things easy, and Paradise as a state of mind is developing a feeling tone of relaxation — domestic, even occasionally comic.[8]

With Book VII the reader enters biblical time. Accommodation is no longer necessary, only "process of speech" transmitting God's immediate acts to human understanding (VII, 176–78), for we are reading about the material world we know so well, often in language we know so well, too. The account of the created universe issuing from the Word of God is essentially an expanded version of the Book of Genesis, presenting the Creation to Adam and to us as an object for heavenly meditation (for instance, VII, 155–60).[9] J. B. Broadbent points out that as it proceeds, language narrows to common experience, and concept is replaced by close images, so that similes arise on the third day, references to things crowd the fifth, and by the sixth we reach into Adam's and Eve's state of mind with all its attendant warnings.[10] If we may say that we encounter the language of the true or normative *mythos* in Book VII, then in Book VIII we discover the new human language of the true *logos*. There man's view and human consciousness dominate, for it is filled with Adam's memories, knowledge, and desires. Each new topic covered by the angel leads to Adam's expression of satisfaction and gratitude, and knowledge is thus surrounded by love. The whole of Book VIII, we may remember, is caused by Adam's desire to keep Raphael with him (perhaps a symbolic act expressive of keeping innocence), and, topic by topic, Adam first desires knowledge, then gets it, and finally cherishes it.

Book IX presents the fall in terms of direct human experience. It is dramatic, like Book II, but now the dramatic is developed by Milton self-consciously into the terms of a human tragic drama. "I now must change / Those Notes to Tragic" (IX, 5–6) not only indicates a new tone and reversal, but becomes a generic indicator as well. Theatrical terms abound (545, 855, for example), and the whole is set out as a five-act tragedy: the antagonist Satan, the protagonists Adam and Eve, the *agon* leading to reversal in Satan's temptation of Eve, the completion of reversal in Adam's decision to join her in sin, and the denouement in the bower. The book is conducted scene by scene, in each case first describing the setting and then reporting dialogue.[11] It is the human voice that predominates, expressing every fallen reader's state of mind at some moment (and mind is presented as microcosm, [1121–26]), voicing truths, half-truths, determination, confusion, vanity, temptation, resistance, yielding, anger, and despair.

Hence it is that, as Christopher Ricks argues, in the latter part of Book IX and in Book X, "with the Fall of Man, language falls too." That is, words are often used before Book IX in their primary etymological signification with neutral connotations in order "to re-create something of the prelapsarian state of language," and are then used later with their common accretions of meaning and dark connotations. Some examples are "error" as merely wandering (IV, 239) and as fault (IX, 1180–81), "wanton" as merely careless (IV, 629) and as unchaste (IX, 516–18), or "liberal" as generous (VIII, 362) and as uncaring (IX, 997).[12] In addition, Anne Ferry notes that Adam, Eve, and the reader start to live in a linguistic universe where image is without further meaning: Eve is a mere literal "rib" (X, 884–85), just as for Satan an "apple" is only an apple; God is too far away to see Eve, she thinks (IX, 810), and to be "naked" starts to mean merely to be without clothes.[13] In Book X, questions about linguistic ontology or the reference of words arise importantly. What is "Death"? A creature? A state of the body? A state of the soul? Another name for Adam ("both Death and I / Am found Eternal, and incorporate both" [X, 815–16])? Likewise, what is a "snake"? A mere animal (490–501)? Satan (180–90)? A typological term (1030–31)? The narrator here acts uncertain, like a mere reporter, prefacing many a statement with "some say" or some such locution (575, 668). The only solution to this linguistic and stylistic uncertainty seems to be to will words into action, in faith; that is what Adam starts to do when he proposes in words that they fall prostrate in repentance and then proceeds to do so, the narrator marking the almost liturgical acting out of words by an unusual echo of Adam's proposal (1086–92) word for word in his own description (1098–1104).

The last two books start to fill language with meaning and certainty once more. The orientation of Book XI is visual: there Michael presents Adam with images for him (and for us) to interpret. Thus the visions of Cain and Abel, the lazar-house, the Cainites and the Sethites gradually redefine "Death" from physical violence to the state of sin; the vision of "War" is redefined from valor to open manslaughter (682–97) and that of "Peace" from tranquillity to easeful corruption. Gradually Adam learns to read these images aright in his steps toward salvation by exegesis: at first mistaken, uncertain, frequently rebuked, by the time of the Flood he has subjected visions to meditation so fully (754–61) that he has become an exegete sufficient to determine unprompted the interpretation that "now I see / Peace to corrupt no less than War to waste" (783–84).

Things seen are now filled with meaning, but it is the "fallen" meaning with which we are familiar, whereby sinful life is a living death, peace corruption, beauty a bait for sin. Such is the postlapsarian state of mind, striving amid difficulty and despite failures toward understanding, and by it toward a unitive vision wherein man, angel, and God can achieve harmony.

As Book XII moves from the world destroyed to the world restored (XII, 3), it moves Adam and the reader from the difficult interpretation of visual events to the easier and more harmonious auditory style of faith. Michael changes his approach from that of presenter to that of narrator (6–12), and built into his words are many indicators of interpretation and response. The auditory style peculiar to Book XII is three-pronged. First of all, it is a style concerned with emotional responses and tonal adjustments, so that Adam's feeling response to Nimrod, for instance, comes to the forefront (63–78), as does his gratitude for grace (469–78); and his responses direct those of the reader, for whom the ending is to produce acceptance and resignation with hope. Second, it is an interpretive style. In his narration, Michael often repeats key words that interpret the action he relates in the very act of relating, as he does by repeating "life" and "death" in his account of the Messiah (385–450) or "spirit" in his account of the regency of the Holy Spirit (510–30). By such means, the nature of the "seed" of Adam which will bruise the serpent's head, formerly cause of such puzzlement (X, 180, 490, 1030), gradually grows in Adam's and our minds, and we realize that it means Christ (XII, 150, 232–35, 310–14, 327–28, 600, 623). Typology is the center of the interpretive style, for by its means an event can be related and at the same time be referred to the fulfillment it points to (230–35, 300–06, for example). Third, it is a unitive style. Since Michael shows forth grace by interpreting as he narrates, Adam's response is always geared to his and wins his approval. Adam becomes the reader's great exemplar. Thus, by means of voices, man, angel, and God can achieve some harmony. That is the promise held out to Adam and the reader as they strive to possess "A Paradise within thee, happier far" (586) by means of faith, hope, and charity.

Generally speaking, the language of *Paradise Lost* undergoes a great shift at the center of the poem. Until it moves into "the light of common day" with the account of the Creation in Book VII, the poem by and large justifies complaints like Samuel Johnson's that "it comprises neither human actions nor human manners,"[14] or Edward Said's that in it "words stand for words which stand for other words. . . . we read Milton's great poem with the disquieting sense that we are witnessing an 'ontology of nothingness'— an infinite regress of truths permanently hidden behind words."[15] In the first six books, narrative time is dislocated, and structure is a matter of contrasting panels. Style and the use of language — especially in Books I–IV— is difficult, and the reader must exert himself in order to grasp the difficult senses of what Hell, Heaven, and Paradise were or were like: by images, by reified concepts, by symbols. The reader's involvement in the epic is itself an epic task of reading; the language he faces line by line is a language of striving.

But as *Paradise Lost* moves into the second phase of its cycle of action, the narrative line smooths out the progress from Creation to Fall to aftermath to a prophesy of the Atonement (as in Scripture). Its subject matter, biblical history, is the history the reader knows and perhaps lives. It begins with the well-known language of the Book of Genesis, proceeds to matters dominated by human consciousness, human desire, human failure down to the Fall ("language begins with the Fall");[16] human responses, both exegetical and emotional, dominate its ending. Events develop in a gradual way, and are conveyed in such language that we fully know — in our own way — what has happened. The reader should no longer be figured as a sort of epic hero of the page, but rather as a common person. Though the matter is often disturbing, the language is that of satisfaction.

## II

At the center of *Paradise Lost*, we experience a change from "divine" or "epic" language to "human" language, from language as striving to language as satisfaction.[17] The crux of the matter of language occurs in Books V and VI, where language is openly discussed in terms of the intersection of the divine and the human, divine instruction and human receptivity. The divine messenger enters the human world. The setting is the meal Raphael shares with Adam and Eve, and throughout Book V the metaphorical associations between eating and knowing (that had been in Milton's mind at least since *Lycidas* and *Areopagitica*) are exploited.[18] Not only do we encounter the occasional pun on such words as "digest," "ruminate," and "nourish" (V, 183), but we also find more sophisticated verbal play like that on "transubstantiate" as an action of digestion (448). Furthermore, the whole book is governed by a rhythm analogous to that of eating: each of its four sections (the talk of Adam and Eve, God's mission to Raphael, the eating scene itself, and Raphael's start of his narrative) proceeds by a rhythm of perceiving (taking in), interpreting (digesting), and relating (flowing out in nourishment).[19] The dream Eve relates near the opening of the book is about eating the fruit of knowledge (51–86), the discourse with Raphael begins with a discus-

sion of eating, human and divine, that leads to the doctrine of accommodation, and Raphael even explains the great chain of being in terms
of eating, whereby "the grosser feeds the purer" (414–33), ending with
a metaphor of sunset as the sun that "sups" with the ocean (426). The
analogy — as well as the whole scene, which Thomas Kranidas finds gently
comic — suggests a kind of naturalness in the act of understanding.[20]

Before the meal begins, before the arrival of the angel, in fact, Adam,
in commenting on Eve's dream and the differences between dreaming
and waking, makes several distinctions between true and false understanding. The waking reason exercises itself in joining the diverse in proper
relations in order to arrive at knowledge, he says, while fancy

> forms Imaginations, Aery shapes,
> Which Reason joining or disjoining, frames
> All what we affirm or what deny, and call
> Our knowledge or opinion.          (V, 105–08)

Reason's operation is hierarchical: itself at the top of a hierarchy supported by the senses and fancy, it subordinates lower to higher in its join-
ings. Fancy, on the other hand, is reason's ape, and operates freely thus
in dreams:

> Oft in her absence mimic Fancy wakes
> To imitate her; but misjoining shapes,
> Wild work produces oft, and most in dreams,
> Ill matching words and deeds long past or late.
> Some such resemblances methinks I find
> Of our last Ev'ning's talk, in this thy dream.          (111–15)

Fancy mixes things up, and produces jumbles of parody, instead of illuminating hierarchical relationships; its extreme, as we see again and
again in the case of Satan, is idolatry.[21] Adam's interpretation and theory
bear the function of restoring the hierarchy that he expressed in his au-
bade (17–25), that was disturbed by Eve's dream (with its imagery of
mingled rise and fall), and that the two of them turn to reassert in their
morning hymn (153–208). Then Raphael arrives as a figure of complete
éclarissement, like a new dawn in the midst of noon (310).

Raphael's speeches reinforce and extend the realm of reason and
understanding. Twice during their mealtime talk, for instance, he sees
fit to explain the nature of his being by characterizing the universe as
hierarchical, by evoking the great chain of being first in terms of eating
(414–33), then in the celebrated plant image presenting creation in terms
of root, stalk, leaf, flower, and scent, stressing "degrees / Of substance"

rather than interdependence (468–90). In each case, while characterizing hierarchy, the angel is showing the action of reason's hierarchical operation in creating analogies, whereby image and idea are separate but related, and image is always in the background, serving idea in the foreground. That fact Adam grasps when he characterizes the created and imaged universe as the mind's road to God (509–12). These two speeches are subtle warnings to Adam to stay obedient (as it appears almost immediately in Raphael's words and Adam's questioning echo [501 and 513–14]), and that warning is the moral which his discourse on the war in Heaven is designed to illustrate (535–43). At the same time the style, using image to clarify idea, leads directly to the doctrine of accommodation that Raphael announces shortly:

> What surmounts the reach
> Of human sense, I shall delineate so,
> By lik'ning spiritual to corporal forms,
> As may express them best, though what if Earth
> Be but the shadow of Heav'n, and things therein
> Each to other like, more than on Earth is thought?     (571–76)

Raphael presents the language of accommodation as capable of two possible interpretations here. Earthly things may be used in the manner of metaphor, casual analogy or "lik'ning," to express events whose reality is ideational, as they were in the description of the cosmos as a plant. This is the traditional doctrine of accommodation as conveyed in biblical commentary, usually centering on ascribing human emotions to God "anthropopathically."[22] Or earthly things may, he avers, be the shadows of heavenly things. There are two current interpretations of "shadow" here. Until recently, most commentators held that it meant a doctrine of correspondences, Neoplatonic Ideas in Heaven reflected imperfectly in matter here on earth, in a manner like that of Plato's cave.[23] But William Madsen has convincingly disproved that interpretation, noting that Adam's words after Raphael has finished his account deny any Neoplatonic correspondence:

> Great things, and full of wonder in our ears,
> Far differing from this World, thou hast reveal'd
> Divine Interpreter.     (VII, 70–72)

Madsen proposes that "shadow" means "foreshadowing" or "adumbration," as it does in the later phrase "From shadowy Types to Truth" (XII, 303), and concludes, "Raphael's account is not a moral allegory, nor is it primarily a metaphorical description of what happened a long time ago in Heaven. It is a shadow of things to come, and more particularly it is a shadow of this last age of the world and of the Second Coming of Christ."[24] The view that Raphael's narrative is typological demands that we take his images seriously, for the linking of image to what it foretells is itself a form of knowledge, while the view that it is mere analogy or metaphor does not. On the one hand, Madsen and Jon S. Lawry propound the typological view. On the other hand, many of the other critics of the war in Heaven assume the analogical or metaphorical view that Raphael's images may, even must, be "discarded" in order to see the reality of the events they show. Such is the view of Joseph Summers, of Arnold Stein who finds in the account many strains of "epic farce," and of Stanley Fish, for whom the battles form a veil, reported with such detail in order to force the reader to construct from its thrusts and parries a working definition of real Christian heroism.[25]

None of the critics have seen fit to look for both analogy and typology operating in Books V and VI. Yet that is precisely what Raphael's specific stylistic maneuvers suggest as he begins his tale. Sometimes Raphael implicitly admits that the reality of which he speaks is inexpressible, as when he uses negatives suggesting godly things by mystical denial (595–99, or 895–900). At other times he evokes human language and feeling and then rejects it, as when he has God speak as a human ruler, worried and ready to fight, and then by the Son's reply shows it to be a joke, spoken "in derision" when applied to him (719–42). At other times he uses mere analogy of resemblence, as when he says that the angels engage in

> Mystical dance, which yonder starry Sphere
> Of Planets and of fixt in all her Wheels
> Resembles nearest, mazes intricate,
> Eccentric, intervolv'd, yet regular
> Then most, when most irregular they seem.          (620–24)

He suggests correspondence when he discusses time, for he treats time in Heaven as corresponding to time on earth as measurement:

> on a day
> (For Time, though in Eternity, appli'd
> To motion, measures all things durable
> By present, past, and future) on such day
> As Heav'ns great Year brings forth.          (579–83)

When the differences between Heaven and earth are stressed, his words approach the typological, for small leads to a comprehension of the great:

> and wider far
> Than all this globous Earth in Plain outspread,
> (Such are the Courts of God).                    (648–50)

And finally, in his use of names, his method is fully typological, wherein past points to future:

> *Satan*, so call him now, his former name
> Is heard no more in Heav'n.                    (658–59)

Since a plurality of methods of accommodation exists in Raphael's verbal details, it seems highly probable that it exists in the entirety of his narrative as well. A case in point is the division of the war in Heaven into three days. As Stella Revard writes, "Milton is distinct among the poets of the Renaissance in that he carefully divides the warfare into three stages, three consecutive days, and carefully assigns a 'kind' of warfare to each day," the first day being single combat, the second the melee, the third the appearance of the Son.[26] The three days are in fact very different: they form three thematic units, in fact, of true Christian heroism, of the vanity of false heroism, of salvation by Jesus Christ. At this point, I should like to offer some observations on the differences among the three days of the war in Heaven, showing the operation therein of both analogy or metaphorical revelation and typology or gradual prophetic revelation. Then I wish to suggest how they go together in a structured way, by reference to scriptural exegesis.

The first day of the war in Heaven naturally shows Raphael striving with difficulty to make heavenly events apprehended; for when he turns from the words angels may share with men to the actions that are of a totally different order, he cries:

> who, though with the tongue
> Of Angels, can relate, or to what things
> Liken on Earth conspicuous, that may lift
> Human imagination to such highth
> Of Godlike Power?                    (VI, 297–301)

The dominant tone, applied both to the matter and to the manner, is pain. His narrative stresses origins here, the difficult emergence into consciousness of something new: "Then *Satan* first knew pain" (327), "Then first with fear surpris'd and sense of pain" (394), the origin of evil (262), of misery (268), of discord especially, as the One seems to divide into oppugnancy. The center here is in definition and redefinition, especially the redefinition of heroic action as "the better fight." When God speaks to Abdiel at the start, he stresses the fact that the Word is mightier than arms, and that the decision "To stand approv'd in sight of God" is the essence of heroic action (VI, 30–40). And Abdiel in response sees the physical battle that is to ensue not so much as a battle in itself as the counterpart to the real war of higher heroism:

> nor is it aught but just,
> That he who in debate of Truth hath won,
> Should win in Arms, in both disputes alike
> Victor.                                    (121–24)

This is a language of analogy—"to what things / Liken on Earth"—in which an image is cast aside once it has been used to clarify a difficult matter. The real meaning of Satan's "physical" wound, for example, is that it tells him he can be wounded—"Gnashing for anguish and despite and shame / To find himself not matchless" (340–41), and flames are "the sign / Of wrath" (58–59). Thus the epic action and its premises are, as mere analogies, downgraded, and will continue to be so. "I might relate of thousands, and their names / Eternize here on Earth," avers Raphael, but then he disposes of the epic need for fame by remarking that he will not relate that, for it is only ignominy that aspires to glory and "through infamy seeks fame" (373–84). After all, it is we readers who know war as part of our fallen lives; it must be explained to Adam by similitudes (68–77). Raphael's language expresses, here, a redoubled difficulty.

The denigration of epic action becomes the center of the second day. Grim comedy, irony, and sarcasm dominate this day, rather than the pity over the origins of painful things. Satan's unveiling of his cannon is surrounded with puns: before, his "scoffing with ambiguous terms" (a language of disaccommodation, [568]) such as the puns on "overture," "discharge," "touch," and "loud"; after, his and Belial's "in pleasant vein . . . scoffing" (629–30) where Satan compares the loyal angels' dismay to a dance and Belial makes puns on "terms of weight," "hard contents," and so on. Part of the comedy is that point of view is restricted, neither party sees or knows beyond its immediate experience, and, hence, surprises abound. So the angel Zophiel can only "conjecture" about what the rebels intend (537–46), and it is Raphael and his cohorts themselves, rather than Adam, who have need of accommodation when the cannon appear:

> Which to our eyes discover'd new and strange,
> A triple-mounted row of Pillars laid
> On Wheels (for like to Pillars most they seem'd
> Or hollow'd bodies made of Oak or Fir
> With branches lopt, in Wood or Mountain fell'd).        (571–75)

Likewise, when the tables are turned and the hills uprooted, it is the rebels whose point of view is constricted, and their surprise evokes the grotesque:

> Amaze,
> Be sure, and terrour seiz'd the rebel Host,
> When coming towards them so dread they saw
> The bottom of the Mountains upward turn'd,
> Till on those cursed Engines' triple-row
> They saw them whelm'd, and all thir confidence
> Under the weight of Mountains buried deep.          (646–52)

It is interesting that Raphael treats gunpowder, cannon, and the hills as actual or literal things here, evoking only an occasional correspondence, as when he comments that Heaven has hills and valleys "much like earth's" (640–41). Even angelic armor is treated as if it were actual, as when he explains that the loyal angels might not have been bowled over by gunshot so easily if it were not for the restrictions of their arms (595–97), or that the rebel host likewise hurt all the more for their armor:

> Thir armor help'd thir harm, crush't in and bruis'd
> Into thir substance pent, which wrought them pain
> Implacable, and many a dolorous groan.          (656–58)

He hints at this point that armor has become a fitting prison for those who began the day by a material creation of gunpowder—"Purest at first, now gross by sinning grown" (661) — and that the rebels, at least, have actually become more material. That is the direction of Arnold Stein's interpretation, for he sees the comedy (which, however, he does not restrict to the second day) as ridicule of Satan's desire for physical might, and thus relates it to Satan's boast in his strength (818) and the Son's later treatment of the rebels as a herd of goats (856–58). Fish and Summers, instead, see it as a deliberate downgrading of human epic and an attempt to evoke in its place true Christian heroism.[27] Certainly, whichever position we choose to accept, what is at the fore here is the grim correspondence (no Neoplatonic shadow) between heavenly war and the reader's earthly experience of war. The grotesque comedy mounts higher and higher, first to the cannon, which are like what we know in our wars, then to the upturned hills absurd beyond our wars, at which point Raphael comments that "War seem'd a civil Game / To this uproar" (667–68). To such a pitch have things risen that God decides he must stop them, and asserts his plan (669–75).

The third day, in contrast to the second, possesses great dignity. There is little battle action here to speak of, neither symbolic nor literal: essentially, the Son merely shows himself in his chariot, and the rebels tumble into Hell. The day is, in fact, entirely ensconced in the action of showing-forth. It begins with God's voice (as quoted by Raphael), as he announces that all we have heard of so far has actually proceeded by his plan —"War wearied hath perform'd what War can do" (695) — and that the time has come for its fulfillment. "Two days are therefore past, the third is thine" (699): it is the time of the Son, and prefigures both his first coming to the toiling nations and his second coming (both of which reflect each other).[28] While the invisible Father announces prefigurement, the Son who is his visible image answers with fulfillment:

> my whole delight,
> That thou in me well pleas'd, declar'st thy will
> Fulfill'd, which to fulfil is all my bliss.          (727–29)

"And the third sacred Morn began to shine" (748): the entire episode is acted out in exalted typological style, with frequent biblical echoes or prefigurings. The mystical description of the Son's "Chariot of Paternal Deity" (750–66) is developed from Ezekiel's vision (Ezek. i, 4–6), which, as Madsen notes, was a type of the Last Day.[29] His first action is to calm the region of heaven in language that suggests the creation of the earth ("At his command the uprooted Hills retir'd" [781]). When he takes over the warfare from the loyal angels he now calls "Saints," the action suggests both the Atonement (for example, in the reiterated "mee," 812–20) and his second coming. Likewise, the cries of the rebel angels at his coming evoke the cries of the wicked at the Last Day (Rev. vi, 16), and the consequent rejoicing of the heavenly host with palm branches and song (882–92) suggests the final moments of the Book of Revelation. The Son's third day thus spans scriptural history, though what is paramount is its shadowing of the Last Days and of the Second Coming of Christ. It is important in the typology of accommodation here that the angels both good and bad keep finding out the specifics of Providence as they are in the midst of acting it out. Thus the rebel angels in hardening their hearts (VI, 791) become like the reprobated who will refuse grace, and the action thus echoes what God had predicted (in Book III, 200). The Son's address to the Saints redefines warfare as faith, its main component to "stand only" (801–12), and it is the power of the *logos* or Word that really overcomes the rebels and makes them in effect destroy themselves.[30] Typological history here transforms the war in Heaven to the acting out of faith, to its showing itself forth as effectual.

Day by day, Raphael's language of accommodation changes in its methods. The first day's language is that of analogy, whereby Raphael struggles to point toward the actual by means of the approximate, so that heroism can be redefined. The second day's language is a literal rather than an accommodated style: only an occasional statement of correspondence is necessary to make clear its appositeness to our situation. The third day is a radiant typological vision, rich in reverberations, whereby truth is progressively revealed. The changes in method take us through the pivot of the whole poem, from language as difficult striving for expression to language as gradual satisfying revelation.

One further point is worth noting here. The events related are all in the past to Adam and to us readers. But Raphael's language accommodates them to the reader in a temporal succession. The first day's recounting is of origins — the beginnings of discord, misery, and pain — and they are spoken of as in our past, before our time, hence difficult to imagine. The language of the second day pulls events into our present, into the literally presented material world of strife, terror, and warfare we know very well. And the language of the third day catapults those past events into our future, as they will appear at the end of our time as a race here on earth.

### III

It is my contention that the three quite different days in Raphael's account of the war in Heaven go together in the manner of different senses of traditional scriptural exegesis, and that such exegesis is the furthest reach of the language by which Heavenly things become accommodated to us on earth.[31]

Adam, we may recall, began Book V with a distinction between reason and its language, which upheld hierarchy, and fancy with its language, which produced parody and implied idolatry. That distinction has some affinity with Edward Said's perception that

man . . . is inserted into Being either *allegorically*, as a linguistic substitute for presence (which language can only allow by the *absence* of *presence*), or, when he continues to insist on his indispensibility to the reality of language, as *parody* — the sheer, endless repetition of himself in the distorting mirrors of social, artistic, psychological, anthropological, historical, or philosophical discourse.[32]

Language, in light of Said's reflection on Adam's sense of things, might be said to proceed along a scale from analogy, which might fall into parody, to its highest form of allegory, which both reveals and reinforces hierarchy. Allegory is the highest form of the language of accommodation.[33] For, when seen in the context of the full history of scriptural exegesis, allegory is basically the most structured or hierarchical way of knowing by extended analogy or accommodation, applying the literal record of an event to the past in the allegorical or historical sense, to the present in the moral sense, and finally to the future in the anagogical or prophetic sense.

The two methods we have observed Raphael using are in fact constitutive of fourfold exegesis. The moral sense grows out of simple analogy: a man should be like the lion in his courage; the soul of man is like Jerusalem only in the fact that both are reviled or praised by God. The allegorical sense grows out of typology but with an element of correspondence in it because it hinges on the comparison of times: Israel's coming out of Egypt corresponds to the New Testament redemption through Christ, as the crossing of the Red Sea corresponds to baptism. And the anagogical sense is that of full-fledged typology, signifying what an event prophesies in the future: Israel's coming out of Egypt foretells "the departure of the sanctified soul from bondage to the corruption of this world" at the end of time, Jerusalem points toward the New Jerusalem.[34] This is like that, this recalls that, this predicts that. Moreover, these methods that had been developed separately in antiquity came together in the formulation of the four senses of Scripture implicitly by St. Augustine and explicitly by John Cassian in the fourth century of the Christian era.[35]

Could the traditional Roman Catholic method of fourfold exegesis exercise any hold on the imagination of John Milton, the Reformation Protestant Calvinist? The claim I would advance is not that Milton was an allegorist but that he applied the four senses as a serial scaffolding for the days of the war in Heaven. The whole matter of Milton and allegory is in need of a full-scale study. But for now, we can assert that we do know that Milton both rejected allegorical interpretation of Scripture and praised allegorical poetry. On the one hand, he writes plainly that "no passage of Scripture is to be interpreted in more than one sense; in the Old Testament, however, this sense is sometimes a compound of the historical and typical."[36] On the other hand, in *Il Penseroso*, he cites Chaucer's *Squire's Tale* as seen through the lens of Spenser's allegorical expansion of it in Book IV of *The Faerie Queene*, and relates it to the general category of bardic tales "Of Forests, and inchantments drear, / Where more is meant than meets the ear" (119–20). And in *Areopagitica* he praises the teaching of two of Guyon's adventures in Book II of *The Faerie Queene* and, while doing so, emphasizes the moral sense of Guyon's descent into the Cave of Mammon as temptation and the allegorical sense of "the bower of earthly bliss."[37]

In *Paradise Lost* itself, we find a variety of allegorical and typological methods; they range from the personification allegory of Sin and Death in Book II, in which the allegorical sense of the historical origins of sin and the moral sense of the wages of sin predominate, to the extensive typological and anagogical renderings of events in Books XI and XII. And in Book V, Raphael's words before he unfolds the doctrine of accommodation suggest that his effort is quite like the allegorical enterprise in revealing secrets and unfolding events presented under a veil:

> how shall I relate
> To human sense th' invisible exploits
> Of warring Spirits; how without remorse
> The ruin of so many glorious once
> And perfet while they stood; how last unfold
> The secrets of another World, perhaps
> Not lawful to reveal?                    (V, 564–70)

While the evidence that exegesis of manifold senses was congenial to Milton as a mode of poetry is by no means conclusive, we do know that such exegesis was not so foreign to his beloved Reformation in England as it might appear. The Reformation was naturally a time of considerable controversy over the nature of Scripture, the validity of allegory in general and of the fourfold method in particular. Roman Catholic thinkers like Erasmus, Bellarmine, and Stapleton used and defended the method as it had been codified by Aquinas. They were defending it, of course, against the Protestant reformers Luther, Calvin, and Tyndale, who insisted that there was only one true sense of Scripture and that it was the literal. Exegesis rigidified rather than advanced in Catholic exegetes, but the Protestant insistence on one true sense had two important and diverse effects.

On the one hand, the Protestants gave new life to typology; for typology was at the same time considered to be part of the literal sense and also an extension of that text beyond its mere words. They developed typological interpretation to unfold the whole range of Providential history by emphasizing the supreme antitype at the end of time as well as the type of the Old Testament and the antitype of the New. And they encouraged extension of Scripture by assimilating the circumstances of contemporary history—both public and private—into typology. As the most recent expositor of this position, Barbara Lewalski, puts it, "The characteristic Protestant approach takes the Bible not as a multi-level allegory, but as a complex literary work whose full literal meaning is revealed only by careful attention to its poetic texture and to its pervasive symbolic mode—typology."[38]

On the other hand, the Reformers did not cast aside the four senses entirely.[39] William Whitaker, for instance, wrote in *A Disputation on Holy Scripture Against the Papists* (1588):

We affirm that there is but one true, proper and genuine sense of scripture, arising from the words rightly understood, which we call the literal; and we contend that allegories, tropologies, and anagoges are not various senses, but various collections from one sense, or various *applications* and *accommodations* of that one meaning. . . . allegorical expositions are not various meanings, but only various *applications* and *accommodations* of scripture. Such allegories, indeed, we may sometimes use with profit and advantage to give pleasure, not to coerce consent.[40]

Whitaker's distinction is akin to the distinction modern literary hermeneutics draws between meaning and significance. According to Emilio Betti as summarized by E. D. Hirsch, meaning is that which is represented by a text (the designation or reference of words, for example, and their ligatures in syntax), and significance is a relation between the text of its meaning and a person, conception, or situation; meaning is determinate, significance boundless and always changing.[41] For Whitaker, the literal sense is the meaning; and trope, allegory, and anagogy are elements of significance one might draw from the meaning or apply it to. His position had the effect of diminishing the authority of the three spiritual senses and at the same time of allowing great freedom in their definition and use: the three senses were freed not only from theology but from scriptural determination as well. They were to be employed flexibly, "quodlibet," so that the spiritual senses or applications of Scripture can be applied and perhaps even *created* by a human being trying to illustrate a point, instead of being derived and determined. As Tyndale put it, "Allegories are no sense of the Scripture, and altogether in the liberty of the Spirit."[42]

Whitaker's was the position taken by the Calvinist William Perkins in his influential book *The Arte of Prophecying* (1592), where he wrote, "There is one onely sense, and the same is literall. An allegory is only a certaine manner of uttering the same sense. The Anagogic and Tropologic are waies, whereby the sense may be applied."[43] And it determined the practice of the preaching of John Donne who, while he insisted that a strict literal interpretation of Scripture is always preferable to a figurative one, at the same time would often add spiritual or moral senses to the literal in an attempt to intensify the usefulness of the text.[44]

English Protestants in general, and the Arminians in particular, while asserting that the traditional senses of exegesis were not properly part of the meaning of Scripture, yet assigned to them an element in the significance of Scripture. They considered the senses beyond the literal as special cases of accommodation in the root sense of that concept, that is, in application, as ways in which a preacher might bring the meaning of Scripture home to the experiences and feelings of his congregation (and Raphael, by the way, might be considered such a preacher to Adam and to us). Thus John Donne will often admit that though an allegorical sense proves nothing about its text, it does add light to it and is allowable in order "to exercise our meditation, and devotion in things."[45] The Calvinist Thomas Adams, also, frequently moves from literal to moral allegorical or metaphorical interpretations of a text as he proceeds from the first part of a sermon or explication to the second part or application, in sermons like *The Rage of Oppression* or *The Spiritual Navigator*.[46]

The Calvinists considered allegory not as hermeneutic in orientation but as rhetorical: that is, it was not part of the meaning of Scripture but rather a way of applying the meaning of Scripture to the people. That is why a fundamentalist and strict literal interpreter of the Bible like John Bunyan could yet be a persistent allegorist in his fictional works incorporating biblical truth and presenting it to his readers. That is why Milton, too, can persistently refuse allegory in his interpretation of Scripture but present favorable attitudes toward pious but humanly created allegory such as Spenser's. And he could use it himself.

If we turn from Milton's theoretical beliefs to his actual practice, we can find a case in point in an episode which various critics have interpreted in all of the traditional senses, separatedly and without labeling them as such. I mean the exemplary action of Abdiel which links Book V with its center in language to Book VI with its center in action filtered through language. Satan has reacted to God the Father's raising his Son to be his equal by parodying God in raising a mount "In imitation" of his (V, 765), from which he harangues his followers about inequality and how it is inconsistent with reason and freedom:

> Thus far his bold discourse without control
> Had audience, when among the Seraphim
> *Abdiel*, than whom none with more zeal ador'd
> The Deity, and divine commands obey'd,
> Stood up, and in a flame of zeal severe
> The current of his fury thus oppos'd.        (V, 803–08)

The significant rising, the argument, and the departure of the angel whose name means "servant of God" has called forth various interpretations. Allan H. Gilbert, Merritt Y. Hughes, and others mark God's approval that "this was all thy care / To stand approv'd in sight of God" (VI, 35–36),

echoing both God's prediction that Adam might fall even though "Sufficient to have stood" (III, 99) and Raphael's implicit warning to Adam
in saying that "we freely love, as in our will / To love or not; in this we
stand or fall" (V, 539–40). From it these critics draw the interpretation
that Abdiel is presented to Adam as an example of proper response to
Satan's wiles.[47] Abdiel comes out especially as a prefigurement of what
Adam is and should be, in his speeches; for calling on reason, he defends
hierarchy, as Adam did in his interpretation of Eve's dream, and in his
words Adam's values extend to their full implications.

    Joseph Summers, Stanley Fish, and others pursue another track. They
note the reiteration of the word "zeal" around Abdiel, and the emphasis
on his standing alone out of harmony with the times:

> but his zeal
> None seconded, as out of season judg'd,
> Or singular and rash.                    (V, 849–51)

They note too his Puritan vocabulary in a statement to Satan on his
loneness:

> there be who Faith
> Prefer, and Piety to God . . .
> . . . my Sect thou seest, now learn too late
> How few sometimes may know, when thousands err. (VI, 143–48)

And they note, finally, God's words to him echoing Matthew XXV, 21,
"Servant of God, well done, well hast thou fought / The better fight"
(VI, 29–30). These critics interpret Abdiel as an exemplum to the Puritan reader of Milton's time, one who marches to a drum different from
that of his time, but whose inner vision will unite him, like Bunyan's
Christian, to God at the end. What is stressed in this interpretation is
the redefinition of heroism for the reader, not as heroic fortitude or personal fulfillment, but as obedience, perseverance through faith or "standing only."[48]

    Finally William Madsen and others emphasize the context of Ab-
diel's action in the light of prefigurement of the Last Day: they point
to the eschatological burden of Matthew XXV, 21, which God's voice
echoes or prefigures, as well as Abdiel's parting millenialist statement,

> I fly
> These wicked Tents devoted, lest the wrath
> Impendent, raging into sudden flame
> Distinguish not.                    (V, 889–92)

Abdiel, in this interpretation, prefigures the conduct of the Just who will resist the Adversary on the Last Day and be received in joy by the Father.[49]

Multiple exegesis is a means of welcoming and structuring diverse and even discordant interpretations. If we allow it to direct our responses, we do not need to choose between single divergent interpretations, but rather to structure them and integrate them. While Hughes points morals, what he really is emphasizing is the allegorical sense; Abdiel's literal "standing up" proliferates allegorical meanings mainly by means of his speeches, which reflect and extend Adam's sense of things, and show him to be a predecessor of Adam in time. The moral sense that Fish and Summers emphasize emerges out of the narrative web toward the reader, and is conveyed mainly by Raphael's interpretive and directive comments, such as V, 896–903. The anagogical sense Madsen perceives comes out mainly in Book VI with God's approval of his actions, his rest with God, and his outstanding conduct in the battle when words become transformed into deeds (VI, 120–26). One sense operates at one time, another at another.

The critical interpretation of Abdiel (himself an accurate interpreter) provides a model for the interpretation of the entire war in Heaven. My final point is that the three days of the war, as presented to the man by the accommodation of the angel, present a gradual unfolding of meaning through one after the other of the exegetical senses. This is not to claim that Milton is an allegorical poet like Spenser or Dante, who tend to present a single event which proliferates all four senses simultaneously, at least in ideal. Rather, I claim that Milton is a poet using the exegetical senses in series, as a structural frame on which to build different modes of revelation.

The conscious model of the three days of the war is the three days of Christ.[50] Among the great predecessors is Spenser's three-day dragon fight at the climax of Book I of *The Faerie Queene*, an episode developed out of Revelation, like Milton's. Day by day the dragon fight's significance unfolds, the first day presenting naturally good man combatting the things of this world, defeated by the sting of concupiscence, and saved by Fortune from death — all concentrating on the tropological or moral sense, *quid agas*, how we are to behave. On the second day the Red Crosse Knight is reborn in baptism, the Dragon is presented as Satanic, and the aura is insistently preternatural: all this suggests the allegorical sense, *quid credas*, or what we are to believe about Christ's combat on earth at his first coming. The third day recalls Easter morning (as does Raphael's third day) and a world newly created: the easy victory enacts a type of Christ's ultimate victory over Satan on the Last Day and foretells *quo tendas,* whither we are going.[51]

It is my contention that the three days in Raphael's account similarly follow a serial unfolding of exegetical significance, one sense emphasized each day: allegorical, moral, anagogical. To show this is merely to codify and relate the differences we have observed before. Raphael's language in his account of the first day is directed more at Adam than the reader: by continual analogies between the situation of the loyal angels, especially Abdiel, and Adam's revealed and perilous situation, and by his insistent redefinition of heroism thereby as "standing only," he reinforces comparison of times or the allegorical sense. This is indeed a warning to Adam; but for us readers following Adam it reinforces our sense of Providential history, of a plan whereby one event reflects another and all events go together in the mind of God. Thus it strengthens our belief. The very emphasis on striving to account for things by means of their origins is, in fact, part of the difficult allegorical language of faith.

The language of the second day makes that day reflect quite directly the grotesqueries and ironies of the reader's postlapsarian present. By presenting war as we know it as pointless and silly, it carries the original redefinition of heroism as inner strength to a point. The moral dimension, in the sense of directives for what to do and what not to do, is thus insistent, and is foregrounded by Raphael's commentary and by God's.

Finally, the third day's language brings anagogy to the fore. Its rich mystical visionary style takes the reader from this time and place to the ultimate place, where truth in all its radiance will be fully and finally revealed. It demands that we be receptive to its suggestions rather than striving to understand them. Its prophetic reach shows us whither we go. Perhaps language can do no more.

Books V and VI at the apex of *Paradise Lost* are the locus of the epic language's struggle to adjust the balance of word and image. It is here, in the language that prompts significance after significance, unfolding along the lines of the exegetical model designed to bring home the Word of God in Scripture to men, that language makes its highest claims. It is here that the striving after significance in words as at its most difficult, its most energetic, and its richest. It is here, too, that such striving modulates toward ease finally, and starts to move downward, as it were, to words that we know well, expressing events and concepts that we understand naturally.

Brown University

NOTES

1. *Milton and His Epic Tradition* (Seattle, 1979), pp. 10–23.

2. See Jon S. Lawry, *The Shadow of Heaven: Matter and Stance in Milton's Poetry* (Ithaca, 1968), pp. 127–30.

3. *Paradise Lost* is cited from *John Milton: Complete Poems and Major Prose*, ed. Merritt Y. Hughes (New York, 1957).

4. "The Style of *Paradise Lost*," in *Milton's Epic Poetry: Essays on "Paradise Lost" and "Paradise Regained*," ed. C. A. Patrides (Baltimore, 1967), p. 291.

5. Thus Moloch's dominant images are of violence, Belial's of physical pain, Mammon's of gold and precious materials.

6. For an analysis of these images, relating them to Books V and VI, see Michael Murrin, "The Language of Milton's Heaven," *MP*, LXXIV (1977), 355–57.

7. On *mythos* and *logos* in seventeenth-century religious writing, especially that of the Puritans, see U. Milo Kaufmann, *"The Pilgrim's Progress" and Traditions in Puritan Meditation* (New Haven, 1966), pp. 25–60. The contrast is a specific case of the Pauline tradition that sight is the sense of reason, hearing that of faith: see Romans X, 17.

8. For an analysis of the gentle comedy of the noontime meal (V, 239–490), see Thomas Kranidas, *The Fierce Equation: A Study of Milton's Decorum* (The Hague, 1965), pp. 143–45.

9. See also Adam's comment on the Creation as the mind's road to God (V, 509–12).

10. *Some Graver Subject: An Essay on "Paradise Lost"* (1960; rpt. New York, 1967), pp. 238–42. Broadbent's book offers a good general account of changes in style.

11. This dramatic cast, noted by many critics, may well be a survival of Milton's original plan for *Paradise Lost* as a tragic drama rather than an epic narrative.

12. *Milton's Grand Style* (London, 1963), p. 109, 110–16.

13. *Milton's Epic Voice: The Narrator in "Paradise Lost"* (Cambridge, Mass., 1967), pp. 117–40.

14. "The Life of Milton" in *Lives of the English Poets*, 2 vols. (London, 1925), I, p. 107.

15. *Beginnings: Intention and Method* (Baltimore, 1975), pp. 280–81.

16. Ibid., p. 280.

17. There seems to have been a long-standing tradition among theologians contrasting the language of God, in which word and deed are one, to the language of men: see, for example, *The Sermons of Master Henrie Smith* (London, 1592), pp. 380–83, 396–98.

18. See *Lycidas*, 125–28, *Areopagitica* (in *Complete Poems*, ed. Hughes), pp. 727–29.

19. This observation I owe to Melita Schaum, University of Notre Dame.

20. *The Fierce Equation*, p. 143.

21. Satan as parodist appears fully in Books I and II, for instance in the raising of Pandemonium or in his issuing from the infernal consult; for Satan as idolator, see, for example, V, 765–71.

22. See Roland M. Frye, *God, Man, and Satan* (Princeton, 1960), pp. 7–13, and C. A. Patrides, "*Paradise Lost* and the Theory of Accommodation," *TSLL*, V (1963), 58–63.

23. See, for example, James Holly Hanford, *A Milton Handbook* (New York, 1926), p. 205, and M. M. Mahood, *Poetry and Humanism* (New Haven, 1950), p. 204. William G. Madsen summarizes and criticizes this view in *From Shadowy Types to Truth: Studies in Milton's Symbolism* (New Haven, 1968), pp. 87–111.

24. *From Shadowy Types to Truth*, pp. 110–11.

25. Joseph Summers, *The Muse's Method: An Introduction to "Paradise Lost"* (Cam-

bridge, Mass., 1962), pp. 119–46; Arnold Stein, *Answerable Style: Essays on "Paradise Lost"* (Minneapolis, 1953), pp. 20–37; Stanley E. Fish, *Surprised by Sin: The Reader in "Paradise Lost"* (London, 1967), pp. 196–97.

26. *The War in Heaven: "Paradist Lost" and the Tradition of Satan's Rebellion* (Ithaca, 1980), p. 182.

27. See note 25.

28. See Lawry, *The Shadow of Heaven*, pp. 207, 209, and 211–12 for a parallel of all three days with Good Friday, Holy Saturday and the grave, and Easter morning, respectively. See also the threefold interpretation of William B. Hunter, "The War in Heaven: The Exaltation of the Son," in *Bright Essence: Studies in Milton's Theology*, by William B. Hunter, C. A. Patrides, and J. H. Adamson (Salt Lake City, 1971), pp. 122–23.

29. Madsen, *From Shadowy Types to Truth*, p. 111, n. 28; see also J. H. Adamson, "The War in Heaven: Milton's Version of the *Merkabah*," *JEGP*, LVII (1958), 690–703.

30. See VI, 848–55; see Broadbent, *Some Graver Subject*, p. 232.

31. It is notable that the Protestant commentator David Paraeus interpreted Revelation xii (the source of Milton's war in Heaven) in accord with this method as the battle of Satan against God in Heaven, as his battle against Christ at the Crucifixion, and as his battle against the Church later, *In divinam apocalypsin S. Apostoli et Evangelistae Johannis commentarius* (Heidelberg, 1618) pp. 560–63; see Revard, *The War in Heaven*, p. 132.

32. *Beginnings*, pp. 332–33; see also Ferry, *Milton's Epic Voice*, ch. 5, "Allegory and Parody."

33. See Joseph Anthony Mazzeo, *Varieties of Interpretation* (Notre Dame, 1978), pp. 140–41.

34. Dante, Letter to Can Grande, in *Literary Criticism of Dante Alighieri*, ed. and trans. Robert S. Haller (Lincoln, Neb., 1973), p. 99.

35. For Augustine's development of the three-term figura, to which Cassian added the moral sense to make four, see Erich Auerbach, "Figura," in *Scenes from the Drama of European Literature* (New York, 1959), pp. 29–44.

36. *De Doctrina Christiana* I, xxx, as translated in *The Student's Milton*, ed. Frank Allen Patterson (New York, 1930), p. 1040. For general discussions of Milton's hermeneutics, see George Conklin, *Biblical Criticism and Heresy in Milton* (New York, 1949), pp. 24–40, and H. R. MacCallum, "Milton and the Figurative Interpretation of the Bible," *UTQ* XXXI (1962), 397–415.

37. *Areopagitica* in *Complete Poems*, ed. Hughes, p. 729.

38. *Protestant Poetics and the Seventeenth-Century Religious Lyric* (Princeton, 1979), p. 117.

39. See George L. Scheper, "Reformation Attitudes toward Allegory and the Song of Songs," *PMLA*, LXXXIII (1974), 51–62. For general comments on the reentry of the four senses into Reformation exegesis, see Kaufmann, *"The Pilgrim's Progress" and Traditions in Puritan Meditation*, pp. 25–41, and Madsen, *From Shadowy Types to Truth*, pp. 18–49, especially p. 38.

40. William Whitaker, *A Disputation on Holy Scripture Against the Papists*, trans. William Fitzgerald (London, 1849), pp. 404, 406; emphases mine.

41. E. D. Hirsch, *Validity in Interpretation* (New Haven, 1967), pp. 7–10; see also Richard E. Palmer, *Hermeneutics: Interpretation Theory in Schleiermacher, Dilthey, Heidegger, and Gadamer* (Evanston, Ill., 1969), pp. 60–64.

42. *The Obedience of a Christian Man* in *Works*, ed. T. Russell, 3 vols. (London, 1831), 1, p. 341.

43. Reprinted in *Works*, 2 vols. (London, 1631), II, p. 651.

44. Dennis Quinn, "John Donne's Principles of Biblical Exegesis," *JEGP,* LXI (1962), 320, 322.

45. *The Sermons of John Donne*, ed. George R. Potter and Evelyn Simpson, 10 vols. (Berkeley, 1953–61), III, 5, 365–78.

46. These two sermons can be found in *The Workes* (London, 1629), on p. 392 and p. 605, respectively.

47. Allen H. Gilbert, *On the Composition of "Paradise Lost"* (Chapel Hill, N.C., 1947), pp. 123–27; Hughes, ed., *Complete Poems*, p. 176.

48. Summers, *The Muse's Method*, pp. 123–30; Fish, *Surprised by Sin*, pp. 189–96.

49. Madsen, *From Shadowy Types to Truth*, pp. 111–12.

50. See ibid., n. 35.

51. See my article "Arthur, Partial Exegesis, and the Reader," *TSLL*, XVIII (1977), 569–70, and the citations of Kaske and Kellogg and Steele therein.

# ABDIEL AND THE SON
# IN THE SEPARATION SCENE

## Diana Benet

R ATHER THAN examining the human parents' dispute in its entirety, readers of the separation scene in the ninth book of *Paradise Lost* usually concentrate on why Eve leaves her husband's side and why Adam permits her to go. Because their disagreement begins and ends with the question of separating or remaining together, it is seen as arising from or responding to tensions in the relationship itself. To explain Eve's departure, most readers turn to the suggestions of Arnold Stein or Joseph Summers: respectively, she is motivated by willfulness and a wish for independence, or by a desire to prove her intellectual equality to her husband.[1] Other readings elaborate on these themes. Barbara K. Lewalski remarks on Eve's lack of maturity in her persistence in a course she knows to be wrong; Don Parry Norford suggests that "latent feelings of inferiority, injured pride, and resentment" underlie her behavior.[2] Stanley Fish comments that she deliberately seeks the occasion to strike a "heroic posture."[3] Only Diane K. McColley and Louis L. Martz suggest that Eve is motivated simply by a wish to do her work as efficiently as possible.[4] Similarly, the commentary on Adam has been restricted to the issues of his responsibility and motivation in agreeing to separation. Readers of the poem who deny Eve's sufficiency to stand alone see his failure to command her obedience as a drastic error that involves him in her fall.[5] Those who affirm Eve's sufficiency see his omission to persuade her to stay as "a tactical and not a moral failure."[6] Most readers account for Adam's behavior by uxoriousness, and assume that he knows the best course for his wife to follow, though he does not insist on it: "He surrenders because of the insecurity of his love, from his fear of not being loved, out of concern for himself rather than Eve."[7]

Analysis of the episode as a whole, however, indicates a different perspective: one of the most important functions of the separation scene is to examine the nature of the spiritual trial that awaits the human couple. Adam and Eve's disagreement does not arise from hidden tensions in their relationship. It is the result of opposing concepts of the anticipated trial, and it is from these concepts that the issue of separation ver-

129

sus togetherness gains impetus and acquires significance. Milton analyzes trial by showing that Adam and Eve expect to emulate the Son and Abdiel, respectively; each model supports a different concept of self and trial, and it is these ideas rather than any personal motivations that fuel the conflict before the temptation. The couple's ideas on trial can come only from Raphael's instruction, but Adam and Eve are very naive interpreters; consequently, their models and the stances they dictate for trial are only dimly understood. Eve proves to be the better (though still imperfect) interpreter of Raphael. Adam, for all his intellectual superiority, is a weak interpreter who is unable to be of much assistance to his wife. Their discussion is an unsettling experience for him because he is forced to recognize that his view is mistaken. When he abandons his model with its corollary concept of trial, he also loses confidence in the wisdom of facing temptation with Eve. He lets her choose whether to go or stay because he does not know which is the better course. Eve goes because she wants to do her work as well as possible, and because her talk with Adam has shown her no compelling reason to stay: her confidence is strong, and the question of her sufficiency is settled, as far, at least, as she and her husband are concerned.

This reading of the separation scene modifies the generally accepted views of Adam and Eve because it demonstrates that both of them act, however mistakenly, from their best understanding of Raphael's instruction rather than from any questionable personal or emotional motives. If the wish to imitate Abdiel, "the positive figure for human emulation" in the poem,[8] underlies Eve's actions, she is not, before the Fall, a figure whose dissatisfaction argues the will to sin against the established order. The reading also challenges the assumption that Adam is the unerring guide whose confident direction Eve can follow. Milton presents him as he presents her: Adam is a fallible individual facing the difficulties of translating divine instruction into the practical sphere. His problems in doing so emphasize the uncertainty that must always attend human effort and the unreliability of the intellect in spiritual matters. Their mistakes and uncertainties notwithstanding, Adam and Eve know everything they need to know in order to face temptation. Without compromising divine providence, Milton uses their errors and falterings to the important end of educating his reader about the nature of spiritual trial.

Eve suggests the separation because of her concern for the work that literally grows overnight. From the beginning of the dispute that ensues, Adam's ideas regarding temptation seem uninfluenced by Raphael's account of the temptation in heaven. They are a blend of reason, unexlained assumption, and confidence that is the more puzzling for following his intelligent tactfulness toward Eve. Responding to her suggestion of working alone, Adam is a model of husbandly sensitivity. Though he rejects efficiency as the most important value in their lives, he expresses approval of Eve's wish to do the work assigned them as efficiently as possible. He is alert even to her unexpressed feelings when he refers to the emotional boredom that he fears might underlie her proposal. Prudently, he points out that safety from the foe must be their primary consideration, but he does this without undervaluing her industry or ignoring her feelings. Adam's reminder to Eve of their danger is timely, and it includes his reason for wanting her to stay with him. Satan, he tells her, hopes to find "His wish and best advantage, us asunder, / Hopeless to circumvent us join'd, where each / To other speedy aid might lend at need" (IX, 258–60).[9] Common sense suggests that Satan probably would prefer to try Adam and Eve separately because it would be easier to entrap one victim rather than two at once. But we must wonder why Adam believes that it is "Hopeless to circumvent us join'd," that together he and Eve are invincible. This is not a conclusion reasonably drawn from Raphael's narrative of events in heaven. Satan circumvented troops of angels who found no moral safety in their number and who failed to profit from the speedy aid of Abdiel's loyal retort. Perhaps Adam thinks he and Eve are invulnerable together because they have the advantage of advance warning. Regardless of its basis, however, his confidence is unjustified and inexplicable in the context of Raphael's instruction.

As Adam goes on, his first description of a simultaneous trial undertaken cooperatively and incapable of failure is subtly revised:

> leave not the faithful side
> That gave thee being, still shades thee and protects.
> The Wife, where danger or dishonor lurks,
> Safest and seemliest by her Husband stays,
> Who guards her, or with her the worst endures.       (IX, 265–69)

Rather than united strength, Adam now emphasizes his individual and greater power to guard Eve. His confidence is firm. At first glance, it might seem that he is willing to sustain failure with Eve if he cannot guard her, but his subsequent remarks indicate that "endure" means "to undergo without succumbing or giving way" (*OED*). Adam distinguishes not between success and failure, but between deflecting trial entirely from Eve and actively involving her in it. His appeal to her is a tender reminder of how truly she is a part of himself. But for all that it is courteously worded, it is a command that reminds her of her secondary status. She hears herself demoted from helpmeet to passive object of the protection of her mate, who sententiously lays down the rule for matronly behavior. Satan is the expected stranger before whom the new proprieties of honor and seemliness must be maintained. Adam is the arbiter of the correct form of behavior in the trial whose outcome is not really in question. It will be safer and more decorous if he protects Eve.

In the course of Adam's first response to Eve, then, he describes two kinds of trial. The first is a simultaneous temptation in which each helps the other to an undoubted success; the second is a single endeavor in which Adam acts alone and succeeds for himself and Eve. He will resolve the seeming contradiction in these two descriptions in due course. For the time being, however, since he is arguing that Eve should not leave his side, it is apparent that he believes their success against Satan will depend on his own power. Adam's confidence in this type of united invincibility is shared by some commentators on the poem: "But Adam would not have fallen if he had met and been tempted by Satan on his own. . . . And if Adam had been with Eve when she was tempted he would likewise not have allowed her to be deceived."[10] It is fruitless to speculate about whether or not he would have fallen if he had met Satan. But the idea that it would be "Hopeless to circumvent" Adam and Eve together because he would not have allowed her to be deceived will require examination later. Already, Adam's anticipation of emulating the Son can be discerned in his desire to face the enemy for his less powerful spouse, and in his confidence.

Once Adam has told Eve what he wants her to do, there is no reason for him to expect a rejoinder from the agreeable spouse who recently said to him: "My Author and Disposer, what thou bidd'st / Unargu'd I obey" (IV, 635–36). But she responds with a "sweet austere composure" (IX, 272), barely concealing her displeasure in Adam's implication that her "firm Faith and Love / Can by [Satan's] fraud be shak'n or seduc't" (IX, 286–87). Adam cannot anticipate Eve's reaction to his gentle command because he does not know that she has her own conception of temptation. It is based on her understanding of Raphael's account of Abdiel, from which she infers several principles. Abdiel appeals to her because he withstood Satan's guiles so heroically and because his status vis-à-vis the tempter and other high-ranking angels corresponds to her own in relation to Adam's. From Raphael's paradigm, Eve concludes that she is not vulnerable to Satan's fraud; that she is not dependent, of necessity, on Adam's protection; and that it is desirable to think for herself. The zealous angel who is "Unshak'n, unseduc't" (VI, 899) proves that unquestioning obedience to one's superior in the hierarchy is not necessarily best, and that a lower place in the scheme does not mean certain moral failure: "Although lesser in intellect and status, Abdiel triumphs, proving himself more than sufficient against the temptings of his superior." [11] Eve rightly concludes that place in the hierarchy instituted by God is not a measure of the capacity for faith and love.

Joan Bennett describes Abdiel as "the true Miltonic revolutionary," [12] but he does not inspire Eve to a domestic rebellion. Her concern is not to challenge Adam's authority, but to correct his perception of herself as a creature inherently more vulnerable to temptation than he is. Because of Raphael's story, she cannot believe that her status in itself entails a disastrous vulnerability that requires Adam's protection. Echoing the adjectives that the sociable angel uses to describe Abdiel, Eve indicates that her dissent is informed by his authoritative voice rather than by the inner voice of discontent. She need not be dissatisfied with her status to understand and appreciate the implication of Abdiel's victory: though lower in standing than Adam, yet she has the capacity to triumph against Satan. Eve's inference is correct, but her assumption that Abdiel's success necessarily predicts and ensures her own is a great error.

While Eve assumes that her experience will follow, undoubtedly, the pattern of Abdiel's, Adam anticipates that he will emulate the Son. Adam is the head of the little human community, and he reasons from that position, expecting to act for Eve while she remains in the background. However, his arguments are weak because they have no foundation in Raphael's teaching, and they are ineffectual because he focuses on a singularly shallow aspect of trial. Rather than warning Eve against the confidence she expresses, he tries to mollify her with the assurance that he knows she would rebuff Satan's attempt on her faith. Her safety, then, is not at issue. Adam wants Eve to stay with him to "avoid / Th'attempt itself" (IX, 294–95), in order to preserve her dignity and reputation:

> For hee who tempts, though in vain, at least asperses
> The tempted with dishonor foul, suppos'd
> Not incorruptible of Faith, not proof
> Against temptation.                    (IX, 296–99)

It may be true that temptation implies the tempter's ill opinion of his victim, but in the circumstances, such nice considerations are incongruous — as incongruous as Adam's earlier concern for seemly behavior before the foe. Reasoning according to imagined aspersions and dishonor, Adam diminishes the significance of trial. He disparages the positive achievement of loyalty when he remarks that even the individual who does not succumb to temptation suffers the injury of imputed dishonor. Superficially focusing on the ignominy of being thought disloyal, he attributes an inflated importance to Satan and disregards the meaning of trial itself. This attitude is more than a momentary lapse. To persuade Eve, he recasts his shallow understanding of trial as mere occasion for Satan's contempt:

> thou thyself with scorn
> And anger wouldst resent the offer'd wrong,
> Though ineffectual found: misdeem not then,
> If such affront I labor to avert
> From thee alone, which on us both at once
> The Enemy, though bold, will hardly dare,
> Or daring, first on mee th' assault shall light.    (IX, 299–305)

Again, Eve is confirmed in her confidence and, again, Adam minimizes the enemy's threat: temptation is an insult from which he gallantly wishes to shield her. Adam's wish to protect Eve is commendable, but his description of trial as an "affront" is a gross underestimation of it. His concern for dignity rather than safety indicates, yet again, that he is as confident as Eve about the outcome of trial. Furthermore, his suggestion that togetherness may be a strategy to avoid trial entirely is contradicted by Raphael's history. But Eve's protector believes that the enemy (who dared to assault legions of angels "at once") will not dare to take on the whole human family of two.

Adam's wish to act for Eve stems from his understanding of his role as her head and protector rather than from any doubt of her single capacity for firmness. His solicitude is touching, but he does not qualify, thus far, as a helpful guide to Eve. Neither his confidence nor his notion of evading trial has a basis in Raphael's teaching. His superior intellect notwithstanding, he seems ignorant of the spiritual enormity of the test they have been warned to expect. The intellectual diminishment of trial effected by his incomprehension extends to his projected imitation of the Son, even as he resolves into a coherent whole his two previous descriptions of the trial. He advises Eve of Satan's subtlety:

> nor think superfluous others' aid.
> I from the influence of thy looks receive
> Access in every Virtue, in thy sight
> More wise, more watchful, stronger, if need were
> Of outward strength; while shame, thou looking on,
> Shame to be overcome or over-reacht
> Would utmost vigor raise, and rais'd unite.    (IX, 308–14)

This formulation of trial clarifies Adam's idea of a joint invincibility to which Eve makes a vital contribution, though only he acts. He argues so persistently for her presence by his side because he believes that *she* is the source of the superior power with which *he* is confident of frustrating Satan.

On the third day of the war in heaven, the Son told the loyal angels to "stand only and behold" (VI, 810). Adam envisions the same kind of scene: Eve is to look on while he acts for her as if she could not act for herself. He believes that he should face and defeat the foe for the weaker "body" as the Son did in heaven. His previously expressed confidence makes sense in this context. He reasons that Satan, having been defeated by one head, will not risk humiliation by confronting another. Adam is so intent on the role in which he thinks his superiority casts him that he forgets his earnest affirmations of Eve's capacity to act for herself. Though he refers briefly to the possibility of her trial "When I am present" (IX, 316), he does so only to persuade her not to leave him. He does not realize, either, that his dependence on Eve invalidates any resemblance between himself and the Son. Thinking to imitate the divine Head, Adam sounds instead like a chivalric hero inspired to great feats by the lady looking on at the contest. His emphasis on shame as the motivation of his "utmost vigor" stresses his overdependence on Eve and his wish to use the trial as an opportunity to please her. Losing sight entirely of the end of faith and loyalty, he sees the trial with a disheartening superficiality: it is an occasion not to affirm his love of God, but to sustain Eve's admiration.

Adam's vision of himself as the champion deriving triumphant strength from the passive Eve is appealingly romantic, but it reduces spiritual trial to the level of courtly tournament. Curiously, readers who have remarked on Eve's "self-concept as heroic"[13] have not noticed that it is matched by Adam's projection of a similarly heroic self. The accuracy of either of these self-images is not as important as their inception in Raphael's narrative. Though the roles that Adam and Eve expect to play in trial are incompatible with each other, their common origin indicates that the opposition between husband and wife does not involve merely personal issues or motivations. Their dispute arises from different interpretations of Raphael's narrative.

When Eve responds to Adam in "heroic" terms, she simply takes up the words and themes that he introduced into the discussion. She counters Adam's superficial perspective on trial with one that is more adequate, in view of Raphael's instruction:

> But harm precedes not sin: only our Foe
> Tempting affronts us with his foul esteem
> Of our integrity: his foul esteem
> Sticks no dishonor on our Front, but turns

> Foul on himself; then wherefore shunn'd or fear'd
> By us? who rather double honor gain
> From his surmise prov'd false, find peace within,
> Favor from Heav'n, our witness from th' event.     (IX, 327–34)

Eve's correction of Adam's misapprehensions can be based only on what she learned from Raphael. The Abdiel episode proves that in itself temptation is neither sin nor dishonor. To the faithful, insult from the enemy is meaningless except as it redounds upon himself to reflect his own foulness. She speaks of the honor to be gained from trial and of a witness because Adam raised the topics, and because she remembers the account of Abdiel's reception and praise in heaven. Adam cast Eve as the spectator of his triumph and proposed himself as the "best witness" of her trial (IX, 317) — if it could not be avoided. Eve rejects this scenario as limited: heaven is the best witness of trial. Implicitly, she criticizes Adam's estimation of herself as central. The central place is properly God's because Satan aims at his glory though he strikes through his creatures.

In the particular context of Adam's remarks, then, Eve's desire to gain favor from heaven cannot be seen as a desire for "self-aggrandizement."[14] She uses Adam's own words to correct his interpretive errors and, in doing so, she evinces her understanding that God's favor is to be sought before anyone else's. Eve does not ignore or deny her proper relationship to Adam; she sets the relationship in the broader context, subsuming it under the primary relationship with God. His approval of Abdiel's aim, "To stand approv'd in sight of God, though Worlds / Judg'd [him] perverse" (VI, 36–37) encourages Eve to make it her own objective. The Father will witness the earthly trial as he did the heavenly, and commend its successful issue. Her desire to please God, though incautious, is admirable; under the specific circumstances, it is an improvement on Adam's wish to please her. It reflects Eve's awareness that what is at issue in temptation is the affirmation of the relationship between the individual creature and his creator, and that in this situation, that relationship must take precedence over any other. The blithe confidence she expresses echoes Adam's and gains impetus from her confutation of the perils of trial as he inadequately identifies them. Eve reasons that if neither unsuccessful temptation nor insult dishonors its target, there is no reason to fear Satan. Her confidence is sadly misplaced but, as we have seen, it does not belong solely to Eve, and it is blameless. As Kathleen M. Swaim suggests, the "condition of innocence makes this security inevitable" for her and her spouse.[15] The only difference in their confidence is that Adam's is in himself as strengthened by Eve's presence, whereas hers is in her individual capacity.

With a simple clarity that eludes Adam, Eve sees into the meaning of trial when she equates its successful outcome with inner peace and favor from heaven. She also brings the argument to its turning point:

> And what is Faith, Love, Virtue unassay'd
> Alone, without exterior help sustain'd?
> Let us not then suspect our happy State
> Left so imperfet by the Maker wise,
> As not secure to single or combin'd.
> Frail is our happiness, if this be so,
> And *Eden* were no *Eden* thus expos'd.          (IX, 335–41)

Eve's reasoning is the most emphatic statement of the confidence she shares with her husband, but it is unnecessary to dwell again on its obvious danger. These lines have been read in part as an argument for the equality of the sexes and the identity of their gifts, or as her insistence "on a virtue that flourishes by trial," [16] but such interpretations misconstrue their emphasis. Eve does not express an eagerness to be tried or the opinion that she is Adam's equal. She opposes Adam's point of view regarding trial with her own. She suggests that faith, love, and virtue are qualities within the individual heart, hers or Adam's. To believe that those qualities can be sustained only by their combined efforts, she argues, is to believe that each is an imperfect creature incapable of maintaining the happiness given by God.

Eve's initial question is the crux of the disagreement, precisely the point at which the stances dictated by her chosen model and her husband's are in conflict. The question arises specifically as a response to Adam's expectation of drawing decisive power from his wife's presence. But, by focusing on the essential nature of spiritual attributes and trial, it challenges his determination to act for her, and his confidence in their united invincibility because of his strength. Clearly, Adam has indicated that he believes he can (and should) undertake the actual temptation for her and himself. Just as clearly, Eve understands trial and the qualities it will test to be strictly individual matters. According to Raphael's instruction and his story of the events in heaven, she is correct. Before telling his auditors about the war, the angel asked: "Can hearts, not free, be tri'd whether they serve / Willing or no, who will but what they must / By Destiny and can no other choose?" (V, 532–34). The essence of trial is free choice: ultimately, Adam cannot will or choose to serve for Eve. The effort to do so, apart from negating for her the possibility of offering the "voluntary service" that God requires (V, 529), is futile. Even in the simultaneous temptation of numberless angels, trial is an individual event whose outcome depends on the hidden motions of the solitary heart. The lonely figure of the "zealous" angel makes the point forcefully. The whole episode stresses the singleness of choice and indicates that one creature cannot determine the outcome of trial for another: one creature cannot have faith, love, and virtue in another's stead. Abdiel's loyalty is not transferable to the other angels; their disloyalty does not compel his. Each of the angels, giving silent assent to Satan's propositions, chooses for himself. Eve suggests that it must be so for Adam and for herself. Faith, love, and virtue exist and stand within or not at all.

Eve's question thoroughly disarms Adam. It dictates his response because it echoes a crucial part of Raphael's instruction, which he had apparently forgotten until now: "stand fast; to stand or fall / Free in thine own Arbitrement it lies. / Perfet within, no outward aid require" (VIII, 640–42). Raphael's final words to Adam confirm Eve's argument for individual sufficiency—his own, at least. He must decide whether or not he really believes in the sufficiency that he has attributed to his wife. Equally important is the light cast by Raphael's statement on Adam's insistence that he and Eve face temptation together. It is all too clear that Adam has been depending on the "outward aid" or "exterior help" of Eve's presence. His expectation that her approbation would raise his "utmost vigor" is exposed as unsound and debilitating. Raphael has expressly told Adam to look to his own inner resources; instead, he has located the source of his strength in Eve and drawn confidence from that support. He has urged her, similarly, to rely not on herself but on him as the external prop to her virtue. The wisdom of such dependence is challenged by Raphael's advice, which implies that Adam is to consider and face trial as a matter whose outcome depends solely on himself.

Adam's realization of his error forces him to correct himself immediately. God's "creating hand," he assures Eve,

> Nothing imperfet or deficient left
> Of all that he Created, much less Man,
> Or aught that might his happy State secure,
> Secure from outward force; within himself
> The danger lies, yet lies within his power.        (IX, 345–49)

Made to remember the injunction to rely only on his perfection, Adam reaffirms Eve's sufficiency: her power to stand against temptation, like his own, is within. He must assume that what Raphael said of him applies to Eve also—he must believe, as Stella Revard points out, that providence could not omit a warning if special conditions were required for her defense.[17] Adam interprets Raphael's statement to mean that Eve's inner perfection, like his, requires no outward assistance, and that interpretation invalidates his understanding of temptation as an occasion in which he must act for her. He must relinquish as inappropriate, in the specific circumstances, the model of the Son, or acknowledge that he has misinterpreted it — and his whole attitude changes accordingly. He becomes, for the first time in this conversation, a good counselor to Eve. He warns her that reason may be misled (as he has good cause to know) and that it is "possible to swerve" (IX, 359). Cautioning and reminding her so carefully of everything she needs to know, he seems to have conceded already that she need not stay with him.

Adam's experience in the discussion with Eve cannot be slighted if we are to understand what follows. Reminded of Raphael's advice, he has empirical proof of the ease with which it can be disregarded and of the perilous consequences of ignoring it: his arguments against Eve's departure sprang from the mistaken dependence on her that the angel meant to undermine. Moreover, the idea of his strength increased by Eve made him confident of victory over the foe. This is the danger the angel sought to avoid with his counsel. Reliance on another can engender a false confidence that weakens the individual defense. In the war in heaven, Raphael remarked that each angel "on himself reli'd, / As only in his arm the moment lay / Of victory" (VI, 238–40). Temptation requires the same attitude. This does not mean that Adam and Eve must face trial separately; like "no outward aid require," it means that even if they are together, each must depend solely on his or her own effort and strength. This attitude is in direct opposition to the one that Adam has expressed and urged his wife to adopt. Because he recognizes his error and the potential problem of overconfidence in unity, he ends as he does, with alternatives:

> Seek not temptation then, which to avoid
> Were better, and most likely if from mee
> Thou sever not: Trial will come unsought.
> Wouldst thou approve thy constancy, approve
> First thy obedience; th' other who can know,
> Not seeing thee attempted, who attest?
> But if thou think, trial unsought may find
> Us both securer than thus warn'd thou seem'st
> Go; for thy stay, not free, absents thee more;
> Go in thy native innocence, rely
> On what thou hast of virtue, summon all,
> For God towards thee hath done his part, do thine. (IX, 364–75)

Certainly, the best course is to avoid temptation, but Adam is no longer certain that it can be eluded by their unity. It is only "most likely" that trial can be avoided together and, in the next instant, altogether unlikely: "Trial will come unsought." As soon as he admits that temptation is unavoidable, his concern shifts to whether meeting it together or alone is best. We have already seen that in the final analysis, the question of togetherness is relatively unimportant — even if they are together, each will be tried. Adam's understanding of this is evident in his concern about which situation will find them *each* best prepared. Barbara K. Lewalski comments that Adam supplies Eve "with a rationale for going which she had not thought of for herself."[18] His own experience of unwise dependence and unwarranted security prompts him. Remembering his own assumption of their united invincibility, he is wary of encouraging a false confidence in Eve, or in himself: security threatens "us both." Urging her to "sever not" from his side, he might be encouraging her to fail to expect trial or to exert her utmost strength against Satan. This is a risk he chooses not to take. He offers her the second alternative, which emphasizes the self-reliance that Raphael recommended, and which avoids entirely the possibility of a potentially ruinous security in dependence.

Most readers agree that Adam decides to let Eve choose whether to stay or go because his love misleads him into caring "more for her immediate approval of him than . . . for her ultimate safety."[19] This means that he "knows his decision is mistaken"[20] because he knows that it would be safest for Eve to stay with him. He knows no such thing. What he does know, as we have seen, is that being together may make them each less careful because dependent on the other. Diane K. McColley suggests that Adam allows Eve to choose because he wishes to preserve her moral freedom: "If 'trial will come unsought' one can approach it freely and with dignity, and Raphael's explanation is still fresh in his mind that obedience can take place only when the will is free."[21] But Eve's freedom to decide for herself is a by-product of Adam's uncertainty rather than the result of his considered policy. She must choose because Adam simply does not know which is the best alternative. Each has something to recommend it, but he can endorse neither as foolproof. The first alternative, while it satisfies his unaltered and loving wish to protect his wife, has been seriously discredited by Raphael's advice and his own experience; the second, while it seems more perilous, urges the self-reliance that Raphael recommends in his narrative and in his parting injunction.

Eve, of course, decides to go. She does not decide "to test her strength,"[22] but to work alone as she wished to do before the discussion with Adam. As Martz suggests, "She means no harm, and she really does have the welfare of her garden at heart."[23] There is no reason not to follow her original inclination. Though, finally, Adam warns her explicitly against "security," he fails to shake the self-confidence that he encouraged earlier in the dispute. He does not persuade her that she is safest with him because he is not certain of it himself. Events beyond Eve's control have given her (and Adam) an enemy who will try her faith — have created, in short, the circumstances that must result in heroism or in catastrophic failure. If temptation comes, she is willing to confront it. She sees it as an opportunity to please God, and she thinks it will be easy. Satan will not "first the weaker seek," she assures Adam, because "the more shall shame him his repulse" (IX, 383–84). Her expectation "to stand approv'd in sight of God" if she is tried is undeniably naive, but it is no more reprehensible than Adam's inability to guide her course with absolute certainty.

Removing the disagreement in the separation scene from the purely emotional and personal realm results in a more balanced view of Adam and Eve, one that is more consistent with their relationship as Milton depicts it in the preceding books of *Paradise Lost*. Eve need not be seen as discontented with the status accorded her by God and, consequently, as predisposed to sin before the temptation. Choosing Abdiel as her model, she responds to Raphel's instruction and thinks to profit from it as she was meant to do. She disagrees with Adam because she has, she thinks, divine authority for her concepts of trial and of herself. Certainly, her understanding is limited, but she is not, therefore, blameworthy. Adam's initial choice of the Son as his model represents his similar effort to interpret the angel's discourse and use it for his and Eve's safety. But his choice is inappropriate and his understanding of trial is inadequate. Milton presents Adam as a weak interpreter of Raphael in order to dispel the assumption that the trial can be circumvented or its outcome determined by intellectual capacity. In Book XII, when Adam asks Michael how God's people will be guided and defended from Satan, the archangel replies:

> the Law of Faith
> Working through love, upon thir hearts shall write,
> To guide them in all truth, and also arm
> With spiritual Armor, able to resist
> *Satan's* assaults, and quench his fiery darts.          (XII, 488–92)

Not intellect but faith and love are the vital weapons against the enemy, and upon them follows the saving truth. Adam is as vulnerable as Eve or, to put it differently, Eve is as capable as Adam of withstanding temptation. His inability to decide whether it would be safest for Eve to stay with him or go stresses the unavoidable uncertainty that characterizes human life. There is no way of knowing beyond question that one situation or another will guarantee spiritual safety. Like the rest of humankind, Adam and Eve must act and choose without the certain knowledge that would make choice easy — and meaningless as an affirmation of faith, love, and obedience.

After he has fallen too, Adam bitterly tells Eve that if she had stayed with him, "we had then / Remain'd still happy, not as now, despoil'd" (IX, 1137–38). He retreats to his first idea that he could have determined the outcome of trial for both. It is a comfortable thought for him, but the reader cannot accept it because Milton has discredited it in the separation scene and in Raphael's narrative. The Son defeats Satan only for the faithful like Abdiel, who have already chosen loyalty and obedience on their own, and who have already fought the enemy to the limits of their own strength and endurance. Even if they had been together, the outcome of Adam's trial would not have determined, necessarily, the outcome of Eve's. Milton uses the separation scene to emphasize those aspects of trial that he dramatizes in the Abdiel episode. No one can confront it for another. It is an inescapably individual matter, and overconfidence is disastrous. To assume its successful issue is perilous and naive, a failure to understand that the possibility of error is the price of free will and the reason for heaven's favor to the obedient.

New York City

## NOTES

1. Arnold Stein, *Answerable Style: Essays on "Paradise Lost"* (Minneapolis, 1953), p. 94; Joseph Summers, *The Muse's Method: An Introduction to "Paradise Lost"* (Cambridge, Mass., 1962), p. 171.

2. Barbara K. Lewalski, "Milton on Women — Yet Once More," in *Milton Studies*, VI, ed. James D. Simmonds (Pittsburgh, 1974), p. 13; Don Parry Norford, "The Separation of the World Parents in *Paradise Lost*," in *Milton Studies*, XII, ed. Simmonds (Pittsburgh, 1978), p. 10.

3. *Surprised by Sin: The Reader in "Paradise Lost"* (Berkeley, 1971), p. 184. Fish suggests only that the dramatic circumstances of Abdiel's temptation mislead Eve. He does not suggest, as I shall, that she considers the triumphant angel her model.

4. Diane K. McColley, "Free Will and Obedience in the Separation Scene of *Paradise Lost*," *SEL*, XII (1972), 114; Louis L. Martz, *Poet of Exile: A Study of Milton's Poetry* (New Haven, 1980), p. 135.

5. Fredson Bowers, "Adam, Eve, and the Fall in *Paradise Lost*," *PMLA*, LXXXIV (1969): "in his role as protector Adam had no right to relieve himself from his responsibility to Eve by making her a free agent. In so doing, he failed in his duty both to her and to

God" (p. 271). Similarly, Dennis H. Burden, *The Logical Epic: A Study of the Argument of "Paradise Lost"* (London, 1967): "For if Adam does not condone her going, then he will have no involvement whatever in her fall" (p. 81).

6. Stella P. Revard, "Eve and the Doctrine of Responsibility in *Paradise Lost*," *PMLA*, LXXXVIII (1973), 73. See also Burton J. Weber, "The Non-Narrative Approaches to *Paradise Lost*: A Gentle Remonstrance," in *Milton Studies*, IX, ed. James D. Simmonds (Pittsburgh, 1976), pp. 99–100, where Burton discusses Adam and Eve's domestic fall and "sin", and Anthony Low, "The Parting in the Garden in *Paradise Lost*," *PQ*, XLVII (1968), 30–35.

7. John C. Ulreich, "'Sufficient to Have Stood': Adam's Responsibility in Book IX," *MQ*, V (1971), 39.

8. William McQueen, "*Paradise Lost*, V, VI: The War in Heaven," *SP*, LXXI (1974), 101.

9. Quotations of the poem are from *John Milton: Complete Poems and Major Prose*, ed. Merritt Y. Hughes (New York, 1957).

10. Burden, *The Logical Epic*, p. 81.

11. Revard, "Eve and the Doctrine of Responsibility," p. 75.

12. "God, Satan, and King Charles: Milton's Royal Portraits," *PMLA*, XCII (1977), 453.

13. S. A. Demetrakopoulos, "Eve as a Circean and Courtly Fatal Woman," *MQ*, IX (1975), 100.

14. Fish, *Surprised by Sin*, p. 184.

15. "'Hee for God Only, Shee for God in Him': Structural Parallelism in *Paradise Lost*," in *Milton Studies*, IX, ed. Simmonds (Pittsburgh, 1976), p. 136.

16. Summers, *The Muse's Method*, p. 172; Burden, *The Logical Epic*, p. 88. Burden suggests (p. 89) that Adam's intellectual error consists of being persuaded by this argument for "virtue that flourishes by trial."

17. "Eve and the Doctrine of Responsibility": "If Eve faces peril from within whenever she is separated from her husband, if she requires his presence in order to stand firm against evil, then Raphael should have specifically warned Adam." If Eve's separateness is "the crucial issue . . . Raphael in not alluding to it is delinquent in his duty to Adam" (p. 72). Revard does not believe that Eve's separateness is the crucial issue, and I agree.

18. "Milton on Women," p. 13.

19. Summers, *The Muse's Method*," p. 174. Similarly, William J. Kennedy, *Rhetorical Norms in Renaissance Literature* (New Haven, 1978): "Suddenly, and for no apparent reason other than that he wants to make Eve happy, Adam reverses his opinion" (p. 183).

20. Ulreich, "'Sufficient to Have Stood,'" p. 39.

21. "Free Will and Obedience," p. 119. See also John Halkett, *Milton and the Idea of Matrimony: A Study of the Divorce Tracts and "Paradise Lost"* (New Haven, 1970), p. 124.

22. Fish, *Surprised by Sin*, p. 184.

23. *Poet of Exile*, p. 135.

# MIDRASH IN *PARADISE LOST:*
# *CAPITULA RABBI ELIESER*

## *Golda Spiera Werman*

FOR MORE than half a century, beginning with the pioneering work of Harris F. Fletcher, readers of *Paradise Lost* with a knowledge of Judaica have noted the resemblance between portions of the epic and Jewish exegesis. However, their efforts to ground their observations on solid scholarly foundations have been largely unsuccessful. They have correctly perceived that Milton's poem and Jewish biblical explication (Midrash) share a number of distinctive similarities of texture and meaning, and they have even pointed to specific Jewish works which contain materials also found in the epic. But because they based their arguments for Milton's use of Jewish sources on the assumption that Milton could read difficult rabbinic texts in the original, these critics failed to convince their readers. From the scattered use of Jewish material in his prose works it is evident that Milton had some knowledge of Hebrew and Aramaic; but there is no indication whatsoever that Milton could make use of intricate Jewish midrashic texts for which literally years of advanced study in Semitics would have been required.[1]

I would like to suggest an approach that bypasses this stumbling block; it is not necessary to turn Milton into a Semitic scholar with a profound knowledge of Jewish sources — an unwarranted, even preposterous notion — in order to explain his use of Jewish midrashic material in *Paradise Lost*. I propose that Milton got the bulk of his Jewish learning, except for the Bible and possibly the Targum, from translations into languages he knew well. Furthermore, I propose a specific translation of a Jewish midrashic work as a possible source used in *Paradise Lost*, Vorstius' Latin translation of *Pirkei* (chapters) *de-Rabbi Eliezer* of 1644. This translation is a particularly good candidate for a midrashic source of the epic because of the inherent interest of the material with which it deals (commentary on Genesis, to a large extent), the religious affiliation of its translator (Arminian, as Milton is thought to have been),[2] the time of its appearance (when Milton was rethinking his religious views and planning his epic), the unusual literary structure of the Midrash (narrative rather than a series of individual statements), the companion piece published in the same volume (a historical book), and the absence of anti-Christian polemic (the polemic is anti-Mohammedan).

According to prevailing opinion, *Pirkei de-Rabbi Eliezer* is an eighth-century Palestinian work also called *Baraita de-Rabbi Eliezer* or *Haggadah de-Rabbi Eliezer*. Written by an unknown Jew living under the Mohammedan conquest of Palestine, it has little of the anti-Christian polemic that characterizes the early talmudic Midrashim or the European medieval commentaries of the Rabbinic Bible, which would have been distasteful to Milton. The book, composed in simple but charming Hebrew, has a poetic and linguistic grace rarely found in midrashic literature as well as a continuous narrative structure which sets it apart from the usual compendia of separate observations which comprise most midrashic works. Midrashic material from many previous works, including the pseudepigraphical books *Enoch* and *Jubilees*, which have been shown by Grant McColley to be close in spirit and details to *Paradise Lost*, are revised and artfully woven into the narrative.[3]

The book as we know it is apparently incomplete; beginning with the history of Eliezer ben Hyrcanus, an important sage of the second century and the putative author of the Midrash, its fifty-four chapters narrate the events from creation until the journeys of the Children of Israel in the wilderness. *Pirkei de-Rabbi Eliezer* makes use of Palestinian materials primarily: the Jerusalem Talmud,[4] the Aramaic Targumim (paraphrases of the Bible) which originated in Palestine,[5] and the Midrashim written in Palestine. Later rabbinic commentators, including Rashi (1040–1105) and Maimonides (1135–1204), cite the work by name. The first Hebrew edition of the Midrash was published in 1514 in Constantinople, and many editions followed, including a modern scholarly Hebrew edition[6] and an English translation with notes.[7]

The translator of the Latin edition of *Pirkei de-Rabbi Eliezer*, Willem (Guilhelmius) Hendrick Vorstius (Vorst), was the son of a well-known Arminian theologian. He was born in Steinfurt, Holland, in 1610, in the same year that his father, Conrad Vorstius, succeeded Arminius as professor of theology in Leiden. After the Synod of Dort (1618–1619) denied the Arminians church services because of their beliefs in conditional rather than absolute predestination, universal atonement, and the possibility of resistance to and relapse from divine grace, Conrad was deposed and persecuted. Willem, who shared his father's views, matriculated as a student of philosophy and rabbinics in Leiden, but had to leave in 1640 because of his religious convictions. In 1642 the influential Arminian, Episcopius, helped him to return to Leiden, where he became a preacher.

*Capitula R. Elieser*, Vorstius' Latin translation of *Pirkei de-Rabbi Eliezer*, appeared together in the same volume with his translation of a larger work, *Zemaḥ David*, a history of the Jews by David Gans.[8] The preface of the Midrash *Pirkei de-Rabbi Eliezer* describes the importance of the work, the identity of Rabbi Eliezer, the use of hyperbole in Midrash, and the nature of Midrash in general. The text of the translation is 150 quarto pages in length. Biblical verses in the text are italicized, and marginal notes give their sources. An extended commentary, *Animadversiones in Pirke R. Elieser*, which starts on page 151 and ends on page 254, is followed by an alphabetic index of fifteen unnumbered pages. In his preface Vorstius states that he used the second printed edition (Venice, 1544) as well as a later edition as his sources. His commentary demonstrates great erudition in Judaica; he quotes from eighteen different tractates of the Mishnah and the Babylonian Talmud, knows the commentaries of Rashi, Kimḥi, and Ibn Ezra, among others, cites the various Targumim, and makes use of many midrashic works. Like Milton he professes a contempt for Jewish "fabulizing," which does not, however, dampen his enthusiasm for translating the book. There are striking affinities between *Pirkei de-Rabbi Eliezer* and *Paradise Lost* which will become apparent in my comparison of the presentation of the invocations, of angels in general and fallen angels in particular, of God and Adam discussing loneliness, of marriage in the Garden, of the seduction of Eve, of work in Eden, and of other more minor points.[9]

## THE INVOCATION

Milton, in his invocation to the Heavenly Muse in Book I, and Eliezer, in his introduction to his explication on creation, give similar reasons for writing their works: both speak of the difficult duty of exalting God and making known His greatness to all men; each recognizes his inadequacy for the task; and both in turn describe the effort as a holy mission which justifies the attempt. Rabbi Eliezer begins with a quotation from Psalm cvi, 2 which asks, "Who can utter the mighty acts of the Lord, or show forth all His praise?" and continues with his own question, "Is there any man who can utter the mighty acts of the Holy One, blessed be He, or who can show forth all His praise?" His answer is a decided No, for even the angels closest to God are incapable of performing such a task: "Not even the ministering angels are able to narrate the Divine praise." How, then, does he presume where angels fail? He justifies his attempt by stressing the importance of the sacred mission: "to investigate a part of His mighty deeds with reference to what He has done, and what

He will do in the future (is permissible), so that His name should be exalted among His creatures, whom He has created, from one end of the world to the other" (Friedlander, 9–10; Vorstius, 3).

Milton begins his explication of the creation with a prayer for guidance from the same Heavenly Muse which inspired Moses on Sinai, "That Shepherd" who first wrote of creation. Like Eliezer, Milton will speak of "Things unattempted yet in Prose or Rhyme." Eliezer's point of reference is the angels; he boldly aims to do what they are only partially capable of, to describe God's works in order to praise Him. Milton's reference is to Greek mythology; he "intends to soar / Above th' *Aonian* Mount" with the daring effort of his "advent'rous Song." Milton, too, recognizes his inadequacy for the task and knows that he will need help to accomplish his goal: "What in me is dark / Illumine, what is low raise and support." Yet, like Eliezer, he feels that despite his insufficiency, he must endeavor to fulfill the sacred duty which he has imposed on himself, to "assert Eternal Providence, / And justify the ways of God to men" (I, 8–26).[10]

## ANGELOLOGY

Both *Pirkei de-Rabbi Eliezer* and *Paradise Lost* reflect their authors' fascination with angels; in each of the works good and evil angels are given important roles and their appearances and actions are described in great detail. Chapter IV of the midrashic work, which is devoted entirely to a description of the angels who surround God's throne, presents some interesting parallels to Book III of the epic, which also describes heaven where God sits "Thron'd inaccessible" (III, 377). Both the midrashist and the poet, responding to the opening verses of the Bible, surmise that God created heaven by spreading His garment to contain the waters below. The Midrash asks, "Whence were the heavens created?" and answers, "From the light of the garment with which He was robed. He took (of this light) and stretched it like a garment" (Friedlander, 15; Vorstius, 4, 151–52). Milton, in his invocation to Light in Book III, speaks of the creation of heaven from the "holy Light" which "at the voice / Of God, as with a Mantle didst invest / The rising world of waters dark and deep" (III, 1–11). Both appear to be based on Psalm civ.

Milton's Almighty Father sits in the pure Empyrean, "High Thron'd above all highth" (III, 58). In *Pirkei de-Rabbi Eliezer* God sits on a throne "high and exalted. His throne is high and suspended above in the air." To the right of Milton's God "The radiant image of his Glory sat" (III, 63). He is surrounded with "all the Sanctities of Heaven . . . thick as Stars" (III, 60–61). In the Midrash, God is likewise surrounded by His angels who are divided into four camps, just as in *Enoch*.[11] The leaders of the four groups of angels are the four archangels who have such important roles in *Paradise Lost*: "the first camp is led by Michael on His right, the second camp is led by Gabriel on His left, the third camp is led by Uriel before Him, and the fourth camp is led by Raphael behind Him" (Friedlander, 22; Vorstius, 6). The New Testament (Rev. iv, 6), by contrast, refers to four beasts before God's throne. In the epic the archangels appear later, but it is likely that Milton got the idea from the *Pirkei de-Rabbi Eliezer* or some other midrashic source, as the New Testament provides the names of only two of the archangels (Michael and Gabriel).

In *Paradise Lost* God sits "invisible / Amidst the glorious brightness" (III, 375–76) with "a cloud / Drawn round about . . . like a radiant Shrine" (III, 378–80). In *Pirkei de-Rabbi Eliezer* "a veil is spread before Him" (Friedlander, 23; Vorstius, 7). In the poem the "brightest Seraphim / Approach not, but with both wings veil thir eyes" (III, 381–82). In the Midrash (based on Isa. vi, 2) "Two Seraphim stand, one on His right and one on His left, each one has six wings, with twain they cover their face so as not to behold the presence of the Shekhinah (God's radiance)" (Friedlander, 25; Vorstius, 7). The Shekhinah seems to be paralleled by Milton's "Begotten Son, Divine Similitude, / In whose conspicuous count'nance, without cloud / Made visible, th' Almighty Father shines / Whom else no Creature can behold" (III, 384–87). Milton describes "Th' Arch-Angel *Uriel*, one of the sev'n / Who in God's presence, nearest to his Throne / Stand ready at command, and are his Eyes / That run through all the Heav'ns, or down to th' Earth / Bear his swift errands" (III, 648–52). *Pirkei de-Rabbi Eliezer* has a similar description: "He [God] has a sceptre of fire in His hand and a veil is spread before Him, and His eyes run to and fro throughout the whole earth, and the seven angels, which were created first, minister before Him" (Friedlander, 23; Vorstius, 7).

The number of resemblances between Milton's heaven and the firmament of *Pirkei de-Rabbi Eliezer*, which house the angels and God, is noteworthy. The number of descriptive parallels is greater between these two works than between either of the two and the Book of Revelation, in which some of the details are found and which most annotators cite as Milton's source.

## SATAN AND THE FALLEN ANGELS

Virtually every important idea connected with Milton's conception of the fallen angels can be found in *Pirkei de-Rabbi Eliezer*. The usual biblical attributions, which must of course be considered important sources for Milton's ideas on Satan and the fallen angels, do not have either singly or collectively as much in common with *Paradise Lost* as does *Pirkei de-Rabbi Eliezer*.[12] The Midrash lacks the poetic vision and epic sweep of the poem, yet all the basic elements in *Paradise Lost* concerning Satan and his fellow rebel angels and the motivation and methods in the seduction of Adam and Eve are found in nascent form in *Pirkei de-Rabbi Eliezer*.

In both works Satan was once chief of the angels in heaven. *Pirkei de-Rabbi Eliezer* refers to Sammael (Satan) as the "great prince in heaven." To make explicit his preeminence over the other angels, the Midrash continues: "the Chajjoth had four wings and the Seraphim had six wings, and Sammael had twelve wings" (Friedlander, 92; Vorstius, 28). *Paradise Lost* describes Satan as one "of the first, / If not the first Arch-Angel, great in Power / In favor and preeminence" (V, 659–61); "high was his degree in Heav'n" (V, 707). In hell he is still called by Beelzebub, "Prince . . . Chief of many throned Powers" (I, 128). Indeed, even in hell Satan sits like a great prince "High on a Throne of Royal State" (II, 1).

Chapter XIII of *Pirkei de-Rabbi Eliezer*, whose subject is the Serpent in Paradise, begins with a quotation from the Mishnah Pirkei Avot (Ethics of the Fathers, iv, 28): "Envy, desire and pride remove man from the world." This is followed immediately with an analysis of the angels' motives for causing man's fall, in which envy, pride, and revenge are stressed. Throughout the chapter the reigning evil angel is called Serpent. In *Paradise Lost*, immediately following the invocation in Book I, the narrator asks who led Adam and Eve to sin, "Who first seduc'd them to that foul revolt?" (I, 33). He answers, as Eliezer had, "Th' infernal Serpent" (I, 34). Even Milton's choice of words to define the Serpent's motives for the perfidy appear to be taken from the quotation from Avot. Vorstius translated the Hebrew as *invidia*, *concupiscentia* (to come later), and *superbia;* Milton comments:

> hee it was, whose guile
> Stirr'd up with Envy and Revenge, deceiv'd
> The Mother of Mankind; what time his Pride
> Had cast him out from Heav'n, with all his Host
> Of Rebel Angels, by whose aid aspiring
> To set himself in Glory above his Peers.          (I, 34–39)

Milton's grand rebel, who sought "to have equall'd the most High, / If he oppos'd; and with ambitious aim / Against the Throne and Monarchy of God / Rais'd impious War in Heav'n and Battle proud" (I, 40–43), has his counterpart in Sammael. *Pirkei de-Rabbi Eliezer* describes him as jealous of God and ready to wage war against Him in the vain attempt to equal God in power: "The Torah began to cry aloud, saying, Why O Sammael! now that the world is created, is it the time to rebel against the Omnipresent? Is this the time that you should lift yourself on high?" (Friedlander, 92; Vorstius, 28). *Pirkei de-Rabbi Eliezer* ends this section with a text from Job (xxxix, 18) in which God laughs mockingly at this endeavor: "The Lord of the world 'will laugh at the horse and its rider.'" Milton, too, has God laugh cynically at Satan's desperate attempt "to erect his Throne / Equal to ours" (V, 725–26) and "to try / In battle, what our Power is" (V, 727–28). The Son says, "Mighty Father, thou thy foes / Justly hast in derision, and secure / Laugh'st at thir vain designs and tumults vain" (V, 735–37).

God's elevation of the Son and the demand that the angels pay him obeisance piques the spite and malevolence of Milton's Satan; he,

> fraught
> With envy against the Son of God, that day
> Honor'd by his great Father, and proclaim'd
> *Messiah* King anointed, could not bear
> Through pride that sight, and thought himself impair'd.
>                                                         (V, 661–65)

On this account Satan organizes his fellow angels to revolt. But Satan's envy is not directed against the Son alone; his speech to his fellow angels in which he urges war reveals his jealousy of man's position as well:

> There went a fame in Heav'n that he ere long
> Intended to create, and therein plant
> A generation, whom his choice regard
> Should favor equal to the Sons of Heaven:
> Thither, if but to pry, shall be perhaps
> Our first eruption.                          (I, 651–56)

And later, when Satan volunteers to carry out the attack on man, he again makes his rancor and vindictiveness against man explicit, declaring that he

> Provokes my envy, this new Favorite
> Of Heav'n, this Man of Clay, Son of despite,
> Whom us the more to spite his Maker rais'd
> From dust: spite then with spite is best repaid.   (IX, 175–78)

In *Pirkei de-Rabbi Eliezer*, too, the angels are angry and jealous of man because God has recognized his unique qualities and honored him by elevating him on earth to the level of angels in heaven.

The ministering angels spake before the Holy One, blessed be He, saying: Sovereign of all Worlds! "What is man, that thou shouldst take note of him?" (Ps. cxliv,

3). "Man (Adam) is like unto vanity" (Ps. cxliv, 4), upon earth there is not his like. (God) answered them: Just as all of you praise Me in the heights of heaven so he professes My Unity on earth, nay, moreover, are you able to stand up and call the names for all the creatures which I have created? They stood up, but were unable (to give the names). Forthwith Adam stood up and named all His creatures. . . . When the ministering angels saw this . . . they said: If we do not take counsel against this man so that he sin before his Creator, we cannot prevail against him. (Friedlander, 91; Vorstius, 28)

Their envy and resentment aroused, the ministering angels of *Pirkei de-Rabbi Eliezer* decide to destroy man, not by fighting him directly but through the devious method of causing him to sin so that God will destroy His own creation. In this way both man and God will suffer.

Milton asserts early in the epic that Adam and Eve are God's special treasures: "Favor'd of Heav'n" (I, 30) and "Lords of the World" (I, 32). At the infernal council, described in Book II, Beelzebub suggests that the "Ethereal Virtues" have a justified resentment against the "new Race call'd *Man*" (II, 348) for his singular position with God: just as the angels of *Pirkei de-Rabbi Eliezer* had disparaged man ("What is man, that Thou shouldst take note of him?"), so Beelzebub disparages man who, despite his deficiency in "power and excellence," is favor'd more / Of him who rules above" (II, 350–51). His advice is to get at God who sits "secure / In his own strength" (II, 359–60) by attacking the more defenseless man. Beelzebub's plan is similar to that of the ministering angels in *Pirkei de-Rabbi Eliezer* who, by causing man to sin, would provoke God to destroy him and thus achieve a double victory. Beelzebub proposes that the fallen angels

> Seduce them to our Party, that thir God
> May prove thir foe, and with repenting hand
> Abolish his own works. This would surpass
> Common revenge.     (II, 368–71)

Later in the epic Satan expresses the same feelings of persecuted injury and insult to honor that had impelled Eliezer's ministering angels to murderous wrath. His angry indignation against God and man is justified, Satan claims, because God, in his spite against the angels,

> Determin'd to advance into our room
> A Creature form'd of Earth, and him endow,
> Exalted from so base original,
> With Heav'nly spoils, our spoils; What he decreed
> He effected; Man he made, and for him built

> Magnificent this World, and Earth his seat,
> Him Lord pronounc'd.                    (IX, 148–54)

Just as Eliezer's ministering angels had been unwilling to accept the divine decree which gave man rather than the angels the earth as an inheritance, so Milton's Satan is unwilling to consent to God's exalting man by making him lord of the earth. "What is man?" Eliezer's ministering angels ask scornfully. Satan replies derisively that man is base, "A creature formed of Earth."

There is agreement between *Pirkei de-Rabbi Eliezer* and *Paradise Lost* on the immense size of the fallen angels. Milton calls them "Giant Angels" (VII, 605). To suggest Satan's extraordinarily large size, the poet describes his accoutrements: a "ponderous shield" (I, 284) whose "broad circumference / Hung on his shoulders like the Moon" (I, 286–87), and a spear so huge that the tallest pine "were but a wand" (I, 294) compared to it. The fallen angels of *Pirkei de-Rabbi Eliezer* are also huge. They declare: "If He bring from heaven the waters of the Flood upon us, behold, we are of high stature, and the waters will not reach up to our necks; and if He bring the waters of the depths against us, behold, the soles of our feet can close up all the depths" (Friedlander, 162; Vorstius, 50). But their size gives Eliezer's fallen angels a false sense of security. Both the fallen angels of *Pirkei de-Rabbi Eliezer* and those of *Paradise Lost* are punished in a pool of flames. This is variously described by Milton as an "inflamed Sea" (I, 300), a "Lake of Fire" (I, 280), a "burning Lake" (I, 210), and a "fiery Deluge" (I, 68). *Pirkei de-Rabbi Eliezer* includes a detailed description of God preparing the burning lake and designates its effects: "What did the Holy One, blessed be He, do? He heated the waters of the deep, and they arose and burnt their flesh, and peeled off their skin from them" (Friedlander, 162; Vorstius, 50).

In *Paradise Lost* the evil angels are all turned into ugly serpents who are made to suffer a horrible double punishment; all food turns to dust in their mouths, and their bodies undergo a painful metamorphosis. Milton gives a vivid description of the serpent's agony as they try to eat the alluring fruit, but

> instead of Fruit
> Chew'd bitter Ashes, which th' offended taste
> With spattering noise rejected: oft they assay'd,
> Hunger and thirst constraining, drugg'd as oft,
> With hatefullest disrelish writh'd thir jaws
> With soot and cinders fill'd.                    (X, 565–70)

The serpents are subjected to this physical transformation for an allotted period every year,

> to undergo
> This annual humbling certain number'd days,
> To dash thir pride, and joy for Man seduc't.          (X, 575–77)

The Bible had nothing to say on this subject; God cursed the snake by decreeing that it was to crawl on its belly and eat dust forever (Gen. iii, 14). *Pirkei de-Rabbi Eliezer* recorded some variations on these curses and added others: God decreed that the serpent "should cast its skin and suffer pain once in seven years in great pain, . . . and its food is turned in its belly into dust and the gall of asps, and death is in its mouth" (Friedlander, 99; Vorstius, 30–31). Here the similarity with Milton's interpretation of the biblical passage is close. The Bible states that the snake would eat dust, and both Milton and Eliezer expand this to the more odious punishment whereby food would turn into ashes in the process of chewing and become bitter and inedible; the Bible makes no mention of the periodic physical change in the serpent to which both *Pirkei de-Rabbi Eliezer* and *Paradise Lost* refer. In both cases the biblical serpent is associated with the fallen angels.

### The Dialogue Between God and Man on Loneliness

It may well have been the *Pirkei de-Rabbi Eliezer* which inspired Milton's conversation between God and Adam in which they discuss the subjects of loneliness and propagation.[13] The Midrash has the following passage in which God soliloquizes about the solitary state and procreation:

And (Adam) was at his leisure in the garden of Eden, like one of the ministering angels. The Holy One, blessed be He, said: I am alone in My world and this one (Adam) also is alone in his world. There is no propagation before Me and this one (Adam) has no propagation in his life; hereafter all the creatures will say: Since there was no propagation in his life, it is he who has created us. It is not good for man to be alone, as it is said (Genesis ii, 18), "And the Lord God said, It is not good for man to be alone; I will make him an help meet for him." (Friedlander, 85–86; Vorstius, 26–27)

In *Paradise Lost* God has a different reason for giving man a mate; having already determined to create Eve, God plays with Adam, who has asked for a companion:

> A nice and subtle happiness I see
> Thou to thyself proposest, in the choice
> Of thy Associates, *Adam*, and wilt taste

> No pleasure, though in pleasure, solitary.
> What think'st thou then of mee, and this my State,
> Seem I to thee sufficiently possest
> Of happiness, or not? who am alone
> From all Eternity, for none I know
> Second to mee or like, equal much less.
> How have I then with whom to hold converse
> Save with the Creatures which I made, and those
> To me inferior, infinite descents
> Beneath what other Creatures are to thee?     (VIII, 399–411)

Adam continues the conversation with a discussion on propagation:

> No need that thou
> Shouldst propagate, already infinite;
> And through all numbers absolute, though One;
> But Man by number is to manifest
> His single imperfection, and beget
> Like of his like, his Image multipli'd,
> In unity defective, which requires
> Collateral love, and dearest amity.     (VIII, 419–26)

These passages in the two works have three elements in common: God discusses man's loneliness with Adam, God justifies Adam's unwedded state by pointing out His own singleness, and both conversations include a discussion of propagation.

### ADAM AND EVE'S MARRIAGE

Both *Pirkei de-Rabbi Eliezer* and *Paradise Lost* describe the wedding. The Midrash emphasizes the wedding canopy:

The Holy One, blessed be He, made ten wedding canopies for Adam in the Garden of Eden. They were all (made) of precious stones, pearls, and gold. Is it not a fact that only one wedding canopy is made for every bridegroom, whilst three wedding canopies are made for a king? But in order to bestow special honor upon the first man, the Holy One, blessed be He, made ten (wedding canopies) in the garden of Eden. . . . The angels were playing upon timbrels and dancing. (Friedlander, 88–89; Vorstius, 27)[14]

Even God and the angels attend the wedding of Adam and Eve in order to honor the first couple and to bless the union. This is a happy and grand occasion. Milton, too, describes a glorious wedding in which all of nature participates in joyous celebration:

> To the Nuptial Bow'r
> I led her blushing like the Morn: all Heav'n,

> And happy Constellations on that hour
> Shed thir selectest influence; the Earth
> Gave sign of gratulation, and each Hill.          (VIII, 510–14)

Milton adopts the view that Adam and Eve had sexual relations before the fall:

> And by her yielded, by him best receiv'd,
> Yielded with coy submission, modest pride,
> And sweet reluctant amorous delay.          (IV, 309–11)

And Milton can be even more explicit:

> Straight side by side were laid, nor turn'd I ween
> *Adam* from his fair Spouse, nor *Eve* the Rites
> Mysterious of connubial Love refus'd.          (IV, 741–43)

The notion of prelapsarian sexual intercourse between Adam and Eve is also found in *Pirkei de-Rabbi Eliezer* (in the ninth hour of the first day) and in other Jewish sources:

The day had twelve hours; in the first hour He collected the dust for (the body of) Adam, in the second (hour) He formed it into a mass, in the third (hour) He gave it its shape, in the fourth (hour) He endowed it with breath, in the fifth (hour) he stood on his feet, in the sixth (hour) he called the (animals by their) names, in the seventh (hour) Eve was joined to him (in wedlock), in the eighth (hour) they were commanded concerning the fruits of the tree, in the ninth (hour) they went up to (their) couch as two and descended as four, in the tenth (hour) they transgressed His commandment, in the eleventh (hour) they were judged, in the twelfth (hour) they were driven forth, as it is said, "So he drove out the man." (Friedlander, 78; Vorstius, 24)

### WORK IN THE GARDEN

Both *Pirkei de-Rabbi Eliezer* and *Paradise Lost* expand on the biblical statement "And the Lord God took the man and put him into the Garden of Eden to work it and to keep it" (Gen. ii, 15). The biblical notion of work in Eden required explanation and midrashic expansion: since the Garden, planted by God, was planned so as to satisfy all of man's needs, why was Adam required to work in it? Furthermore, the work that was Adam's punishment for his sin—"In the sweat of thy face shalt thou eat bread" (Gen. iii, 19) — was not to be confused with his prelapsarian activity in the Garden. *Pirkei de-Rabbi Eliezer* (Chapter XII) interprets the work allegorically; Adam and Eve were required to labor diligently so as to acquire the knowledge and understanding of God's laws which would enable them to keep his commandments. The Midrash begins by asking the question: "What work was there in the Garden that the text should say, 'to work it and keep it'?" and proceeds by giving an answer which interprets work literally, "There was work to be done in the Garden of Eden, namely, to prune the vines in the vineyards, to plough the ground, to cast out the stones, to stack the sheaves, to harvest." But this answer is not satisfactory to the author; it contradicts the reality of the Garden, for "Did not all the trees grow of their own accord?" Eliezer next posits another possibility: "Perhaps you will say, There was some other work (to be done) in the garden of Eden, (such as) to water the garden." This he also dismisses: "But did not a river flow through and issue forth from Eden and water the garden, as it is said, 'And a river went out of Eden to water the garden' (Gen. ii, 10)?" The author concludes that the work demanded of Adam and Eve required a metaphoric explanation: "What then is the meaning of this expression: 'to dress it and keep it' . . . except (in the sense) of being occupied with the words of the Torah and keeping all its commandments, as it is said, 'to keep the way of the tree of life' (Gen. iii, 24) and the tree of life is nothing other than Torah" (Friedlander, 84–85; Vorstius, 26). Work is the allegorical representation of devotion to study and the moral life.

In Milton's Paradise everything grows in lush profusion: "Out of the fertile ground he caus'd to grow / All Trees of noblest kind for sight, smell, taste" (IV, 216–17). The Garden is watered by "a fresh Fountain" (IV, 229), and there is no dearth of sun to warm the trees, fragrant with "odorous Gums and Balm" (IV, 248) and rich with "fruit burnisht with Golden Rind" (IV, 249). Nor does the Garden lack shady retreats "o'er which the mantling Vine / Lays forth her purple Grape" (IV, 258–59). What work is there for Adam and Eve in this Garden? Milton insists that there was a great deal to be accomplished; it was not meant for man to be idle: "Man hath his daily work of body or mind / Appointed, which declares his Dignity" (IV, 618–19). The poet gives a literal description of the tasks they must perform "to reform / Yon flow'ry Arbors, yonder Alleys green / . . . with branches overgrown" (IV, 625–27). Yet the labor is too much for them; the Garden has a continual tendency to overabundance and wildness which Adam and Eve cannot hope to control. Adam knows that all their efforts have no appreciable effect on the Garden's wanton growth which mocks their "scant manuring" (IV, 628).

Milton could not have intended Adam and Eve's labors to be an empty pursuit; God would not have assigned them a hopelessly frustrating and unnecessary task. Some other meaning must be attached to the work, and indeed this meaning becomes clear in Book IX where Adam and Eve's labors in controlling the Garden can be related to the effort required in

controlling their own temptations. While they labor in the Garden together, Adam and Eve manage to maintain control over temptation, to
keep within the bounds God set for them. When Eve insists on breaking
away from Adam, arguing for greater efficiency in their work, she demonstrates a lack of understanding of the purpose of their labors; Adam,
on the other hand, understands that their work has a moral purpose that
has nothing to do with their productivity in the fields. But he cannot
persuade Eve of this. Milton emphasizes work as an aspect of life in Eden
as *Pirkei de-Rabbi Eliezer* had done; and, as in the Midrash, *Paradise
Lost* gives both a literal description of the work required and a demon-
stration of its allegorical meaning.

It is significant also that both books describe the Garden of Eden
in sexual terms; this metaphorical interpretation is particularly bold in
*Pirkei de-Rabbi Eliezer*, which comments on the biblical verse "of the
fruit of the tree which is in the midst of the garden" (Gen. iii, 3):

here "tree" only means man, who is compared to the tree, as it is said," For man
is the *tree* of the field" (Deut. xx, 19). . . . "in the midst of the garden" is here
merely an euphemism (referring to that which is in the middle of the woman),
for "garden" means here merely woman, who is compared to a garden, as it is
said, "A garden shut up is my sister, a bride" (Cant. iv, 12). Just as with this garden, whatever is sown therein, it produces and brings forth, so (with) this woman,
what seed she receives, she conceives and bears through sexual intercourse. (Friedlander, 150; Vorstius, 47)

This passage is followed by Sammael's sexual seduction of Eve. More sub-
dued, and without Eliezer's explicit allegorization, Milton's graphic description of the Garden's fertility is also charged with sexual imagery:

> On to thir morning's rural work they haste
> Among sweet dews and flow'rs; where any row
> Of fruit-trees overwoody reach'd too far
> Thir pamper'd boughs, and needed hands to check
> Fruitless imbraces: or they led the Vine
> To wed her Elm; she spous'd about him twines
> Her marriageable arms, and with her brings
> Her dow'r th' adopted Clusters, to adorn
> His barren leaves.            (V, 211–19)

### THE SEDUCTION OF EVE

Milton's poetic conception of the seduction of Eve in Book IX has
many parallels in Chapter XIII of *Pirkei de-Rabbi Eliezer*, which narrates the fall of Adam and Eve. The Midrash tells the story very simply
in comparison to the epic, in which the incidents are expanded and the

episodes dramatized. Yet the similarities are remarkable; particularly note-worthy are those structural resemblances and analogous details for which the Bible gives no clues. In both accounts the seduction begins with Satan's choice of an animal in which to hide so as to avoid discovery. Both follow the Bible: "Now the serpent was more subtile than any beast of the field which the Lord God had made" (Gen. iii, 1). In *Pirkei de-Rabbi Eliezer*, Satan "descended and saw all the creatures which the Holy One, blessed be He, had created in His world and he found among them none so skilled to do evil as the serpent" (Friedlander, 92; Vorstius, 28). Milton similarly, writes of the careful search made by Satan before choosing the serpent:

> thus the Orb he roam'd
> With narrow search; and with inspection deep
> Consider'd every Creature, which of all
> Most opportune might serve his Wiles, and found
> The Serpent subtlest Beast of all the Field.          (IX, 82–86)

The notion that Satan meticulously examines the animal kingdom be-fore making his selection is not found in the Bible. But Milton is not sat-isfied with this bare idea; he develops the conception that the snake is known to be wily and crafty and would therefore not arouse suspicion by unusually clever behavior:

> Fit Vessel, fittest Imp of fraud, in whom
> To enter, and his dark suggestions hide
> From sharpest sight: for in the wily Snake,
> Whatever sleights none would suspicious mark,
> As from his wit and native subtlety
> Proceeding, which in other Beasts observ'd
> Doubt might beget of Diabolic pow'r.          (IX, 89–95)

The *Pirkei de-Rabbi Eliezer* relates a parable, designed to illustrate that the serpent was merely a vessel to contain Satan (Friedlander, 93; Vor-stius, 28). Milton's Satan enters his vessel, the serpent, through its mouth (IX, 187). Eliezer's snake is described as having the appearance of a camel, which Satan mounts and rides.[15]

After his choice of an animal through which to enact his evil deed, the Satan of *Pirkei de-Rabbi Eliezer* decides on a plan of action. Aware of man's intellectual superiority, he knows that he cannot fool Adam with his hypocritical glozing; he therefore determines to attack the woman verbally:

The serpent argued with itself, saying: If I go and speak to Adam, I know he will not listen to me, for a man is always hard (to be persuaded). . . . but I will speak to Eve, for I know that she will listen to me; for women listen to all crea-tures. (Friedlander, 94; Vorstius, 29)

Just so, Milton's serpent knows that Adam is a "Foe not informidable" (IX, 486), the "higher intellectual" (IX, 483) whom he must shun. Con-sequently, Satan is delighted to find Eve, the weaker intellectual, alone: "Beyond his hope, *Eve* separate he spies" (IX, 424). Like the Eve in *Pirkei de-Rabbi Eliezer*, she will be easy to convince: "The Woman, opportune to all attempts" (IX, 481).

The Satans in both accounts introduce the idea of God's envy. On hearing Eve repeat the prohibition concerning the forbidden fruit, the Satan of *Pirkei de-Rabbi Eliezer* suggests that God will not share the se-cret of creation because he is envious:

This precept is nought else except the evil eye [envy, as translated by Vorstius], for in the hour when ye eat thereof, ye will be like Him, a God. Just as He creates worlds and destroys worlds, so will ye be able to create worlds and destroy worlds. Just as He slays and brings to life, so also will ye be able to kill and bring to life, as it is said: "For God doth know that in the day ye eat thereof, then your eyes shall be opened" (Gen. iii, 5). (Friedlander, 94–95; Vorstius, 29)

The Satan of *Paradise Lost* likewise introduces the idea of God's envy:

> Why then was this forbid? Why but to awe,
> Why but to keep ye low and ignorant,
> His worshippers; he knows that in the day
> Ye Eat thereof, your Eyes that seem so clear,
> Yet are but dim, shall perfetly be then
> Op'n'd and clear'd, and ye shall be as Gods.     (IX, 703–08)

Milton's Satan actually uses the word *envy* when he asks, "is it envy?" (IX, 729) which motivates God to deny the fruit to Adam and Eve. But having planted the idea, Satan craftily dismisses it: "can envy dwell / In heav'nly breasts?" (IX, 729–30). In the Midrash, to become like God is interpreted by Satan as having the knowledge to create and destroy; Milton's Satan also introduces this idea:

> And what are Gods that Man may not become
> As they, participating God-like food?
> The Gods are first, and that advantage use
> On our belief, that all from them proceeds;
> I question it, for this fair Earth I see,
> Warm'd by the Sun, producing every kind,
> Them nothing: If they all things, who enclos'd
> Knowledge of Good and Evil in this Tree,

> That who so eats thereof, forthwith attains
> Wisdom without their leave?                    (IX, 716–25)

Satan implies that the knowledge gained from eating the fruit will give
Eve the wisdom of the gods.

In *Pirkei de-Rabbi Eliezer* the serpent convinces Eve to eat the fruit
by touching the tree and proving to her that it does not call down God's
wrath and the threatened punishment of death: "The serpent said to the
woman: Behold, I touched it but I did not die; thou also mayest touch
it, and thou wilt not die" (Friedlander, 95; Vorstius, 29). The snake of
*Paradise Lost* convinces her with the same ploy: "look on mee, / Mee who
have touch'd and tasted, yet . . . live" (IX, 687–88).

Immediately after the Eve of the Midrash touches the tree, she real-
izes that she may die. This thought produces a most unexpected response:
not fear and sadness at her own imminent death, but an overwhelming
jealousy at the possibility of being replaced by another woman in Adam's
life: "The woman went and touched the tree, and she saw the angel of
death coming towards her; she said: Woe is me! I shall now die, and the
Holy One, blessed be He, will make another woman and give her to Adam"
(Friedlander, 95; Vorstius, 29). To prevent such an eventuality, Eve determines to make Adam sin with her: "I will cause him to eat with me; if
we shall die, we shall both die, and if we shall live, we shall both live.
And she took of the fruits of the tree, and ate thereof, and also gave (of
its fruits) to her husband, so that he should eat with her." [16] Milton's Eve
is motivated by the same emotion. After eating the fruit, she wonders
whether to tell Adam or not. If she keeps her sin a secret, her superior
knowledge might win his greater love and respect. But she is afraid that
she will die; then Adam would be given another Eve:

> but what if God have seen,
> And Death ensue? then I shall be no more,
> And *Adam* wedded to another *Eve*,
> Shall live with her enjoying, I extinct.        (IX, 826–29)

Here, as in *Pirkei de-Rabbi Eliezer*, Eve's emotional response to her impending death is jealousy of a new mate for Adam; she does not begrudge
his remaining alive without her, but she is jealous at the thought of his
bliss with a new wife. Milton's Eve decides therefore, for the same reasons as the Eve of the Midrash, to give the apple to Adam: "Confirm'd
then I resolve, / *Adam* shall share with me in bliss or woe" (IX, 830–31).

In *Pirkei de-Rabbi Eliezer* Adam's response to his own evil deed is
first anger with Eve for causing him to sin and then sorrow at the loss

of his innocence. He bewails the penalty of death which his transgression has introduced into the world, to be shared by all future generations:

When Adam had eaten of the fruit of the tree, he saw that he was naked, and his eyes were opened, and his teeth were set on edge. He said to her: What is this that thou hast given me to eat, that my eyes should be opened and my teeth set on edge? Just as my teeth were set on edge, so shall the teeth of all generations be set on edge. (Friedlander, 95–96; Vorstius, 30)

These same ideas, greatly augmented, are found in *Paradise Lost*; Milton adds the intoxicating lust which follows the sin. Adam declares:

> since our Eyes
> Op'n'd we find indeed, and find we know
> Both Good and Evil, Good lost, and Evil got,
> Bad Fruit of Knowledge, if this be to know,
> Which leaves us naked thus, of Honor void,
> Of Innocence, of Faith, of Purity.                    (IX, 1070–75)

Both authors follow the biblical statement "And the eyes of them both were opened, and they knew that they were naked" (Gen. iii, 7), and expand on it. Milton, like Eliezer before him, adds Adam's anger and resentment; he blames Eve from a "distemper'd breast" (IX, 1131), "estrang'd in look and alter'd style" (IX, 1132). Milton's Adam feels that he might bear his own deserved punishment, but like Eliezer's Adam he rues the penalty his progeny will have to pay:

> The misery, I deserv'd it, and would
> My own deservings; but this will not serve;
> All that I eat or drink, or shall beget,
> Is propagated curse. O voice once heard
> Delightfully, *Increase and multiply*,
> Now death to hear!                                     (X, 726–31)

Almost every important point in the structure of the narrative of Satan's seduction of Eve in *Paradise Lost* has a parallel in *Pirkei de-Rabbi Eliezer*. Indeed, Chapter XIII of the *Pirkei de-Rabbi Eliezer* could be used as an outline of Book IX of *Paradise Lost*. Both follow the brief biblical account as related in Genesis iii, 1–7, and each progressively embellishes and enriches the skeletal Scripture story of seven terse verses. Both the Midrash and the epic have Satan choose the serpent as the appropriate animal through which to operate; both Satans choose the woman as their victim because of her intellectual inferiority; both attack innocence through fraud and deception; both accuse God of wishing to keep man ignorant because of envy; both convince Eve to taste the apple, either by touching the tree (*Pirkei de-Rabbi Eliezer*) or by claiming to have done so (*Paradise Lost*). In both accounts Eve decides to give the apple to Adam because of jealousy of a future wife. And in both accounts Adam is angry with Eve for her betrayal and miserable in the knowledge that he has betrayed all future generations.[17]

There are many interpretations of the Genesis story from which Milton could have chosen details that appealed to him. In this case, in which the two elaborated accounts of the seduction legend share so many of the same amplifications of the original text, it is reasonable to assume that Milton, in his later rendition, borrowed from the earlier work, particularly when the evidence points to the Midrash being both attractive and accessible.

### PARALLELS IN THE TREATMENT OF SOME VERSES OF GENESIS VI–XI

Milton devotes the first ten books of *Paradise Lost* to an explication of the first three chapters of Genesis and then summarizes the rest of the Bible in the final two books of the poem. *Pirkei de-Rabbi Eliezer*— incomplete in all the editions we have—devotes twenty out of fifty-four chapters to Genesis i–iii. As is to be expected, there are many more points of contact between Milton and Eliezer on the Adam and Eve story than on the later biblical material; yet there are some interesting parallels in the events subsequent to the expulsion from Eden. Both works describe man's evil state before the flood, stressing sexual promiscuity and violence as outstanding features.

In interpreting the biblical verse "The sons of God saw the daughters of men that they were fair; and they took them wives of all which they chose" (Gen. vi, 2), both authors understand this to mean that the sons of God succumbed to the strategies of the daughters of men who lured them through sexual wiles. *Pirkei de-Rabbi Eliezer* elaborates: "The angels who fell from their holy place in heaven saw the daughters of the generations of Cain walking about naked, with their eyes painted like harlots, and they went astray after them" (Friedlander, 160; Vorstius, 49). In Milton's epic the sons of God lost their virtue to

> A Bevy of fair Women, richly gay
> In Gems and wanton dress.
>
> . . . . . . . .
>
> The Men though grave, ey'd them, and let thir eyes
> Rove without rein, till in the amorous Net
> Fast caught.                                    (XI, 582–87)

*Pirkei de-Rabbi Eliezer* gives a specific account of the lust of the generations of Cain: "they defiled themselves with all kinds of immorality, a man with his mother or his daughter, or the wife of his brother, or the wife of his neighbor, in public and in the streets, with evil inclination which is in the thoughts of their heart" (Friedlander, 159; Vorstius, 49). Milton defines their lust similarly:

> Marrying or prostituting, as befell,
> Rape or Adultery, where passing fair
> Allur'd them.                                    (XI, 716–18)

Pirkei de-Rabbi Eliezer depicts the biblical "mighty men . . . men of renown" (Gen. vi, 4) who were the products of these illicit matings as "giants who walked with pride in their heart, and who stretched forth their hand to all (kinds of) robbery and violence, and shedding of blood" (Friedlander, 160–61; Vorstius, 50). Milton portrays "the product / Of those ill-mated Marriages" (XI, 683–84) as false heroes, soldiers who are admired though they kill and plunder:

> Such were these Giants, men of high renown;
> For in those days Might only shall be admir'd,
> And Valor and Heroic Virtue call'd;
> To overcome in Battle, and subdue
> Nations, and bring home spoils with infinite
> Man-slaughter, shall be held the highest pitch
> Of human Glory.                                   (XI, 688–94)

The two works agree about the specific qualities of evil in man for which God destroyed the world by flood.

The Noah episodes in both the epic and the Midrash differ from the Bible in portraying Noah as a preacher who pleads with the people to change their ways. Pirkei de-Rabbi Eliezer has Noah exhort: "Turn from your ways and evil deeds, so that He bring not upon you the waters of the Flood, and destroy all the seeds of the children of men" (Friedlander, 161–62; Vorstius, 50). Paradise Lost depicts Noah as a "Reverend Sire" who "of thir doings great dislike declar'd, / And testifi'd against thir ways" (XI, 720–21). Milton's Noah preached over a long period of time:

> hee oft
> Frequented thir Assemblies, whereso met,
> Triumphs or Festivals, and to them preach'd
> Conversion and Repentance, as to Souls
> In Prison under Judgments imminent.               (XI, 721–25)

But the people did not repent; his preaching was "all in vain" (XI, 726). In Pirkei de-Rabbi Eliezer Noah builds the ark over a period of "fifty-two years, so that they should repent of their ways" (Friedlander, 165; Vorstius, 51).

The Bible is silent on the issue of how the animals were gathered together before they were brought into the ark; it states merely that they went "unto Noah into the ark, the male and the female, as God commanded" (Gen. vii, 9). In *Pirkei de-Rabbi Eliezer* Noah cries out to God: "Sovereign of all the world! Have I then the strength to collect them unto me to the ark?" (Friedlander, 166; Vorstius, 51). God hears his call and provides a solution through messengers: "The angels appointed over each kind went down and gathered them, and with them all their food unto him to the ark" (Friedlander, 166; Vorstius, 51). Milton implicitly addresses himself to the same problem of how the animals were gathered into the ark and finds a similar miraculous solution:

> when lo a wonder strange!
> Of every Beast, and Bird, and Insect small
> Came sevens, and pairs, and enter'd in, as taught
> Thir order.                                    (XI, 733–36)

"Taught / Thir order." By whom? By heavenly intervention, clearly.

It is of significance that both *Pirkei de-Rabbi Eliezer* and *Paradise Lost* greatly expand the three brief references to Nimrod in the Bible: he was a "mighty one in the earth," "a mighty hunter before the Lord," and "the beginning of his kingdom was Babel" (Gen. x, 8–10). Both works turn Nimrod into an important symbolic figure, the prototype of the tyrannous and rebellious king who gains illegal sovereignty by subjecting a weak people to his ambitious designs. God, according to the midrashic work, was the first king; "the second king was Nimrod, who ruled from one end of the world to the other" (Friedlander, 80; Vorstius, 25). Milton similarly comments that Nimrod claimed "second Sovranty" (XII, 35) from heaven. Eliezer further declares that the people "cast off the Kingdom of Heaven from themselves, and appointed Nimrod king over themselves; a slave son of a slave. Are not all the sons of Ham slaves? And woe to the land when a slave rules" (Friedlander, 174; Vorstius, 54). Milton states in the same vein that since man

> permits
> Within himself unworthy Powers to reign
> Over free Reason, God in Judgment just
> Subjects him from without to violent Lords;
> Who oft as undeservedly enthral
> His outward freedom: Tyranny must be,
> Though to the Tyrant thereby no excuse.
> Yet sometimes Nations will decline so low
> From virtue, which is reason, that no wrong,

> But Justice, and some fatal curse annext
> Deprives them of thir outward liberty,
> Thir inward lost: Witness th'irreverent Son
> Of him who built the Ark, who for the shame
> Done to his Father, heard this heavy curse,
> *Servant of Servants*, on his vicious Race.     (XII, 90–104)

The "irreverent Son" is Ham, Nimrod's grandfather, who has been cursed by Noah as "a servant of servants" (Gen. ix, 25).

   *Pirkei de-Rabbi Eliezer* cites a parable describing a ruse used by Nimrod to deceive the people into thinking that he had special powers; he wears the garments which God had made for Adam and Eve, and all the animals prostrate themselves before him. His countrymen, impressed, "thought that this was due to the power of his might; therefore they made him king over themselves" (Friedlander, 175; Vorstius, 54). In *Paradise Lost* Nimrod is similarly depicted; he is a man

> Of proud ambitious heart, who not content
> With fair equality, fraternal state,
> Will arrogate Dominion undeserv'd
> Over his brethren, and quite dispossess
> Concord and law of Nature from the Earth.     (XII, 25–29)

Both the Midrash (Friedlander, 175; Vorstius, 54) and the epic (XII, 38–45) charge Nimrod with building the Tower of Babel; the Bible does not do so. This idea, however, is rather commonplace among biblical commentators. Milton follows the biblical statement "And the Lord came down to see the city and the tower which the children of men builded" (Gen. xi, 5), but adds an interesting aside about God's frequent descents:

> God who oft descends to visit men
> Unseen, and through thir habitations walks
> To mark thir doings.     (XII, 48–50)

This is reminiscent of a statement in *Pirkei de-Rabbi Eliezer*: "Ten descents upon the earth were made by the Holy One, blessed be He" (Friedlander, 97; Vorstius, 30). Regarding His coming down to see the building of the Tower of Babel, the Midrash states: "This was the second descent" (Friedlander, 177; Vorstius, 55). The entire Nimrod episode, so briefly treated in the Bible, is very much elaborated in the two works; both portray Nimrod as the type of evil king who usurps God's rightful power by devious means from an insufficiently holy people; in both he is accused of instigating the building of the Tower of Babel.

These parallels between *Pirkei de-Rabbi Eliezer* and *Paradise Lost* have been selected from a list of over one hundred such correspondences which I have compiled.[18] In addition to the similarities in design and purpose in the two works, there are remarkable resemblances in the emphasis on the first three chapters of Genesis, the invocations, the shared interest in astronomy and angelology, particularly in Satan, the acceptance of prelapsarian sex, the jealousy of the serpent, Eve's jealousy, the interpretation of work in the Garden, and the Nimrod episodes. To this must be added the marked congruence of the seduction scenes as well as a large number of details scattered throughout the books.

Although many of the parallels noted are widespread in midrashic literature, nowhere else are they found in such abundant concentration or in the singularly attractive and unique narrative style of *Pirkei de-Rabbi Eliezer*; some are only to be found in that source. Moreover, *Pirkei de-Rabbi Eliezer* contains most of the material from *Josippon, Enoch, Jubilees*, and Rashi which have, until now, been considered Milton's major Jewish sources. Unlike the pseudepigraphic literature, however, this work was available to Milton in Latin, in Vorstius' translation, as well as in Hebrew.

The numerous resemblances between *Pirkei de-Rabbi Eliezer* and *Paradise Lost* strongly suggest that the Midrash was a possible source for Milton. Moreover, since there is little evidence to make us believe that Milton had an extensive knowledge of Semitics, the availability of *Pirkei de-Rabbi Eliezer* in a Latin translation lends even stronger support to the suggestion. Two questions remain, however; how would Milton have known about the *Pirkei de-Rabbi Eliezer*, and why was the connection between the Midrash and *Paradise Lost* not seen previously?

The first question cannot be answered with certainty, but a number of conjectures can reasonably be posited: among other ways, the poet might have learned of the book through his Dutch connections, or through his interest in the historical material in the first half of the volume (Vorstius' translation of Gans's *Ẓemaḥ David*), or through his Arminian contacts, or through his reading of Buxtorf's translation of Maimonides' *Guide for the Perplexed*, which mentions this Midrash.

The answer to the second question is simpler. Few Milton scholars have the necessary background in Judaica and Hebrew to make the connection between Eliezer's Midrash and the epic; furthermore, the Latin translation is now rare and appears to be known only to midrashic scholars. Nonetheless, the connection has been noted previously. A Christian Hebraist, Richard Laurence, pointed to Vorstius' translation as a source for many elements of *Paradise Lost* as far back as 1819. But he published his views in the afterword of a book which would not ordinarily be read by literary scholars, his English translation of the apocryphal *Ascension of Isaiah*.[19] Don Cameron Allen did come across this reference and published it in a short paper in 1948,[20] but his hastily written note was hardly convincing, and his finding was largely ignored.

I have pointed out the characteristics that make *Pirkei de-Rabbi Eliezer* a good candidate for a source of some of the midrashic material in *Paradise Lost*: along with the large number of shared details must be included the unusual narrative form of this Midrash, with its emphasis on the early chapters of Genesis. Furthermore, this work was influenced by *Enoch*, previously thought to have been the origin of midrashic elements in *Paradise Lost*. *Pirkei de-Rabbi Eliezer*, written under Moslem rule, has none of the anti-Christian polemic found in other suggested sources which would have been disturbing to Milton. And finally, the contemporary Latin translation by Vorstius provided Milton access to the midrashic material. Short of an actual citation by the poet, this combination of factors makes *Pirkei de-Rabbi Eliezer* the most likely midrashic source known for Jewish material in the epic.

Nevertheless, even if unconditional proof of Milton's use of the Vorstius translation were to be found, perhaps in a marginal note in the poet's hand in one of the extant texts, the problem of the Jewish sources of *Paradise Lost* would not be solved. There are many midrashic ideas in the poem which are not found in *Pirkei de-Rabbi Eliezer*; nor can they be accounted for by Milton's reading of the Church Fathers, who used Jewish materials freely. It seems reasonable to assume that Milton used other sources containing Jewish midrashic material in translation, particularly in Latin; an investigation of these works for possible influence on Milton would be a logical next step to the points raised in this essay.

Jerusalem

## NOTES

1. Fletcher's works include "Milton and Yosippon," *SP*, XXI (1924), 496–501; *Milton's Semitic Studies* (1926; rpt. New York, 1966); and *Milton's Rabbinic Readings* (Urbana, Ill., 1930). Fletcher argues that Milton was familiar with the Hebrew medieval commentaries through his reading of Buxtorf's Rabbinic Bible and that many of the poet's ideas came from this source. Denis Saurat, *Milton: Man and Thinker* (New York, 1925), made the extravagant claim that all of Milton's important ideas are taken from the kabbalistic

work the *Zohar*. Edward C. Baldwin, "Some Extra-Biblical Semitic Influences Upon Milton's Story of the Fall of Man," *JEGP*, XXVIII (1929), 366–401, offers numerous examples of Milton's use of Jewish legendary material, but does not deal with the problem of how Milton got to these sources. R. H. West, *Milton and the Angels* (Athens, Ga., 1955) deals, among other things, with the Jewish sources of Milton's angelology. Harold Fisch, "Hebraic Styles and Motifs in *Paradise Lost*," in *Language and Style in Milton*, ed. R. D. Emma and J. T. Shawcross (New York, 1967), pp. 34–35, and Jason Rosenblatt, "A Revaluation of Milton's Indebtedness to Hebraica in *Paradise Lost*" (Ph.D. diss., Brown University, 1969), maintain that Milton got his Jewish materials from the medieval Jewish commentator, Rashi. J. M. Evans, *Paradise Lost and the Genesis Tradition* (Oxford, 1968) gives a general survey of the Genesis story in Jewish as well as Christian sources.

For a skeptical discussion of the claims made by scholars for Milton's interest in rabbinical sources in Hebrew, see Robert M. Adams, *Milton and the Modern Critics* (1955; rpt. Ithaca, 1966), pp. 133–47. Adams goes to the opposite and equally unreasonable extreme, however, in proposing that the poet invented all the material which had previously been attributed to Jewish sources. For Milton's knowledge of Hebrew see E. C. Baldwin, "Milton and the Psalms," *MP*, XVII (1919), 457–63; M. H. Studley, "Milton and His Paraphrases of the Psalms," *PQ*, IV (1925), 361–72; H. S. Gehman, "Milton's Use of Hebrew in the *Doctrina Christiana*," *Jewish Quarterly Review*, n.s. XXIX (1938), 37–44; and W. B. Hunter, Jr., "Milton Translates the Psalms," *PQ*, XL (1961), 485–94. The term *Midrash* applies to the method of biblical interpretation as well as to the specific exegetical work (plural *Midrashim*); a single statement of biblical interpretation is a *midrash*.

2. Dennis Danielson, "Milton's Arminianism and *Paradise Lost*," in *Milton Studies*, XII, ed. James D. Simmonds (Pittsburgh, 1978), pp. 47–73, and Maurice Kelley, "The Theological Dogma of *Paradise Lost*, III, 175–202," *PMLA*, LII (1937), 75–79, show how the ideas in the epic conform to Arminian thinking.

3. "The *Book of Enoch* and *Paradise Lost*," *Harvard Theological Review*, XXXI (1938), 21–39.

4. There are hints that the Babylonian Talmud was also used by the author. See Leopold Zunz, *Die gottesdienstlischen Vortrage der Juden historisch entwickelt* (1832; trans. into Hebrew from the 2nd ed., 1892, by M. A. Zak, Jerusalem, 1947), ed. H. Albeck, p. 420, n. 29.

5. The Targumim based on the Pentateuch, Pseudo-Jonathan (Targum Yerushalmi I), and the fragmentary Targum Yerushalmi (II).

6. David Luria (Radal) (Warsaw, 1852).

7. Gerald Friedlander (1916; rpt. New York, 1970). For the convenience of the reader I give the pagination of this English edition with every quotation from *Pirkei de-Rabbi Eliezer*, even when the translation is my own. I also give the pagination of the Latin translation by Vorstius. See note 8.

8. The edition, *Capitula R. Elieser* (Leiden, 1644), is now rare, but copies can be found as follows: the Union Catalogue lists ten copies in libraries throughout the United States; the British Library has one; the Bodleian has one; Trinity College, Dublin, has one; the Bibliothèque Nationale in Paris has two; the Bibliotheca Rosenthaliana, Amsterdam, has one; the University Library at Leiden has one; the State and University Library in Frankfurt am Main has one; and the National and University Library in Jerusalem has three. I thank Professor Peter Lindenbaum of Indiana University and Dr. A. K. Offenberg of the Universiteits Bibliotheek of Amsterdam for tracing copies for me in Europe.

9. Both works also reflect their authors' interest in and wide knowledge of the astronomy of their day. Milton speaks of sunspots (III, 588–91), the courses of the sun and

moon, (IV, 660–88), the topographic features of the moon (I, 290–91), the planets of Jupiter (VIII, 148–51), and Venus (VII, 366). Eliezer deals with the separation of the functions of the sun and moon (VI), the role of stars as servants of the seven planets, the order of appearance of the planets both by day and by night, the constellations of the Zodiac, the cycles of the moon (VII), the conjunction of the moon and the sun, and the heavenly path of the moon.

10. For quotations from *Paradise Lost* I have used *John Milton: Complete Poems and Major Prose*, ed. Merritt Y. Hughes (New York, 1957).

11. *Enoch* and *Pirkei de-Rabbi Eliezer* share a great deal of material which the later Midrash probably borrowed from *Enoch*. See pp. XXVII–XXXVI of the Friedlander translation of *Pirkei de-Rabbi Eliezer* for a long list of parallels.

12. The usual biblical attributions are: for Satan who was hurled from heaven (I, 45), Isaiah xiv, 12, "How art thou fallen from heaven, O Lucifer, son of the morning," and Luke x, 18, "I beheld Satan as lightning fall from Heaven"; for the "Adamantine Chains and penal Fire" (I, 48), Matthew xiii, 39 and xxv, 41, which speak of the everlasting fire prepared for the devil, and 2 Peter ii, 4, "God spared not the angels that sinned but cast them down to hell, and delivered them into chains of darkness"; for the war in heaven, Jude i, 6, where Michael the archangel contends with the devil. The fullest biblical treatment is in Revelation xii, which speaks of a war in heaven in which Michael and his angels fought against the dragon and his angels. The great dragon was called the Devil and Satan, and he and his cohorts are cast out of heaven into the earth. There the dragon persecutes the woman who brought forth the man child (not Eve but Mary). The rest of the angelology in Revelation is not followed by Milton. In Revelation xx the devil is "cast into the lake of fire and brimstone."

13. This has been incorrectly attributed to *Josippon* by James H. Hanford, *A Milton Handbook*, 4th ed. (New York, 1961), p. 245. E. C. Baldwin, "Some Extra-Biblical Semitic Influences upon Milton's Story of the Fall of Man," cites the source as *Jerahmeel*, unaware that this Midrash was unavailable in a printed version in Milton's time; ironically, he notes on page 367 that the legend is borrowed from *The Book of the Chronicles of Rabbi Eliezer, the Son of Hyrqanus*. Alfred Möller, "Zu Miltons rabbinischen Studien," *Anglia Beiblatt*, XL (1933), 158, cites *Pirkei de-Rabbi Eliezer*, Ch. XII, as the source.

14. The Hebrew word *ḥuppah* is now used for wedding canopy but also means bridal chamber (see TB Kiddushin 5a, which states that bringing the bride into the *ḥuppah* [wedding chamber] constitutes legal marriage). Vorstius renders *ḥuppah* as "thalamus," a bride's room, a marriage bed, or wedding. Don Cameron Allen, "Milton and Rabbi Eliezer," *MLN*, LXIII (1948), 262–63, comments on this passage and connects *Paradise Lost* with *Pirkei de-Rabbi Eliezer*.

15. Maimonides, *Guide for the Perplexed*, trans. Michael Friedlander, 3rd ed. (1881; rpt. New York, 1946), also talks of a camel in connection with Satan: "The serpent had a rider, the rider was as big as a camel and it was the rider that enticed Eve; this rider was Samael" (p. 217).

16. This legend is found in Genesis Rabbah XIX, 5, *Jerahmeel* XXII, 2, and Rashi on Genesis iii, 6. Arnold Williams, *The Common Expositor* (Chapel Hill, N.C., 1948), p. 123, cites Fereus, Mercerus, and Peter Martyr, who ascribe the legend to "some Jews."

17. Milton probably did not get the idea of Satan's sexual jealousy of Eve from *Pirkei de-Rabbi Eliezer*, in which the devil actually has sexual relations with Eve and she conceives (Friedlander, 150). The notion of Satan's lust for Eve is common in Jewish sources: see Genesis Rabbah XVIII, 6; XLIX, 3; *Avot de-Rabbi Nathan* A, I, 5; *Tosefta* Sotah iii, 17; TB Sotah 9b.

18. See the appendix to my dissertation, *"Paradise Lost* and Midrash" (Indiana University, 1982).

19. *Ascensio Isaiae Vatis* (Oxford, 1819), a work of mixed Jewish and Christian elements, which Laurence translated from Ethiopian. For information on this work see R. H. Charles, *The Ascension of Isaiah* (1900; rpt. London, 1917).

20. Allen, "Milton and Rabbi Eliezer," pp. 262–63. Alfred Möller, "Zu Miltons rebbinischen Studien," also makes the connection between *Paradise Lost* and *Pirkei de-Rabbi Eliezer* and knows of the Latin translation; in his view, however, Milton used the Hebrew original.

# THE COURSE OF TIME:
# A CALVINISTIC *PARADISE LOST*

## *Julie Nall Knowles*

---

### I

IN 1827, Robert Pollok, a young Scottish Presbyterian preacher, published a long blank verse poem titled *The Course of Time* — a work that sought to present "the Course of Time, / The second birth, and final doom of man" (*CT* I, 11–12).[1] As the poem first gained notice, Pollok died, and etched on his tombstone near Southampton in England is an Ozymandian prophecy: "His immortal poem is his monument."

Feeling confident of the poem's immortality, admirers placed this inscription on Pollok's tombstone. Like T. Walker in *The North American Review*, numerous critics voiced a belief that "a high place will be assigned him among the gifted sons of song."[2] John Wilson, whose remarks regarding Wordsworth, Coleridge, and Keats were scarcely kind, wrote of Robert Pollok as a "true poet" and a "gifted spirit."[3] Pollok was even called "the Scotch Dante,"[4] and his work was hailed by many avid readers as a religious epic greater than *Paradise Lost*.

On the whole, Timothy Flint expressed the opinion of many when he insisted, "He often reaches, and it seems to us, sometimes almost surpasses the grandeur of Milton."[5] *Blackwood's Edinburgh Magazine* felt that *The Course of Time* was "of deep and hallowed impress, full of noble thoughts and graphic conceptions — the production of a mind alive to the great relations of being."[6] An "Introductory Notice" to the poem predicted:

It is not an ephemera. It has in it the seeds of immortality. . . . The name of the Author will hereafter be associated with those of the noblest bards of England; even cold and careless readers will often mention it together with Cowper and Milton; and there will seldom be wanting those who will decidedly prefer the poetry of Pollok.[7]

About the same time, A. Norton of *The Christian Examiner and General Review* asserted, "The great popularity of Mr. Pollok's production is a sufficient pledge of its merit."[8]

For the most part, the public liked *The Course of Time* because it was a long poem filled with personal reminiscences; many read it as an autobiography, for they were especially intrigued with its author. The poem may be said to have value, first, as a narrative poem composed from personal experiences in the life of an extraordinary man. Readers were impressed with

> The lonely bard [who] enjoyed, when forth he walked,
>
> · · · · · · ·
>
> the distant tops of thoughts,
> Which men of common stature never saw,
>
> · · · · · · ·
>
> gazing through the future, present, past, [he]
> Inspired, thought linked to thought, harmonious flowed
> In poetry — the loftiest mood of mind.        (CT V, 360–96)

The poem was immensely popular for several decades. As George Gilfillan observed, "Still we do not think . . . that a tissue of wordy worthlessness would run like wildfire,— pass through some score of editions in less than eighteen years."[9]

If the public rationalized in considering The Course of Time great because of numerous editions, so did the publishers. William Blackwood, writing to his son William (March 13, 1827), said, "Pollok's Course of Time and Aird's Characteristics are two extraordinary books, and you will be better able to read them after reading the reviews in the June No."[10] Succeeding letters to William continued:

[Jan. 27, 1828] I published about a fortnight ago a second edition of the poem, and have already sold off the whole impression, consisting of 1500 copies. I have a third edition at press.
[June 30, 1828] Poor Pollok's poem, the Course of Time, has had a most extraordinary sale. I have disposed of four editions, making altogether nearly 6000 copies, and I am now printing another edition of 3000 copies. I have large orders already for copies, so that I expect to sell all these very soon.[11]

On December 13, 1828, Alexander Blackwood, in a report to his brother William, wrote, "We have had some very good selling books this season: of Pollok's Course of Time 12,000 copies have been sold, and it is selling as fast as ever."[12] By 1867, twenty-five editions had been published,[13] and in 1868 the seventy-eight-thousandth copy was published in Edinburgh. Perhaps equally as many copies were published in the United States, for more than twenty editions came from presses in New York, Boston, and Philadelphia.[14]

One of the earliest books illustrated by Blackwood, The Course of Time was "committed to the hands of Mr. Robert Lauder . . . who was wildly enthusiastic about it, knew half of the poem by heart, and threw his whole soul into the drawings."[15] In 1857 a gift edition was placed before the public — for twenty-one shillings.[16] The binding of red and gold design, indeed beautiful, complemented a book "profusely illustrated by the best talent which the art of Design can place at the service of Poetry."[17] The illustrations were by Birket Foster, John R. Clayton, and John Tenniel; they were engraved by Edmund Evans, Dalziel Brothers, John Green, and H. N. Woods. These artists (particularly John Tenniel, illustrator of *Alice in Wonderland* and *Through the Looking-Glass*) were admired and well known and probably received a good price for their work. (Some of the illustrations are remarkably like several in *Through the Looking-Glass*.) Of this illustrated edition, *Bell's Messenger* commented:

At last this superb poem has received an honour too long deferred, of being presented in a form commensurate with its intrinsic value. There has been no modern poem in the English language of the class to which *The Course of Time* belongs, since Milton wrote, that can be compared with it.[18]

## II

It is in this, its contrast with the work of John Milton, that *The Course of Time* would seem to have significance for the modern reader, for basically it is a Calvinistic version of *Paradise Lost*. In fact, Pollok deliberately referred to Milton (*CT* IX, 479–511) and actually quoted from *Paradise Lost* (*CT* VI, 68–69; IX, 507). The style is clearly imitative of *Paradise Lost*; particularly in the first two books, it is quite obvious that Pollok echoes Milton's sentence rhythms and many of Milton's expressions. Since from the age of eighteen, Pollok read from *Paradise Lost* almost every day,[19] it is little wonder that the two poems are so like in style. In theology and in structure, however, *The Course of Time* departed widely from *Paradise Lost*.

In holding that "every Christian must feel that *Paradise Lost* is not of a character to answer the great religious end in view," the editors of *The Spirit of the Pilgrims* were not alone.[20] A. Norton remembered that "The Reverend Mr Balwhidder . . . had the design of writing 'an orthodox poem, like *Paradise Lost*, by John Milton,' wherein he proposed to treat more at large of original sin, and the great mystery of redemption."[21] The implication of this passage is that since *Paradise Lost* was not an orthodox poem, someone needed to write one that was. Thomas McNicoll also thought that "notwithstanding [the] high general estimate of the *Paradise Lost*. . . . the author does not always surmount the great difficulties of his subject with . . . ease or with uniform success."[22]

Through his course of study at Glasgow University, Pollok became an "unhesitating Calvinist"[23] and found that he could not accept many of John Milton's ideas. His intention was to rewrite *Paradise Lost* so that "truth" would be presented satisfactorily. It was this, the religious fervor with which the poem was composed, that merited the highest praise. Observed *The Spirit of the Pilgrims*, "We are indebted to Mr. Pollok for having presented . . . some of the leading principles of the Orthodox faith."[24] In particular, *Blackwood's Edinburgh Magazine* (June 1827) praised *The Course of Time* as a work filled with the "sublime simplicity of our religion."[25]

Immediately the question arises, why would Pollok have considered *Paradise Lost* unorthodox? The relatively simple answer is that beginning with his divorce pamphlets (1643), Milton departed from dominant Presbyterianism. Repelled by Protestant "orthodoxy" that laid stress upon man's worthlessness instead of his worth, Milton set forth a basically non-Calvinistic, essentially non-Presbyterian creed. It was Milton's idea of free will, his attitude that man possessed a spark of the divine even after the fall, and his rejection of the doctrines of limited atonement, reprobation, and predestination that put *Paradise Lost* at variance with Presbyterianism.

One major doctrinal difference involved the controversy over predestination. Since God foresaw that man would fall, predestination, to Milton, extended only to the means of man's redemption:

> For Man will heark'n to his [the Devil's] glozing lies,
> And easily transgress the sole Command,
> Sole pledge of his obedience: So will fall
> Hee and his faithless Progeny: whose fault?
> Whose but his own? ingrate, he had of mee
> All he could have; I made him just and right,
> Sufficient to have stood, though free to fall.
> . . . . . . . .
> They therefore as to right belong'd,
> So were created, nor can justly accuse
> Thir maker, or thir making, or thir Fate;
> As if Predestination over-rul'd
> Thir will, dispos'd by absolute Decree
> Or high foreknowledge; they themselves decreed
> Thir own revolt, not I: if I foreknew,
> Foreknowledge had no influence on their fault,
> Which had no less prov'd certain unforeknown. (*PL* III, 93–119)

According to Milton, Christ offered mankind a general election. Christ's redemption was offered to all who would accept by their own free will, not to an elect or predestined number:

His [Adam's] crime makes guilty all his Sons, thy merit
Imputed shall absolve them who renounce
Thir own both righteous and unrighteous deeds,
And live in thee transplanted, and from thee
Receive new life.                    (*PL* III, 290–94)

But because of his unbending Calvinism, Pollok could foresee nothing but eternal damnation for non-Calvinists. Discovery in *The Course of Time* of basic Calvinistic tenets is no difficult task. Concerning predestination, John Calvin had written in the *Institutes of the Christian Religion*:

We call predestination God's eternal decree, by which he determined with himself what he willed to become of each man. For all are not created in equal condition; rather, eternal life is foreordained for some, eternal damnation for others. Therefore, as any man has been created to one or the other of these ends, we speak of him as predestined to life or to death. . . . God by his secret plan freely chooses whom he pleases, rejecting others. . . . as the Lord seals his elect by call and justification, so by shutting off the reprobate from knowledge of his name or from the sanctification of his Spirit, he, as it were, reveals by these marks what sort of judgment awaits them.[26]

Thus Pollok wrote of the divine foreordination of God:

Thou sitst on high, and measurest destinies,
And days, and months, and wide-revolving years;
And dost according to thy holy will;
And none can stay thy hand, and none withhold
Thy glory; for in judgment, Thou, as well
As mercy, art exalted, day and night.
Past, present, future, magnify thy name.     (*CT* VI, 669–75)

Even the elders do not understand God's foreordination:

The elders round
The Throne conversed about the state of man,
Conjecturing—for none of certain knew—
That Time was at an end.
They gazed intense
Upon the Dial's face, which yonder stands
In gold, before the Sun of Righteousness,
Jehovah, and computes time, seasons, years
And destinies, and slowly numbers o'er
The mighty cycles of eternity;
By God alone completely understood.     (*CT* VI, 436–46)

In the sanctity and glory of Heaven, according to Pollok, "naught but angel's foot, or saint's elect / Of God, may venture there to walk"

(*CT* I, 73–74). As could be expected of an "unhesitating Calvinist," the doctrine of reprobation was one of Pollok's strongest beliefs. Writing of the reprobate, Pollok described his hopelessness:

> And oft in dreams, the reprobate and vile,
> Unpardonable sinner, — as he seemed
> Toppling upon the perilous edge of hell, —
> In dreadful apparition, saw, before
> His vision pass, the shadows of the damned;
> And saw the glare of hollow, cursed eyes
> Spring from the skirts of the infernal night;
> And saw the souls of wicked men, new dead,
> By devils hearsed into the fiery gulf;
> And heard the burning of the endless flames;
> And heard the weltering of the waves of wrath;
> And sometimes, too, before his fancy passed
> The Worm that never dies, writhing its folds
> In hideous sort, and with eternal Death
> Held horrid colloquy, giving the wretch
> Unwelcome earnest of the wo to come.          (*CT* V, 584–99)

Still another objectionable doctrine in *Paradise Lost* was the doctrine of religious toleration (a corollary of the doctrine of general election), which Milton advocated to the point of implying that God's grace might be given even to Roman Catholics. In *Paradise Lost*, Milton suggested that Catholics might exist in eternity in a "Paradise of Fools" (*PL* III, 440–99), which is scarcely the same as hell. To Pollok, Catholics were not at all numbered among God's elect. He pictured the Catholic standing before God on Judgment Day:

> With crucifixes hung,
> And spells, and rosaries, and wooden saints,
> Like one of reason reft, he journeyed forth,
> In show of miserable poverty,
> And chose to beg — as if to live on sweat
> Of other men, had promised great reward;
> On his own flesh inflicted cruel wounds,
> With naked foot embraced the ice, by the hour
> Said mass, and did most grievous penance vile;
> And then retired to drink the filthy cup
> Of secret wickedness, and fabricate
> All lying wonders, by the untaught received
> For revelations new. Deluded wretch!
> Did he not know, that the most Holy One
> Required a cheerful life and holy heart?     (*CT* VIII, 195–209)

Specifically referring to the theological doctrines in *The Course of Time*, Pollok said: "It has my mother's divinity — the divinity that she taught me when I was a boy. . . . in writing the poem, I always found that hers formed the groundwork, the point from which I set out. I always drew on hers first, and I never was at a loss."[27] Reminders of the religious inheritance left by the Presbyterians in the hills of southern Scotland had permeated Pollok's life, for his mother was directly descended from the Covenanters of 1660–1688. Because he felt that *Paradise Lost* seemed not to "answer the great religious end in view," Pollok deliberately sought to write a poem "in which a Calvinistic poet shall represent his God."[28]

Weakened by his studies at Glasgow University, by pulmonary tuberculosis, a disease with which he had long been affected, and by an attack of rheumatic fever in March 1824,[29] Pollok must have recognized that he did not have much time in which to accomplish his purpose. Like Milton, Pollok first intended to become a minister, but overcome by physical weakness, he found himself unable to preach. Thus, in order to convey his message, he poured his years of study into writing.

### III

Pollok rewrote *Paradise Lost* into a narrative of "things to come / As past" (*CT* I, 10–11), altering three major elements of *Paradise Lost*: (1) he rejected the formulas for epic poetry that Milton used; (2) whereas Milton made all action in *Paradise Lost* lead forward and backward to the fall, Pollok pointed his complete poem to "the final doom of man"; and (3) Pollok replaced Milton's conception of the Trinity (Holy and unholy) with essentially Calvinistic theological ideas.

First, Pollok rose "fearlessly above the old artificial prescription for making up a poem."[30] Classical requirements for an epic poem placed stress, first, upon the word *man*. Homer began the *Iliad*, "An angry man — there is my story." Vergil began the *Aeneid*, "Arms, and the man I sing." Explaining the epic pattern of *The Faerie Queene*, Spenser wrote: "The generall end therefore of all the booke is to fashion a gentleman or noble person in vertuous and gentle discipline. . . . In which I have followed all the antique poets historicall."[31] Milton followed classical example in beginning *Paradise Lost* with the word *man:*

> Of Man's First Disobedience, and the Fruit
> Of that Forbidden Tree, whose mortal taste
> Brought Death into the World, and all our woe,
> With loss of *Eden*, till one greater Man
> Restore us, and regain the blissful Seat,
> Sing Heav'nly Muse.                    (*PL* I, 1–6)

Rejecting the classical formula, Pollok began *The Course of Time* with an invocation to the "Eternal Spirit! God of truth!" (*CT* I, 1). Actually, according to Pollok's theology, no such creature as a "vertuous man" existed after the fall of Adam. Pollok believed

> That man, that every man of every clime
> And hue, of every age and every rank
> Was bad, by nature and by practice bad.    (*CT* II, 296–98)

For this reason, according to Pollok, "who writes the history / Of men, and writes it true, must write them bad" (*CT* III, 735–36). Thus, instead of writing of one man, Pollok wrote of *all* men — from the creation of the world to and into eternity.

A second classical formula followed by Milton in *Paradise Lost* was the invocation of a muse. Milton began his epic with a prayer to the "Heav'nly Muse" (*PL* I, 6–13) — both Urania, ninth of the Greek muses and the patroness of astronomy, and the Holy Spirit. Pollok deliberately rejected a muse:

> The muse, that soft and sickly woos the ear
> Of love, or chanting loud in windy rhyme
> Of fabled hero, raves through gaudy tale
> Not overfraught with sense, I ask not.    (*CT* I, 13–16)

Pollok's reason for rejecting a muse was that "such / A strain befits not argument so high" (*CT* I, 16–17). A. Norton also felt that "The sacredness of his subject . . . led the author to reject all the profane arts of poetry."[32] Instead of calling to his aid the combined pagan and Christian muse invoked by Milton, Pollok prayed:

> Eternal Spirit! God of truth! . . . inspire my song;
>     .   .   .   .   .   .   .   .   .
> Hold my right hand, Almighty! and me teach
> To strike the lyre, but seldom struck, to notes
> Harmonious with the morning stars, and pure
> As those by sainted bards and angels sung,
> Which wake the echoes of Eternity.    (*CT* I, 1–26)

Like Homer and Vergil, Milton began *Paradise Lost* with a third common epic convention, a plunge into "the middle of things"— the point where the fallen angels who rebelled against God were "rolling in the fiery Gulf" (*PL* I, 52). Their foregoing crises Milton related later when Raphael described the war in heaven and the subsequent expulsion of the rebel angels from heaven.

Instead of beginning *in medias res*, Pollok made a major change in

Milton's narrative by beginning *The Course of Time* at the *end* of things. He opened his story at an indefinite point in eternity: "Long was the day, so long expected, past / Of the eternal doom, that gave to each / Of all the human race his due reward" (*CT* I, 29–31). Pollok created a beatified Spirit — a "Calvinistic divine"[33] — to tell two inquiring seraphs and another blessed spirit the story of "the course of time." The blessed spirit, newcomer to heaven from a distant world, had inquired about the place of torment that he had found when he veered off course in his flight toward heaven. Since the two seraphs who welcomed him to heaven could not explain the mystery, the three visited the beatified spirit. The beatified spirit related the fall, redemption, and final judgment of mankind — the full "course of time"— in explanation of the "final doom of man" recently seen by the newcomer to heaven:

> So shalt thou find, as from my various song,
> That backward rolls o'er many a tide of years,
> Directly or inferred, thy asking, thou
> And wondering doubt, shalt learn to answer, while
> I sketch in brief the history of man.          (*CT* I, 484–88)

This "brief sketch" of the "history of man" comprised the remaining nine books of *The Course of Time*.

Unlike Milton, Pollok had no desire to write an epic, a "windy rhyme / Of fabled hero . . . [a] gaudy tale / Not overfraught with sense" (*CT* I, 14–16). He envisaged a poem which would imitate "the solemn brevity of the sacred historian [Moses], never substituting the light of his own invention."[34] Thus, in imitating the brevity of Genesis, he accepted God's ways without subtle question or examination. In *Paradise Lost* Milton devoted 7,500 lines — three-quarters of his poem — to the story of creation, the fall of man, and the Son's redemption. In *The Course of Time* Pollok restricted the corresponding account in the "history of man" to only 152 lines (*CT* II, 1–152).[35]

The second major change that Pollok made in *Paradise Lost* involved "things to come" (*CT* I, 10). In his opening lines, Milton referred to Moses, "That Shepherd, who first taught the chosen Seed, / In the Beginning" (*PL* I, 8–9); Pollok referred instead to John, the prophet who saw "the future pass / Before him" (*CT* I, 5–6). For Milton's emphasis on Genesis — the beginning — Pollok substituted Revelation — the end. He considered Milton's avowed purpose in writing *Paradise Lost*, "That . . . I may assert Eternal Providence, / And justify the ways of God to men" (*PL* I, 24–26), to be improper, and he wrote *The Course of Time* so "That fools may hear and tremble, and the wise / Instructed, listen, of ages yet to come" (*CT* I, 27–28).

In *Paradise Lost* Milton restricted his description of the day of Christ's coming "in the Clouds from Heav'n" to seven lines (*PL* XII, 545–51). In contrast, Pollok devoted more than half of *The Course of Time* to lengthy, detailed descriptions of the Battle of Armageddon, the Millennium, the Resurrection, and Judgment Day. He also moved Milton's account of the war in heaven from the beginning to the end of time in order to present his belief in a Millennial Reign of Christ before the final Judgment Day.

In his account of the war in heaven, Milton mixed literal action with metaphorical details drawn from pagan accounts of ancient history. Milton's angels fought a battle similar to that told by Hesiod between the gods and the Titans; Milton's warriors literally

> pluckd the seated Hills with all thir load,
> Rocks, Waters, Woods, and by the shaggy tops
> Uplifting bore them in thir hands.          (*PL* VI, 644–46)

St. Augustine, St. Thomas Aquinas, and even rabbinical tradition accepted the idea of a conflict in heaven. In telling of an actual war in heaven, Milton combined Revelation xii with Revelation xvi so that the battle would be equated with the Battle of Armageddon.[36] Thus, the Battle of Armageddon, to Milton, had already taken place.

A strict Calvinist would have objected to Milton's use of classical writings and Revelation as proof that the war in heaven occurred before the beginning of time, for Calvin referred only to Peter and Jude in discussing the nature of the devils. Besides, Calvin had admonished:

what concern is it to us to know anything more about devils or to know it for another purpose? Some persons grumble that Scripture does not in numerous passages set forth systematically and clearly that fall of the devils, its cause, manner, time, and character. But because this has nothing to do with us, it was better not to say anything, or at least to touch upon it lightly. . . . Therefore, lest we ourselves linger over superfluous matters, let us be content with this brief summary of the nature of devils: they were when first created angels of God, but by degeneration they ruined themselves, and were made the instruments of ruin for others.[37]

Even though Pollok recognized that some form of pre-Genesis conflict may have existed (*CT* X, 156–57, 347–48, 433–36), he did not speculate upon the duration of the battle or in any way describe that war. In giving only a "brief summary of the nature of devils" Pollok was strictly Calvinistic.

Besides, Pollok believed that the last battle between the powers of

good and evil and a Millennial Reign of Christ would come before the
actual end of time:

> A time there came,
>
> . . . . . . .
>
> A time foretold by Judah's bards in words
> Of fire; a time, seventh part of time, and set
> Before the eighth and last, the Sabbath day
> Of all the earth, when all had rest and peace. (*CT* V, 788–96)

Then,

> The seven fierce vials of the wrath of God,
> Poured by seven angels strong, were shed abroad
> Upon the earth and emptied to the dregs;
> The prophecy for confirmation stood:
> And all was ready for the sword of God.        (*CT* V, 867–71)

Pollok did use Milton's description of the war in heaven in his own account of the Battle of Armageddon. Milton's war lasted three days; "Three
days the battle wasting slew" (*CT* V, 901), Pollok also declared. Following the vision or series of visions in Revelation, Pollok wrote of a battle
that raged to the extent that weapons were "drunk with blood," the blood
that "came out of the winepress [God's wrath], even unto the horse bri-
dles" (Rev. xiv, 20), in "Hamonah's vale" (*CT* V, 902–04), the symbolical
place near which evil is to be defeated (Ezek. xxxix, 16). By shifting Milton's war in heaven to the end of time, Pollok was able to include in *The
Course of Time* a detailed description of Christ's reign on earth during
the thousand years of peace following the Battle of Armageddon (*CT*
V, 907–1100).[38]

## IV

Pollok's rejection of epic conventions and his emphasis upon "things
to come" involved structural changes which distinguish *The Course of
Time* from *Paradise Lost*. Theological differences furnish a third major
contrast. Seeking to replace Milton's views of the Godhead with Calvinistic ideas of the Trinity, both Holy and unholy, Pollok expressed a religious point of view considerably different from Milton, whose God was a

> Fountain of Light . . . invisible
> Amidst the glorious brightness where [He] sit'st
> Thron'd inaccessible,
>
> . . . . . . .
>
> [So bright] that brightest Seraphim
> Approach not, but with both wings veil thir eyes.
>
> (*PL* III, 375–82)

Before the beginning of time God revealed to the angels his unrestricted gift of freedom of will to his creatures, declaring that he made man

> just and right,
> Sufficient to have stood, though free to fall.
> Such I created all th' Ethereal Powers
> And Spirits, both them who stood and them who fail'd;
> Freely they stood who stood, and fell who fell.    (*PL* III, 98–102)

In recompense, all God required was love and willingness to serve Him:

> I form'd them free, and free they must remain,
> Till they enthrall themsevles: I else must change
> Thir nature, and revoke the high Decree
> Unchangeable, Eternal, which ordain'd
> Thir freedom: they themselves ordain'd thir fall.
> The first sort by thir own suggestion fell,
> Self-tempted, self-deprav'd: Man falls deceiv'd
> By th' other first: Man therefore shall find grace,
> The other none: in Mercy and Justice both,
> Through Heav'n and Earth, so shall my glory excel,
> But Mercy first and last shall brightest shine.    (*PL* III, 124–34)

To Milton, God was a god of mercy. The ultimate force in the service of God was love.

Pollok presented a considerably different concept of God — a god of wrath and judgment. When

> the sons of men
> . . . . . . . .
> Beheld the glorious countenance of God,
> All light was swallowed up, all objects seen
> Faded; and the Incarnate, visible
> Alone, held every eye upon him fixed;
> The wicked saw his majesty severe;
> And those who pierced Him saw his face with clouds
> Of glory circled round, essential bright!
> And to the rocks and mountains called in vain,
> To hide them from the fierceness of his wrath.
> Almighty power their flight restrained, and held
> Them bound immovable before the bar.    (*CT* X, 377–89)

There was good reason for the wicked to seek shelter among the rocks and mountains (Rev. vi, 16), for, at the Day of Judgment, when God's angel decreed "that Time / Should be no more" (*CT* VII, 128–29),

> there was silence in the vault
> Of heaven; and as they stood and listened, they heard
> Afar to the left, among the utter dark,
> Hell rolling o'er his waves of burning fire,
> And thundering through his caverns, empty then,
> As if he preparation made, to act
> The final vengeance of the fiery Lamb.      (*CT* IX, 1178–84)

It was then that God, the eternal judge,

> Pronounced the sentence, written before of old,
> 'Depart from me, ye cursed, into the fire,
> Prepared eternal in the Gulf of Hell,
> Where ye shall weep and wail forevermore.'      (*CT* X, 446–49)

> the righteous heard the groan,
> The groan of all the reprobate, when first
> They felt damnation sure! and heard Hell close!
> And heard Jehovah, and his love retire!      (*CT* X, 484–87)

Justly punished by God, all "felon spirits" (*CT* VII, 266) were thus cast into hell, a literal place of torment where all those sinful beings must remain forever.

Pollok's hell was not in the center of the earth, as was Dante's; like Milton's, it was in space, but in a somewhat different location. The blessed spirit, newcomer to heaven, reported:

> Long was my way, and strange. I passed the bounds
> Which God doth set to light, and life, and love;
> Where darkness meets with day, where order meets
> Disorder, dreadful, waste, and wild; and down
> The dark, eternal uncreated night
> Ventured alone. Long, long on rapid wing,
> I sailed through empty, nameless regions vast,
> Where utter Nothing dwells, unformed and void.
> .   .   .   .   .   .   .   .
> This passed, my path, descending, led me still
> O'er unclaimed continents of desert gloom
> Immense, where gravitation shifting turns
> The other way; and to some dread, unknown,
> Infernal centre downward weighs: and now,—
> Far travelled from the edge of darkness, far,
> As from that glorious mount of God to light's
> Remotest limb,— dire sights I saw.      (*CT* I, 151–73)

Impelled by curiosity, the blessed spirit peeped over hell's fiery adamantine wall to behold

> beings damned for evermore,
> Rolling, and rolling, rolling still in vain,
> To find some ray, to see beyond the gulf
> Of an unavenued, fierce, fiery, hot,
> Interminable, dark Futurity!
> And rolling still, and rolling still in vain! (*CT* IX, 1170–75)

As George Gilfillan pointed out, "His Hell is not Milton's hell, nor Quevedo's, nor Dante's, nor Bunyan's. It is Pollok's own, and came to him in the night visions of his own spirit."[39]

Pollok's second major theological revision of *Paradise Lost* concerned the character of the Son. Milton maintained that the Son existed in the beginning, before the creation of earth. God, speaking to the assembled angels, announced the exaltation of the Son (*PL* V, 600–12) as God's vicegerent, exalted to sit on the right hand of the Father. As vicegerent, the Son was commanded by God to expel the rebel angels from Heaven (*PL* VI, 680–716) and to create another world, the earth (*PL* VII, 131–67).

Milton distinguished between Christ's generation, first in heaven, as the vicegerent, and second on earth, as the propitiator of man's sin. Pollok first attested to the generation of the Son on earth:

> When man had fallen, rebelled, insulted God,
>
> .  .  .  .  .  .  .
>
>          God was made flesh,
> And dwelt with men on earth! The Son of God,
> Only begotten and well beloved, between
> Men and his Father's justice interposed;
> Put human nature on.          (*CT* II, 129–41)

Thus, after man fell, God's Son was begotten on earth, "Making his soul an offering for sin" (*CT* II, 143). Pollok also rejected Milton's view that in heaven the Son was exalted as the vicegerent of God, maintaining that the Son did not share God's throne, for God sat alone:

> Of old thou builtst thy throne on righteousness,
> Before the morning Stars their song began,
> Or silence heard the voice of praise. . . .
>
> .  .  .  .  .  .  .
>
> Mysterious more, the more displayed, where still
> Upon thy glorious Throne thou sitst alone,
> Has sat alone, and shalt for ever sit
> Alone, Invisible, Immortal One!          (*CT* VI, 640–48)

In this instance, Pollok was more literally biblical than Milton; he used a literal interpretation here of Revelation iv, 9, v, 1–9, and xx, 11. The foremost difference between Milton's and Pollok's views of the Son was a matter of emphasis. Milton's Son was a victorious warrior who defeated the enemies of his Father. Pollok's was the Saviour of man, who went "to Calvary, / To be insulted, buffeted, and slain" (*CT* X, 345–46).[40]

The difference in Milton's and Pollok's treatment of the Holy Spirit was also a matter of emphasis. Instead of providing man with "spiritual Armor" (*PL* XII, 491), Pollok's Holy Spirit, "the third / In the eternal Essence" (*CT* II, 316–17),

> open[s] the intellectual eyes,
> Blinded by sin; . . . bend[s] the stubborn will,
> Perversely to the side of wrong inclined
> To God and his commandments, just and good.
>
> (*CT* II, 321–24)

Relying upon the Calvinistic doctrine of irresistible grace, Pollok thus assigned the Holy Spirit the role of extending the grace of God, or salvation, until "the last elect / Was born, [to] complete the number of the good" (*CT* VI, 490–91).

## V

The next major area of Pollok's theological revision of *Paradise Lost* concerned Milton's unholy trinity — Satan, Sin, and Death. After God appointed the Son vicegerent, Milton pictured Satan as sulking in his palace, the "Mountain of the Congregation" (*PL* V, 766) in the "Quarters of the North" (*PL* V, 689). Milton followed medieval theological tradition in describing Satan as being moved by pride to revolt against God. Since his theme was to "assert Eternal Providence, / And justify the ways of God to men," he sought to show that God's actions in punishing Satan were unquestionably just.

Pollok accepted God's actions without any attempt at justification. He did not try to explain, therefore, why Satan was filled with the pride that made him refuse to bow before God. Instead, he admonished,

> Ask not how pride, in one created pure,
> Could grow; or sin without example spring,
> Where holiness alone was sown.          (*CT* IX, 910–12)

Pollok merely represented Satan as a being who

> by other name, once [held]
> Conspicuous rank in heaven among the sons
> Of happiness, rejoicing, day and night.
> But pride, that was ashamed to bow to God,

Most High, his bosom filled with hate, his face
Made black with envy, and in his soul begot
Thoughts guilty of rebellion 'gainst the throne.

. . . . . . .

   the Devil chose to disobey
The will of God, and was thrown out from heaven,
And with him all his bad example stained.   (*CT* IX, 901–29)

Nor did Pollok attempt to explicate Satan's temptation of Adam and Eve. Rather, Pollok emphasized that, throughout "the course of time," Satan, "like a roaring lion, up and down / The world, destroying, though unseen . . . raged" (*CT* IX, 1004–5), tempting *all* men.

As Pollok was mute on the cause of Satan's rebellion, he also made no attempt to determine the origin of Sin: "Ask not how . . . sin without example [could] spring" (*CT* IX, 910–11). However, he did follow Milton in allegorizing Sin:

Oh, cursed, cursed Sin! traitor to God,
And ruiner of man! mother of Wo,
And Death, and Hell! wretched, yet seeking worse;
Polluted most, yet wallowing in the mire;

. . . . . . .

Thing most unsightly, most forlorn, most sad,
Thy time on earth is passed, thy war with God
And holiness.

. . . . . . .

Thou sittst in hell, gnawed by the eternal Worm,
To hurt no more, on all the holy hills!   (*CT* II, 474–93)

Pollok alluded to Milton's description of Sin's torment by the hell-hounds in one line: "Slander, the foulest whelp of Sin" (*CT* VIII, 716). Whereas Milton's Sin was tormented by hell-hounds, Pollok visualized Sin as being tormented by the perpetual gnawing of the "eternal Worm." His description of this "Worm" (conscience) recalls the gruesomeness of Milton's Sin:

Of worm or serpent kind it something looked,
But monstrous, with a thousand snaky heads,
Eyed each with double orbs of glaring wrath;
And with as many tails, that twisted out
In horrid revolution, tipped with stings;
And all its mouths, that wide and darkly gaped,
And breathed most poisonous breath, had each a sting,
Forked, and long, and venomous, and sharp;

> And, in its writhings infinite, it grasped
> Malignantly what seemed a heart, swollen, black
> And quivering with torture most intense;
> And still the heart, with anguish throbbing high,
> Made no effort to escape, but could not; for
> Howe'er it turned—and oft it vainly turned—
> These complicated foldings held it fast.
> And still the monstrous beast with sting of head
> Or tail transpierced it, bleeding evermore;
> . . . . . . . .
> A voice—from whence I knew not, for no one
> I saw—distinctly whispered in my ear
> These words: This is the Worm that never dies. (*CT* I, 183–204)

Pollok's caricature of the third being in the unholy trinity, Death, is also reminiscent of Milton's, although Pollok depicts this figure only indirectly:

> Who sees it once shall wish to see't no more.
> For ever undescribed let it remain!
> Only this much I may or can unfold.
> Far out it thrust a dart that might have made
> The knees of Terror quake, and on it hung,
> Within the triple barbs, a being pierced
> Through soul and body both. Of heavenly make
> Original the being seemed, but fallen,
> And worn and wasted with enormous wo.
> And still, around the everlasting lance,
> It writhed, convulsed, and uttered mimic groans;
> And tried and wished, and ever tried and wished
> To die, but could not die. Oh, horrid sight!
> I trembling gazed, and heard this voice
> Approach my ear: This is Eternal Death.     (*CT* I, 207–21)

Since his theme was "the final doom of man," Pollok naturally was more concerned with the man on Death's dart than with Death's relationship to Satan and Sin. Pollok therefore described Death more as the eternal foe of all men than as a member of the unholy trinity:

> Each son of Adam's family beheld,
> Where'er he turned, whatever path of life
> He trode, thy goblin form before him stand,
> . . . . . . . .
> With sithe, and dart, and strength invincible,

Equipped, and ever menacing his life.
He turned aside, he drowned himself in sleep,
In wine, in pleasure; travelled, voyaged, sought
Receipts for health from all he met.

. . . . . . . .

But still thy gloomy terrors, dipped in sin,
Before him frowned, and withered all his joy.
Still, feared and hated thing! thy ghostly shape
Stood in his avenues of fairest hope;

. . . . . . . .

Still, on his halls of mirth, and banqueting,
And revelry, thy shadowy hand was seen
Writing thy name of — Death.          (*CT* VII, 705–38)

## VI

To Robert Pollok, Death was more than dogma. As he described
Death, he was only reading the "handwriting on the wall" of his own
early death. During the composition of *The Course of Time*, Pollok was
bedridden most of the time. As Gilfillan suggested, his poem

is, verily, written with his heart's blood. We find the same quality in a work of
far more artistic, though fragmentary merit, written, too, by a dying hand, namely,
'Hyperion,' where the splendours are all hectic, and the powers projected forward from eternity.[41]

After *The Course of Time* was published on March 24, 1827, Pollok
was persuaded that he could afford a voyage to Italy for his health. In
the summer, he set out from Moorhouse, his home in Renfrewshire, Scotland, for Italy, but by the time he reached Edinburgh his doctors pronounced him too weak for the trip. Encouraged to go to southern England
instead, he proposed to rest at Southampton, where he found a cottage
at Shirley Common. He enjoyed the atmosphere for a few days, but by
September it became apparent that there was no hope for his recovery.
In the early morning, on Tuesday, September 18, 1827, at twenty-nine
years of age, Robert Pollok died, "exchanging, we trust, the fast bright-
ening blaze of earthly fame for the glories of Immanuel's land,"[42] amidst
eulogies of *The Course of Time*.

Besides its autobiographical interest, *The Course of Time* was at first
praised so exceedingly because it reflected the tone of early-nineteenth-
century sentiment. Pollok's affection for the humble folk of rural Scotland and his love of "Scotia's northern battlement of hills" (*CT* V, 486)
are traits of pure romanticism. A prime characteristic of the romantics,
a meditative love of nature, was clearly echoed in *The Course of Time*:

Nor is the hour of lonely walk forgot,
In the wide desert, where the view was large.
Pleasant were many scenes, but most to me
The solitude of vast extent, untouched
By hand of art, where Nature sowed, herself,
And reaped her crops; whose garments were the clouds,
Whose minstrels, brooks; whose lamps, the moon and stars;

. . . . . . . .

Whose banquets, morning dews; whose heroes, storms;
Whose warriors, mighty winds; whose lovers, flowers;
Whose orators, the thunderbolts of God;

. . . . . . . .

And from whose rocky turrets, battled high,
Prospect immense spread out on all sides round,
Lost now between the welkin and the main,
Now walled with hills that slept above the storm     (*CT* V, 340–56)

In what other age might these lines be placed, if not in the romantic period?

*The Course of Time* was widely accepted during the first half of the nineteenth century also because, like the revivalist movements then occurring in Great Britain and in America, it placed emphasis on "The second birth, and final doom of man" (*CT* I, 12). This poem, then, being an account of the life and firm religious convictions of "the Evangelical bard,"[43] offers to the twentieth century an explanation of the early-nineteenth-century religious milieu. By 1861, Thomas McNicoll recognized *The Course of Time* as "the Evangelical Epic" because it was representative of a neo-Puritan age.[44] Around the beginning of the nineteenth century, many people were deeply influenced by fundamentalism, a great religious movement emphasizing a return to beliefs of the Puritans. Spreading to America, the evangelical movement swept across the United States in the 1820s. Even the name of the magazine that reviewed *The Course of Time* most favorably, *The Spirit of the Pilgrims*, reflected the general return to orthodoxy. Hence, "Robert Pollok . . . intended to measure all literature against the strictest Evangelical standards."[45] This statement by Hoxie Neale Fairchild in 1957 is the generally accepted twentieth-century evaluation of Robert Pollok and his "immortal poem."

Clearly, *The Course of Time* was an important nineteenth-century poem. Its primary significance lies in its specific relationship to *Paradise Lost*. So far as doctrine is concerned, Milton might well have written such a poem had he not rejected Calvinism before writing *Paradise Lost*; Pollok's poem highlights the extent to which Milton actually departed from orthodox Calvinistic theology. *The Course of Time* gives to its reader an insight into the problems that Milton faced in rejecting Calvinism — and a much better realization of the greatness of *Paradise Lost.*

University of Alabama

NOTES

1. All quotations from *The Course of Time* are taken from Robert Pollok, *The Course of Time* (Philadelphia, 1864) and are designated in the text by book and line number. The quotations from *Paradise Lost* are from *John Milton: Complete Poems and Major Prose,* ed. Merritt Y. Hughes (New York, 1957) and are also designated by book and line number in the text.

2. Review of *The Course of Time, The North American Review,* xxviii (April 1829), 341–42.

3. *Blackwood's Edinburgh Magazine,* XXVII (April 1830), 677–78, and XXXVI (August 1834), 268.

4. Sarah Warner Brooks, *English Poetry and Poets* (1890), p. 492, as cited in *The Library of Literary Criticism of English and American Authors,* ed. Charles Wells Moulton (New York, 1935), V, p. 73.

5. Review of *The Course of Time, The Western Monthly Review,* II (November 1828), 354–59.

6. "Pollok's Course of Time," *Blackwood's Edinburgh Magazine,* XXI (June 1827), 846.

7. "Introductory Notice" to Robert Pollok, *The Course of Time* (Philadelphia, 1864), pp. xxvi–xxvii.

8. Review of *The Course of Time, The Christian Examiner and General Review,* VI (March 1829), 86.

9. "Robert Pollok," in *Sketches of Modern Literature, and Eminent Literary Men* (New York, 1846), I, p. 363.

10. In Mrs. [Margaret Oliphant Wilson] Oliphant, *William Blackwood and His Sons* (New York, 1897), II, p. 77.

11. Ibid., II, pp. 81, 84.

12. Letter from Alexander Blackwood to his brother William Blackwood, ibid., II, p. 94.

13. Ian Jack, *English Literature: 1815–1832* (Oxford, 1963), p. 597.

14. S. Austin Allibone, ed., *A Critical Dictionary of English Literature . . .* (1872; rpt. Detroit, 1965), II, p. 1618.

15. Oliphant, II, p. 269.

16. "Books Published by Messrs Blackwood and Sons, Edinburgh and London [advertisement]," in *The Ballads of Scotland,* ed. William Edmondstoune Aytoun (Edinburgh, 1858), I, p. 12.

17. "Memoir" to Robert Pollok, *The Course of Time: A Poem,* illustrated ed. (Edinburgh, 1857), p. xxiv.

18. *Bell's Messenger,* quoted in "Books Published by Messrs Blackwood and Sons, Edinburgh and London [advertisement]," in Aytoun, ed., *Ballads of Scotland,* I, p. 12.

19. David Pollok, *The Life of Robert Pollok* (1843), p. 19, as cited in Raymond Dexter Havens, *The Influence of Milton on English Poetry* (1922; rpt. New York, 1961), p. 411.

20. *The Spirit of the Pilgrims*, I (October 1828), 538.

21. Norton, review of *The Course of Time*, p. 86.

22. "Sacred Poetry; Milton and Pollok," in *Essays on English Literature* (London, 1861), p. 77.

23. David Patrick, ed., *Chambers's Cyclopaedia of English Literature* (Philadelphia, 1902), II, p. 792.

24. *The Spirit of the Pilgrims*, I, (October 1828), 525–26.

25. "Pollok's *Course of Time*," *Blackwood's Edinburgh Magazine*, XXI (June 1827), 846.

26. *Institutes of the Christian Religion*, 3.21.5–7, ed. John T. McNeill, trans. Ford Lewis Battles (Philadelphia, 1960), II, pp. 926–31.

27. "Memoir" to Pollok, *The Course of Time* (1857), p. ix.

28. Norton, review of *The Course of Time*, p. 93.

29. "Memoir" to Pollok, *The Course of Time* (1857), pp. xvi–xviii.

30. "Introductory Notice" to Pollok, *The Course of Time* (1864), p. xxv.

31. Edmund Spenser, "A Letter of the Authors Expounding His Whole Intention . . . to . . . Sir Walter Raleigh . . ." in *The Complete Poetical Works of Spenser*, ed. R. E. Neil Dodge (Boston, 1936), p. 136. H. T. Swedenberg, Jr., *The Theory of the Epic in England, 1650–1800* (Berkeley, 1944), pp. 53, 64–65, argues that emphasis on a "vertuous man" is the first requirement for an epic.

32. Norton, review of *The Course of Time*, p. 94. In rejecting classical or "pagan" mythology, Pollok represented a widely held theory that has a long history. The Dutch, in particular, objected to Milton's use of "heathen idols." See Herman Scherpbier, *Milton in Holland. A Study in the Literary Relations of England and Holland Before 1730* (Amsterdam, 1933), p. 84. Samuel Johnson, in his criticism of *Lycidas*, similarly objected to the presence of "heathen deities" in a Christian poem: see *Lives of the English Poets* (London, 1961), I, p. 96. The objections appeared frequently in eighteenth and nineteenth-century criticism.

33. Norton, review of *The Course of Time*, p. 86.

34. Walker, *North American Review*, XXVIII (April 1829), p. 346.

35. Adam and Eve's occupancy of the Garden of Eden is described by Pollok in forty-one lines (*CT* II, 37–77); he did not explain or discuss the actual temptation and fall, stating only that "Man sinned; tempted, he ate the guarded tree; — / Tempted of whom thou afterwards shalt hear" (*CT* II, 87–88). Pollok did not mention Adam and Eve again until, briefly, they are described as appearing at the Day of Judgment (*CT* VII, 496–500).

36. See Austin C. Dobbins, *Milton and the Book of Revelation: The Heavenly Cycle* (Tuscaloosa, Ala., 1975), especially pp. 26–52.

37. *Institutes*, 1.14.16, I, p. 175.

38. Calvin did not believe in the Millennium (*Institutes*, 3.25.5; II, pp. 994–995). In this, Pollok followed not Calvin but the Chiliasts.

39. *Sketches of Modern Literature*, I, p. 369.

40. This emphasis was also Calvin's. See *Institutes*, 2.12.4–5; I, pp. 467–70.

41. *Sketches of Modern Literature*, I, p. 366.

42. Ibid., p. 380.

43. Hoxie Neale Fairchild, *Religious Trends in English Poetry*, IV: *1830–1880, Christianity and Romanticism in the Victorian Era* (New York, 1957), p. 30.

44. *Essays on English Literature*, p. 97.

45. Fairchild, *Religious Trends in English Poetry*, p. 43.

# LANGUAGE AS WEAPON IN MILTON'S
## *PARADISE REGAINED*

## *Leonard Mustazza*

---

MOST CRITICS writing on Milton's *Paradise Regained* have focused on such important issues as the poem's epic structure and subject (some even question whether it is an epic at all), the nature of the debates, the poem's style (especially in contrast to *Paradise Lost*), the meaning of Christ's repudiation of classical learning, and the like. But few critics have explored what I consider to be an equally important issue—the extent to which the epic "conflict" concerns the nature and uses of language itself. Clearly, the epic battle in this poem, unlike that of any other epic, brief or diffuse, is fought almost exclusively with words. Moreover, words are used here not only as weapons, but sometimes as the fortresses in which Satan takes refuge and from which he tries to besiege his opponent, and sometimes as the prizes he offers his opponent in return for obeisance. The Son, of course, refuses such prizes and, armed with his own words as well as the Word, he proceeds to tear down Satan's linguistic fortresses until the Devil is left unprotected in "shameful silence" at the end of the second and longest temptation. The final scene, as we shall see, is somewhat different from those that precede it, for it is the least verbal. Rather, it is an "action scene" where pernicious words give way to overt violence both in Satan's homicidal placement of Christ on the pinnacle of the temple and in Satan's own plunge following it. In this regard, the last scene certainly contains the most dramatic and viscerally moving moments in the poem.

My objective in this essay is to examine Satan's uses of language against the Son and the Son's repudiations of Satan's offers, his assaults on false words by means of his own prudent words, and the silence toward which the poem inexorably moves: Satan's silence signifying defeat, and Christ's signifying both his victory over his adversary and his acceptance of the Father's will. Rather than consider the entire debate, moreover, I would like to discuss only those passages where the Son and Satan consider the uses and abuses of language itself, thereby showing their acute awareness (and, by implication, Milton's awareness) of the destructive and constructive uses to which language can be put. I want

finally to consider the effects of words on the protagonist and the antagonist, effects which can be discerned not so much from what they say as
from the narrator's descriptions of them between speeches. With respect
to Satan especially, these descriptions show most clearly the poem's movement from garrulity to silence, a movement which culminates in violent
action. Before we consider these points, however, it would be useful to
look at what others have had to say on this topic.

Although he does not treat language as such, Merritt Y. Hughes makes
an interesting point in one of his footnotes to *Paradise Regained*. He observes that whereas in Job Satan is called *Adversary*, in the New Testament he is often called *false accuser,* which is what the word *devil* means.[1]
According to the *Oxford English Dictionary*, *devil* is etymologically derived from the Greek word *diabolos*, which signifies "slanderer," "calum-
niator," "accuser," or "traducer." Of course, this point sheds an important
light on the verbal contest, especially if we consider that Christ is the
*Logos*, the Word made flesh. Hence, what we are listening to in the poem
is not merely a contest between Good and Evil, but also between the Word
and the Devil, whose name itself denotes linguistic dishonesty.

Lee Sheridan Cox, on the other hand, claims that Milton's primary
concern in *Paradise Regained* is with the "nature and office of the Word
incarnate and of the word."[2] Although her focus is on "food-word" imagery, and is therefore considerably different from my thesis here, she notes
that "word imagery encircles the poem,"[3] and she examines some of the
references I shall consider shortly.

Louis Martz also notices the language theme at work, although he
chooses to focus more on style than on Christ's and Satan's many references to language itself. He shows how Milton manipulates the different
styles in which the epic combatants speak, "a contest in which the flights
of poetic splendor are consistently drawn back by the prevailing net of
a frugal, georgic style to the ground of renunciation and temperance."[4]
I agree with Martz's assertions, but I would like to show that Christ's
words defeat Satan's not only by *how* he speaks (style), but also by *what*
he says about language.

Stanley Fish, finally, claims that there are two plots in the poem —
one dramatic or narrative, and one verbal: "On the verbal level there
is a progressive diminishing, first of the complexity of language and then
of its volubility, until finally . . . there is only silence. . . . Milton's heroes characteristically perform actions or make decisions which in context affirm the claims of God at the expense of the self until that self
exists only in terms of its reliance on God. And when that happens the
voice of the individual is heard no more."[5] Fish's point about the progres-

sion in the poem toward silence is somewhat similar to mine. However, although I agree with Fish that the subordination of self to God's will is at work in Milton's major poems, especially in the main plot of *Paradise Lost* and in *Samson Agonistes*, I do not think it operates in the same way in *Paradise Regained*. For one thing, Christ never places his interests above those of the Father; the concept of *kairos*, in God's time, is constantly operative in the poem. Moreover, since Satan is incorrigible and unregenerate, his defeat is not meant to be corrective, and his silence in the end is therefore not a yielding of his will (self) to God, but a defeat, pure and simple, by a higher power. Unlike Adam and Samson, he yields by necessity, not voluntarily.

As Lee Sheridan Cox says, word imagery encircles the poem, and, indeed, we begin to see the effects of words from the very beginning. First we hear John the Baptist, "the great Proclaimer with a voice / More awful than the sound of Trumpet" (I, 18–19), calling people to baptism, and after he has baptized Christ, the voice of God "From Heav'n pronounc'd him his beloved Son" (I, 32). Satan, who apparently has been present for these proceedings, is not affected by the "Proclaimer's" words, but the Father's words disturb him profoundly:

> That heard the Adversary, who roving still
> About the world, at that assembly fam'd
> Would not be last, and with the voice divine
> Nigh Thunderstruck, th'exalted man, to whom
> Such high attest was giv'n, a while survey'd
> With wonder, then with envy fraught and rage
> Flies to his place.                    (I, 33–39)

His distress at the divine proclamation is visible, and he flies off to confer with his fellow demons. Barbara Lewalski comments on "Nigh Thunderstruck" that "this metaphor also carries the further suggestion that in the present conflict Satan is and will be thunderstruck not by the power of God but simply by the voice divine, the Word."[6] To put it another way, unlike the conflict in heaven depicted in *Paradise Lost*, where Christ as the Father's agent forcibly conquered the rebel angels and ejected them from heaven, here the weapon will be language. If we look ahead to the end of the poem, we find that this idea of divine words being used to vanquish Satan really frames the poem, for in the angels' song at the end, the angels, in an apostrophe, tell Satan that Christ "all unarm'd / Shall chase thee with the terror of his voice" (IV, 626–27).

In turn, Satan's disturbing news greatly disconcerts the mid-air Consistory. Paralleling the Father's and the Son's replacement of force with

language to conquer the foe, Satan suggests to his fellows that to oppose
the Son they must use "Not force, but well couch't fraud, well woven
snares" (I, 97) — that is, linguistic stratagems and guileful words. The infernal throng, at least initially, is not sanguine about the prospects:

> He ended, and his words impression left
> Of much amazement on th'infernal Crew,
> Distracted and surpris'd with deep dismay
> At these sad tidings.                    (I, 106–09)

A great deal of irony pervades this entire first scene. The infernal Crew,
particularly their leader, are masters of linguistic guile. In *Paradise Lost*,
whose temptation scene is frequently recalled in the mid-air council, the
Father of Lies used seductive language to effect the downfall of Eve. In
*Paradise Regained*, however, we realize quite early that Satan is being
opposed with his own weapons, words. The devils are amazed, distracted,
surprised, and dismayed by their leader's words, and he is nearly thunderstruck by the Father's. "Their Great Dictator" (I, 113) will nevertheless try to oppose the Son with words, but in the end, when he places
Christ on the pinnacle, he does resort impotently to force, although he
acknowledges early on the inefficacy of such force.

The final aspect of this matter is an analogous "council in heaven"
(also reminiscent of parallelism in *Paradise Lost*), where God tells Gabriel that the time has come to permit Satan to tempt and "assay" the Son:

> To show him worthy of his birth divine
> And high prediction, henceforth I expose
> To Satan; let him tempt and now assay
> His utmost subtlety, because he boasts
> And vaunts of his great cunning to the throng
> Of his Apostasy.                    (I, 141–46)

Here we see very clearly the figures in the contest about to begin: the
Son, the Messiah of "high prediction," versus Satan, the boaster and
vaunter, the slanderer, the abuser of language. And underscoring the linguistic nature of the conflict is the song of the angels around the heavenly throne:

> Victory and Triumph to the Son of God
> Now ent'ring his great duel, not of arms,
> But to vanquish by wisdom hellish wiles.          (I, 173–75)

Although strictly speaking, wisdom and wiles need not be linguistic, they
mean little else in this poem.

Just prior to Satan's arrival in the wilderness, the Son, who has spent forty days there alone and fasting, is seen contemplating his true identity. His soliloquy reveals his questions about himself, and we discover that all he knows he has felt within, heard, or read about.[7] His self-examination leads momentarily to doubt:

> What from within I feel myself, and hear
> What from without comes often to my ears,
> Ill sorting with my present state compar'd.     (I, 198–200)

Gradually, however, he remembers that all his life his spirit has aspired to heroic acts — to free Israel from the Roman yoke, to suppress tyranny, to restore Truth, to establish equity on earth — and he also remembers the way in which he will effect these ends:

> Yet held it more humane, more heavenly, first
> By winning words to conquer willing hearts,
> And make persuasion do the work of fear.     (I, 221–23)

It is interesting to note that both Satan and Christ go about their work in exactly the same way. Neither considers force efficacious, and both seek to gain disciples with "winning words." This similarity, if such it can be called, is important not only because of the disparity in their intentions, but because the Son, by using words to save souls, is in effect redeeming words, which seem to have fallen along with Adam and Eve. Eve hearkened to the serpent's words, and therefore both the serpent and Eve, who tempted Adam after her own fall, have marred the purpose of speech. Now Christ will use words to redeem mankind and thus restore the integrity of language.

Satan first appears to Christ as "an aged man in Rural weeds" (I, 314) asking what Christ is doing in the wilderness and, of course, yearning to discourse with him. He claims to have seen Christ's baptism because those who dwell in the wilderness sometimes go into towns and villages to hear news. Characteristically, Satan's emphasis is constantly on "hearing." Nowhere does he say, as one might expect, that such country fellows go into town to *see* the sights; all of his interest centers on hearing things ("aught we hear" [333]), the curiosity to hear news ("curious are to hear / What happ'ns new," [333–34]), and hearing rumors ("Fame also finds us out" [334]). Christ's response to the "aged man" is surprisingly laconic and rude: "Who brought me hither / Will bring me hence, no other Guide I seek" (335–36).

This first response is important and suggestive in many ways. We learn shortly that Christ has seen through Satan's disguise, and his response here sets the tone of scorn with which he will treat his adversary.

Satan is scornful as well, but he will try to keep his composure and genial tone, and he is somewhat successful until the end of the second day, when he loses patience with his unyielding opponent. The Son, however, is never patient or cordial with Satan. Why should he be? Moreover, the Son's response reveals that the idea of *kairos* is present from the outset. His life is in the Father's hands, and he does things when the Father wills them done. Finally, the simplicity and dignity of his answer subtly evokes respect in the reader. We have seen that Satan uses gregariousness and garrulity to win confidence, whereas Christ means to use "winning words" to save mankind. Satan resorts to the usual tricks of his trade against the Son, but the Son needs no winning words here, for he does not seek to "save" Satan. Hence, his first response is short, to the point, not cordial.

Following quickly this exchange is the first temptation, and, once again, Christ's retort reveals his knowledge of Scripture, his great reverence for the Father, and his awareness of the power of language:

> Think'st thou such force in Bread? is it not written
> (For I discern thee other than thou seem'st)
> Man lives not by Bread only, but each Word
> Proceeding from the mouth of God, who fed
> Our Fathers here with Manna?                    (I, 347–51)

The combat has now been engaged. In his entire response to this temptation, (II, 346–56), the Son utters four sentences, three of which are rhetorical questions. These questions serve to express his scorn for Satan's intelligence as well as to taunt him. "Do you think there is force in mere bread?" "Do you not know what has been written in Holy Scripture?" "Do you think I don't recognize you?"— all of these questions (and Christ asks many rhetorical questions in his responses to Satan throughout the poem) reflect Christ's contempt for his adversary. Perhaps the Fiend's stratagems here and elsewhere seem brilliant to the reader, but not in comparison to the real wisdom of his opponent. What is more, as Cox points out, "in both Scriptural accounts of the temptation, Christ bases all of his rejections on the Word,"[8] and Milton follows the Gospels (Matt. iv, 4; Luke iv, 4) in this dialogue. By referring to Scripture, Christ suggests both his knowledge of and dependence on the Word of God, thereby emphasizing his own humanity, not his divinity. For if the Son were depicted as divine, he could not fall to Satan's temptations, and therefore there would be no epic struggle. Moreover, the Son's equation of God's words and Manna — God's words as sacred food, in effect — subtly contrasts with Satan's profane and mundane words and the mundane bread he requests.

Stanley Fish raises an interesting point about this first temptation and Christ's response: "Rather than deal with the issues Satan's challenge raises, Jesus seizes on what is almost a literary quibble to make a very special point. He takes 'save thyself' in its spiritual significance and proceeds as if hunger were not a reality but a metaphor. As a result the dialogue becomes a vehicle of *non*-communication; we hear two voices supposedly addressing each other, but they issue from wholly different points of reference."[9] Fish's point that language becomes a "vehicle for *non*-communication" is well noted, for Christ and Satan are in fact speaking on different planes of meaning. But then this question comes up: are they really trying to communicate with each other? As Fish often points out in his interpretations of Milton's poetry, the reader is an intricate component in Milton's art, and, if anyone is being communicated with, it must be the reader. Communication implies many things, including persuasion of one's auditor and some degree of understanding between communicants. Christ, however, neither seeks to persuade nor to understand his opponent (he understands him all too well); Satan seeks both to learn about his opponent and to persuade in order to entrap and destroy him. Thus, the only effect of Christ's words on Satan is to frustrate and enrage him. Fish makes us aware of the opponents' non-communication, but we must also bear in mind that the combatants are engaged in an epic battle of words—words that are meant to destroy the enemy.

Moreover, Fish's reference to a "literary quibble" is somewhat misleading. It is true that Christ seizes on the metaphorical meanings of "hunger" and "save" to make his point, but it is not so abrupt or incoherent a shift as Fish seems to imply. The line "Think'st thou such force in Bread" (347) serves as his transition between literal and figurative meanings, and this transition lends coherence to Christ's interpretation. For that matter, the Son provides similar interpretations in each temptation scene, for he constantly proposes prudent theological concepts and often substitutes metaphorical for literal meanings in Satan's mundane offers.

Many of Christ's and Satan's exchanges following the first temptation and the unmasking of the antagonist center on words, especially Satan's influence on oracles and his lying. Satan claims—although one knows that he does not truly believe it—that he has done the Father's work by, for example, tempting Job and placing lying, flattering prophets around Ahab:

> And when to all his Angels he propos'd
> To draw the proud King *Ahab* into fraud
> That he might fall in *Ramoth*, they demurring,
> I undertook that office, and the tongues
> Of all his flattering Prophets glibb'd with lies
> To his destruction, as I had in charge.      (I, 371–76)

In effect, he is saying that he and the Son do the Father's work, albeit using different methods. He tries to gain the Son's sympathy by claiming he works for the Father, with the Father's permission, and, in a way, this is true. What he fails to mention is that his lies and his inspiring others to lie are not designed, for his part, to help the Father, but to win those souls for hell.

Christ's response, as one might expect, is to expose Satan for what he really is, to bring truth to bear on the Adversary's half-lies, and to establish his own role as the silencer of oracles, and therefore of Satan. Constantly, the Son's emphasis is on language—lying oracles, silence, truth—and Satan's abuses of it. He begins by exposing Satan's lies and negating the role his opponent ascribes to himself:

> Deservedly thou griev'st, compos'd of lies
> From the beginning, and in lies wilt end;
> Who boast'st release from Hell, and leave to come
> Into the Heav'n of Heavens; thou com'st indeed,
> As a poor miserable captive thrall.          (I, 407–11)

Christ points out that although Satan was released from hell and permitted to effect the Fall of Man, as well as to roam the world, this is no reason to boast, for Satan is God's prisoner, his slave. As we saw earlier, God permits Satan to assay the Son, just as he permitted him to assay Adam and Eve, Job, and all men until this time. However, now he meets his superior, who will expose him and eventually defeat him.

Even more to the point, Christ acknowledges Satan's role as the influencer of oracles, but he also removes the respectable varnish with which Satan has painted over his true role:

> The other service was thy chosen task,
> To be a liar in four hundred mouths;
> For lying is thy sustenance, thy food.
> Yet thou pretend'st to truth; all Oracles
> By thee are giv'n, and what confest more true
> Among the Nations? That hath been thy craft,
> By mixing somewhat true to vent more lies.
> But what have been thy answers, what but dark,
> Ambiguous and with double sense deluding,
> Which they who ask'd have seldom understood,
> And not well understood, as good not known?      (I, 427–37)

This is, I think, one of the great speeches of *Paradise Regained*. Christ not only exposes his adversary here, but, in clear and direct language, he contrasts his and his Father's truth to his opponent's lies. What is more, with extraordinary brevity (a mere eleven lines), the Son conveys a great many ideas: (1) that Satan's service, although it works well into God's plans, was not solicited, but done for Satan's own gain; (2) that Satan is both the originator of lies, and lives on lies (here we see Cox's word-food metaphor); (3) that the world's oracles are influenced by Satan, but, again, for his own purposes, not God's; (4) that Satan's method, as we so often see in the poem, is to mix some truth with his lies in order to seduce and entrap the unwary; and (5) that Satan abuses language by investing words with dark, ambiguous, delusive meanings, which are seldom understood. This last point is particularly suggestive, for it shows Christ's direct awareness of Satan's abuse of language and, by implication, the correct ways in which words should be used. In effect Christ shows himself to be a linguistic theorist. One of the major themes of the poem here comes to the surface. Both Christ's and Satan's uses of language are, for the first time in the poem, shown and pitted against each other.

Finally, Christ announces that the days of the oracles will soon be over, and those who go, for example, to "Delphos" will find the Satan-inspired oracle mute. For Christ has come not only to redeem man and his language, but also to silence the oracles. Hereafter, he goes on to say, true oracles will exist only within the hearts of the pious:

> God hath now sent his living Oracle
> Into the World to teach his final will,
> And sends his Spirit of Truth henceforth to dwell
> In pious Hearts, an inward Oracle
> To all truth requisite for men to know.          (I, 460–64)

The concept of the "oracle within" should be familiar to readers of *Paradise Lost*, where the lost Eden is replaced with a "Paradise within" (*PL* XII, 587) for Adam and Eve and all their descendants. Christ as judge in *Paradise Lost* emphasizes this internalization process. For example, after he has judged Adam and Eve, the Son dresses them in the skins of beasts (*PL* X, 216–17), and he dresses their "inward nakedness, much more / Opprobrious, with his Robe of righteousness" (X, 221–22). He does a similar thing here with oracular words; he will silence the oracles, who derive their inspiration from Satan, and will replace them with internal oracles which dwell only in the hearts of the pious. Hence, language takes on an even newer dimension here, for in addition to its function of conveying truth outwardly, it will also dwell within the faithful.[10]

Of course, Satan cannot understand what the Son means, although he should understand. If we turn again to *Paradise Lost*, we hear Satan himself express the notion of the "hell within" in the Niphates soliloquy: "Which way I fly is Hell: myself am Hell" (IV, 75). The Satan of *Paradise Regained* is somewhat different from that of *Paradise Lost*. Milton's later Satan is a materialist, whose mind cannot (or at least does not) reach beyond what is immediately tempting and practical. Cox points out Satan's "lack of perception when he can praise the words of oracles and not hear the words of the 'living Oracle.'"[11] His first response is feeble rationalization for his actions:

> where
> Easily canst thou find one miserable,
> And not enforc'd ofttimes to part from truth,
> If it may stand him more in stead to lie,
> Say and unsay, feign, flatter, or abjure? (I, 470–74)

Again, all of Satan's supposed remedies for his misery concern the abuse of language. This is his attempt to "reason" with his unyielding opponent, and, of course, it fails. He then slips very smoothly from this lament into flattery, another linguistic stratagem:

> Hard are the ways of truth, and rough to walk,
> Smooth on the tongue discourst, pleasing to th'ear,
> And tunable as Silvan Pipe or Song;
> What wonder then if I delight to hear
> Her dictates from thy mouth? (I, 478–82)

That he is insincere, as all flatterers are, is clear to the reader and to the Son. But his professed delight in hearing the Son's truthful words is, in effect, a promise that he will return and try again. The battle lines are now distinctly drawn, and the antagonist will return for another attempt, this time with smoother language, a smoother appearance, and greater offers.

The language theme occurs only sporadically in Book II, which is taken up mostly with the second demonic council and the initial temptations of the second day. In the council, Satan tells his followers that the Son will not be as gullible a victim as Eve (not Adam, who "by his Wife's allurement fell," [II, 134]). This Satan is quite different from the boastful adversary of *Paradise Lost* and even from the Satan who appears in Book I of this very poem. He tells his fellows that he may well have found his match, and, if so, their demise may be imminent. Boasting has now given way to fear, and for once he uses language clearly and directly so that his followers will understand the present danger:

> Therefore I am return'd, lest confidence
> Of my success with *Eve* in Paradise
> Deceive ye to persuasion over-sure
> Of like succeeding here.                    (II, 140–43)

He eventually becomes more hopeful, however, when he seizes on a new plan — one that will also employ linguistic guile, this time in the form of offering popular praise, "Rocks whereon greatest men have oftest wreck'd" (II, 228). Apparently, he still fails to understand the power of his opponent and the real threat he poses. Earlier, Satan accused Belial, who wanted to tempt the Son with women, of judging others by what he himself likes. Now he proposes a plan that is almost as feeble. Satan, who has watched the Son for the past thirty years and suspects that he is about to enter the public phase of his life, thinks that no public figure can resist fame, especially one who has kept himself retired for so long.

But Satan does not offer fame first when he appears to the Son on the second day, "seemlier clad, / As one in City, or Court, or Palace bred" (II, 299–300). Using "fair speech," he offers the Son the sensuous (and sensual) banquet. This Christ quickly and economically rejects, condemning Satan's specious gifts as "guiles" (391). Satan then, as is his wont throughout the second day's temptations, "sweetens the pot," and offers riches, which Christ also rejects as specious and needless. The emphasis in Book II is not on language, but on material things. In Books III and IV, however, Satan's offers of langauge — both in terms of popular praise for the Son and his offer of eloquence — will build to a crescendo until, later in Book IV, Satan has no words left, and he resorts to overt violence.

Louis Martz regards the offer of riches as the center of the poem and the beginning of Satan's rhetorical attack: "From this steadfast center of the poem . . . Satan now attempts to move the hero by rhetorical and imagistic elaborations that gradually rise toward the height of Milton's grand style. The temptation of glory begins on a higher pitch of rhetorical insinuation than anything we have seen earlier, especially in contrast with the long, straightforward, temptation speech we have just heard."[12] Indeed, Satan, briefly at a loss for words, collects "all his Serpent wiles" and "with soothing words" tries again at the beginning of Book III.

As one might expect, he first uses flattery, praising Christ's words in another futile attempt to gain his sympathy:

> I see thou know'st what is of use to know,
> What best to say canst say, to do canst do;

> Thy actions to thy words accord, thy words
> To thy large heart give utterance due, thy heart
> Contains of good, wise, just, the perfect shape.    (III, 7–11)

Once again, Satan is lying in his own way, mixing truth with lies. All he has to say about the Son in these beautifully rounded phrases is true, but, of course, he does not believe these things, and, even if he does, his intention is to destroy the Son. Moreover, what better way to preface the offer of glory than with praise itself? Irene Samuel claims that Satan "first flatters the intellectual pride of his opponent, as the Sophist always flatters the instinct on which he plans to work,"[13] and Satan does become at this point every bit the Sophist "teacher," not only in his use of flattery, but also by "selling," as the ancient Sophists did, information that is useful for worldly success.

I think the temptation of glory is important for a number of reasons. First of all, Satan reveals himself to be rather foolish, for after all he has heard what the Son says about lying and flattery in Book I, yet he still persists in using flattery and offering the Son more flattery in the form of popular praise. Christ's rejection shows his irritation, and, in a voice radically different from that of Matthew's and Luke's accounts of Christ's ministry (perhaps closer to his voice in John's Gospel), the Son first criticizes Satan's arguments and then attacks the concept of popular praise itself:

> For what is glory but the blaze of fame,
> The people's praise, if always praise unmix't?
> And what the people but a herd confus'd,
> A miscellaneous rabble, who extol
> Things vulgar, and well weigh'd, scarce worth the praise?
> . . . . . . . . .
> And what delight to be by such extoll'd,
> To live upon thir tongues and be thir talk,
> Of whom to be disprais'd were no small praise?    (47–56)

This attack on the people has met with about as much critical dismay as Christ's later rejection of classical learning. Martz, for example, claims that Christ's response is bitter, out of line with his temperance, and hears in this tirade Milton himself voicing disillusionment over the Stuart restoration.[14] This may be, but we still must deal with Christ's words here. Does he hate the rabble, as some political leaders do? I do not think so. What he seems to hate is empty talk—flattery, lies, rumors, ephemeral praise, and the like—which is what Satan depends upon to do his work. To such praise, Christ opposes "true glory," the praise and applause of

God and his angels in heaven. External mundane praise is empty, like the riches Christ has already rejected: real riches must lie inward; true praise is God's alone. Hereafter, Christ's attacks on empty, ephemeral words will intensify.

Two more points need to be made about the language theme in Book III before we proceed to the crucially important aspects of it in Book IV. After Satan's temptation of glory is rebuffed, he stoops even lower than he has hitherto done, showing his stupidity even more. He "murmurs" (another sign of his weakness) the accusation that the Father seeks glory from men and angels for all his good works. In effect he accuses the Father of exchanging deeds for words, an exchange which depreciates the deed. Of course we are here reminded of Christ's reference to Scipio Africanus, who refused such mere words of praise (III, 101–04). Satan leaves himself wide open for Christ's response, which also concerns language. The Son "fervently" replies that the Father well deserves such glory, but glory is not the Creator's prime concern:

> since his word all things produc'd,
> Though chiefly not for glory as prime end,
> But to show forth his goodness, and impart
> His good communicable to every soul
> Freely.                                         (III, 122–26)

He goes on to say that such glory, in view of all that the Father has done, is easy to give.

Many suggestions are packed into these lines: the "murmurer" is being put down by the "fervent" respondent; empty praise is being pitted against deserved glory; ephemeral words of praise are being contrasted with "easy" thanks; and, by implication, vicious words are being contrasted with the "good communicable." Moreover, it is significant that Christ's references to the Father are concerned with language—the Father's creation of the world by his "Word," and the fact that the Father's goodness is verbally and nonverbally "communicable to every soul." Here we see most clearly Christ's redemption of language. Not only does he remind us that language, from the Father's mouth, has been used to create everything and everyone, but he shows that the "good" is communicable between God and man and, beginning especially with Christ's ministry, between man and man. The Satanic use of language is about to be superseded by the Christian use.

Finally, toward the end of Book III, Christ becomes somewhat exasperated with Satan's vain attempts to seduce him, and he once again uses clear, direct, unadorned language to expose Satan's schemes and to

comment on "time," an important theme in the poem. He begins by reiterating the uselessness of Satan's ploys, his "talk," to achieve the Son's
destruction:

> and in my ear
> Vented much policy, and projects deep
> Of enemies, of aids, battles and leagues,
> Plausible to the world, to mee worth naught.     (III, 390–93)

He then proceeds to comment on Satan's prediction that the predictions
about Christ will "unpredict" him — that is, the predictions will prove
erroneous, and the Son will be undone. Christ is playing with words and
again contrasting sacred words (the divinely inspired predictions of the
Hebrew prophets) with Satan's profane interpretation of these predictions (perhaps akin to the words of Satanically inspired oracles). Satan
cannot be expected to understand all Christ's meanings, but he does understand Christ's warning that when his time comes, Satan's time will
run out. This is what the Adversary has feared all along. Hence, the Son's
words again silence Satan, and Milton reveals his conscious manipula-
tion of this "silencing" theme in the closing lines of Book III, where Christ
makes "void all his wiles. / So fares it when with truth falsehood contends" (442–43).

The beginning of Book IV, of course, continues the temptation of
the kingdoms, which culminates in Christ's second biblical rejection at
line 175. Prior to this rejection, we hear what are pretty much reitera-
tions of Christ's and Satan's positions on language. When, for example,
Satan offers the Son Rome, whose rule he can obtain by expelling Sejanus,
old Tiberius' deputy, Christ's rejection includes, among other things, the
fact that such rule would perforce include his having to listen to the empty,
boring words of foreign emissaries:

> then Embassies thou show'st
> From Nations far and nigh; what honor that,
> But tedious waste of time to sit and hear
> So many hollow compliments and lies,
> Outlandish flatteries?                           (IV, 121–25)

He finds the hollow language of the court offensive. But even more offensive is the rhetorical tutor of the world's courts, and, as he did at the
end of his rejection of Parthia (III, 386–440), Christ includes in this rejection a direct threat to his adversary (IV, 125–29). For the second time,
the Son not only attacks Satan's language, but threatens him personally.

But in contrast to the end of Book III, where Satan is temporarily silenced, here he grows "impudent" (154), either not understanding or, more likely, choosing to ignore for the moment the Son's threat. He thinks that Christ's rejections and threats are nothing more than linguistic sparring: "Nothing will please the difficult and nice, / Or nothing more than still to contradict" (IV, 157–58). There is something here of the psychological defense mechanism of denial. He refuses to acknowledge the threat, which he seemed to be keenly aware of in both demonic-council scenes.

The impudence ends, despite all of Christ's rejections and threats, in Satan's announcement of his condition: the Son will have all the kingdoms of the world if he will fall down and worship Satan as his superior. The way Milton handles this scene is very interesting, for it exactly parallels the pattern of the Son's rejections of Satan's words, his claim to follow the Father's time, and his threat to Satan at the end of Book III.

He begins by having the Son attack Satan's "talk":

> I never lik'd thy talk, thy offers less,
> Now both abhor, since thou hast dar'd to utter
> Th'abominable terms, impious condition.          (IV, 171–73)

Stanley Fish makes the important point that "the drama of the temptation is counterpointed by the sustained attack on talk," and, indeed, we have seen Christ's repeated attacks on hollow words. Even more significantly, Fish claims that "Satan talks and talks and talks, and at every opportunity the Son displays his scorn for the productions of the tongue."[15] Here we see Christ's most overt attack on Satan's "talk."

The second point here is Christ's reiteration that he works according to the Father's time, not his own: "But I endure the time, till which expir'd, / Thou hast permission on me" (174–75). Thus, the Son's patience and his dependence on the Father are once again established.

The third part of the response is Christ's biblical answer to Satan (IV, 175–77). Again Milton follows the Bible's phrasing "It is written" (Luke iv, 8, Matt. iv, 10; Milton follows Luke's order), which also obliquely points to the language theme of the entire poem, for it emphasizes the repeated distinction between sacred and profane words.

The fourth and final aspect of this scene is the Son's threat to Satan:

> And dar'st thou to the Son of God propound
> To worship thee accurst, now more accurst
> For this attempt bolder than that on *Eve*,
> And more blasphemous? which expect to rue.          (IV, 178–81)

For the third time in some two hundred lines (III, 396–97; IV, 129; IV, 181), Christ links his attacks on Satan's words (or on Satanically inspired words) with a direct threat to his adversary, and the message is beginning to sink in. Satan remains silent in the first instance (III, 442), grows impudent in the second (IV, 154), and now answers apologetically "with fear abasht" (IV, 195). Although he is not frightened enough to desist, he is beginning to understand the power of his foe and the threat he poses. Barbara Lewalski writes that Satan answers fearfully "in an effort to placate Christ's formidable ire, and also to win continuing opportunity for his temptation."[16] I think Lewalski is right, but I also think that Satan actually is somewhat afraid at this point.

He grows bolder, however, as he begins the temptation of Athens. It is almost as though he derives strength and courage from his own words, and, as Lewalski points out, he makes his final offer "in the most persuasive and eloquent terms — in language itself evoking and imitating the elegance, nobility, and loveliness of the ideal described."[17] Instead of realizing that his rhetorical legerdemain will not work on *this* adversary, Satan uses his grandest language in his grandest temptation.

Satan begins the temptation of Athens by shifting grounds and claiming that he knows the Son is not inclined to the kingdoms of this world since they are transitory (he did not seem to think this on the offers of Parthia and Rome). He says he knows this because he watched the Son in his dispute with the Doctors earlier in his life, when he was

> addicted more
> To contemplation and profound dispute,
> As by that early action may be judg'd,
> When slipping from thy Mother's eye thou went'st
> Alone into the Temple; there wast found
> Among the gravest Rabbis disputant
> On points and questions fitting *Moses'* chair
> Teaching not taught.                                    (IV, 213–20)

He goes on to offer him "persuasion," with which to rule the Gentiles, hold conversations with them using their own terms, reason with them, and refute their "Idolisms, Traditions, Paradoxes" (229–34). And he ends by using a martial image for the language he will give the Son: "Error by his own arms is best evinc't" (235). This is not a new idea in the poem. Earlier, when Satan proposed in his council the necessity for wiles, not force, to combat Christ, and Christ announced that he would conquer the world not by force, but with winning words, both equated words with arms. Here, Satan proposes exactly what Christ had in mind earlier, but the emphasis is very different. Satan's word-arms only conquer the enemy in order to win a personal victory. "Satan's invitation to value talk," Fish writes, "is an invitation to value the self."[18] On the other hand, Christ's winning words, *his* word-arms, would serve to instill universal peace and to effect salvation after death. His word-arms would save the Gentiles, not destroy them.

Satan, of course, does not really understand Christ's real mission, save that his presence threatens him and his demonic crew. So he proceeds to offer the Son the learning of Athens: the Olive Grove of *Academe*, the schools of ancient Sages, music, odes, epic poetry, tragedy, oratory, and philosophy. He offers the Son what *he* thinks the Son wants, a monarchy within to prepare him for the monarchy without: "These rules will render thee a King complete / Within thyself, much more with Empire join'd" (IV, 283–84). This point is particularly suggestive, for it indicates that Satan's only knowledge of what the Son "wants" is derived from what the Son has said. Earlier the Son claimed that the monarchy within is better than external kingship, so here Satan incorporates that suggestion, thinking Christ wants both external and internal kingship. Hence he offers this knowledge of Athens not as a prize in itself — a materialist could never understand such a motive — but as a preparation for mundane rule.

Since so many of Satan's offers in the Athens temptation are related to language (eloquence, poetry, and the like), the Son's rejections naturally entail repudiations of such language. He begins with the general category of readings:

> However, many books
> Wise men have said are wearisome; who reads
> Incessantly, and to his reading brings not
> A spirit and judgment equal or superior
> (And what he brings, what needs he elsewhere seek)
> Uncertain and unsettl'd remains
> Deep verst in books and shallow in himself.     (IV, 321–27)

Much of what the Son says here is familiar to us by now, but some of it is rather perplexing. For example, Christ claims in his parenthetical comment (325) that the wise man who brings spirit and judgment to his reading really does not need to read since he already has the knowledge most men seek in books. Thus, for the wise, reading is redundant. What makes this comment even more perplexing is the fact that the Son himself seems to be quite familiar with biblical and classical works; indeed, up until this point in his life he has been a scholar. Are we then to conclude that he is not among the wise men he describes above? Since he clearly does possess such wisdom, the intent of this aside remains mysterious.

The Son then proceeds to become a literary critic, asserting among other things that the poetry of his native language sounds sweeter than that of the Greeks, that the Greeks derived their poetic eloquence from the Hebrews, that the Greeks "ill-imitate" the original, and that the portrayal of their gods is ridiculous. Even more to the point, the beauty of Greek verse, if it has any beauty, rests on the surface. It is all show and no substance:

> Remove their swelling Epithets thick laid
> As varnish on a Harlot's cheek, the rest,
> Thin sown with aught of profit or delight,
> Will far be found unworthy to compare
> With Sion's songs.                              (IV, 343–47)

Much rests below the surface of these lines. Many critics are disturbed by the Son's (or Milton's) repudiation of classical poetry, and, indeed, the lines are distrubing when they are taken out of context. First of all, it is somewhat misleading to assume, as many critics have, that the Son expresses Milton's sentiments here, and therefore to conclude that Milton himself is repudiating the study of those classics to which he devoted so much of his life. Such biographical extrapolation serves merely to break the fiction. Strictly speaking, Milton himself is no more the protagonist of this poem than he is the blind Samson or the blind poet-narrator of *Paradise Lost*. These *personae* are above all fictional, and to point out that one or another character shows what appears to be Milton's own sentiments is interesting, but dramatically superfluous. Christ *is* repudiating the classical arts, but that repudiation tells us little about Milton's own beliefs.

The second point about the Son's criticism also concerns dramatic context. We should not be surprised that Christ rejects classical learning because it is merely one facet of this second day's sweeping repudiation of virtually all the classical world's achievements — political, military, and artistic. The judgment the Son makes here is perfectly predictable in light of what has preceded it. Moreover, in light of the Son's constant attacks on the emptiness and dishonesty of Satan's words, what else can he do but condemn Satan's offer of eloquence? He knows that such language is empty, delusory, akin to Satan's verbal legerdemain, and eloquence of that sort he rejects.

Finally, Christ criticizes the Greek orators, "The Top of Eloquence, Statists indeed" (354), and he compares them to the Hebrew Prophets, who can better teach "The solid rules of Civil Government" (358). His praise of the Prophets and his criticism of the Orators is related not only to the subjects they teach, but especially to their medium of communication — oratorical style. The Prophets can teach (and instruction is the goal of the true orator) more effectively "In thir majestic unaffected style / Than all the Oratory of *Greece* and *Rome*" (IV, 359–60). Neither the subject nor the style of the classics is suitable for Christ's purposes. He therefore not only rejects the offer of Athens: he condemns it as useless, in much the same way as he condemned Satan's banquet in the wilderness at the beginning of this day. Satan earlier argued that Christ needed the right language in order to rule the Gentiles by persuasion. By this point, it becomes clear that he already possesses the "winning words" with which to win the hearts of the faithful, and the words that Satan tries to peddle here are useless to his purposes. Christ "has almost completely . . . undercut Satan's argument of persuading the heathen by means of their knowledge," writes Arnold Stein. "Christ has that knowledge and finds it inadequate for wisdom, as the concept of persuasion dependent on that knowledge is for him inadequate."[19]

Once again, Satan is silenced ("Quite at a loss, for all his darts were spent" [IV, 366]), and then he grows angry and says that Christ will be sorry for his refusals. Satan feigns disappearance, and waits for the Son to fall asleep so that he can trouble the Son's dreams. Words have begun to fail the Fiend; he can no longer use his linguistic wiles, and so he decides to resort to force. First he mounts a psychological offensive in order to weaken the Son's will for the third day's trial.

The Son's Satan-induced dream is significant in several ways. For one thing, it reminds us of Eve's Satan-induced dream in Book IV of *Paradise Lost*. There he is seen "Squat like a Toad, close at the ear of *Eve*" (*PL* IV, 800), using his "Devilish art to reach / The Organs of her Fancy" (801–02). He uses both flattering language and tempting images, as Eve tells Adam at the beginning of Book V. In *Paradise Regained*, however, the thrust is different. He has already tried flattering words and enticing images on the Son, and they have failed. Thus, the dream here is meant to frighten the Son, not entice him. So Satan raises around Christ "Infernal Ghosts, and Hellish Furies," "some howl'd, some yell'd, some shriek'd" (IV, 422–23). Articulate language has given way to howls, yells, and shrieks — irrational noises. When Satan's weapons were rational words, Christ fought him with better words. What does Christ now oppose to these inarticulate shrieks? Silence: "thou / Satt'st unappall'd in calm and sinless peace" (424–25).

The enraged Satan appears on the morning of the third day, in

Hughes's words, "as an ill-concealed murderer."[20] He claims that if the Son does not heed his advice, the "terrors, voices, prodigies" of the ominous night just past can be taken as a "sure foregoing sign" of his failure. The Son's response is by now quite familiar. He says that Satan's signs, "though noising loud," could not do him any harm, and therefore he never feared them. Just as the Son condemns Satan's words and offers, so he condemns his "noises." Satan's smooth words have now given way to noises, and finally to silence and "swoln rage" (499). Christ also ends in silence, the silence of peace and truth.

But the battle of words and Satan's final defeat are still not over. Once Christ is placed on the pinnacle of the temple, Satan scornfully dares him to stand, if he can, and then the Fiend tries to turn Christ's own weapons against him by quoting Scripture. According to Holy Scripture, he claims, God will command his angels to save Christ if he falls, and Satan prefaces this dare with a veritable parody of Christ's earlier words, "For it is written" (556). Christ is undanted by his tormenter and would-be murderer. He answers tersely, "Also it is written, / Tempt not the Lord thy God" (560–61). Although Milton has derived Satan's quotation of Scripture from the Bible (Matt. iv, 6; Luke iv, 10), he gives it added significance here by manipulating the linguistic contest — not only of words, but *about* words as well — throughout the poem. Satan thinks he is turning the Son's weapons on his foe, but in fact these prove to be his own final words before his fall. Christ has also uttered his last words, but again the contrast in the types of silence that prevail is quite striking. Whereas Satan is silenced, Christ remains silent; whereas Satan's word-weapons are all spent, Christ no longer has need for his. Finally, Milton ends *Paradise Regained* by emphasizing the language theme. He compares Satan's fall to that of the Sphinx, "that *Theban* Monster that propos'd / Her riddle, and him who solv'd it not, devour'd" (IV, 572–73), thereby again figuratively equating language and violence. Like Oedipus, who solved the Sphinx's riddle and caused her to cast herself from "th'*Ismenian* steep," the Son, "the divine Word, destroys the monster whose riddles threaten all human life."[21] Many critics have observed that this scene shows the inability of the adversaries to communicate. Hughes claims that Satan "cannot even understand Christ's plain words and unconsciously translates them into a kind of double-talk of his own."[22] Lee Sheridan Cox argues that "one of the reiterated implications in the New Testament and one of the basic points of Milton's poem is Satan cannot communicate with Christ: he lacks the language."[23] And Edward LeComte is even more emphatic: "Quite apart from his deliberate deceptions and lies, 'his weak arguing and fallacious drift' (III, 4), Satan is confusing and confused, a would-be Christologist who grapples with some real problems — and loses. Things of the spirit are beyond him, and the only way to convince him of anything (*convince* means *conquer*) is to . . . knock him down."[24]

I agree with these commentators, but would add one thing: neither Christ nor Satan ever tries to communicate, in any meaningful sense, with the other. Words for them are weapons designed to vanquish the foe. Satan is always on the offensive while the Son seems often to be on the defensive, but, ultimately, Christ wins the epic battle of words. At the end of the second day, we saw Satan's words lapse into the inarticulate yelling of his demons. And it is on this distinction between Christ's words and Satan's noises that the poem finally comes to rest in the angelic song addressing Satan:

> hereafter learn with awe
> To dread the Son of God: hee all unarm'd
> Shall chase thee with the terror of his voice
> From thy Demoniac holds, possession foul,
> Thee and thy Legions; yelling they shall fly,
> And beg to hide them in a herd of Swine,
> Lest he command them down into the deep.     (IV, 625–31)

Pennsylvania State University

NOTES

1. Merritt Y. Hughes, ed., *John Milton: Complete Poems and Major Prose* (Indianapolis, 1957), p. 483, 33 n. This edition is cited throughout.

2. "Food-Word Imagery in *Paradise Regained*," *ELH*, XXVIII (1961), 226.

3. Ibid., p. 229.

4. *The Paradise Within: Studies in Vaughan, Traherne, and Milton* (New Haven, 1964), p. 187.

5. "Inaction and Silence: The Reader in *Paradise Regained*," in *Calm of Mind: Tercentenary Essays on "Paradise Regained" and "Samson Agonistes" in Honor of John S. Diekhoff*, ed. Joseph Anthony Wittreich, Jr. (Cleveland, 1971), p. 27.

6. *Milton's Brief Epic: The Genre, Meaning, and Art of "Paradise Regained"* (Providence, R.I., 1966), p. 341.

7. It is interesting to note the degree to which the Son himself has been dependent on language. He does not know who he is instinctively, but learns gradually by means of conversations with his mother, discourses with Teachers of the Law, his readings of the Bible, and "searching what was writ / Concerning the Messiah" (I, 260–61).

8. "Food-Word Imagery," p. 225.

9. "Inaction and Silence," p. 34.

10. Another example of internalization is Christ's claim, later in the poem, that "he who reigns within himself, and rules / Passions, Desires, and Fears, is more a King" (II, 466–67).

11. "Food-Word Imagery," p. 237.

12. *The Paradise Within*, p. 190.

13. *Plato and Milton* (Ithaca, N.Y., 1947), p. 123.

14. *The Paradise Within*, p. 190.

15. "Inaction and Silence," pp. 39–40.

16. *Milton's Brief Epic*, p. 28.

17. Ibid.

18. "Inaction and Silence," p. 41.

19. *Heroic Knowledge* (1957; rpt. Hamden, Conn., 1965), p. 106.

20. Hughes, ed., *John Milton*, p. 479.

21. Ibid., p. 477.

22. Ibid.

23. "Food-Word Imagery," p. 241.

24. "Satan's Heresies in *Paradise Regained*," in *Milton Studies*, XII, ed. James D. Simmonds (Pittsburgh, 1978), p. 263.

# THE HEROIC TRADITION OF MILTON'S
## *SAMSON AGONISTES*

## *John Mulryan*

T HE TRADITIONAL elements of heroism in *Samson Agonistes* have always posed problems for the interpreters of Milton's work. *Samson Agonistes* is a Greek tragedy about a Hebrew judge, but the poem is chiefly neither Greek nor Hebraic. Most of the forms of Greek tragedy are observed, but the Greek dread and cynical acceptance of an indifferent fate do not dominate the tragedy. Many critics have also had difficulty accepting the Samson of biblical tradition as a viable protagonist for the work, because of his reputed brutality and thirst for revenge; and those critics who have looked to the classical tradition, in particular to the legend of Heracles, have fared little better; in effect, they have merely substituted a pagan womanizer and brute for a Hebrew one.

It is the purpose of this essay, yet once more, to attempt to disentangle the strands of Greek and Hebrew heroic tradition in the poem;[1] to demonstrate that Milton's choices of traditional elements for *Samson Agonistes* were judiciously made and deftly employed; to suggest that the two major figures that Milton selected from traditional lore as models for his Samson were indeed the biblical Samson and the Greek Heracles; and to point to a secondary but nonetheless significant employment of the legends of Oedipus and Sisyphus.

### THE BIBLICAL SAMSON

A review of Old Testament scholarship on the Book of Judges in general and on Samson in particular may prove useful in overcoming what has been a basically unsympathetic view, among literary critics, of Samson as a hero. The problem, for many critics, is a question of verisimilitude — how can a stupid ox like Samson, a selfish practical joker, be at once the "deliverer" of Israel in the Bible and the instrospective hero in *Samson Agonistes*?[2] Indeed the notion of the biblical Samson as a kind of thug or stupid muscle man has received almost universal approbation among Milton critics. Or, as Professor Anthony Low puts it, "In this century, critical opinion has emphasized almost unanimously that in *Samson Agonistes* Milton has cleaned up the originally disreputable folk hero of

217

the Book of Judges and made him presentable to his readers." J. H. Hanford says that "the hero of the Hebrew chronicle is a naïve and semi-humorous märchen figure, whose sluggish intellect is far removed from any capability of spiritual conflict." For D. C. Allen, he is "that primitive ruffian of a half-savage legend" whom Milton raised "to nobler heights than the compilers of the Book of Judges could possibly imagine." For A. S. P. Woodhouse, he is "the sanctified barbarian of the Book of Judges"; for Arthur Barker, he is the hero who, before Milton got to him, had no "awareness of new faculties that, as Hebraic Hercules, he stupidly never dreamed he potentially had." For G. A. Wilkes, he is "fumbling and uncomprehending"; for John Carey, he "finds self-fulfillment, as Harapha habitually does, in bombast and violence." For F. Michael Krouse, he is a "boastful brawler"; for Louis Martz, the "primitive hero." And W. R. Parker praises Milton because, from Parker's Hellenic perspective, "the prankish, rather fantastic fellow of the Biblical story never once puts in his appearance."[3]

Critics have also generally been in accord with the view that the Old Testament Samson seeks vengeance. Again, Low summarizes the difficulty: "Few aspects of *Samson Agonistes* have more disturbed the modern reader than its apparent insistence on the theme of vengeance." Woodhouse, in comparing *Samson Agonistes* with Hamlet, notes that "a dominant motive" for both is "revenge."[4] And Carole S. Kessner, the most recent and vocal exponent of this thesis, pursues the biblical Samson with a "vengeance":

The climactic verse 28 of Judges xvi renders the biblical Samson absolutely antithetical to Milton's imagined Samson: "And Samson called unto the Lord, and said, O Lord God, remember me, I pray thee, and strengthen me, I pray thee, only this once, O God, That *I may be avenged of the Philistines for my two eyes*" (italics added).[5]

As we have seen, many critics have dismissed the biblical account of Samson as too crude, barbaric, and incredible to sustain him as a hero or even as a man of sense. However, recent biblical research has taken just the opposite approach — depicting Samson as a witty character who was based on a real person, reasserting the fact of his judgeship, giving more credit to the Deuteronomist's ability as a storyteller. The problem of his supposed vengeance has been reinterpreted as a problem of translation: "deliverance" now takes the place of "vengeance" as the motivating force behind Samson's actions. Let us compare the old and new translations of the pertinent passage emphasized by Kessner:

O Lord God, remember me, I pray thee, and strengthen me, I pray thee, only this once, O God, that I may be at once avenged of the Philistines for my two eyes. . . . And Samson said, Let me die with the Philistines.     (xvi, 28, 30)

Lord Yahweh! Please remember me! Please strengthen me! Just this once! God! Let me deliver myself with one deliverance — on account of my two eyes — from the Philistines![6]

In his introduction to the Anchor Bible edition of *Judges*, Robert G. Boling explains the shift in meaning from vengeance to deliverance:

The verb *nāqam*, in the Hebrew Bible as in the Amarna letters, stands for the Suzerain's exercise of his executive prerogatives in the world — vindication, not "vengeance." The result of such vindication, in Israel as at Amarna, was deliverance. All this casts an entirely new light upon the tragic end of Samson's life, where the Philistines have unwittingly submitted themselves to Yahweh's judge, and Samson prays to Yahweh for deliverance.[7]

As Harris Fletcher and others have pointed out, Milton was conversant with Hebrew, and it is certainly within the realm of possibility that he understood the meaning of *nāqam* and employed it to spectacular advantage in *Samson Agonistes*.[8] Such intimate knowledge of the text, on Milton's part, might also explain why he never uses the term *vengeance* in any of his other writings on the biblical hero.

Where Boling has emphasized the lawfulness of Samson's action, James L. Crenshaw has upheld the power and depth of Samson's character, as well as the sophistication of the Hebrew narrative:

The Samson saga demonstrates Israelite narrative art at its zenith. . . . An author, or several perceptive writers, freely drew upon the full range of stylistic devices that constituted *belles lettres* in ancient Israel. . . . Heroes in this exciting age were not simpletons. Capable of considerable skill at repartee, Samson sought to impress Philistines with his wit. To do so, he chose the appropriate means — a riddle contest. . . . [It was] Essentially a test of worth.[9]

Thus, in terms of modern biblical scholarship, Hanford's references to Samson's "sluggish intellect," Allen's "primitive ruffian," Woodhouse's "sanctified barbarian," Krouse's "boastful brawler," and Wilkes's "fumbling and uncomprehending" hero simply cannot be supported. After all, as Crenshaw has pointed out, Samson does triumph over the Philistines most of the time, and as often by his wits as by his physical strength.

Therefore, within the biblical narrative, Milton would have found a strong, intelligent, resourceful hero who is loyal to his god and a distinguished exemplar of the culture from which he emerged. He does not appear to be introspective, but he is something of a loner, alienated by his superhuman strength from the Hebrews as well as from the Philistines. Still, his last act was a kind of passive resistance, attacking a building instead of the Philistines, delivering the Hebrews, as Christ delivered mankind, by taking death upon himself.

## THE LEGEND OF HERACLES

As we have seen, in examining the meager details of the Samson narrative in the Book of Judges, the account speaks volumes in its silence: unencumbered by editorial comment, the Bible leaves the poet free to develop his character in a variety of ways.[10] The Heracles legend, however, is almost never presented without commentary, whether in the Greek and Roman plays where Heracles appears, or in the pages of the mythographers, who write their own glosses on the classical texts. Thus Milton may well have noted, with all of the other students of Scripture of his age, the close resemblance between the account of Samson in the Book of Judges and the treatment of Heracles in the Greek drama, and then employed the Greek mode of commentary, but shifted it from Heracles and applied it to Samson.

The conventional analogy between Samson and Heracles has been well stated by R. C. Jebb:

The central idea of Samson's history, and, in harmony with that history, the central idea of Milton's poem, is the idea of a national champion, first victorious, then abased, then finally triumphant in a national cause. The feeling uppermost in Samson's mind is this—that the strength entrusted to him for the honour of God and Israel has, through his own weakness, been betrayed and crushed; and that the great cause which he was commissioned to uphold has thereby been dishonoured. When Samson has perished in the temple of Dagon it is Manoah's comfort that this stain has been effaced (448–71, 1669–1720). The central idea of the story of Herakles is that of a champion of the whole human race, persecuted throughout his mortal life by a cruel destiny. In his supreme agony—when the robe anointed by the unsuspecting Deianeira with the poisoned blood of the Centaur Nessus is burning into his flesh, as he writhes in his torment by the altar at Cenaeum, whence he is borne to his fiery death on Mount Oeta—his foremost thought is this, that the strength which had been used for all mankind has been overcome by an unworthy adversary through the workings of destiny. Samson in his death triumphs over the Philistines; Herakles in his last agony is the victim of fate.[11]

Jebb stresses the heroic Heracles, the champion of mankind; however, an analysis of individual plays reveals comic and sensual elements in the Heracles legend that Jebb does not take into account.

Sophocles wrote two plays about Heracles, the *Trachiniae* and the *Philoctetes*;[12] of the two, the *Trachiniae* offers the best parallel to the story of Samson; at the same time, however, the play reveals the limitations of the Greek hero and the superior heroic qualities of Milton's Samson. Where Milton's Samson is supposed to be a deliverer, he actually causes a great deal of grief for the Hebrew people; Heracles has no such noble calling, and his acts are even more negative than Samson's. Both heroes have difficulties with their women, but Heracles' Deianira, while she praises her husband's heroic qualities, often seems to hold him in contempt. When their son Hyllus notes that Heracles "served as bondsman to a Lydian dame [Omphale]," she responds with incredible cynicism: "Naught would surprise me if he sank so low" (70–71). Where Samson allows his life to be forfeited in order to obtain deliverance for his people, or, alternatively, satisfaction for the judgment of God, the Heracles of the *Trachiniae* seeks suicide as a respite from pain. Moreover, while Samson literally kills himself, Heracles is reduced to asking others to do him in. The cowardly, complaining Heracles of the *Trachiniae* bears little relation to Milton's Samson except by way of contrast. Milton's Samson cries out in anguish over his guilt and failure to act as God's elect:

> let me here,
> As I deserve, pay on my punishment;
> And expiate, if possible, my crime,
> Shameful garrulity.[13]                 (488–91)

Sophocles' Heracles never blames himself for anything and sacrifices both his dignity and his self-possession to the prospect of freedom from pain:

> For you I laboured hugely and spent myself, to free
> Your land from ravening beasts of prey and monsters of the sea;
> And now in long drawn agony ye leave me to expire.
> Will none of you deliver me with sword or kindly fire?
> .  .  .  .  .  .  .  .  .  .
>         look all of you
> On this poor maimèd body, and declare
> Was ever wretch so piteous as I.          (1011–14; 1079–81)

His sense of the ingratitude of his people is more highly developed than Samson's, but he also sees himself as a deliverer, and actually asks deliverance for himself (1013), knowing all the while that the hero stands alone in his trial. Milton's Samson is a majestic ruin; Sophocles' Heracles is a dying, dangerous animal.

In contrast to the *Trachiniae*, the *Philoctetes* of Sophocles presents a deified Heracles who reconciles conflicting personal goals and needs to the service of the state, calming Odysseus and Neoptolemus, reassuring Philoctetes. He serves both as the calm, detached deity and the suffering hero, reminding Philoctetes that his poisoned foot may be the gateway to Paradise:

> But first I'll mind thee of my own career,
> How, having laboured hugely and endured,
> I won immortal glory, as thou seest.
> Know that thy fortune like to mine shall be,
> Through suffering to glorify thy life.          (1418–22)

In *The Children of Hercules* of Euripides, the character of Heracles is emphasized less than the horrible aftermath of his deeds and the difficulty of assigning praise or blame to the various "heroes" who have survived Heracles himself.[14] Even the gods are suspect, for the great Zeus has allowed the family of Heracles to suffer egregious pain at the hands of Eurystheus, and his only boon is the capture of Eurystheus, to which Alcmena responds with the appropriate sarcasm: "Zeus, late on mine affliction hast thou looked; / Yet thank I thee for all that thou hast wrought" (869–70). Mere lip service is paid to the divinity of Heracles, for with its declaration comes the knowledge that he is wedded to a divinity, pursuing, as usual, his own pleasure:

> He hath died not!—to heaven hath risen
> Thy scion, great queen.
> Tell me never that Hades' dim prison
> His long home hath been!
> Nay, he soared through the flames leaping round him;
> And with honour the Spousal-god crowned him,
> And to Hebe with love-links he bound him,—
> Zeus' son to Zeus' daughter,—where glisten
> Heaven's halls with gold-sheen.          (910–18)

Alcmena does not even bother to reply.

Eurystheus, the "villain" of the piece, defends himself with dignity and courage ("Woman, be sure I will not cringe to thee, / Nor utter any word beside, to save / My life, whence cowardice might stain my name" [983–85]), and his villainy is further undermined by the bloodthirsty revenge of Alcmena: "Hence with him, thralls. When ye have slain him, then / To dogs 'twere good to cast him" (1050–51).

The net effect of the play is to reduce Heracles to human terms, perhaps even to emphasize the futility of his actions. Unlike Milton's Samson, who is surrounded by weaklings and well-meaning but ineffectual advocates like Manoa and the chorus, Heracles is dead, and the only real

courage is displayed by the old man, Iolaus. In fact, strength is dissoci-
ated from courage — mere girls like Macaica die without a qualm, while
the whole of Athens vacillates before the determined hatred of Alcmena
for Eurystheus.

   *The Madness of Hercules* by Euripides explores the paradox of a
strong man whose strength is his undoing. His strength allows him to ter-
rorize those who might prevent him from murdering his own wife and
children; it also adds an extra indignity to his suffering, for the strong
man must suffer in silence and live up to the persona of the hero that
has been thrust upon him by circumstance, as the exchange between Theseus and the weeping Heracles makes clear:

> Theseus: Art thou so all-forgetful of thy toils?
> Hercules: All toils endured of old were light by these.
> Theseus: Who sees thee play the woman thus shall scorn.
> Hercules: Live I, thy scorn? Once was I not, I trow!
> Theseus: Alas, yes! Where is glorious Hercules?          (1410–14)

Unlike Milton's Samson, Heracles is a religious skeptic, and thus can find
no meaning for his suffering except in the personal struggle for self-
determination:

> And Zeus, who'er Zeus be — . . .
>
>           .   .   .   .   .   .   .
>
> Ah, all this hath no pertinence to mine ills!
> I deem not that the Gods for spousals crave
> Unhallowed: tales of God's hands manacled
> Ever I scorned, nor ever will believe,
> Nor that one God is born another's lord.
> For God hath need, if God indeed he be,
> Of naught: these be the minstrels' sorry tales.
> Yet thus I have mused — how deep soe'er in ills —
> *"Shall I quit life, and haply prove me craven?"* (1263; 1340–48)

The Heracles of *The Madness of Hercules* is full of the anguish, suffering, and pride of Milton's Samson, but also salted with the bitterness of a
man without values that extend beyond the strength of his own personality.

   The tradition of Heracles represented thus far has been of Heracles
the ruthless and the powerful; in moving on to the *Alcestis* of Euripides,
we are confronted with Heracles the comic, the stupid, indeed Heracles
the generous, the good-hearted buffoon. Similarly, while Milton emphasizes the dignity of Samson, and what one might call his heroic sense of
loss, to the superficial eye he is an object of scorn and ridicule: filthy,
a slave, the most powerful of men overpowered by a weak woman, a stage

Israelite. For while it is true that Milton has chosen to isolate the most redeeming features of Heracles from the many strands of the tradition, even among the Greek tragedians there was always a hint of inappropriateness about Heracles—he might do just the wrong thing, or react as a creature of appetite when some more exalted emotion was called for. In the *Alcestis* of Euripides he does both—even in the midst of a heroic act, bringing Alcestis back from the dead for Admetus, he makes a pretense along the lines of his own grotesque imagination, saying that he has just won some woman in battle on the level of a horse or some other animal:

> Horses there were for them to take which won
> The light foot's triumph; but for hero-strife,
> Boxing and wrestling, oxen were the guerdon;
> A woman made it richer. Shame it seemed
> To hap thereon, and slip this glorious gain.          (1029–33)

He also pretends not to understand the grief of Admetus for the death of Alcestis, and reduces the loss of a noble woman to the lack of a bed partner: "How?—wilt not wed, but widowed keep thy couch?" (1089). This is the clumsy, grossly physical Heracles of the tradition, but even this Heracles is kind-hearted and means only the best. It is difficult to imagine the Heracles of the *Alcestis* following Milton's Samson in brooding over his sins, or sacrificing himself for someone else, but there is a certain sense of loyalty and generosity, even in this drunken hulk:

> O that such might I had as back to bring
> To light thy wife from nethergloom abodes,
> And to bestow this kindness upon thee!          (1072–74)

This is the Heracles who uses his brute strength to make amends for his boorishness, but who is also something of a boaster:

> But the man lives not who shall ever see
> Alcmena's son flinch from a foeman's hand.          (505–06)

But at the same time he does not linger for a celebration of his brute battle with Death, merely saying obliquely, "I closed in conflict with the Lord of Spirits" (1140). The drunken Bacchanalianism, which dominates the first half of the play, evolves into an account of a loyal friend who exchanges his few moments of respite from the mastership of Eurystheus for the praises of a friend. He wrestles with and defeats gods, but he has yet to understand fully even the affairs of men.

The final example of the Heracles tradition in drama is drawn from a Latin play, the *Hercules Furens* of Seneca.[15] Seneca leaves us with an ambivalent description of Heracles — he has many negative features, but Seneca does not depict them as such. The sense of awe and sublimity aroused by his character is reminiscent of the majesty of Milton's Samson, but the cruelty, the sheer danger of the man represents a different tonal approach to the hero than we find in Milton. One feels, somehow, that even the greatest of human beings, or demigods, can be crushed by fate.

Seneca reaffirms the majesty and power of Heracles, but at the expense of recording some unflattering speeches from the mouth of his enemy, Lycus, particularly the following:

Are we to call him brave from whose shoulders fell the lion's skin and club, made present for a girl, and whose side shone resplendent, decked out in Tyrian robes? Call him brave, whose bristling locks dripped with nard, who busied those famous hands with unmanly strummings on the tambourine, whose warlike brow a barbaric turban crowned? (465–71)

The speech of Lycus on Heracles' enslavement by Omphale resembles the taunt of Harapha to Samson; at the same time it exposes some of the more disgraceful accounts of Heracles, particularly his effeminacy, which Milton's Samson relates to his defeat by Dalila: "foul effeminacy held me yok't / Her Bondslave; . . . / What boots it at one gate to make defense, / And at another to let in the foe, / Effeminately vanquish't?" (410–11; 560–62).

It is interesting to note that the ego of Seneca's Heracles never sleeps. We are, after all, tricked into thinking that his delusions of grandeur would last only as long as the fit of madness was upon him. When Juno takes away his senses, he raves at heaven and threatens to hurl mountains at both heaven and the gods; but when he awakens, his first thought is of his own superiority: "Who has gained so great spoils of me, and has not shuddered at even a sleeping Hercules?" (1154–55); "ah, now my own weapons do I recognize. No need to ask the hand that used them! Who could have bent the bow or what hand drawn the string which scarce yields to me?" (1196–98).

Heracles' yearning for suicide is combined with a threat to pull the city down upon himself, much as Samson did in fact pull down their city upon the Philistines: "I shall find a path to death. . . . or else all the dwellings of Thebes with their households and their masters, the temples with all their gods, I will pull down upon myself and lie buried 'neath a city's wreck" (1245; 1287–90). One does not know how to respond to this — is it the agony of a man transformed to a dying animal, or the petulance of an adolescent trying to inflict hurt on others to compensate for his own rage and shame?

There is also a parallel between Manoa and Amphitryon: both fear that they have been cuckolded by a divine power. Amphitryon has two children, Heracles and Iphicles, but he learns from an oracle, before the children are born, that his wife has had intercourse with a god while he was away at war. By placing snakes in their cradle, he discovers that Heracles is really the child of Zeus. Similarly, Manoa becomes suspicious of his own paternity when an angel prophesies to him that his wife will bear the godlike Samson. However, even though he is supposed to be the father of the child, and there is no indication on Manoa's part of suspicion in either the Book of Judges or in *Samson Agonistes*, Josephus introduces this aspect of the story in his analysis of the Hebrew hero:

The woman, when her husband arrived, reported what she had heard from the angel, extolling the young man's comeliness and stature in such wise that he in his jealousy was driven by these praises to distraction and to conceive the suspicions that such passion arouses. But she, wishing to allay her husband's unreasonable distress, entreated God to send the angel again that her husband also might see him. . . . But the husband, on beholding the angel, even then did not desist from his suspicion, and he requested him to repeat to him all that he had revealed to his wife. (V. 279–81)[16]

Milton was no doubt aware of the account of Manoa in Josephus, and of the parallel account of Amphitryon in Greek legend, and while he did not draw directly from them, critics' perception of Manoa as ineffectual[17] may be related to Manoa's absurd posture as a potential cuckold.

Thus the Latin play reinforces and repeats many of the traditions of Heracles to be found in Greek tragedy. Its strongest resemblance to Milton's play lies in the Manoa-Amphitryon parallel, and the use of long, meditative, declamatory speeches. Neither *Samson Agonistes* nor *Hercules Furens* was intended for the stage, and thus both belong to the tradition of closet drama.

The dramatic tradition of Heracles was certainly available to Milton, and certainly used by him. However, there was another source of Heraclean lore, the mythographies and the emblem books, which provided symbolic interpretations of the myths, as well (in the case of the mythographies) as a summary of their different versions, from Homeric to late classical times. These accounts include views of Heracles not found in the dramatic tradition, views which may explain the cerebral orientation of Milton's Samson. For example, in Vincenzo Cartari's *Imagini*

(Venice, 1571),[18] and in the *Emblemata* of Alciati (Leiden, 1591),[19] Heracles is depicted as drawing men in chains emanating from his mouth. He is an aged, bald figure, but the power of rhetoric and wisdom, usually associated with Mercury, has compensated for his lack of physical strength. He is also a symbol of eloquence, a fact which may explain the fluid speeches of Milton's Samson, which have no precedent either in the biblical account of Samson or in the more traditional accounts of Heracles.

Even the more offensive acts of Heracles are allegorized and excused by Natale Conti in his *Mythologiae* (Frankfurt, 1581).[20] He attempts to impose a Christian interpretation of the violent acts of Heracles, and distorts the myth to make it appear that Heracles is actually conquering the passions that are the mark of the Heraclean hero:

Man must neutralize the first of all these monsters: pride, anger, arrogance, and the raging of the soul. This is the Nemean lion, and he grazes in the uncharted forests of our soul, and ravages all of our strengths. And even after these stirrings of the soul have been quieted, we do not move on to tranquillity for our entire life, for there are many hidden kinds of desires that rise up against us. Thus after he tamed the lion, the Thespian daughters were given to Hercules, and he deflowered them all in one night. ("Concerning Hercules," Vll, i, Y3)

Although Milton was aware of this Christianizing tendency in the mythological interpretations of Heracles, he remains constant to the pagan heroic tradition, and Dalila applies in vain for pardon and forgiveness, since pitiless anger is part of the greatness of the Heraclean hero, no matter how unchristian it might seem:

> And Love hath oft, well meaning, wrought much woe,
> Yet always pity or pardon hath obtain'd.
> Be not unlike all others, not austere
> As thou art strong, inflexible as steel.
> If thou in strength all mortals dost exceed,
> In uncompassionate anger do not so.                    (813–18)

But Dalila's plea falls on deaf ears, suggesting that strange mixture of pagan and Christian elements that dominates the action and defines the character of Milton's Samson: he espouses a Christian humility toward God but a pitiless, Heraclean anger against his enemies, and a Heraclean contempt toward the commonality. The Heraclean hero, as Eugene Waith has told us, goes his own way on his divine mission without regard for social pressures, and with a grand disregard of the consequences of his actions, particularly where women are concerned.[21] There is no need to elaborate here on the theme of feminine betrayal in *Paradise Lost*, or the imperviousness of Christ to female charms in *Paradise Regained*; parallels in the Heracles story which receive particular emphasis from the mythographers include his vengeful pursuit by Hera or Juno, a female deity often associated with Tyche or Fate, and the fact that women were forbidden to enter the temple of Heracles, a prohibition resulting from a time when a female devotee of the goddess Bona Dea denied Heracles water because no woman could serve a man on her special day.[22]

The mythographic accounts also give the lie to the narrow definition of Heracles as a musclebound warrior. Mental anguish and the tortures of the spirit are not the emotions we associate with such a type, but they are appropriate and salutary when they are lodged in the bosom of a judge of Israel, or a defender of virtue, a man of greatness of soul (and thus of mind) as well as body, a man like the Heracles Conti creates in his *Mythologiae*.

Obviously, there has definitely never been any other person who depicted the glory of virtue better than Hercules, the tamer of all monsters, bandits, and evil men; for to the extent that his name and glory were observed among all men, to that extent no state was able to cause any destruction. Temples, altars, sacrifices, and ceremonies were instituted in his honor. For no amount of family nobility, physical power, or imperial sway could compete with him without wisdom and greatness of soul. ("Concerning Hercules," Vll, i, V2)

Finally, the mythographic accounts of Heracles may suggest a new approach toward Harapha. Although Harapha is usually associated with the *miles gloriosus*,[23] it is at least possible that Milton was also thinking of Heracles' love of the taunting and cursing of his frightened enemies. Cartari provides an account of a man who would not and could not fight Heracles, and so cursed him instead, like the "Tongue-doughty Giant" Harapha (1181):

Hercules took by force from a peasant (who did not want to sell them) the two oxen the peasant was using to plow the earth, and he and some of his companions ate them. The poor man, desperate over the loss of his oxen, and not being able to exact any other kind of vengeance, turned to curse and blaspheme Hercules and to say all the evil things in the world to him and to his companions.

Hercules kept laughing at that, and said that he never ate with such delight as he did on hearing that one saying so many evil things about him. And when he was made a god the people of the country dedicated an altar to him called the yoke of the ox, and at a specific time they sacrificed a pair of oxen to him with the yoke on their necks. And the priest kept cursing all the time, and others that happened to be there, blaspheming, and saying all kinds of evil things; for they believed that that was the way to renew for Hercules the pleasure that he had had when he felt himself blasphemed and cursed by the peasant whose oxen he ate. ("Mercury," 2V2–2V2ᵛ)

### OEDIPUS AND SISYPHUS

A survey of the dramatic tradition would not be complete without a discussion of Milton's adaptation of Sophocles' Oedipus to the character of Samson. Milton's view of Samson as a suffering hero certainly owes something to Sophocles' *Oedipus at Colonos*,[24] and the parallels presented here indicate the eclectic nature of Milton's borrowings from Greek tragedy. The character of Oedipus, in his approach to his fate and in the background of his dilemma, is remarkably similar to Milton's Samson. Both are victims of a fate decided by others; both are alienated, concerned with old age and death, and guilty of broken promises. Where Samson fears that "a sedentary numbness [will] craze my limbs / To a contemptible old age obscure" (571–72), Oedipus poses a cynical acceptance of the same state:

> For I am taught by suffering to endure,
> And the long years that have grown old with me,
> And last not least, by true nobility.                    (6–8)

Where Samson is punished for breaking a vow made in his behalf (drink no strong drink, keep your hair unshorn), Oedipus is guilty of committing taboo acts (killing his father and marrying his mother) because others have concealed from him his own identity. Oedipus is also fulfilling the curse of the house of Labdacus, while it could be argued that Samson is being punished because "the children of Israel did evil again in the sight of the Lord."[25] In other words they are both scapegoats, taking the punishment of others upon themselves. They are further alienated and transported from their own lands, Oedipus from Thebes to Colonos, Samson from Israel to Gaza. Both are inimical to their own lands—Samson does not really liberate the Hebrews from the Philistines by his act of self-destruction,[26] and Oedipus can only bring a curse on his own land:

> "There," said he [Phoebus], "shalt thou round thy weary life,
> A blessing to the land wherein thou dwell'st,
> But to the land that cast thee forth, a curse."          (91–93)

> When time had numbed my anguish and I felt
> My wrath had all outrun those errors past,
> Then, then it was the city went about
> By force to oust me, respited for years.                  (437–41)

And Samson has experienced a similar fate, for his own people delivered him in bonds to the Philistines:

> I willingly on some conditions came
> Into thir hands, and they as gladly yield me
> To the uncircumcis'd a welcome prey,
> Bound with two cords.                    (258–61)

The emphasis on Samson and Heracles has caused critics to overlook another interesting parallel — that of Samson and Sisyphus. Like Samson, Sisyphus has revealed the secrets of the gods. Like Samson, he is a trickster (the father of the wily Odysseus),[27] a womanizer, and a talebearer. Where Samson blabs the secret of his strength in exchange for peace and the love of Dalila, Sisyphus tells Asopus that Zeus abducted his daughter Aegina in exchange for a permanent spring for Corinth. And while Sisyphus engages in the meaningless activity of pushing a stone up a hill, only to watch it tumble down again, Samson grinds grain like an animal, "Eyeless in *Gaza* at the Mill with slaves" (41). Where Samson uses riddles to outwit his foes, Sisyphus outwits the gods themselves, and defeats death through a well-planned ruse, as Natale Conti explains:

for he deceived the demons who say that he, dead, came to the underworld where he then deceived Pluto. Just before he died he ordered his wife to cast away his body without burying it. After she had done that he then begged Pluto to allow him to return to earth and punish his wife for so neglecting him, promising that he would return immediately. When Pluto consented, he went back to the upper world with no intention of ever returning to the lower world. ("Concerning Sisyphus," V1, xvii, R3ᵛ)[28]

Like Samson, Sisyphus had been favored by the gods and had returned treachery for preferment; as Conti puts it: "For in fact when Sisyphus had been made cognizant of the gods' secrets, he suffered a well-deserved, severe punishment for accepting their favors and then breaking faith with them" (Ibid., R4). Milton, alluding to the Sisyphus myth, makes a similar point:

> And expiate, if possible, my crime,
> Shameful garrulity. To have reveal'd
> Secrets of men, the secrets of a friend,
> How heinous had the fact been, how deserving
> Contempt, and scorn of all, to be excluded
> All friendship, and avoided as a blab,
> The mark of fool set on his front? But I
> God's counsel have not kept, his holy secret
> Presumptuously have publish'd, impiously,

> Weakly at least, and shamefully: A sin
> That Gentiles in thir Parables condemn
> To thir abyss and horrid pains confin'd.[29]          (490–501)

The chorus agrees with Samson's self-evaluation and the horror of his punishment:

> To violate the sacred trust of silence
> Deposited within thee; which to have kept
> Tacit, was in thy power; true; and thou bear'st
> Enough, and more the burden of that fault;
> Bitterly hast thou paid, and still art paying
> That rigid score.          (428–33)

Samson's desire for purposeful action, coupled with a contradictory yearning for inner peace, is mirrored in one of the traditional interpretations of Sisyphus, again cited by Conti:

Others believed that the stone of Sisyphus represented the zeal of man, the hill (or mountain) the course of human life, and the top of the mountain toward which Sisyphus attempted to push the stone as the tranquil and peaceful spirit; the underworld to be men, and Sisyphus to be the soul. ("Concerning Sisyphus," R4[v])

Thus, while Sisyphus or the soul exercises his zeal in pushing the stone along the "course of human life," to reach the "tranquil and peaceful spirit" of the mountain, away from the underworld or the concerns of men, Samson follows his heavenly destiny by using his divinely sent energy to crush the stones of the temple and escape from the Philistine underworld to the "calm of mind" promised to all who fulfill God's divine ordinance.

## CONCLUSION

It has been my purpose in this essay to survey the complexity and richness of the traditional materials of heroism that Milton drew upon in writing *Samson Agonistes*, and to suggest that earlier criticism has been forced to choose between a Hebraic and a Greek bias in evaluating sources. As an artist, Milton was no apologist for either tradition, and *Samson Agonistes* presents as fine an integration of rival traditions as one is likely to find. Samson, Heracles, Oedipus, and Sisyphus are all "loners"— flawed heroes rejected by their own people, punished by their gods, but still capable of positive action, even when that action appears futile, as in the case of Sisyphus. Both the biblical Samson and the classical Heracles are more intelligent and less barbaric than Milton critics have been willing to recognize, and as the play comes to a close, Milton's Samson, like the Hebrew judge and the Greek hero, has expiated his guilt, achieved true heroism, frustrated female treachery, excited the wonder and stilled the criticism of the mob, and regained his senses. He is now ready to depart this life, with "calm of mind, all passion spent" (1758).

St. Bonaventure University


## NOTES

I would like to record here my special thanks to John C. Ulreich, Jr., and Albert C. Labriola for reading and evaluating this paper before it was submitted for publication.

1. While some critics would disagree, it is my view that the materials in Aeschylus' *Prometheus Unbound* and the Book of Job function as persuasive analogues to Milton's *Samson*, but not within the heroic tradition as the term is employed in this paper; hence they are not discussed here.

2. On the problem of verisimilitude for the biblical poet, see Barbara K. Lewalski, *Milton's Brief Epic: The Genre, Meaning, and Art of "Paradise Regained"* (Providence, R.I., 1966), p. 73.

3. Low, *The Blaze of Noon: A Reading of "Samson Agonistes"* (New York, 1974), p. 36; Hanford, "*Samson Agonistes* and Milton in Old Age," in *Twentieth Century Interpretations of "Samson Agonistes,"* ed. Galbraith M. Crump (Englewood Cliffs, N.J., 1968), p. 18; Allen, "The Idea as Pattern: Despair and *Samson Agonistes,*" in ibid., p. 52; Woodhouse, "Tragic Effect in *Samson Agonistes,*" in *Milton: Modern Essays in Criticism,* ed. Arthur E. Barker (New York, 1965), p. 451; Barker, "Structural and Doctrinal Pattern in Milton's Later Poems: *Samson Agonistes,*" in Crump, p. 81; Wilkes, "The Interpretation of *Samson Agonistes,*" *Huntington Library Quarterly,* XXVI (1962), 375; Carey, *Milton,* Arco Literary Critiques (New York, 1970), p. 144; Krouse, *Milton's Samson and the Christian Tradition* (Princeton, 1949), p. 83; Martz, "Chorus and Character in *Samson Agonistes,*" in *Milton Studies,* I, ed. James D. Simmonds (Pittsburgh, 1969), p. 130; Parker, *Milton's Debt to Greek Tragedy in "Samson Agonistes"* (N.Y., 1969), p. 200; see also Murray Roston, "Milton's Herculean Samson," *MQ,* XVI, 4 (Dec. 1982), pp. 85–93.

4. *The Blaze of Noon,* p. 185; *The Heavenly Muse: A Preface to Milton,* ed. Hugh MacCallum (Toronto, 1972), p. 309.

5. "Milton's Hebraic Herculean Hero," in *Milton Studies,* VI, ed. Simmonds (Pittsburgh, 1974), p. 247.

6. In *The Anchor Bible: Judges,* introduction, translation, and commentary by Robert G. Boling (Garden City, N.Y., 1975), p. 247.

7. Ibid., p. 25.

8. Cf. Harris Fletcher, *Milton's Semitic Studies and Some Manifestations of Them in His Poetry* (Chicago, 1926), and two articles by Samuel S. Stollman, "Milton's Samson and the Jewish Tradition," in *Milton Studies,* III, ed. James D. Simmonds (Pittsburgh, 1971), pp. 185–200, and "Milton's Rabbinical Readings and Fletcher," in *Milton Studies,* IV, ed. Simmonds (Pittsburgh, 1972), pp. 195–215. It must, however, be admitted that the evidence of Hebrew scholars in or near Milton's time is against his understanding *nāqam* cor-

rectly. Both Johann Buxtorf (*Lexicon Hebraicum et Chaldaicum Complectens omnes voces* [Basel, 1615]) and Henricus Opitus (*Novum Lexicon Hebraeo-Chaldaeo-Biblicum* [Leipzig, 1692]) translate *nāqam* as "revenge." However, in the *Testamenti Veteris Biblia Sacra* (n. pl., 1607) of Franciscus Junius and John Immanuel Tremellius, a work well known to Milton (see *A Milton Encyclopaedia*, ed. William B. Hunter, Jr., et al. [Lewisburg, Pa., 1980], VIII), the authors suggest, in a note to the passage rephrasing Samson's prayer, that Samson is bringing the judgment of God upon the Philistines, rather than seeking his own revenge:

> Ac proinde virium, quas de integro tu in me instauras explicandarum commoditas tanta oblata est: fac ut iniuriam hanc mihi effossione oculorum illatam & damnum irreparabile quo me affecerunt ad vltiones tuas impedidendas, semel nunc demum praestent. (2D^v)

> [Since now so great an opportunity has been presented of unfolding the strength which you gave me anew, let them now finally pay for this injury inflicted on me through the ruination of my eyes, and this irreparable damage with which they have afflicted me, in order to impede your revenge.] (Translation mine)

And in the *Biblia Sacra Polyglotta* of Brian Walton (London, 1657; facs. rpt. Graz, Austria, 1964), the word has three different translations: *vindictam* (defense, vengeance) from the Syriac; *ultionem* (vengeance) from the Arabic; and *retributionem* (repayment, requital) from the Greek (*antapodōso, antapodōsin*, requital, to requite). See also Malka Milo, "*Samson Agonistes* et les commentaires bibliques," *Revue de littérature comparée*, XLIX (1975), 260–70.

9. *Samson: A Secret Betrayed, a Vow Ignored* (Atlanta, 1978), pp. 149–50.

10. On the lack of critical commentary in biblical narrative, see Herbert N. Schneidau, *Sacred Discontent: The Bible and Western Tradition* (Berkeley, 1977).

11. "*Samson Agonistes* and the Hellenic Drama," in *Milton: "Comus" and "Samson Agonistes": A Casebook*, ed. Julian Lovelock (New York, 1975), p. 181. See also Low, pp. 176–79, who elaborates on the similarities of the two heroes outlined by Jebb, and Woodhouse (*The Heavenly Muse*, pp. 297–98), who sees Christianity, and not Hebraism, as the element that distinguishes Milton's Samson from the Greek tradition.

12. All references are to the English translations by F. Storr in the Loeb series (Cambridge, Mass., 1967), and will be given in the text.

13. All citations of Milton's poetry are from *John Milton: Complete Poems and Major Prose*, ed. Merritt Y. Hughes (New York, 1957).

14. All references to the plays of Euripides are to the English translations of Arthur S. Way in the Loeb series (Cambridge, Mass., 1964, 1971), and will be given in the text.

15. All references to the *Hercules Furens* are to the English translation by Frank Justus Miller in the Loeb series (New York, 1927), and will be given in the text.

16. Flavius Josephus, *Jewish Antiquities*, text and trans. by Ralph Marcus, in the Loeb series (Cambridge, Mass., 1950), V, p. 127.

17. Cf. Nancy Y. Hoffman, "Samson's Other Father: The Character of Manoa in *Samson Agonistes*," in *Milton Studies*, II, ed. James D. Simmonds (Pittsburgh, 1970), pp. 195–210.

18. "Mercury," 2T3. All references are to my own (unpublished) translation of the *Imagini*, based on this edition. Signature references are to the Italian text.

19. 4th ed., ed. Cl. Mignault, emblem 180, p. 631. See also Achilles Bocchi, *Symbolicarum Quaestionum* (Bologna, 1574), II, symb. 43, pp. 92–93. This is the Gallic Heracles, first discussed in Lucian's *Heracles*, who connected him with the Celtic god Ogmios

and named him as the Celtic god of rhetoric; see the Loeb edition, trans. A. M. Harmon (New York, 1921), I, pp. 63, 65. The emblem also appears in the *Recueil d'emblemes divers avec des discours* of Jean Baudoin (Paris, 1638), pp. 532–41, together with a long prose analysis which paraphases, for the most part, the account found in Lucian, but without recognizing the humor. See also Arthur Henkel and Albrecht Schöne, eds. *Emblemata: Handbuch zur Sinnbildkunst des XVI. und XVII. Jahrhunderts,* 2nd ed. (Stuttgart, 1976), cols. 1651–52, and "De l'Ogmios de Lucien à l'Ogmios de Dürer," in F. Le Roux, *Les Druides: Collection mythes et religions* (Paris, 1961). On the relation of the Gallic Heracles to *Paradise Regained,* cf. Kathleen M. Swaim, "Hercules, Antaeus, and Prometheus: A Study of the Climactic Epic Similes in *Paradise Regained,*" *Studies in English Literature,* XVIII (1978), 137–53; Robert A. Stein, "Eloquence as Power: Another Dimension of the Hercules Simile, *Paradise Regained,* IV, 562–68," *MQ,* IV (1970), 22–24; and Lewalski, *Milton's Brief Epic,* p. 241.

20. All references are to the translation by the present writer and Steven Brown, to be published by Cornell University Press, and are to the Frankfurt, 1581 edition, the copy text of the translation. Signature references are to the Latin text.

21. *The Herculean Hero in Marlowe, Chapman, Shakespeare and Dryden* (New York, 1962), p. 24. See also John M. Steadman, *Milton and the Renaissance Hero* (Oxford, 1967).

22. See Conti, VII, 1, "Concerning Hercules," Y2, and Cartari, "Mercury," 2V4–2V4$^V$.

23. Cf. Daniel C. Boughner, "Milton's Harapha and Renaissance Comedy," *ELH,* XI (1944), 297–306.

24. All references are to the English translation of the *Oedipus at Colonus* by F. Storr in the Loeb series (Cambridge, Mass., 1968), and will be given in the text.

25. Judges xiii, 1 and *passim,* a habitual phrase used to describe God's disappointment with the conduct of the chosen people.

26. Crenshaw, *Samson: A Secret Betrayed,* pp. 136–37.

27. This is Conti's version. The accepted tradition is that Ulysses was the grandson of the thief Autolycus. Cf. *Odyssey,* 19, 394; *Iliad,* 10, 267.

28. It should be noted that Heracles also triumphs over death, not only on the funeral pyre, but also in his relationship with Alcestis, as Conti notes: "but it was also rumored that Hercules frightened away Death, when he came to the deceased Alcestis, and restored her to her husband alive, as Euripides wrote in the tragedy of Alcestis" ("Concerning Hercules" [Vll, i, X5]).

29. Hughes associates these lines with Tantalus rather than Sisyphus (p. 563 n.); however, unlike Sisyphus, Tantalus is not a trickster and does not cheat death.

# GRAECI CHRISTIANI:
# MILTON'S SAMSON AND
# THE RENAISSANCE EDITORS
# OF GREEK TRAGEDY

## Margaret J. Arnold

M ILTON'S DEBT to Greek tragedy and his adaptations of the tragic genre have received deserved attention.[1] But F. M. Krouse's suggestion of 1949 still awaits a critical response. Krouse states that we will understand Milton's use of his classical predecessors

> only when someone has carefully studied the Greek plays in the forms in which Milton and his age knew them. . . . No one has yet studied the commentaries in the Renaissance editions of Aeschylus, Sophocles, and Euripides to find what interpretations of their plays Milton was accustomed to. . . . Thus far we know nothing of Sophocles Christianus.[2]

This study is a preliminary attempt to read Greek tragedy in Krouse's terms, examining Renaissance editions and commentaries on four plays: Sophocles' *Ajax* and *Trachiniae,* Euripides' *Heracles,* and Aeschylus' *Prometheus Bound.* Milton was influenced by the observations of sixteenth- and seventeenth-century Christian commentators; however, he went beyond his reading to transform Samson into a figure "not less but more Heroic" by Renaissance standards than his classical predecessors.[3]

The commentators approached classical tragedy in general as work which contained fragments of truth but which was superseded by Christian revelation. Hugo Grotius, introducing passages from selected Greek tragedies and comedies, expresses the idea most clearly when he compares the Greek works to fragments of a shipwreck from which one may glean truths about "the one God, about his most pure nature separate from the world . . . about eternal providence, about freedom of choice in human actions . . . and about the true worship of God." However, one must add faith because "there are many things, especially concerning divine matters, which cannot be reduced to clarity by the investigation of reason alone."[4] In other words, Renaissance commentators read the tragedies in the light of faith. This study will compare Milton's Samson with such Christian readings of Sophocles' Ajax, Sophocles' and Euripides' Heracles, and Aeschylus' Prometheus. In general, commentators on the *Ajax* and *Trachiniae* saw Sophocles' heroes as men of great outward valor who were also great sinners, brought low by pride and lust. Annotators of Euripides' *Heracles* praised and pitied a man who, after a devastating shock, redefined his heroism. Commentators on Aeschylus' Prometheus considered the Titan a noble spirit and also a sinner, a type of Adam and Christ, and a character in a trilogy whose liberation would come through Heracles.

Milton gives Samson the outward strength of an Ajax or Heracles but has him repudiate his own pride and lust, substituting an arduous mental struggle for the Greek heroes' physical labors. From Euripides he borrows the concept of redefining heroism but makes Samson's task more difficult by placing the labor of expiation for a crime early in the play rather than at the end. From the annotations of the Renaissance Prometheus and from his own reading he adapts the concept of internal suffering and the analogies with Adam and Christ. In each case he also isolates his hero from family and friends, and — in the comparison with Prometheus — from the natural world. Finally, as though he were responding to speculations about Prometheus' place in a trilogy, he provides the reader with the scope of a trilogy in his treatment of Samson.

## I

To the commentators, Sophocles' Ajax and Heracles were figures of great outward fortitude who had not conquered their internal desires. The most frequently translated Sophoclean tragedy was the *Ajax*, in part because of the contrast of Ajax's *fortitudo* with Odysseus' *sapientia*.[5] Vitus Winshemius, pupil of Melanchthon and professor of Greek at Wittenberg, makes the two characters contrasting kinds of political figures, the martial hero who is ambitious for outward confirmation of his glory, and the "senator" who is modest and sympathetic to his enemies:

In Aiace, hoc est, homine militari, describitur immensa gloriae cupiditas, sive Ambitio & contumacia, ac impatientia repulsae, quibus vitiis plerumq; obnoxii sunt homines magnanimi. In Senatore vero, hoc est, in Ulysse, modestia in rebus secundis describitur, & compatientia in calamitate inimici, ac moderatio in cupiditate vindictae.

[In Ajax, that is, the military man, there is represented an immeasurable desire for fame, or ambition and arrogance that cannot bear rejection, flaws to which many great-souled men are liable. Truly in the senator, that is, in Ulysses, modesty in good fortune is represented and compassion for the injury of an enemy, and moderation in a desire for vengeance.][6]

Samson, to be a truly Christian hero, must serve both as the military leader and the man of *sapientia,* but he must not be guilty of the sins of pride and contempt of the deity attributed to Ajax. Georgius Rotallerus, Frisian lawyer and senator, calls Ajax "Deorum contemptorem" ("despiser of the Gods") and suggests that Athena's turning his *furor* toward the flocks at the beginning of the play is an example of God's care of the other Greeks.[7] Ioannes Lalamantius, after indicating Ajax's stature as a military figure in single combat with Hector, questions the nature of his fortitude since he loses self-control so quickly after Odysseus is awarded Achilles' arms, suggesting that Ajax had, perhaps, only a *simulacrum* of fortitude.[8] Related to Ajax as a man of fortitude and superior to him in his disdain of weapons and his use of his strength for all men is the Heracles of Sophocles' *Trachiniae.* However, he is a great sinner, brought low by his immoderate lust. Rotallerus, for example, sees him as a warning against intemperance in that vice: "Quam turpis, quamque noxia sit libidinum intemperantia, hic exemplo Herculis admonemur" ("Here we are reminded by the example of Hercules how unseemly, and how harmful is the excess of passions"),[9] and Winshemius attributes his fall to his "vaga libido" ("wandering lust").[10]

Samson is like Ajax and Heracles in his desire to choose the terms upon which he continues to live, and, if possible, to make further choices concerning his life and death. As Parker notes, Samson, like Ajax, does not wish to be seen.[11] Also, his ironic submission to the Public Officer (1403–07) echoes Ajax's deceptive acceptance of the mutability of human and natural processes just before his suicide in the *Ajax.*[12] Samson's stature as the Hebraic and Christian Hercules has been noticed by others.[13] What is remarkable is the way in which he outstrips his predecessors as they are presented in the Renaissance commentaries. In the first place, he repudiates their vices — the excessive pride of Ajax and the lust of Heracles — asserting that he is more free grinding at the mill than in loving Dalila:

> These rags, this grinding, is not yet so base
> As was my former servitude, ignoble,
> Unmanly, ignominious, infamous,
> True slavery, and that blindness worse than this,
> That saw not how degenerately I serv'd.     (415–19)

He has spoken of a time when his outward fortitude was intact; essentially he is making his present misery more heroic than the Herculean victories the Chorus has recalled. Further, Sophocles' Ajax and Heracles do not ask why they suffer. Substituting internal for external labors, Samson must speculate about his disproportionate shares of wisdom and strength (53–54, 206–08). In fact, he probes the mystery of creation and of human fragility:

> why was the sight
> To such a tender ball as th'eye confin'd?
> So obvious and so easy to be quench't.          (93–95)

It is true that he must move beyond such questions.[14] It is important, however, that, unlike his Greek counterparts, he is using his reason and opening his way to further thought, "for opinion in good men is but knowledge in the making."[15] Both Ajax and Heracles define the terms by which they live and impose their wills. Ajax, shamed, determines that "whoever is well-born must nobly live or nobly die" (479–80),[16] deciding to end his life rather than live in shame, and instructing his young son to live by his father's values (545–56). Heracles passes condemnation upon his unwitting wife Deianeira and imposes his will on his son Hyllus, in order to die by his own design on the pyre on Mt. Oeta and to order his son to marry Iole, the object of the father's own lust. Both Ajax and Heracles impose their wills and insist on their own terms, but there is no mental struggle. Samson, on the other hand, must constantly think and choose. First, when he might have blamed his mental slowness and when the Chorus' comments about female deception (210–11) might have allowed him to blame *eros*, he takes more responsibility than most readers would give him. He judges himself rigorously: "But what avail'd this temperance not complete?" (568). Further, he designs his life within narrow limits, drawing distinctions worthy of a judge rather than merely a strong warrior. His rejection of Manoa's offer is more than the rejection of an unheroic life: it shows a willingness to serve, even though Samson cannot see the goal of service:

> To what can I be useful, wherein serve
> My Nation, and the work from Heav'n impos'd.          (564–65)

To his countrymen he distinguishes between slavery and freedom:

> But what more oft in Nations grown corrupt,
> And by thir vices brought to servitude,
> Than to love Bondage more than Liberty,
> Bondage with ease than strenuous liberty.          (268–71)

To Dalila he draws the distinctions between true and false penitence (754), wickedness and weakness (834), love and lust (838), and true and false gods (898–99). He also reaches to the universal law of nature and of nations (889–90) to distinguish obligations to a spouse from obligations to a country.[17] To Harapha he defends his stature as a public person "rais'd / With strength sufficient and command from Heav'n / To free my Country" (1211–13) in contrast to the countrymen who gave him up. He has also answered his earlier tormenting questions. His strength, no longer "hung" only in his hair (59), is now "diffus'd / No less through all my sinews, joints and bones" (1141–42),[18] God, who has been silent, is one "Whose ear is ever open; and his eye / Gracious to re-admit the suppliant" (1172–73). Moreover, Samson's contrast with Ajax, Heracles, and Prometheus is marked when, instead of feeling shame, he invites Harapha to stare carefully at him (1229). To the demands of the Public Officer, too, he uses his reason as a judge, explaining the lawful use of his strength in the service of his enemies:

> but by labor
> Honest and lawful to deserve my food
> Of those who have me in thir civil power. (1365–67)

He retains a sense of his own dignity while showing his private remorse when he refuses

> to be thir fool or jester
> And in my midst of sorrow and heart-grief
> To show them feats, and play before thir god. (1338–40)

Only when he has labored inwardly to the full extent of his human powers, accepting due blame, defining civil and moral terms, choosing God and choosing to live on his own terms, do the "rousing motions" summon him to his final triumphant service. He has used his mind freely, only to answer a call for obedience to a God no classical hero is asked to serve. When the Chorus sings of "plain heroic magnitude of mind" they testify, in their partial view, to Samson's transcendence of divided *sapientia* and *fortitudo* to attain true magnanimity, "when in the seeking or avoiding, the acceptance or refusal of riches, advantages, or honors, we are actuated by a regard to our own dignity, rightly understood."[19] John Steadman has clearly expressed the internal nature of Samson's heroism:

His drama is largely a drama of the mind; his story a narrative of spiritual crisis. . . . he stresses the inner conquests that precede heroic action. . . . Milton portrays his hero's virtue not simply in deed but, first and foremost, in analysis and choice.[20]

It is important, though, that Milton, as if responding to the classical tragedies, has his hero repudiate the vices of Ajax and Heracles and con-

vert their outward intransigence to the stubborn inward dignity with
which Samson maintains his position.

## II

Before considering the significance of other elements of the *Ajax* and
the *Trachiniae* Milton chose not to use, one must add Euripides' *Heracles*
to the classical models he transformed. The commentators did not condemn the pride or lust of Euripides' hero; they pitied him. Gasparus
Stiblinus, whose commentary is printed in Milton's copy of Euripides,
refers to the *Heracles'* sad and deadly reversals ("spectes funestas et atroces
rerum conversiones"),[21] noting that Heracles has just been celebrated for
saving his family from a tyrant when he is stricken with *ate*, kills his wife
and children, and wishes to kill himself. Although Samson's heroism ultimately transcends that of Heracles, several of Stiblinus' comments provide useful comparisons. For instance, he sees in the persecution of
Heracles' family the willingness of nations in general to forget the services of great men, a weakness with which Samson reproaches his people,
who gave him up when his "deeds themselves, though mute, spoke loud
the doer" (247). Further, Stiblinus internalizes Heracles' attack by Madness, suggesting that she represents the torments of conscience: "nihil aliud
quam horrores, tumultus et cruciatus inquietae conscientiae" ("nothing
other than the terrors, disturbances, and afflictions of a restless conscience").[22] Carole Kessner rightly sees Euripides' hero as one whose darkness, care for his father, and internal growth compare with Samson's,[23]
but Samson, in contrast to Heracles, must fight his battle alone. The commentators praise Heracles for choosing to live on in his weakness, but
he has the understanding support of his father, Amphitryon, and the bond
of *philia* Theseus extends to him.[24] Milton himself paid tribute to friends
by quoting Theseus from Euripides' play:

> Lend your hand to your devoted friend.
> Throw your arm around my neck, and I will conduct you
>     on the way.[25]                                               (1398–1402)

Samson gains stature, in comparison, because he must instruct his father
and because he is isolated, without a *philos*. Also, even though Heracles
redefines the Olympian powers which have destroyed him, uttering a proverb the commentators often draw attention to, "If God is truly God, he
has need of nothing" (1345–46), he does not draw strength from faith
but from human ties. The Renaissance commentators indicate that his
final journey to Athens is to expiate his crime.[26] In a sense, he ends his

growth with expiation while Samson begins the process of expiation for sin early in the action of *Samson Agonistes* when he resolves to

> pay on my punishment;
> And expiate, if possible, my crime,
> Shameful garrulity.                    (489–91)

Samson has yet to face Dalila, Harapha, the Public Officer, and the Philistine multitudes alone.

Thus, Samson must repudiate sins Sophocles' Ajax and Sophocles' and Euripides' Heracles do not acknowledge, and fight stronger mental and spiritual battles than they do. Further, his isolation deserves emphasis because Milton achieves an effect of timelessness by removing his hero from figures in an earthly community.[27] Amphitryon's role in Heracles' recovery has been observed, but it is worth fuller comment. In a sense Heracles learns to redefine the deities from his father's example. Amphitryon has already repudiated the idea of Zeus as a god who cares for human suffering: "I, a mortal, while you are a god, conquer you in virtue (*arete*) / For I have not abandoned Heracles' sons" (342–43). Heracles confirms Amphitryon's claim by choosing his earthly rather than his heavenly father, "for I count you as my father before Zeus" (1265). Because the structure of *Heracles* shows no connection between Heracles' deeds and his punishment, the cosmos is disorderly, and the human bond stands paramount as the play ends. In Samson's case, though, deeds and punishment, however disproportionate he and Manoa may consider them, are causally related. When Samson refuses the efforts of his earthly father, finally responding to the "motions" of his heavenly father, he leaves Manoa and the reader feeling that the universe has order and meaning.[28]

Sophocles' Ajax and Heracles also have human ties Milton denies his hero. Ajax can instruct his son Eurysaces to live as a hero, thus perpetuating his ties to a community in which such heroism will be of use; Heracles in the *Trachiniae* lays the same obligation on Hyllus. Further, both *Ajax* and Euripides' *Heracles* include characters who are capable of putting themselves figuratively in the heroes' place. Odysseus, although he is Ajax's opponent, can see his own mortal lot in the argument over giving Ajax burial rites: "For I too shall come to that need" (1365). Theseus, in Euripides, reaches out to Heracles, who considers himself polluted by his crimes: "There is no curse (*alastor*) between friend and friend" (1234). Samson has no one to reach out and imagine what it is like to be Samson. The effect not only increases his heroic burden and emphasizes obedience and service to God as values above humanistic *philia;* it also places the action of Milton's drama beyond any circumscribed time.[29] Eurysaces, Hyllus, Odysseus, and Theseus can apply their understanding of the hero to specific Grecian communities so that the heroes' *arete* is perpetuated in definite times and places, times and places which precede the Christian revelation. God may be uncertain—"If God is really God . . ."—but the human ties are secure. In *Samson Agonistes* the human benefit is uncertain. God, through Samson, has liberated his people, but they may not take advantage of that liberation:

> To *Israel*
> Honor hath left, and freedom, let but them
> Find courage to lay hold on this occasion.                    (1714–16)

The effect is to turn the reader back to Samson's lonely struggle in which he affirms his faith, performs his obedience, and acts as his "own deliverer." The effect is timeless because the action leaves God certain and leaves the memory of a struggling individual finding service, victory, and peace through him. It is an individual struggle, a challenge for each reader to emulate.

## III

The permanent and cosmic implications of Samson's *agones* are even clearer in Milton's response to the Renaissance Prometheus. Commentators considered him as an individual, as a type of Adam and Christ, and as a character peforming in one section of a trilogy. Milton echoes some of his speeches and the commentators' glosses; he makes use of the differences between Samson and Prometheus to define Samson's more difficult heroism; he permits his reader to draw the parallels with Adam and Christ; and he gives the effect of a trilogy within his "five-act" structure.

Prometheus as an individual hero was both a great soul and a great sinner to the men who annotated the plays. Petrus Victorius, the editor who first restored the text of the *Oresteia* (1557), admires him, commenting on the rhetorical appropriateness of Prometheus' response to Hermes, "Be sure, I would never exchange my misery / For your servitude" (966–67):[30]

Aeschylus . . . caused Prometheus, a noble character who had not been tamed by the huge troubles he was enduring and had not allowed them to break his spirit in any way, to reply to Mercury [in the same way that Cicero had rebuked an opponent]. . . . he says that he would not exchange his unfortunate condition for Mercury's good fortune and the servitude he was enduring. . . . At the end he adds that, because Mercury set the pattern for the violence in his speech, it is right for him to repay like with like.[31]

Samson, replying to Dalila's assault with his consciousness of her betrayal and enmity, is allowed a very similar rejoinder:

> This Gaol I count the house of Liberty
> To thine whose doors my feet shall never enter.     (949–50)

Mattheus Garbitius, professor of Greek at Tübingen, allegorizes Prometheus on several levels. On one level he sympathizes, comparing Prometheus to great thinkers such as Democritus and Anaxagoras, making a metaphor of their internal suffering when he says that they inhabit their own Caucasus, tormented and worn by contemplation, as if an eagle were feeding on their livers. The final earthquake represents a period of withdrawal, isolation, or repression, from which only a God can free them.[32] Although Milton does not give Samson the mind of a Democritus, he does show his hero figuratively as well as literally imprisoned, with "thoughts my tormentors, arm'd with deadly stings" (623), and

> Myself my Sepulcher, a moving Grave,
> Buried, yet not exempt
> By privilege of death and burial
> From worst of other evils, pains and wrongs.     (102–05)

Garbitius' application, moreover, is to the end of Aeschylus' play. Samson's mental imprisonment begins the action and serves to illustrate by its placement the spiritual and mental struggles still to be overcome by Milton's hero.

Commentators considered Prometheus a sinner because he was defying Zeus, whom they sometimes equated with God. When Francesco Robortello objected to the play in the process of applying Aristotle's *Poetics* to it, he admitted that spectators would feel pity, but inappropriately: "Since he is a good man and suffering unjustly, men are enraged against Jupiter and the gods as if they were most cruel tyrants." The play possesses *pathos*, but it is "full of impiety against the gods."[33] Garbitius sees Prometheus' theft to benefit mortals as an act of pride, as a sin (*delictum*) and as overbold (*authadēs*) against God.[34] At the same time both men appear to recognize Prometheus' divided nature: his stature as an immortal prophet who can see the future and his periods of suffering as though he were mortal.

Milton purifies Samson's struggle in contrast to Prometheus'. Unlike Prometheus, Samson does not defy God even though he lacks Prometheus'

knowledge of the future. Parker rightly noticed the parallels of both characters' opening laments.[35] Prometheus, however, can lapse into his knowledge of the future:

> And yet, what do I say? All that is to be I
> knew well and in advance.                                    (101–02)

Samson is limited in not knowing God's purposes. At a parallel point in
his lament he must increase his heroic burden by absolving God of responsibility, an admission Prometheus does not make: "Whom have I to
complain of but myself?" (46). Further, although Prometheus admits that
he has transgressed Zeus' decree (ēmarton [268]), he does not repent the
fact that he has given mortals fire and the accompanying arts of civiliza-
tion (447–557). Indeed, he is proud that he dared to do so (ego d'etolmēs
[237]). Samson, in contrast, must repent his act of disobedience and confess that he has failed God as well as his countrymen and himself:[36]

> Father, I do acknowledge and confess
> That I this honor, I this pomp have brought
> To *Dagon*, and advanc'd his praises high
> Among the Heathen round; to God have brought
> Dishonor, obloquy. . . .
> . . . . have brought scandal
> To *Israel*, diffidence of God, and doubt
> In feeble hearts.                                            (448–55)

Prometheus can prophesy to Io that she will be the ancestress of Heracles,
his deliverer (871–72). Prometheus has only to remain with unbent knee,
stubbornly holding his secret about Zeus. Samson, on the other hand,
is lying "carelessly diffus'd," having betrayed God's secret, making his
choices in "Some narrow place enclos'd" (1117), until he rises to act as
a deliverer who has not had the privilege of foreseeing the call he will
receive.[37]

Milton further increased Samson's heroic burden by evoking a universe in which God is creator and lord of nature. Prometheus maintains
his stance in a world of metaphysical fracture. Zeus' law and the rest of
nature (*nomos* and *physis*) are separate from each other. Zeus has not
created Prometheus. In fact, the powers of nature—the elements Prometheus invokes (88–93); his mother, Themis, the Earth; Oceanus; and the
chorus of ocean nymphs—give him sympathy and support. Thomas Stanley, the great British editor of Aeschylus, appears to have understood this
affinity when he approved Prometheus' invocation of the elements.[38] In
such a world Zeus is not infallible and may modify his nature. Prome-

theus even predicts such a change, foreseeing a Zeus who, "eager, will come to meet my eagerness" (195) and will behave gently with the currently oppressed mortal Io (848–52). Garbitius even sees a pagan foreshadowing of the Virgin Birth in the lines about Zeus' gentle touch.[39]

Samson's God, in contrast, is the creator of the natural world, of the physical and spiritual light from which Samson is exiled:

> O first created Beam, and thou great Word,
> "Let there be light, and light was over all";
> Why am I thus bereav'd thy prime decree?     (83–85)

He is the source of "sun or shade" and the author of "The breath of Heav'n fresh-blowing, pure and sweet" (10). Some readers see his power in the "wind" (1070) which blows Harapha toward Samson and in Dalila's "floating" entrance (1072).[40] Samson cannot hold himself obdurate, as Prometheus does, and wait for God and nature to evolve. His task is harder than Prometheus'. Because he has disobeyed his Creator, he must change, confessing his sin, imploring pardon, choosing to serve God even in his maimed condition until the "rousing motions" confirm that his bond with his Creator is restored. His final words to the Chorus suggest that Samson is at peace with his Creator; after his exile and struggle he is also at peace with himself: by obeying his Creator he has become Samson again:

> ·     expect to hear
> Nothing dishonorable, impure, unworthy
> Our God, our Law, my Nation, or myself.     (1423–25)

The messenger's description of the catastrophe evokes a Samson who, no longer exiled from nature, acts in God's service like a natural force:

> straining all his nerves he bow'd;
> As with the force of wind and waters pent
> When Mountains tremble.     (1646–48)

Thus Samson, without Prometheus' defiance, without his foreknowledge, and also without his superior support, moves himself with divine help from dejection to triumph.

Renaissance commentators also found in the *Prometheus Bound* allegorical shadowings of Adam's fall and Christ's redemption. In Prometheus' disobedience of a "far superior and primary mind" to seek knowledge and to confer benefits on others, Garbitius sees an image of "our first parent, who, created by God for simplicity and rectitude, through eating of the forbidden fruit of the tree of knowledge of good and evil, hurled himself and all posterity into perpetual difficulties and miseries."[41] Garbitius is not alone. We may get a glimpse of the way the play was read and taught in the manuscript annotations William Alabaster, Cambridge student and poet in the 1580s, made in his copy of Henricus Stephanus' edition of Aeschylus: "Fabula Promethei mythologi de hominis casu" ("The story of the Prometheus myth is about the fall of man").[42] Samson, of course, repeats Adam's sin by disobeying God to reveal his secret, showing pride when he considered himself a "petty God" (529) and yielding to uxoriousness with Dalila.[43] Because Prometheus saved the human race from extinction and benefited it, he was also a type of Christ. Milton's countryman Thomas Stanley makes the point explicit: "Some of the holy fathers compare the legendary chains with the passion of our Lord. . . . Christ is the Logos, the wisdom of the Father. . . . the name of Prometheus is not inconsistent with this idea: both are helpers of mankind."[44] He also defines leōrgos (knave, miscreant [5]) as "one who dies for the people" and calls attention to the apparatus by which Prometheus is crucified. Garbitius refers to Christ as the possessor of true prometheia but interprets Heracles, Prometheus' eventual deliverer, as the Christ-figure in the work. Heracles is a "man outstanding in courage (virtus) and wisdom. . . . But I incline more in this direction: I think he means heavenly liberation by the son of God, about which redeemer of mankind the poet doubtless knew certain things from the prophets."[45] Anthony Low has discussed the allusions, culminating in the phoenix, which led readers to consider Samson a type of Christ: "His humanity is preserved because, although Samson acts the part of Christ, he does so not only imperfectly, but unknowingly, lacking a full consciousness of the nature and potency of his vicarious sacrifice and lacking the knowledge of Christian life after death."[46] Garbitius' reference to Hercules' liberation of Prometheus may be applied to Christ's liberation of Samson. Samson may do a Christ-like deed in serving God and liberating his people, but Samson, as one of the believers preceding Christ, is himself redeemed by Christ as the discussion of Old Testament figures in chapter xi of the Epistle to the Hebrews suggests.

## IV

The speculations of the early editors about the structure of Aeschylus' play and its place in a trilogy are interesting in themselves. Further, they shed light on the scope of Milton's undertaking because he manages, within the scope of one play, to suggest the outlines of a trilogy about Samson. The commentators on the Aeschylean trilogy also help us understand their conception of tragedy. Apart from consideration of the scope of a trilogy, Milton's readers could have found a discussion of the *Prometheus Bound* which noted a succession of scenes unconnected by an outward chain of causation. Francesco Robortello, in his nineteen objections to the play, criticized the structure, saying that the Io scene was not related to the central action and that, in fact, the series of episodes did not lead naturally from one encounter to the next.[47] Similarly, Milton gives no essential motivation for the visits of Manoa, Dalila, and Harapha on the day of the Dagonalia. Both Aeschylus and Milton use episodic design to illustrate the mental states of their heroes. Prometheus moves from a patronizing dismissal of Oceanus' offer to help, through increased indignation over Io's plight, to resolute defiance of Zeus after Hermes' visit. Samson, in contrast, rejects Manoa's efforts but confesses his sins; challenges Harapha, testifying to his renewed faith; rejects the Public Officer, using his human reason; and receives the "motions" from God, leading to his chosen obedience and ultimate triumph.[48]

Milton and his readers would also have found, in the work of the early editors, evidence about the trilogy of which the *Prometheus Bound* was a part, particularly about fragments from the *Prometheus Unbound* (*Luomenos*). Henricus Stephanus, one of the learned scholar-printers, reports in his 1557 *Aeschylus* that a passage Galen had attributed to the *Prometheus Bound* describing Heracles' journeys must belong to the play which followed. He notes, too, that Earth and Heracles are listed as characters for the second play and conjectures that Heracles comes to kill the eagle, freeing Prometheus.[49] Stanley conjectured that Zeus freed Prometheus or that Themis and Heracles contrived the liberation.[50] Their speculations resemble those of modern editors.[51] Since Milton considered other titles for other parts of the Samson story in the Cambridge manuscript, and since he shows his readers a Samson both bound and freed, the idea that he compressed the action of a trilogy into *Samson Agonistes* is an attractive one. In Samson's and the Chorus' account of Samson's career before his fall, Milton gives a suggestion of *Samson Hybristes*. The action of *Samson Hybristes* includes Samson's state of innocence before he knew his limitations, before he was tested and found wanting:

> I was his nursling once and choice delight,
> His destin'd from the womb,
> Promis'd by Heavenly message twice descending.
> Under his special eye
> Abstemious I grew up and thriv'd amain;
> He led me on to mightiest deed
> Above the nerve of mortal arm
> Against th'uncircumcis'd, our enemies.          (633–40)

To this period belongs the mighty warrior whose deeds the Chorus celebrates:

> whom unarm'd
> No strength of man, or fiercest wild beast could withstand;
> Who tore the Lion, as the Lion tears the Kid,
> Ran on embattled Armies clad in Iron,
> And weaponless himself,
> Made Arms ridiculous. (126–131)

Samson explicitly refers to his ignorant self-confidence, the *hybris* which led to his disobedience and fall:

> Full of divine instinct, after some proof
> Of acts indeed heroic, far beyond
> The Sons of *Anak*, famous now and blaz'd,
> Fearless of danger, like a petty God
> I walk't about admir'd of all and dreaded
> On hostile ground, none daring my affront.
> Then swoll'n with pride into the snare I fell. (526–32)

The fallen Samson then struggles throughout the *agones* of the play, refusing options, drawing mental distinctions, and, at last, openly testifying to God as a merciful Father who gave him his strength and purpose (1140–42; 1170–73). After Samson's encounters with Manoa, Dalila, and Harapha, the choral lines help the reader contrast the new Samson with the old:

> This Idol's day hath been to thee no day of rest,
>> Laboring thy mind
> More than the working day thy hands. (1297–99)

When Samson has used his human reason fully, the "rousing motions" summon him to an action which recalls his youthful strength but demands the control of his newly awakened mind. The younger Samson is recalled in the choral benediction:

> Send thee the Angel of thy Birth, to stand
> Fast by thy side, who from thy Father's field
> Rode up in flames. (1431–33)

The new Samson is one who can control himself, "patient but undaunted" (1624) in his performance before the Philistines. He combines human choice and obedience when he stands

> as one who pray'd,
> Or some great matter in his mind revolv'd.[52] (1637–38)

Samson's long struggle ends, his will united with the motions of grace, while Manoa and the Chorus simply hear the noises and groans from the temple. In the great images of light and inward vision, it is as if Milton wrote *Samson Pursophorus*, another Samson play he had mentioned in the Cambridge manuscript, to interpret the effect of Samson's renewal for his countrymen and for Christian readers for whom the phoenix has further resonance:

> With inward eyes illuminated
> His fiery virtue rous'd
> From under ashes into sudden flame,
>
> .   .   .   .   .   .   .
>
> His cloudless thunder bolted on thir heads.
> So virtue giv'n for lost,
> Deprest, and overthrown, as seem'd,
> Like that self-begott'n bird
>
> .   .   .   .   .   .   .
>
> From out her ashy womb now teem'd,
> Revives, reflourishes, then vigorous most
> When most unactive deem'd,
> And though her body die, her fame survives,
> A secular bird ages of lives.                    (1689–1707)

The *Prometheus Bound* ends with Prometheus' defiant words of suffering as a cataclysm sends him to Tartarus; the *Trachiniae* ends with Hyllus observing his father's pyre and saying, "There is nothing here which is not Zeus" (1278). The effect of each is to leave the reader meditating the significance of the final violent act and casting his mind backward over the steps which led to it. Milton takes his readers not backward but forward, when the reader, with the Chorus, sees the flame of inward vision, witnesses the noontime rebirth of Samson's heroic *arete*, and meditates the meaning of a symbol of resurrection.[53] This combination of past, present, and future in 1,758 lines transcends the scope of any one Attic drama. Although he does not extend the point, A. S. P. Woodhouse has commented upon this broader view: "Milton has chosen the much more difficult task of displaying in four acts a gradual change of mind in his hero comparable in extent to the whole development of Oedipus from the time when he stood before the palace blinded and desperate."[54] Milton not only shows us Samson's change of mind; he also permits his Chorus and reader to explore the significance of that change in the final lines before dismissing them with "calm of mind, all passion spent" (1757). The effect is that of a trilogy: the pride and fall of the protagonist; his struggle and suffering to achieve a death worthy of him; and the cosmic reconciliation which follows that event.

Given the spiritual victory and cosmic reconciliation, has Milton written a tragedy? Without entering contemporary disputes about the nature of Christian tragedy, one may say that the Renaissance commentators would have included Milton's play within the genre. Q. S. F. Christianus defends the *Philoctetes*, in which a suffering hero is recalled to service in the Trojan War, as tragic.[55] More significant is Thomas Stanley's comment on the final play of an extant trilogy, Aeschylus' *Eumenides*:

It is not essential for a tragedy always to have fearful conclusions, deaths, murders, and poisonings. The *Alcestis* of Euripides has an ending which is entirely happy, for it shows Alcestis, the wife of Admetus, freed from death by the help of Hercules. However, there are two things which characterize a tragedy: First, the characters, who should be Gods or heroes or kings or distinguished men, but certainly not from the common people or of a lower rank. . . . Secondly, the events which are represented should not be drawn from common life but should be lofty and serious. If these things are in a play, whatever the conclusion is, it is a tragedy.[56]

Milton certainly portrayed lofty and serious events from the life of a distinguished man and hero in *Samson Agonistes*. But Stanley's application of *tragoedia* to the *Eumenides* is even more significant than the criteria he stipulates. He thus permits a play in which the hero is freed, in which the cosmic order is renewed, and which ends with choruses of rejoicing to be considered tragic. In an even more serious way Milton permits his hero to fulfill his life's purpose in freedom, leaving the Chorus to chant in joy, and answering the earlier painful questions about God's ways with a reconciled acceptance of the cosmic order Samson's death has affirmed,

> With God not parted from him, as was fear'd,
> But favoring and assisting to the end.
> Nothing is here for tears, nothing to wail
> Or knock the breast, no weakness, no contempt,
> Dispraise or blame, nothing but well and fair,
> And what may quiet us in a death so noble.          (1719–24)

Stanley's and Milton's reconciliation of spiritual renewal with "that sort of dramatic poem which is call'd tragedy" suggests that they were willing to leave the tragic boundaries broader than many current readers do.[57]

## V

In responding to Greek tragedies, then, Milton portrayed his hero purging himself of former pride and lust, giving him an internal struggle and internal victory which surpassed those of his models. For "senseless" defeats, such as Euripides' Heracles experienced, he substituted a divinely guided, orderly world. Instead of channeling his hero's energy into a com-

# Milton's Samson and the Editors of Greek Tragedy 251

munity of *philoi*, he isolated him, making his action a model for all time. In place of the farseeing Prometheus, he substituted a determined, fallible human whose will ultimately conformed with that of nature and nature's God. In the process he attained the spaciousness of a trilogy and the triumphant effect of the close of an Aeschylean sequence. One must conclude that he succeeded in meeting his youthful aspiration "that what the greatest and choicest wits of Athens, Rome, or modern Italy, and those Hebrews of old did for their country, I, in my proportion, with this over and above of being a Christian, might do for mine."[58]

University of Kansas

NOTES

1. The classic study of Milton's echoes of all the Greek tragedies is William Riley Parker, *Milton's Debt to Greek Tragedy in "Samson Agonistes"* (Baltimore, 1937). For a comparison of prophecies in *Samson* with the oracles of the *Trachiniae*, see J. C. Maxwell, "Milton's Samson and Sophocles' Heracles," *PQ*, XXXIII (1954), 90–91. A. S. P. Woodhouse, "Tragic Effect in *Samson Agonistes*," in Arthur E. Barker, ed., *Milton: Modern Essays in Criticism* (New York, 1965), pp. 447–66, contrats Samson and the Oedipus of *Oedipus at Colonus*, indicating that the old Oedipus does not need to change his nature in Sophocles' play. Martin Mueller, "'Pathos' and 'Katharsis' in *Samson Agonistes*," *ELH*, XXXI (1964), 156–74, indicates the difference of Milton's drama from "Aristotelian" Greek tragedies. Mueller notes further parallels and contrasts with the *Trachiniae* and the *Philoctetes* in "Time and Redemption in *Samson Agonistes* and *Iphigenie auf Tauris*," *UTQ*, XLI (1972), 227–45. Anthony Low, *The Blaze of Noon: A Reading of "Samson Agonistes"* (New York, 1974), notes parallels with Heracles and Philoctetes, pp. 21, 54–55, and 176–77. Carole S. Kessner, "Milton's Hebraic Herculean Hero," in *Milton Studies*, VI, ed. James D. Simmonds (Pittsburgh, 1974), pp. 243–58, discusses parallels between Milton's Samson and Euripides' Heracles. For contrasts between Greek and Christian tragedy, see Northrop Frye, "Agon and Logos," in *Spiritus Mundi: Essays on Literature, Myth and Society* (Bloomington, Ind., 1976), pp. 201–28; Thomas B. Stroup, "'All Comes Clear at Last' but 'the readiness is All,'" *Comparative Drama*, X (1976), 61–75; Morris Freedman, "Waiting for Samson: The Modernity of *Samson Agonistes*," *MQ*, XIII (1979), 42–45; and M. V. Rama Sarma, "'The Unsearchable Dispose of Highest Wisdom': *Samson Agonistes*," *MQ*, XIII (1979), 85–89.

2. *Milton's Samson and the Christian Tradition* (Princeton, 1949), p. 10 and n. 17.

3. *Paradise Lost* IX, 14, in *John Milton: Complete Poems and Major Prose*, ed. Merritt Y. Hughes (New York, 1957). All citations of Milton's work are from this edition.

4. *Excerpta ex Tragoediis et Comoediis Graecis* (Paris, 1626), "quia multa sunt, praesertim de rebus divinis, quae sola rationis indagine ad liquidum perduci nequeunt. . . . de Deo uno, de eius purissimae et a rebus aliis secreta natura, de Dei opere Mundo, de perpetua providentia, de libertate humanarum actionum . . . et de vero Dei cultus," sigs. a ii[v] and a iii[r]. I have translated the Latin from the commentaries.

5. *Ajax* appeared separately in Greek (Paris, 1530); Ioannes Lonicerus published

a Latin version in 1533 (Basel); and Balthazar Stolbergius added a lengthy commentary to this version in 1668. Joseph Scaliger also translated the work into Latin without a commentary (Paris, 1573). This version was reprinted in Heidelberg in 1574, 1591, and 1600 and in Strassburg in 1587. Wolfhart Spangenberg produced a German translation (Strassburg, 1608), and G. Giustiniano translated it into Italian from the Latin of Georgius Rotallerus (Venice, 1603). Rotallerus' *Ajax, Antigone,* and *Electra* in Latin appeared in 1550 (Lyons), and Thomas Naogeorgus' *Ajax* and *Philoctestes* followed in 1552 (Leipzig). Joachim Camerarius translated *Ajax* and *Electra* when he published a commentary on all of the plays (Basel, 1556). Every commentator marks the contrast of Ajax's *fortitudo* and Odysseus' *sapientia.* For discussions of these qualities in *Samson Agonistes* from perspectives different from mine, see A. B. Chambers, "Wisdom and Fortitude in *Samson Agonistes, PMLA,* LXXVIII (1963), 315–20, and John M. Steadman, *Milton and the Renaissance Hero* (Oxford, 1967), pp. 154–60.

6. *Interpretatio Tragoediarum Sophoclis ad Utilitatem Iuventutis* (Frankfurt, 1549), pp. 2–3.

7. *Tragoediae Sophoclis* (Antwerp, 1552), sig. A7ᵛ.

8. *Sophoclis Tragicorum . . . Tragoediae* (Paris, 1557), p. 11.

9. *Tragoediae Sophoclis,* p. 359.

10. Winshemius, *Interpretatio Tragoediarum Sophoclis,* p. 305.

11. Parker, *Milton's Debt to Greek Tragedy,* notes this parallel as well as Ajax's despair and brooding about his disgrace, pp. 116–17.

12. All of the editions note Ajax's deception of Tecmessa and the Chorus.

13. See especially Low, *The Blaze of Noon,* pp. 21 and 176–77. For a reading of other Renaissance traditions about Hercules, see Raymond B. Waddington, "Melancholy Against Melancholy: *Samson Agonistes* as Renaissance Tragedy," in *Calm of Mind: Tercentenary Essays on "Paradise Regained" and "Samson Agonistes" in Honor of John C. Diekhoff,* ed. Joseph A. Wittreich, Jr. (Cleveland, 1971), pp. 259–287.

14. John Huntley, "A Revaluation of the Chorus' Role in *Samson Agonistes," MP,* LXIV (1966–67), sees Samson's question as an effort to teach God a better kind of creation. I agree in part but see the process of questioning and probing the depths of suffering as essential to Samson's final attainment of renewed heroic stature.

15. Milton, *Areopagitica,* ed. Hughes, p. 743.

16. Sophocles, *Ajax,* in *Sophocles: The Plays and Fragments,* ed. R. C. Jebb (Cambridge, Eng., 1896). Line numbers for Sophocles are from this edition. Translations of the Greek are mine. I am indebted to William Arrowsmith for this conception of the Sophoclean hero. The old Oedipus also imposes his own definitions and distinctions, preferring his daughters to his sons in faithfulness and judging Theseus reverent, fair, and honest (1125–26), worthy to receive his *philia* and his blessing.

17. Joan S. Bennett, "Liberty Under the Law: The Chorus and the Meaning of *Samson Agonistes,"* in *Milton Studies,* XII, ed. James D. Simmonds (Pittsburgh, 1978), p. 156, notes that Samson's conception of God is universal rather than tribal in this scene.

18. Waddington, "Melancholy Against Melancholy," also makes this point (p. 276).

19. *Christian Doctrine,* II, ix, ed. Hughes, p. 1019.

20. *Milton and the Renaissance Hero,* p. 160.

21. *Euripides Poeta Tragicorum Princeps* (Basel, 1562), p. 626.

22. Ibid., p. 628.

23. "Milton's Hebraic Herculean Hero," p. 248.

24. Stiblinus translates and calls attention to Heracles' support from Amphitryon (p. 629). He also admires Theseus' faithful friendship (p. 626).

25. Milton, *Second Defense*, in Hughes, p. 827. Line numbers from Euripides are from *Euripides*, ed. and trans. Arthur W. Way, III (London, 1912). With the exception of these lines translated by Milton, the translations of Euripides are my own.

26. Joshua Barnes's *Euripides* (Cambridge, Eng., 1694) is later than most of the commentators cited in this study, but he cites the comments of Stiblinus, Grotius, and others. He is clearest on the motive of expiation, saying that Theseus leads Heracles to Athens for this purpose (p. 355).

27. Mueller, "'Pathos' and 'Katharsis,'" makes this point, but I have extended the implications and differ in seeing the *pathos* as tragic.

28. Stanley Fish, "Question and Answer in *Samson Agonistes*," *Critical Quarterly*, XI (1969), 237–64, identifies this effect for the reader (p. 263). For a sympathetic reading of Manoa's strengths and limitations in perceiving the significance of Samson's struggle, see Nancy Y. Hoffman, "Samson's Other Father: The Character of Manoa in *Samson Agonistes*," in *Milton Studies*, II, ed. Simmonds (Pittsburgh, 1970), pp. 195–210. I put more emphasis on Manoa's perception after Samson's death that God's world is orderly.

29. For a reading of *Samson* which contrasts classical and Christian concepts of time, see E. W. Tayler, "Milton's *Samson*: The Form of Christian Tragedy," *ELR*, III (1973), 306–21.

30. References to the *Prometheus Bound* are from *Aeschylus*, ed. and trans. Herbert Weir Smyth, I (London, 1922). Unless otherwise noted, I have translated the Greek.

31. Victorius, Var. Lect. XXVI, 7, cited by Stanley in his manuscript addenda to his 1663 Aeschylus. Stanley's citation appears in Samuel Butler's reprint of his work *Aeschyli Tragoediae quae Supersunt* (Cambridge, Eng., 1809): "qui et ipse fecit, gravem personam, Prometheum, et quem mala ingentia quae sustinebat non domuerant, nec spiritus ipsius ullam in partem contuderant, eodem pacto respondere Mercurio qui ipsum laeserat. . . . Inquit igitur, se non commutaturum statum suum illum malum, cum ipsius secundis rebus, ministerioque quod obibat; satiusque esse adfixum illi scopulo haerere, quam nuntium esse Jovis, mandataque ipsius fideliter exequi. Ad extremum vero addit, quod vim illius suae orationis aperit ac constituit, decere par pari referre, et contumeliam illatam, contumelia refellere" (I, p. 200).

32. *Aeschli Prometheus* (Basel, 1559), pp. 280–82.

33. *Scholia in Aeschyli Tragoedias Omnes* (Venice, 1552), "nam spectatores homines potius inducuntur in odium Iovis, qui illorum commodis invidens Prometheum poena afficit. . . . Hominibus ciet quidem sed, bonus cum sit, immerito patitur, et homines indignanter in Iovem, et Deos, tanquam crudelissimos tyrannos. . . . Nullam habet peripetiam, neque agnitionem, pathos tantum, atque illud impietatis in Deos plenum" (sig. 6ᵛ).

34. *Aeschli Prometheus*, sig. B5ʳ.

35. Parker, *Milton's Debt to Greek Tragedy*, pp. 178–79.

36. Parker was the first to point this out (ibid., p. 37).

37. See Huntley's discussion of Samson's posture: having lain flat at the beginning, he is sitting when he addresses Dalila and standing in the scene with Harapha ("A Revaluation of the Chorus' Role," p. 142).

38. Thomas Stanley, *Aeschyli Tragoediae Septem* (London, 1663), p. 720.

39. Garbitius, *Aeschli Prometheus*, p. 243.

40. For the idea that these episodes follow an "inner" rather than an "outer" logic, see Anthony Low, "*Samson Agonistes*: Theology, Poetry, Truth," *MQ*, XIII (1979), 96–102.

41. Garbitius, *Aeschli Prometheus*, "de primo parente, qui ad simplicitatem & rectitudinem a Deo creatus, per esum vetiti fructus de arbore scientiae boni & mali, se & omnem posteritatem in perpetuas difficultates & miserias praecipitavit" (pp. 20–21).

42. Alabaster's notes are in Adv.c.26.1 in the Cambridge University Library, a copy of Stephanus' edition (1557), p. 12.

43. For Samson's resemblance to the first and second Adam, see Sherman H. Hawkins, "Samson's Catharsis," in *Milton Studies*, II, ed. Simmonds (Pittsburgh, 1970), p. 228.

44. Stanley, *Aeschyli Tragoediae Septem*, "Nonnulli e sanctis Patribus Promethei vincula Fabulosa cum Passione Domini nostri conferunt, hisce forsan aut similibus rationibus perducti: Christus est ho Logos, sophia Patros . . . eo non abludit Promethei nomen; ambo philanthropoi" (p. 714).

45. Garbitius, *Aeschli Prometheus*, "qui sit futurus magnus & excellens virtute & sapientia vir. . . . Huc tamen magis inclino, & puto cum intelligere liberationem coelestem per filium Dei, de quo redemptore generis humani Poeta haud dubie cognorat quaedam ex prophetiis & sapientia Hebraeorum" (p. 282).

46. *The Blaze of Noon*, p. 31.

47. *Scholia in Aeschyli Tragoedias Omnes*, "Episodia non ducuntur ex iis, quae praecedunt actionem, uti debent duci, et ex aliis circunstantiis haerentibus actioni, sed omnia ducuntur ex consequentibus quibusdam, et parum cohaerentibus, tolli enim possent, nec manca appareret actio, hoc vero summum vitium in ipsis Episodiis" (sig. 8ʳ).

48. See Low, "*Samson Agonistes*," p. 101, and Hawkins, "Samson's Catharsis," p. 225, for the idea that no outward logic connects these episodes.

49. Stephanus in Petrus Victorius, ed., *Aeschyli Tragoediae VII* (Geneva, 1557), pp. 356–58.

50. Canter's conjectures are reprinted in Stanley's 1663 Aeschylus, p. 686.

51. See C. J. Herington's appendix to Aeschylus, *Prometheus Bound*, trans. James Scully and C. J. Herington (New York and London, 1975), pp. 97–100.

52. For a reading in which "either-or" becomes "both-and," see Anthony Low, "Action and Suffering: *Samson Agonistes* and the Irony of Alternatives," *PMLA*, LXXXIV (1969), 514.

53. For the resonances of the phoenix symbol, see Albert R. Cirillo, "Time, Light, and the Phoenix: The Design of *Samson Agonistes*," in *Calm of Mind*, ed. Wittreich, pp. 209–33, and Anthony Low, "The Phoenix and the Sun in *Samson Agonistes*," in *Milton Studies*, XIV, ed. Simmonds (Pittsburgh, 1980), pp. 219–33.

54. "Tragic Effect in *Samson Agonistes*," p. 461.

55. *Sophoclis Tragoedia Philoctetes* (Paris, 1586). "Species huius Tragoediae est ethike, & tota laeta, ut desinant nugari Grammaticorum purgamenta, qui turbidum semper finem tristemque exitum Tragoediae assignant, nec aliter eam definiunt" (p. 44).

56. Stanley, *Aeschyli Tragoediae Septem*, "Non est Tragoediae necessarium ut semper habeat horrendos rerum exitus, et mortes et caedes et venena; Alcestis Euripidis in exitu omnia habet laeta; ostendit enim Alcestin Admeti uxorem a morte auxilio Herculis liberatam. Quae vero Tragoediam charakterizousi duo sunt. Primo, Personae, quas esse oportet aut Deos, aut Heroas, aut Reges, aut viros clarissimos, non vero e plebecula aut notae inferioris. . . . Secundo, Res quae repraesentatur, quam non oportet esse e communi vita depromptam, sed grandem et severam. Haec si succedant Fabulae, quiscunque exitus sit, Tragoedia est" (p. 832).

57. Helen Damico, "Duality in Dramatic Vision: A Structural Analysis of *Samson Agonistes*," in *Milton Studies*, XII, ed. Simmonds (Pittsburgh, 1978), pp. 91–116, finds parallels between the structure of *Samson Agonistes* and Greek Old Comedy. Her observations also fit the structure of the *Eumenides*. For links between Aeschylean trilogy and Old Comedy, see C. J. Herington, "Aeschylus: The Last Phase," *Arion*, IV (1965), 387–403.

58. Milton, *The Reason of Church Government*, ed. Hughes, p. 669.

# THE ROLE OF RAPHAEL
# IN *SAMSON AGONISTES*

*Philip J. Gallagher*

<br>

Or if Virtue feeble were,
Heav'n itself would stoop to her.

M ARY A NN R ADZINOWICZ has recently argued that "the fullest response to Milton's poetry . . . comes from interpreting its
meaning in relation to its evolution within the corpus of his works."[1] As
my title implies, I endorse Radzinowicz's belief in the centrality to Milton
studies of author-contextual criticism, upon whose assumptions I rely in
the following comparative study of regeneration in *Paradise Lost* and *Samson Agonistes*.[2] I also accept, along with the vast majority of Milton
scholars, the traditional chronology according to which *Samson* is the last-
composed of Milton's poems.[3] Chronology aside, however, my intention
to read the tragedy in the light shed upon it by the epic is the more plausible given the fact, as Joseph Wittreich has observed, that "even if [*Paradise Lost, Paradise Regained,* and *Samson Agonistes*] were not composed
sequentially, they were published that way," and so (presumably) intended
to be read in the order of publication.[4] In the *Christian Doctrine* Milton
writes, apropos of scriptural exegesis, that "difficult texts . . . must be explained by many clearer passages which resemble them; for clear things
are not elucidated by obscure things but obscure by clear."[5] Exactly this
relationship appertains between *Samson Agonistes* and *Paradise Lost*: since
the God of the play is so much a deus absconditus as to have been omitted from the dramatis personae, and since the play lacks "normative characters,"[6] and since there is "no narrator authorized by God to guide our
human response"[7] to the exfoliation of its plot, its meanings are sometimes
more elusive than those of *Paradise Lost*, wherein the ways of God are
often enough rendered less than inscrutable by the definitive analyses of
the epic bard. If both epic and tragedy proceed from essentially the same
poetic and religious sensibility, the more leisurely exposition of the former
ought to provide a telling context in which to resolve doubts and ambi-
guities in the latter.

255

To be specific, I will argue that excepting differences necessitated by the formal demands of genre, the descent of Raphael in *Paradise Lost* is precisely analogous to the marriage of Samson to the Woman of Timna in *Samson Agonistes*. Both angel and woman are embodiments of prevenient grace sent by the deity to initiate the regeneration of fallen man before he has fallen. Both therefore corroborate Anthony Low's assertion that "secretly guiding and shaping the action [of *Samson*] is the hidden providence of God."[8] Unlike the fall of a sparrow, there is special providence in the falls of Adam and Samson: through the mediation of Raphael and the Timnite, Milton's God preveniently renders these sinners inexcusable for sins they have yet to contemplate committing. He thereby lovingly hastens their regeneration by enabling them to internalize that conviction of guilt without which spiritual renovation cannot occur.

Before developing this thesis, I think it best to elaborate on the two methodological hypotheses that will comprise my exegetical approach. First, I assume, given the sequential publication of *Paradise Lost* and *Samson Agonistes*, that Milton expects us to approach the tragedy from the normative perspective of fall and regeneration enumerated in the diffuse epic. It is, however, theoretically just as likely that he regards *Samson* as a revisionary critique of *Paradise Lost*, or that both poems are to be judged against the ethical and aesthetic axioms of *Paradise Regained*, which Milton deliberately interposed between them. Arthur E. Barker has said of the brief epic and the tragedy that "in some sense we are involved with the last two items in a trilogy," but his probing analysis fails to specify whether and how the poems are "properly sequential."[9] Both Balachandra Rajan and Mary Ann Radzinowicz have discerned that *Samson* is a fitting sequel to *Paradise Regained*, but neither addresses the appropriateness of using *Paradise Lost* as a scholium upon the drama.[10] Joseph Wittreich has attempted to read all three poems as mutually illuminating, but his conclusions as to their interrelatedness differ radically from mine. According to Wittreich *Paradise Lost*

serves as a gateway into the brief epic and the tragedy; yet these poems are much more than recapitulations of the diffuse epic, and certainly they are not redactions of one another's visions. In no case does the perspective of one poem duplicate that of the other: the diffuse epic is a focusing of orthodoxies that *Paradise Regained* proceeds to demolish; the brief epic is a formulation of a new system of religion, more perfect and enduring than the one it supersedes. . . . having shown how the paradise within may be achieved, [it] is complemented by a tragedy that shows how it may be lost, and the effects of its being lost.[11]

For Wittreich indeed "*Paradise Regained* finds its demonic parody in *Samson Agonistes*, Milton's tragedy showing not a man freeing other men from the cycles of history but a 'hero' binding men down to them."[12] The brief epic thus negatively illuminates both its predecessor and its sequel — especially the latter, wherein one finds recapitulated neither the redemptive paradigm of Christ in the wilderness nor the regenerative experiences of Adam and Eve in the Garden. Given these considerations, what (if anything) justifies my assumption that *Samson* should be read in the supposedly definitive context of *Paradise Lost?*

The assumption derives support from my second methodological hypothesis, namely, that the diffuse epic and the biblical tragedy are poetically and spiritually homologous, standing as twin monuments to Milton's unchanging mind. If they are of a piece, then the fall and regeneration of Adam ought to be repeated chapter and verse in the career of Samson, and *Paradise Lost* ought in many ways to clarify what is obscure in *Samson Agonistes*. But are the poems isomorphic? I recognize the pitfalls of beginning with this assumption, so my analysis will try assiduously to validate it by ransacking both poems in search of exemplary homologues. Here I will pause only to comment on the striking and suggestive analogy between Genesis and Judges that Milton draws in *Paradise Lost* as Adam and Eve arise after their first postlapsarian coitus:

> So rose the *Danite* strong
> *Herculean Samson* from the Harlot-lap
> Of *Philistean Dalilah*, and wak'd
> Shorn of his strength, They destitute and bare
> Of all thir virtue.                                   (IX, 1059–63)

Apart from the fact that the Dalila of *Samson Agonistes* is married to Samson, whereas here she prostitutes herself to him, this passage suggests that in Milton's mind, Adam and Samson are alike in punishment as in their crime — and perhaps also in the dialectic of their regeneration, as I shall argue. At the very least the hint of congruence between epic and drama asserted in Milton's simile is surely worth tracking to its inmost cell. Among the immediate dividends of doing so will be the opportunity to understand how *Samson* can at once adhere to the formal generic norms of Greek tragedy as Aristotle understood them, and yet redefine the moral parameters of tragic experience, thereby to eliminate the self-extenuating I-am-a-man-more-sinned-against-than-sinning propensities latent in Aristotle's definition of tragic *hamartia* as involving "the sort of man who is not conspicuous for virtue and justice, and whose fall into misery is not due to vice and depravity, but rather to some error";[13] and to allow for the regeneration of the tragic hero, in fact his categorical restoration to divine favor, so that one's final response to a completed tragic action can resemble Manoa's asseveration, at the end of *Samson Agonistes*, that

> Nothing is here for tears, nothing to wail
> Or knock the breast, no weakness, no contempt,
> Dispraise, or blame, nothing but well and fair,
> And what may quiet us in a death so noble.[14]          (1721–24)

Irene Samuel has argued eloquently against Manoa's position by conjoining the Aristotelian bias of the prefatory note to *Samson Agonistes* with the *Poetics'* definition of *hamartia* to assert that "Milton called [his drama] a tragedy, not a martyr play; its subject cannot be Samson restored to divine favor."[15] The possibility remains, however, that Milton's indebtedness to Aristotle and the Greek tragedians extends only to formal features, such as the presence of a Chorus, the measure of the verse, and observance of the three unities. Matters such as these constitute the primary concern of the prefatory epistle, and here as elsewhere Milton cites the opinion of David Paraeus that no less joyful a book than Revelation itself, given its "solemn scenes and acts" interspersed "with a sevenfold chorus of hallelujahs and harping symphonies," deserves on these structural grounds alone to be called "a high and stately tragedy."[16] It is, moreover, probable that Milton wishes his reader to understand tragedy conceptually (as opposed to formally) in precisely the terms in which he couches it in *Paradise Lost*. There, as he reluctantly essays to narrate the fall of man, the poet offers a view of the tragic entailing, *contra* Aristotle, the case of one whose misfortune comes about through "vice and depravity"; there, Milton's Christian tragic notes recount not Hellenic *hamartia* but

> foul distrust, and breach
> Disloyal on the part of Man, revolt,
> And disobedience: On the part of Heav'n
> Now alienated, distance and distaste,
> Anger and just rebuke, and judgment giv'n.[17]          (IX, 6–10)

If, as I believe, *Paradise Lost* and *Samson Agonistes* are conceptually complementary, then the tragic fall of the Danite will recapitulate the tragic Adamic paradigm, and the regeneration of Samson may proceed, on the analogy with the restoration of Adam, without any oxymoronic violation of the norms of tragic experience as Milton (not Aristotle) conceived of them.

My point in thus entering into questions of generic definition is to engage my reader's sympathy toward the prima facie plausibility of supposing *Samson Agonistes* as in some sense a redundant repetition of *Paradise Lost*. If the epic's explicitness can alert us to Milton's preferring, in typical departure from the predilections of the Greeks, to write a tragedy of regeneration,[18] it can just as likely contribute to the adjudication of other disputes about the meaning of *Samson Agonistes*. If the diffuse epic can make us see that the possibility of Samson's regeneration is not a priori outlawed by Milton's definition of tragedy, *Paradise Lost* can also offer compelling external evidence that such regeneration is in fact accomplished in the play. The issue is more than a quibble, for much recent criticism has sought to depreciate the traditional view that Samson finishes his career as the reinstated faithful champion of God. To the already cited testimony of Joseph Wittreich and Irene Samuel may be added the witness of other twentieth-century commentators for whom *Samson Agonistes*, in Wittreich's words, criticizes "men and civilizations that have repeatedly reverted to the ways represented by Samson from which Jesus, as an example, provided them with a release."[19] The most extreme statement of this revisionist position is perhaps that of John Carey, for whom the climax of the play "is indeed morally disgusting": Samson's "last bloody act of vengeance, which the surface voice of the drama invites us to applaud, is condemned, at a deeper level, by the progression of imagery." To Carey, far from achieving spiritual regeneration, "the weak-minded, vengeful hero" is reduced "to the level of Dalila and the Philistines."[20] The purveyors of this and similar views tend to deny the essential rationality of *Samson Agonistes*, whose catastrophe — even if they applaud it — seems to them inscrutably bizarre. A decade ago Stanley Fish argued that although Milton's God is just, "we cannot infer his benevolence or validate his justice from the known facts" of the play; more recently Lawrence W. Hyman has found us forced by the absence of viable alternatives to rely on the admittedly inadequate Choral explanation of the plot's significance; and John C. Ulreich, Jr., has maintained that "neither the action of [*Samson*] nor its argument is fully coherent on its own terms," for "letter [i.e., action] and spirit [i.e., argument] remain irreconcilably opposed to one another."[21]

In opposition to the revisionist readings of Wittreich, Carey, and Samuel, and to the fideistic or skeptical hermeneutics of Fish, Hyman, and Ulreich, I shall argue that Samson is indeed a regenerate hero and that the Chorus of *Samson Agonistes*, no less than the narrator of *Para-*

*dise Lost,* accurately avers that "Just are the ways of God, / And justifiable to men" (293–94). My thesis is not new but my evidence is, for much of it will come from *Paradise Lost.* I shall begin with a discussion of certain problems in the descent of Raphael arising in the main from the foreknown fact that the angel's admonitions to Adam and Eve will be ignored; solution of these problems will be found by contrasting Raphael to his Hesiodic, Homeric, and Vergilian literary forebears and by showing how God, given his divine prescience and the special providence whereby he decrees the predestined redemption of Adam, sends the archangel to him to facilitate his regeneration before he falls. I shall then turn to *Samson Agonistes.* After comparing it with certain analogues in Judges xiii–xvi, knowledge of which helps the reader discern the providential hand of God lovingly manipulating the play's bewildering succession of Miltonic ironies, I shall study the Woman of Timna, whose career must be understood as the repetition on a finer tone of the restorative descent of Raphael. In the event, blessed angel and heathen woman will prove, to cite Mary Ann Radzinowicz again, that "the ways of [Milton's] God are just and merciful," while "the ways of the poet are particularly merciful . . . his greatest pity [being] reserved for the discovery that chastened remorse may be among the purest and least ambivalent responses to life of which the individual is capable."[22]

## I

The circumstances of Raphael's descent from Heaven are these: Satan has tempted Eve in a dream that has distressed her, but from the painful effects of which Adam has been able quickly to restore her. After lengthy morning orisons our father and mother have hastened to their garden work and, so occupied, have become the focus of divine attention:

> Them thus imploy'd beheld
> With pity Heav'n's high King, and to him call'd
> *Raphael,* the sociable Spirit.                    (*PL* V, 219–21)

Out of celestial condescension God sends the archangel on a mission whose protocols repay the closest scrutiny:

> *Raphael,* said hee, thou hear'st what stir on Earth
> *Satan* from Hell scap't through the darksome Gulf
> Hath rais'd in Paradise, and how disturb'd
> This night the human pair, how he designs
> In them at once to ruin all mankind.
> Go therefore, half this day as friend with friend
> Converse with *Adam,* in what Bow'r or shade

> Thou find'st him from the heat of Noon retir'd,
> To respite his day-labor with repast,
> Or with repose.[23]                                    (224–33)

In langauge reminiscent of the conciliar prediction by which he has already announced the fall of man to the assembled angels (III, 86–128), God enjoins Raphael to

> advise [Adam] of his happy state,
> Happiness in his power left free to will,
> Left to his own free Will, his Will though free,
> Yet mutable; whence warn him to beware
> He swerve not too secure: tell him withal
> His danger, and from whom, what enemy
> Late fall'n himself from Heaven, is plotting now
> The fall of others from like state of bliss.          (234–41)

Faithful angel that he is, Raphael will execute these orders to the last jot and tittle. His motive is obedience: "nor delay'd the winged Saint / After his charge receiv'd" (247–48);[24] God's is "*to render Man inexcusable*" (The Argument) for a crime he has as yet scarcely thought of perpetrating:

> this let him know,
> Lest wilfully transgressing he pretend
> Surprisal, unadmonisht, unforewarn'd.                 (243–45)

The proximate consequence of the mission (and hence its apparent rationale) will be to clear God's "*own Justice and Wisdom from all imputation*," he "*having created Man free and able enough to have withstood his Tempter*" (III, The Argument): "So spake th' Eternal Father," Milton concludes, "and fulfill'd / All Justice" (V, 246–47).

Now, as I see it, and as the literature on the subject amply attests, at least the following objections can be raised to Raphael's journey: (1) it seems redundant, Adam having already been warned by God himself to "swerve not too secure"; it is a mission either (2) impossible or (3) beside the point, God's unerring prescience of Adam's fall having assured that Raphael's admonitions, however vehemently reiterated, will be ignored; and (4) it is allegedly conceived in "pity" but in reality executed in "Justice," a "Justice" moreover so odious that Thomas Greene has concluded, in a searching criticism of the role of Raphael in *Paradise Lost*, that "when it is scrutinized, God's generosity in dispatching [the angel] turns out to be not at all a true magnanimity but a petty legalistic self-righteousness."[25]

The first two of these objections are easily disposed of: as to the first, even if Adam has already been told by God that he will die if he eats the forbidden Fruit (IV, 419–32), and even if he knows already of his free estate (V, 548–49), this knowledge is, in Adam's innocence, of purely "academic" interest, so to speak: witness his naive reference to the "easy charge" (IV, 421) and his incredulous question "can we want obedience then / To [God], or possibly his love desert [?]" (V, 514–15). Raphael's mission is designed in part to persuade Adam of the real and present danger of disobedience — and of Satan: the angel is to "*admonish him . . . of his enemy near at hand; who he is, and why his enemy*" (The Argument). So his descent is not redundant. As to the second difficulty, although there may be certain missions impossible in *Paradise Lost*, Raphael's is not one of them:[26] as commissioned, he communicates, in language accommodated to Adam's human understanding, matters of fact, principles of philosophy, and specific warnings, all of which our father readily comprehends.

As to Raphael's "Venial discourse" (IX, 5) being beside the point, God having long since "*fore[told] the success of Satan in perverting mankind*" (III, The Argument), this is a more weighty objection. For although God enjoins Adam at his creation not to eat the Fruit of the Tree of Knowledge, and though Raphael cautions Adam to beware by the example of Satan, a warning he twice reiterates, and though Satan cannot "deceive" the archangel Uriel "once warn'd" (IV, 124–25), nevertheless, Adam will certainly repudiate Raphael's advice and "easily transgress the sole Command" (III, 94). Given these foreknown facts the angel's mission would appear to be an exercise in futility.

That it is futile seems even more evident when one considers the descent of Raphael in the context of its classical prototypes. The mission corresponds to a part of the epic repertoire studied by Thomas Greene and (more recently) by Francis C. Blessington.[27] Among relevant analogues, Greene cites the descent of Hermes in the Vth *Odyssey*, the suasive purpose of which is to convince Calypso to facilitate the captive Odysseus' return to Ithaca, and the appearance of Mercury to Aeneas in the IVth *Aeneid*, wherein he twice enjoins Aeneas to free himself from uxorious bondage to Queen Dido. Greene finds the Vergilian examplar a particularly apt Miltonic source because of the ethical urgency with which it is suffused: Mercury's descent, like Raphael's, takes the form of a categorical imperative, the god demanding "that the self be made an *imperium*."[28] Common to both Homeric and Vergilian usage, however, is the foreknown fact that the divine admonitions will speedily be heeded, whereas in *Paradise Lost* the reverse is true. Sensing perhaps the latent absurdity of Raphael issuing warnings that both he and God foreknow will be ignored, Greene is persuaded finally to deny the legislative motive of his mission: the angel "is dispatched neither to prod nor to encourage nor to punish," he writes, "but to explain, almost indeed to lecture."[29] Greene's denial of the mission's admonitory rationale is unconvincing, but is not our only alternative to dismiss Raphael's injunctions as patently futile?

So at any rate they have seemed to a number of Milton scholars. The vague sense of dissatisfaction with Raphael that Arthur E. Barker expressed when he wrote that the angel "learns much in his effort to respond adequately to his call"[30] becomes a firm if temperate judgment of failure in a later essay: the angel's "somewhat Platonized and uncertain account of past history should prepare Adam (and Eve) for the trial to come," Barker writes, "but somehow fails of doing so adequately."[31] And Thomas Greene's attempt to rationalize by denial has been seconded recently by Robert Crosman: "the pretext of Raphael's visit to warn Adam is *perceived* by us as a pretext," he claims, because "Adam can't be helped to resist the Fall but only to repair its effects afterwards."[32] In the final analysis these criticisms may reflect their authors' grasp of the properly legislative role generally assigned to prophetic utterances in the later Renaissance: "after Tasso," Joseph Wittreich writes, "legislative responsibility becomes increasingly more of an obsession to the poet, especially after epic joins with prophecy. . . . Like the epic poet the prophet may recount history; but his purpose is less to record it than to bring it to an apotheosis."[33] In the matter of Raphael's prophetic utterances, however, both he and the reader foreknow that their presumed world-transforming functions will be vitiated, Adamic apotheosis being contingent upon an obedience (V, 493–505) that will be honored only in the breach. Ought not therefore Raphael (and Milton) to have preferred a blameless silence before the futile office of hopeless admonition?

Yes, assuredly—*if* one endorses the parsimonious assumption that the reiterated warnings of *Paradise Lost* ought to have been motivated by the hope (if not the certainty) that they would be heeded. Although a moment's reflection will suffice to lay bare the illogic of this misconception, the fallacy that to be adequately forewarned is ipso facto to be insuperably forearmed merits further discussion, for it is attractive enough to have insinuated itself into the impassioned plea for help that, in distant anticipation of Raphael's descent, escapes from the lips of *Paradise Lost*'s narrator at the imminent intrusion of the Evil One into the sacred precincts of Eden:

O for that warning voice, which he who saw
Th' *Apocalypse*, heard cry in Heav'n aloud,
Then when the Dragon, put to second rout,
Came furious down to be reveng'd on men,
*Woe to the inhabitants on Earth!* that now,
While time was, our first Parents had been warn'd
The coming of thir secret foe, and scap'd
Haply so scap'd his mortal snare.          (IV, 1–8)

One cannot but be struck by the audacity of this prayer. If, on the one hand, in a rare suspension of narrative omniscience, Milton does not fore-know that Raphael's mission is in the offing, his supplication hovers on the edge of blasphemy, for its contrary-to-fact modality implies that God neglected "innocent frail man" (11) in the aboriginal human crisis. If, on the other hand, Milton is deliberately anticipating the descent of the archangel, his prayer seems at best disingenuous (since it implies that Raphael never come to warn Adam), and at worst a proleptic disquali-fication of the angel's stewardship (since Milton desiderates the voice of Revelation xii, 10–13, not Raphael's). Overwhelmed with the sense of Heaven's desertion, the poet appears to conceive of adequate forewarn-ing and the supposed infallibility of "our first Parents" as being anon twin halves of one august but tragically unrealized event: for "had" Adam and Eve "been warn'd / The coming of thir secret foe," they would have "scap'd / . . . so" (i.e., thereby, by means of the warning): as if, in a com-plete reversal of Raphael's priorities, Milton would substitute external admonition for internal self-sufficiency as the sine qua non of human perseverance.

But, on the other hand, Milton — the prophetic Milton who, in the hallowed tradition of Isaiah and Jeremiah, published on the eve of the Restoration *The Ready and Easy Way to Establish a Free Commonwealth,* a tract whose impassioned admonitions he knew to a moral certainty would fall on deaf ears — assuredly knew that timely warnings are often ignored. That is why he carefully wrote not "scap'd / . . . so scap'd" but "scap'd / *Haply* [i.e., perhaps, by chance] so scap'd": the doublet "Haply so" oxymoronically signals the absence of any relevant connection between Raphael's (or God's) admonitions and Adam's standing (or his sufficiency to have stood). Is the relationship between warning and standing casual (*Haply*) or causal (*so*)? But the question is absurd! The two events are not at all related, though they have appeared to be the yolk and white of one shell. Aware of this, Raphael would not expect God's charge to him to follow the illogical pattern "Go therefore, converse with Adam, tell him of Satan, *lest he transgress*"— for the italicized words constitute a non sequitur that would indeed make the angel's mission an impossible exercise in futility. Milton takes certain risks in *Paradise Lost* IV, 1–8 in order to admonish not Adam but the reader, whom he cautions not to be shocked upon learning that Raphael is sent to warn Adam not lest he wilfully transgress, but "Lest wilfully transgressing he pretend / Surprisal." Far from requiring, as the condition of sufficiency, the insights about Satan he acquires from Raphael, Adam need not even know of the Devil's existence.

This brings me to the final difficulty with the role of Raphael in *Paradise Lost*—that it seems motivated by a legalism less indicative of divine magnanimity than of pharisaic self-righteousness: "*God to render Man inexcusable sends* Raphael *to admonish him*" (V, The Argument). Given the apparently defensive rigor of the deity, Thomas Greene seems entitled to complain that "the majesty of Raphael's descent can only be appreciated if the awkwardness of its motive remains half-forgotten."[34]

Greene and others like him might nevertheless have judged Milton's God less harshly had they considered the two most relevant classical parallels to Raphael's mission. The first occurs in Hesiod's *Works and Days* when Zeus sends Hermes to punish Epimetheus' reception of the gift of fire from Prometheus: the blacksmith god Hephaistos having created Pandora, and Hermes having "into her heart . . . put lies, and wheedling words of falsehood, and a treacherous nature," Zeus sends Maia's son to present the first woman to mankind: "the Father sent the gods' fleet messenger, Hermes, to Epimetheus, bringing her, a gift, nor did Epimetheus remember to think how Prometheus had told him never to accept a gift from Olympian Zeus, but always to send it back, for fear it might prove to be an evil for mankind. He took the evil, and only perceived it when he possessed her."[35] This account bears intimately upon Milton's practice in *Paradise Lost* insofar as it is a paradigm instance in classical literature of a timely warning being issued notwithstanding the certainty that it will be ignored: just as Adam forgets to remember the high injunction (endlessly reiterated by Raphael) not to taste the forbidden Fruit, so Epimetheus foolishly, absent-mindedly, and in blatant disregard of the warnings of Prometheus, neglects to repudiate Pandora. But in Hesiod Zeus *intends* that the admonitions of his enemy the fire-bringer be ignored: Pandora is a "sheer, impossible deception" (83), and the messenger god is an accessory to his father before and during the tragic fact: "to Hermes . . . [Zeus] gave instructions to put in Pandora the mind of a hussy, and a treacherous nature" (68–69). The celestial descent in the *Works and Days* is designed to ruin mankind, whose fall from grace proceeds (if I may be permitted a theological anachronism) in the harshest supralapsarian tradition of Calvinist predestination. The bottom line on the mission of Hermes is indeed that "there is no way to avoid what Zeus has intended" (105).[36]

For these reasons Milton is at great pains in *Paradise Lost* to dissociate himself from Hesiod's so-called "theodicy"— precisely to discredit the intimate Wittgensteinian family resemblance between pagan myth and Christian mystery. As Adam and his wife enter their "blissful Bower" (IV, 690) Milton articulates a simile that carefully distinguishes Hesiod's narrative from his own:

> Here in close recess
> With Flowers, Garlands, and sweet-smelling Herbs
> Espoused *Eve* deckt first her Nuptial Bed,
> And heav'nly Choirs the Hymenaean sung,
> What day the genial Angel to our Sire
> Brought her in naked beauty more adorn'd,
> More lovely than *Pandora*, whom the Gods
> Endow'd with all thir gifts, and O too like
> In sad event, when to the unwiser Son
> Of *Japhet* brought by *Hermes*, she ensnar'd
> Mankind with her fair looks, to be aveng'd
> On him who had stole *Jove*'s authentic fire.          (708–19)

In this simile "*Eve*," "the genial Angel," Adam ("our Sire"), and God are comparable to "*Pandora*," "*Hermes*," Epimetheus ("the unwiser Son / Of *Japhet*"), and "*Jove*"; moreover, in both Hesiod and Milton woman is given to man "to be aveng'd / On him [Prometheus/Satan] who had stole *Jove*'s [Jehovah's] authentic fire."[37] But the perfection of naked Eve, who is "Virtue-proof" (V, 384), far excels Pandora's in all real dignity, and Milton's God, unlike Hesiod's Zeus, intends Eve to rectify man's "single imperfection," not to destroy him (VIII, 423–51). Milton, *pace* Hesiod, laments that Eve and Pandora are "O too like / In sad event"— in outcome, that is, when Adam's wife, "for thee ordain'd / A help, *became* thy snare" (XI, 164–65; emphasis mine) through acquired (not innate) perversity. Eve thus becomes (in a true Aristotelian peripeteia) what Pandora always is, and Adam, who "not deceiv'd," nevertheless permits himself to be "fondly overcome with Female charm" (IX, 998–99), thus becomes our true Epimetheus.[38] Milton's simile is a precise exercise in close discrimination that by implication condemns the descent of Hermes in the *Works and Days* as blasphemously prejudicial to both the goodness and greatness of God: however awkward the mission of Raphael may appear to his modern detractors, it becomes a work of genuine magnanimity when compared to the pusillanimous machinations of Hesiod's Zeus and Hermes.[39]

The mission's equanimity is likewise evinced when it is compared to a second celestial descent ignored by Greene and others—that alluded to by Zeus in the opening lines of the *Odyssey*. Odysseus is trapped on the island of Calypso, victim at once of the goddess's lust and of the implacable hatred of Poseidon, whose son Polyphemos the man of many turns has years ago blinded in self-defense. At the insistence of his benefactress Athena, who pleads Odysseus' case by appealing to fair play, Zeus promises to dispatch Hermes to secure the hero's release. First, however, the god recalls (by way of anticipatory contrast and in order to clear his own justice) the legal circumstances surrounding the retributive murder of Aigisthos:

> The father of men and gods began to speak among them.
> In his heart he was remembering excellent Aigisthos
> Whom Agamemnon's son, far-famed Orestes, had slain.
> Thinking of that man, he made his speech to the immortals:
> "Well now, how indeed mortal men do blame the gods!
> They say it is from us evils come, yet they themselves
> By their recklessness have pains beyond their lot.
> So this Aigisthos married beyond his lot the lawful
> Wife of the son of Atreus, and killed him on his return;
> Knowing he would be destroyed, since we told him beforehand:
> We had sent sharp-eyed Hermes, the slayer of Argos,
> To tell him not to kill the man and not to woo his wife,
> Or payment would come through Orestes, descendant of Atreus,
> As soon as he came of age and longed for his own land.
> So Hermes told him, but though of good mind himself, he did not
> Change Aigisthos' mind. And now he has paid for it all."[40]

If the *Odyssey* was composed after the *Works and Days*[41] its author—whoever he was—may have invented the above passage with Hesiod in mind. It certainly represents a dramatic jurisprudential advance over the crude casuistry of the Boeotian shepherd. It is also a corrective codicil to the *Iliad*: the "speech of Zeus implies a belief radically different from that found in the *Iliad*," writes Hugh Lloyd-Jones. "There the god puts evil ideas, no less than good ideas, into men's minds; that is how men's *moira*, the portion assigned them by the gods, comes to be fulfilled. When the god wishes to destroy a man, he sends Ate to take away his wits. But now Zeus denies that the gods put evil ideas into the minds of men, and even claims that they warn men against evil ideas they themselves have thought of."[42]

For these reasons, it is certain that Milton vastly preferred the *Odyssey*'s theodicy to those in the *Works and Days* and the *Iliad*: he concludes his analysis "Of Predestination" in the *Christian Doctrine* by twice citing "even a heathen like Homer" to the effect that man's own free will self-corrupted is the adequate and sufficient cause of his disobedience (YP VI, 202). Milton's proof-texts are, first, the observation that Odysseus' companions "lost their own lives because of their recklessness" (*Odyssey* I, 6–9) in ignoring Teiresias' and Circe's abjurations not to eat the cattle of Hyperion (*Odyssey* XI, 84–117; XII, 127–41), and second, Zeus's disclaimer that the gods are responsible for the destruction of Aigisthos — or indeed of any man. Milton evidently regarded the descent of Hermes in *Odyssey* I, 28–43, as a rare pagan instance of perfectly realized distributive poetic justice. As Maia's son to Aigisthos, so Raphael to Adam: Zeus/God to render Aigisthos/Adam inexcusable sends Hermes/Raphael to admonish man of his obedience. Their cautionary warnings fall on deaf ears but serve the noble purpose of "fulfill[ing] / All [distributive] Justice" (*PL* V, 246–47). Given the evident isomorphism of the two episodes, it is patently unfair to accuse Milton of awkwardly motivating the mission of Raphael: by using it to clear God's "*own Justice*" (III, The Argument) he is merely emulating the *Odyssey*'s justification of the ways of Zeus to Aigisthos, and no one (to my knowledge) has taken exception to the Greek narrative as an unsatisfactory theodicy characterized less by divine justice than by self-justifying paranoia and pharisaism.

In the *Odyssey*, nevertheless, the justice we encounter is rather more often retributive than distributive: Hermes "did not / Change Aigisthos' mind. *And now he has paid for it all*" (I, 42–43; emphasis mine) — and witness also the gruesome vengeance exacted of the suitors of Penelope at *Odyssey* XXII and XXIV. Were *Paradise Lost* to recapitulate exactly the Greek archetype, the descent of Raphael would eventuate in retribution for Adam's and Eve's transgression that would make the fate of Aigisthos seem paradisiacal by comparison; for in addition to adultery and murder our grand parents commit a plethora of offenses including blasphemy and genocide.[43] Milton, however, never merely recapitulates his Hellenic and Roman forebears:[44] unlike Zeus vis-à-vis Aigisthos, Milton's God beholds unfallen Adam and Eve "with pity" (V, 220) *and therefore* sends Raphael paradoxically to satisfy "All Justice" (247). Since Messiah has already "offer'd himself to die" in vicarious atonement of "man's offense" (III, 409–10), precisely "to appease [God's] wrath, and end the strife / Of Mercy and Justice in [his] face discern'd" (406–07), and since the Father has already accepted the offer, "as is most just" (294), it is possible in *Paradise Lost* to distinguish most of God's judgments into mercies. Although divine retribution of the sort meted out to the fallen angels (V, 600–615) and to incorrigibly hard-hearted men (III, 198–202) is purely punitive, it is also atypical: even immediately after Adam's and

Eve's fall, when Milton has led us to expect not pity but "distance and distaste, / Anger and just rebuke, and judgment giv'n" (IX, 9–10), we encounter instead a "gracious Judge" (X, 118) who dispenses "Mercy colleague with Justice" (59) in ample fulfillment of God's earlier assurance that "Mercy first and last shall brightest shine" (III, 134). The foreknown death of Messiah having repaid man's debt of retribution measure for measure (214–15), the dispensation of justice to Adam can be exclusively restorative:[45] It is therefore less justice than—in Jon Lawry's apt description—"the sharp right profile of Mercy."[46]

This is nowhere more true than with respect to the role of Raphael. His mission is a work of special providence consequent to God's eternal prescience of Adam's fall and dependent upon the decision of "his Heart [not *mind*] / Omniscient" (X, 6–7), through infinite pity, to ameliorate that catastrophe before it happens by predestinating Adam to salvation according to rubrics spelled out in the *Christian Doctrine* I, iv:

The principal SPECIAL DECREE of God which concerns men is called PREDESTINATION: by which GOD, BEFORE THE FOUNDATIONS OF THE WORLD WERE LAID, *HAD MERCY ON THE HUMAN RACE*, ALTHOUGH IT WAS GOING TO FALL OF ITS OWN ACCORD, AND, TO SHOW THE GLORY OF HIS MERCY, GRACE, AND WISDOM, PREDESTINED TO ETERNAL SALVATION, ACCORDING TO HIS PURPOSE or plan IN CHRIST, THOSE WHO WOULD IN THE FUTURE BELIEVE AND CONTINUE IN THE FAITH. (YP VI, 168; emphasis mine)

Thus in *Paradise Lost* God, foreseeing that man will fall (III, 92–99), *"declares his purpose of grace towards him"* (The Argument) by publishing the decree of predestination: "Man therefore shall find grace" (131). The decree entails the foreknown death of Messiah, whose willing expiation of Adam's crime (211–12) enables God's predestinating words to become flesh, so to speak: "man shall find grace," Messiah cries, "And shall grace not find means[?]" (227–28). The "means" are, first, Christ's redemptive death, but also, and most importantly in the context of the descent of Raphael, the renovation of Adam's and Eve's "lapsed powers" (176) through quite ordinary psychological processes that, in the *Christian Doctrine* I, xix, Milton calls "recognition of sin, contrition, confession, abandonment of evil and conversion to good" (*YP* VI, 468). Precisely these stages occur in Book X of *Paradise Lost* when, in what seems a wholly natural sequence of events, Adam and Eve eventually acknowledge their mutual sinfulness, confess their mutual guilt to God, and beg his "pardon" "with tears" and "sighs" "sent from hearts contrite" (X, 1101–03). We then learn (as we ought to have expected after reading III, 185–90) that their rehabilitation has been mediated by "Prevenient Grace descending" that "remov'd / The stony from thir hearts" (XI, 3–4).[47]

Now the ways of regeneration in *Paradise Lost* are the key to the role of Raphael. In the matter of Adam's rehabilitation he is the *angelus* ex machina in a renovative plot requiring three instances of visible divine intervention, the other two being by Messiah (X, 47–102) and Michael (XI, 99–225). Visiting unfallen Adam, Raphael *is* "Prevenient Grace descending"—"descending from the Thrones above" (V, 363) — in anticipation not only of man's repentance (the ostensible function of prevenient grace) *but of his fall as well.* Shall not predestinated man find grace? And shall not grace find means? Enter Raphael. Through him Adam will "oft be warn'd / [His] sinful state" (III, 185–86) before he has sinned! Or more precisely, he will be admonished of Satan's imminent intentions, so that once fallen he will be forced, so to speak, by ineluctable evidence to convict himself of grievous sin. Raphael descends, in short, to soften Adam's stony heart before it has hardened, to initiate his postlapsarian regeneration before he lapses.[48] Insofar as he is sent to render man inexcusable his mission may appear petty, legalistic, and self-righteous; his function nevertheless is not so much to clear God's justice as to hasten Adam's repentance by making it crystal-clear to him that God "made him just and right, / Sufficient to have stood" (III, 98–99). The "Justice" that God "fulfill'd" in dispatching Raphael is thus less fair play than a merciful work of supererogation, assuring Adam of the Original Justice of his creation and fulfilling "*All* Justice"— even that which a fallen, sinful, and self-extenuating creature might unreasonably expect — by warning him above and beyond the demands of distributive jurisprudence.[49]

Do Adam and Eve need Raphael? As our father is about to fall he is said to "*extenuat[e] the trespass*" (IX, The Argument), and later both he and Eve engage in "mutual accusation," "neither self-condemning" (IX, 1187–88). Adam subsequently extenuates in the very presence of God, attributing his fall to Eve (X, 125–43) — a specious allegation he reiterates in a vicious barrage of misogyny directed both at her (X, 867–908) and later about her (XI, 632–33). He also blames God for having made him (X, 743–52), for having made Eve (888–95), for having commanded an impossible obedience (750–52), and for having punished all men for his offense (822–24). Given these epidemic extenuating propensities, Milton's remark about Adam's and Eve's falling to variance with one another seems entirely apposite: "of thir vain contest appear'd no end" (IX, 1189).

Do Adam and Eve need Raphael? Short of a more direct act of divine intervention in the form perhaps of some irresistible grace (like that which converts Saul at Acts ix), some such intermediary as Raphael seems requisite to put an end to the vicious cycle of self-extenuating summarized above—if, that is, Adam and Eve are to be redeemed. Fallen Eve blames her Satanic seduction on Adam, who erred, she argues, in permitting her that fateful morning to garden solitarily—whence, she erroneously thinks, her fall (IX, 1155-61). Adam's rejoinder, however ill-motivated, shows that shortly before Eve's transgression he did for her exactly what Raphael had done for both of them:

> I warn'd thee, I admonish'd thee, foretold
> The danger, and the lurking Enemy
> That lay in wait; beyond this had been force,
> And force upon free Will hath here no place. (1171-74)

Had Raphael been permitted to converse with Adam after the fall, he might well have spoken the same words to him. Even without them, however, his mission eventually has precisely the desiderated effect: thanks to Raphael, dim beginnings of *metanoia* are scattered amidst Adam's fallen ravings: "I deserv'd it" (X, 726), he says, "Be it so, for I submit, [God's] doom is fair" (769). The first substantive breakthrough toward full conviction of guilt occurs, however, after Adam acknowledges the justice of his Original Sin's hereditary penalties (821-28). The admission marks the terminus not, to be sure, of Adam's regeneration, but of the infinite pity that has sought so lovingly *"to render Man inexcusable"*:

> [God] after all Disputes
> Forc't I absolve: all my evasions vain
> And reasonings, though through Mazes, lead me still
> But to my own conviction: first and last
> On mee, mee only, as the source and spring
> Of all corruption, all the blame lights due. (828-33)

Raphael has thus been privileged to play a pivotal role, as the harbinger of prevenient grace, in the redemption of Adam and Eve. No wonder Milton calls him "the sociable Spirit" (V, 221), and no wonder the "affable Arch-angel" (VII, 41) so speedily and unreluctantly (V, 247-48) executes his aery purposes: his motive has been a true *imitatio Christi*: "immortal love / To mortal men, above which only shone / Filial obedience" (III, 267-69). The finest commentary on his descent from Heaven was composed preveniently by the sage and serious Edmund Spenser, with whose unconscious tribute to Raphael I hasten to conclude this section:

And is there care in heauen? and is there loue
In heauenly spirits to these creatures bace,
That may compassion of their euils moue?
There is: else much more wretched were the cace
Of men, then beasts. But O th' exceeding grace
Of highest God, that loues his creatures so,
And all his workes with mercy doth embrace,
That blessed Angels, he sends to and fro,
To serue to wicked man, to serue his wicked foe.

How oft do they, their siluer bowers leaue,
To come to succour vs, that succour want?
How oft do they with golden pineons, cleaue
The flitting skyes, like flying Pursuiuant,
Against foule feends to aide vs millitant?
They for vs fight, they watch and dewly ward,
And their bright Squadrons round about vs plant,
And all for loue, and nothing for reward:
O why should heauenly God to men haue such regard?[50]

To resolve the dilemma posed in Spenser's concluding alexandrine, and
to show also how and how universally Milton's God has "such regard"
to the "wicked" sons of Adam, I turn now to the examplary case of Samson and the Woman of Timna in *Samson Agonistes*.

## II

In a convincing clarification of Christ's strategic allusion to Deuteronomy vi, 16 ("Tempt not the Lord thy God") in *Paradise Regained* IV,
560–61, Irene Samuel asserts that in matters of biblical exegesis "the direction of Milton's nonconformities was never toward greater mystery, greater
miracle, but rather always toward greater rationality, greater availability as a guide in living."[51] Her point is as true of *Samson Agonistes* as
it is of the brief epic. F. Michael Krouse has hedgingly averred that "one
can say that Milton's interpretation of the Samson story *is ostensibly* an
example of rationalistic literalism,"[52] but I will argue the far stronger
hypothesis that Milton's reconstruction of Judges xiii–xvi is designed part
and parcel to rehabilitate a highly embarrassing biblical narrative. My
primary proof-text will be the poet's recasting of Samson's relation to the
Woman of Timna, whom in Judges he marries at the urging of "the LORD,
that he sought an occasion against the Philistines: for at that time the
Philistines had dominion over Israel" (xiv, 4). Milton's God, I shall
demonstrate, has additional, nonterritorial reasons for motivating the mar-

riage: he does so, first, to make sense of Samson's subsequent marriage to Dalila, and second (on the analogy with the descent of Raphael in *Paradise Lost*), to facilitate his regeneration before he falls. *Samson Agonistes* thereby transforms a signally awkward episode in the Judges saga into yet another instance of God's loving providence.

Let us begin by briefly enumerating those features of the Old Testament folk hero that required Milton to accommodate the details of his life and death to a pious interpretation; for even if the poet saw in the biblical Samson a ready-made and divinely sactioned alter ego through whom to sublimate his personal anxieties about having gone blind, he saw little else worth emulating or commemorating in the boorish, womanizing Danite of Holy Writ. J. Blenkinsopp has summarized part of the case against Samson in a brilliant study of the saga's structure: the Judges plot "revolves around an explicitly religious theme," he writes, "that of the broken vow. . . . Samson is a *nazir*. The regulations for the Nazirite [Num. vi, 1–21] specify that he must avoid contact with a dead body, must not drink wine or *sekar* and, most important, must not allow his hair to be cut for the whole period of the vow."[53] According to Blenkinsopp, Samson's marriage to the Timnite involves a threefold rejection of his vocation: (1) his taking a Philistine wife (xiv, 1–3) "is an implicit repudiation of the vow in intent," marriage with a Canaanite being expressly forbidden by Deuteronomy vii, 1–3; (2) his eating honey from the carcass of a lion he has killed (xiv, 5–9) involves ritual defilement by forbidden contact with the dead; and (3) his "alliance with the alien woman leads inevitably to his taking part in a marriage feast at the heart of which is a 'drinking bout'" (citing Judges xiv, 10).[54] These violations are compounded (4) when Samson destroys a contingent of Philistines with the jawbone of an ass (xv, 9–17), (5) when he traffics with a prostitute at Gaza (xvi, 1–3), (6) when he lusts after Dalila (xvi, 4), and (7) — most egregiously — when he reveals to her the secret of his strength, whereupon Dalila divests him of both his power and his Naziriteship, her shearing of Samson's locks being the symbolic equivalent of terminating his affiliation with the select group of *nazirim*. To this litany of sins may be added at least the following corollary offenses: (8) Samson obeys — without demur — the Philistines' command to entertain them at the festival of Dagon (xvi, 25), thereby violating the Mosaic prohibitions against idolatry (Exodus xxii, 5 and xxiii, 24); (9) he commits suicide when he declares, just before destroying the pagan temple, "Let me die with the Philistines" (xvi, 30); and (10), perhaps worst of all, he expresses not an iota of remorse for any of the nine offenses just cited.

Now in spite of the biblical Samson's dubious record, the author of the Epistle to the Hebrews found him worthy of mention (along with the likes of Abel, Abraham, and Moses) as an Old Testament hero of faith (Heb. xi, 1–32). Perhaps for this reason St. Jerome's Vulgate expunges from the authoritative Masoretic text the hero's suicidal valediction;[55] perhaps for this reason the marginal glosses of the Geneva Bible — as George W. Whiting and Jackie DiSalvo have shown — exculpate Samson of all sin save revelation of his strength's secret springs;[56] perhaps for this reason — perhaps for others — Milton likewise adjusts the biblical text in *Samson Agonistes* to eliminate the ethical inconveniences of most of Samson's behavior. Reserving offenses (1), (7), and (10) for later — and fuller — discussion, I offer the following examples to illustrate the poet's rehabilitative compositional strategy: (1) as to Samson's twice ritually defiling himself, Milton nowhere mentions the incident with the dead lion, and while both the Chorus and Samson allude briefly to the proverbial ass's jawbone, they do so only to evidence the Danite's strength and his probity in assaulting Philistines (142–45, 261–64); (2) as to his becoming intoxicated at his bachelor party — if in fact Milton was aware of it — again both Samson and the Chorus affirm his perpetual abstinence;[57] (3) in the matter of the harlot of Gaza, *Samson Agonistes* never refers to this lustful episode (though the poet willingly records its immediate consequence, the strong man's prodigiously carrying the doorposts of the Gaza city gates to the top of a steep hill (146–50); (4) as to Samson lusting after Dalila, Milton, as I indicated earlier, transforms his promiscuity into married love; (5) in the matter of attendance at the Dagonalia, Milton's Samson — unlike his biblical prototype — *thrice* refuses to accompany the Public Officer to the spectacle (1319–47), and when at last he capitulates, he justifies doing so on impeccable casuistical grounds;[58] and (6) the problem of Samson's suicide is likewise resolved casuistically, both in The Argument (wherein a Messenger "*relat*[*es*] *the Catastrophe, what* Samson *had done to the* Philistins, *and by accident to himself*") and twice in the text (1586–89, 1660–68). A skeptical reader might protest one or more of these face-saving modifications, but their cumulative weight suggests a deliberate and systematic rehabilitative effort. To clinch the point, I might mention a final relevant (but apparently quite minor) Miltonic variation on a biblical theme: in Judges xv, 8, having smitten many Philistines in revenge for their murder of the Woman of Timna, Samson "went down and dwelt in the top of the rock Etam." The text does not say why — perhaps Samson is merely resting, perhaps he has withdrawn, Achilles-like, to sulk over the death of his Timnite bride — but in any event he is not about his heavenly Father's business, so to speak. In *Samson*

*Agonistes* Milton adjusts the biblical account to eliminate the implicit charge of dereliction of duty: *his* Samson

> Safe to the rock of *Etham* was retir'd,
> *Not flying*, but forecasting in what place
> To set upon [the Philistines], what advantag'd best.
>
> (253–55; emphasis mine)

It is as if the hero has the text of Judges at hand and seeks to set the historical record straight by filling in the inspired (but elliptical) paratactic transitions of Judges with a pious hypotactic scholium; certainly Milton at least has this purpose in mind.

The same is true with respect to Samson's marriage to the Woman of Timna. Judges xiv, 4 claims — awkwardly, given the xenophobic tenacity with which Deuteronomy prohibits mixed marriages — that Yahweh has arranged the union to create a subterfuge for harrying Philistines. Providentially, the stratagem works: in devastating response to his bride's betrayal of him (xiv, 15–18), Samson slays thirty Ashkelonites (xiv, 19), destroys Philistine crops and vineyards (xv, 4–5), occasions the immolation of the Timnite and her father (xv, 6), indulges in a general rampage (xv, 8), and dispatches "a thousand men" with "the jawbone of an ass" (xv, 15–17). So important is his vendetta that it requires fully a fifth of the biblical narrative (21 of 96 verses) to recount the bloodbath triggered by Samson's marriage.

Now *Samson Agonistes* acknowledges these violent consequences but it radically deemphasizes them: less than 8 percent of the tragedy (129.5 of 1,758 lines) alludes to Samson's retaliation, most of the references are peremptory, and one incident — that involving the three hundred foxes (xv, 3–5) — is omitted entirely. On the other hand, whereas Judges motivates the marriage almost offhandedly, devoting only a single verse (xiv, 4) to supernaturalizing what would otherwise appear to be a case of lust at first sight, Milton takes relatively greater pains (52 lines) to scrutinize the union's origins: he is apparently less than edified with Samson the scourge of God and more than a little anxious to reconcile his hero's Timnite interlude with the matrimonial caveats of the Mosaic code. Thus, early in the play, in response to Choral doubts (215–18), Samson justifies his marriage (219–26) "on the basis of the casuistical concept of the significance of the intention, surrounding circumstances, and probable consequences of an action."[59] Although Manoa expresses lingering ambivalence as to whether his son was prompted by "Divine impulsion" (422) to marry a gentile, which he will neither confirm nor deny,[60] Samson's account satisfies the Chorus, which repeats the rationale of Judges xiv,

4 (315–21) and later justifies its endorsement of the marriage (239) by invoking the dispensational prerogatives of God:

> [He] made our Laws to bind us, not himself,
> And hath full right to exempt
> Whom so it pleases him by choice
> From National obstriction, without taint
> Of sin, or legal debt;
> For with his own Laws he can best dispense.[61]        (309–14)

In sum, there is ample warrant in the play for accepting Samson's analysis of his first marriage — and no reason to fault him for the union, as at least one critic has done.[62]

On the other hand, Milton's redaction differs importantly from the Bible's in at least this respect: whereas Judges never says that Samson knew God was urging him to marry the Woman of Timna — only that his parents did *not* know — the hero of *Samson Agonistes* married her in obedient response to an inner prompting that grew daily upon him:

> The first [woman] I saw at *Timna*, and she pleas'd
> Mee, not my Parents, that I sought to wed,
> The daughter of an Infidel: they knew not
> That what I motion'd was of God; I knew
> From intimate impulse, and therefore urg'd
> The Marriage on; that by occasion hence
> I might begin *Israel's* Deliverance,
> The work to which I was divinely call'd.        (219–26)

This most striking departure from Holy Scripture is a modification consistent with Milton's intention throughout *Samson Agonistes* to associate the inward light of God's Spirit with reasoned deliberation and critical self-awareness. Moreover Samson's intuition of the divine will enables the poet to utilize the Timnite marriage — with extraordinary dramatic economy — for purposes never dreamed of by the redactors of Judges. Proximately, it motivates Samson's marriage to Dalila: the Woman of Timna "proving false," Samson explains,

> the next I took to Wife
> (O that I never had! fond wish too late)
> Was in the Vale of *Sorec*, *Dalila*,
> That specious Monster, my accomplisht snare.
> I thought it lawful from my former act,
> And the same end; still watching to oppress
> *Israel's* oppressors.        (227–33)

In Judges Samson's assignation with Dalila is a private and selfish affair, lust (or perhaps love) having led him to interrupt his vocation as Israel's judge to sport with yet another gentile in the shady vineyards of Sorec. By having *his* Samson *marry* Dalila for *public political* reasons, Milton neatly eliminates the implicit censoriousness of the scriptural version. His Samson "interpreted intuition by analogy,"[63] and so decided to marry a second Philistine woman, "still watching to oppress / *Israel's* oppressors." What a far cry from the backsliding *nazir* of the Old Testament!

Now it is clear — given my hypothesis that *Samson Agonistes* is a rehabilitative reconstruction of Judges — that for Milton the Timnite marriage is explained as exculpating Samson from an array of embarrassing charges ranging from lust through ritual defilement and intoxication to military desertion. But the matter is not that simple, for Milton's decision to use the first marriage to motivate the second also entails an inconvenience quite absent from the Bible: it appears to make God's original "intimate impulse" (223) responsible for Samson's fall: God causes the Timnite wedding, which causes the marriage with Dalila, which causes the hero's blindness, humiliation, and despair — the state of affairs with which *Samson Agonistes* commences. Although this sort of thinking is easily refuted as an instance of the post hoc, ergo propter hoc fallacy, and although — in contravention of *Paradise Lost* III, 120–23 — it would make God the author of sin, it is so attractive an error as to pervade Milton's play, especially discussion of Samson's second bride. Early on, Samson parenthetically laments that he married her (228), as if the fact of marriage were synonymous with his downfall; much later the Chorus similarly yokes the two events when, in a veiled allusion to Dalila, it speciously describes Samson's sin as the ineluctable consequence of his wedding a Philistine (1044–45). Manoa is more explicit, alleging in a final comment that his son was as good as blind the moment he married the Woman of Timna: "The Virgins," he concludes,

> also shall on feastful days
> Visit [Samson's] Tomb with flowers, only bewailing
> His lot unfortunate in nuptial choice,
> From whence captivity and loss of eyes.　　　(1741–44)

No wonder Manoa has earlier declared, in a rare and uncharacteristically laconic litotes, that he "cannot praise thy marriage choices, Son" (420).

Nevertheless Samson's father has got things all wrong: in point of fact Samson's marriages do not necessitate his blindness — even if they have appeared to be twin halves of one lamentable and tragically realized

Aristotelian peripeteia. Just as, in *Paradise Lost* IV, 1–8, Milton takes certain risks to exorcise the specious assumption that to be adequately forewarned is to be insuperably forearmed, in *Samson Agonistes* he venti-
lates the kindred misogynistic fallacy that to marry at all is at all events
to miscarry. Loving father that Manoa is, he would extenuate Samson's
trespass by assigning its etiology to a union arranged by God. Yet not
God either: rather than attribute such a catastrophe to the inducing motions of a providential deity, Manoa finds a more convenient scapegoat
in Samson's "lot" ( = Greek *moira*) "unfortunate" ( = Greek *tyche*), which
he thus characterizes, oxymoronically, as the foreordained outcome of
some chance destiny. But Manoa has got things all wrong.

When, however, he speaks of Samson's "lot unfortunate in nuptial
*choice*" Manoa approximates a partial truth, for Samson was indeed free
to hear and heed or to neglect and scorn God's call to marry the Woman
of Timna: to Milton the divine motions are not at all irresistible impulses.
Moreover, Manoa seems vaguely to comprehend a fuller truth, namely,
that Samson's first and second marriages alike are related to his malfea-
sance only contiguously, as its necessary but not its sufficient conditions:
thus his initial stumbling analysis of his son's espousals is punctuated by
a more or less coherent effort to sort out the tangled web of responsibility
for them:

> I cannot praise thy marriage choices, Son [wrongly implying
>     that they caused Samson's fall],
> Rather approv'd them not [implying pique that Manoa's advice
>     fell on deaf ears]; but thou didst plead
> Divine impulsion prompting how thou might'st
> *Find some occasion* to infest our Foes [confirming Judges xiv, 4].
> I state not that [implying doubt whether God would urge such
>     disasters upon Samson]; this I am sure; our Foes
> *Found soon occasion* thereby to make thee
> Thir Captive, and thir triumph; thou the sooner
> Temptation found'st, or over potent charms [wrongly implying that
>     Samson could not resist Dalila's blandishments]
> To violate the sacred trust of silence
> Deposited within thee [correctly identifying his son's
>     transgression]; which to have kept
> Tacit, was in thy power; true [reluctantly conceding that
>     Samson was sufficient to have stood though free to fall].
>                                        (420–30; emphasis mine)

This most interesting oscillation between the obligation to censure his
suffering son and the desire to extenuate his trespasses correctly names

Samson's marriages as *the occasion* of his downfall — for they comprise the fact, event, or state of affairs that made it possible — without, however, necessitating it (a distinction Manoa repeats in lines 1714–16). The concept of occasional causality rescues God from complicity in Samson's sin, which is why Milton arranges for Manoa to invoke it — even if the old man cannot apply it consistently to the case of conscience that continues to perplex him.

The reader of *Samson Agonistes*, however, forearmed with the prescience conferred upon him by the Book of Judges, and sensitized to the subtle intricacies of special providence as incarnated in the descent of Raphael in *Paradise Lost*, can apply the concept of occasional causality more rigorously than Manoa can to render a full account of the Woman of Timna motif in the play: for if she is the distant occasion of Samson's fall, she is also the near occasion of his regeneration (just as, mutatis mutandis, Raphael triggers from afar the revivification of Adam and Eve). Milton's God (no less than the Bible's) urges Samson to marry the Timnite as a pretext for harrying Philistines — foreknowing however that given the Danite's military zeal, he will interpret the marriage as precedent-setting and so marry Dalila. God also foreknows that given the bias of Samson's free inclinations he will, having wed a second time, sin mortally by "divulg[ing] the secret gift of God" (201) to his wife. Now God could have prevented the sin by removing its near occasion (Dalila) by removing its distant occasion (the Timnite), just as he could have prevented Adam's and Eve's transgressions by eliminating from *their* world certain "specious object[s] by [Satan] suborn'd" (*PL* IX, 361) — namely, fallen Eve and "the spirited sly Snake" (613) respectively. But the gracefully prevenient motions of Milton's God never violate the free agency of his rational creatures (III, 120–23), however catastrophic the foreseen contingent consequences of their choices may be. God therefore urges Samson to initiate a chain of events that involves, in a first marriage, innocent publication of one secret (Samson's), but in a second, wrongful publication of another (God's). Foreseeing these contingencies, God all the while utilizes them, through the mighty wings outspread of his predestinating Spirit, to effect his hero's salvation *if only he will repent*. Shall not predestinated Samson find grace? And shall not prevenient grace find means? Enter the Woman of Timna. God sends her first, I repeat, to seek occasion against the Philistines, but second, given his prescience of the marriage's medium-range implications, to render Samson inexcusable for "publish[ing]" "God's . . . holy secret" (496–99) to Dalila. In thus preveniently reducing to absurdity the hypothetical claim of circumstantial extenuation as regards Samson's fall, God hastens his regeneration (as he does Adam's and Eve's) by educing from him the conviction of sin that is regeneration's critical first step.

Consequently, in startling and suggestive contrast to its biblical proto-type, *Samson Agonistes* can, in nine well-defined stages, rehearse the psychology of guilt and sorrow even unto superfluity: nearly every utterance of Samson is steeled with the sense of ire merited and affliction self-wrought. His opening soliloquy contains a first admission that exonerates God and identifies with astonishing precision the nature of Samson's "own default" (45),

> Who this high gift of strength committed to me,
> In what part lodg'd, how easily bereft me,
> Under the Seal of silence could not keep,
> But weakly to a woman must reveal it,
> O'ercome with importunity and tears.
> O impotence of mind, in body strong!         (47–52)

The seriousness of Samson's offense is implied in the diction with which he later describes it: he has violated the "hallow'd pledge / Of all my strength" (535–36), a crime he characterizes in language reminiscent of the fall of Adam. Indeed, Samson precisely recapitulates our grand father's Original Sin: just as Adam succumbs to "effeminate slackness" (*PL* XI, 634) and profanes the interdicted Tree, the "Sole pledge of his obe-dience (III, 95), so Samson has surrendered to "foul effeminacy" (*SA* 410) and "profan'd" his hair, "The Mystery of God giv'n me under pledge / Of vow" (377–79). Apart from the inheritability of Adam's transgression, his and Samson's sins are virtually identical.

The crucial difference is that whereas conviction of guilt is wrested as it were from Adam in a tortuous self-extenuating dialectic, Samson is first and last his own harshest critic: the mere presence of the Chorus elicits from him a second confession (195–202); when it offers misogynis-tically to extenuate his trespass by blaming Dalila (210–12), Samson guilt-ily insists that "She was not the prime cause, but I myself" (234); and when Manoa alleges that the punishment of blindness does not fit his son's crime, he having merely "through frailty err[ed]" (369), Samson dog-gedly dissents, discerning in the conviction of sin reasons to justify God's judgments from the insulsity of his father's mortal tongue:

> Appoint not heavenly disposition, Father,
> Nothing of all these evils hath befall'n me
> But justly; I myself have brought them on,
> Sole Author I, sole cause: if aught seem vile,

As vile hath been my folly, who have profan'd
The mystery of God giv'n me under pledge
Of vow, and have betray'd it to a woman,
A *Canaanite*, my faithless enemy. (373–80)

This is a remarkable third confession: though spoken by the guilty accused, it achieves the juridical objectivity of the detached judge — in fact of Milton himself, whose rigorous analysis of the falls of Adam and Eve in *Paradise Lost* X, 1–16 applies equally well to Samson's offense:

Meanwhile the heinous and despiteful act
Of *Satan* done in [Sorec's Vale], and how
Hee [through gold] had perverted [Dalila],
Her Husband shee, to [cut his fatal locks],
Was known in Heav'n; for what can scape the Eye
Of God All-seeing, or deceive his Heart
Omniscient, who in all things wise and just,
Hinder'd not [Dalila] to attempt the mind
Of [Samson], with strength entire, and free will arm'd,
Complete to have discover'd and repulst
Whatever wiles of Foe [i.e., Satan] or seeming Friend
[i.e., Dalila].
For still [he] knew, and ought to have still remember'd
The high Injunction [God's secret ne'er to tell],
Whoever tempted; which [he] not obeying,
Incurr'd, what could [he] less, the penalty,
And manifold in sin, deserv'd to fall.

That the Samson we encounter even thus early in Milton's tragedy would endorse these opinions chapter and verse is evident (1) from the vaguely incremental repetition whereby, echoing God's specification of angels and men as "Authors to themselves" (*PL* III, 122) of their own sins, the blind hero calls himself "Sole Author I, sole cause" of his misery; (2) from the hint of poetic justice expressed in his conditional chiasmus, "if aught seem vile, / As vile hath been my folly"— a hint Samson quickly elaborates when he castigates his "servile mind / Rewarded well with servile punishment" (412–13); and (3) from the pitilessness with which he thrice identifies his Philistine accomplice, not indeed to lessen his offense (408–09), but rather to weigh in justice's scales the gravity of his crime: Samson has capitulated to "a woman" (bad enough), to "A *Canaanite*" (worse still), and to "my faithless enemy" (worst of all). How unlike the Ciceronian entanglements of fallen Adam who, in a parallel situation, *and in God's very presence,* makes straight seem intricate, to extenuation swift:

> This Woman whom thou mad'st to be my help,
> And gav'st me as thy perfet gift, so good,
> So fit, so acceptable, so Divine,
> That from her hand I could suspect no ill,
> And what she did, whatever in itself,
> Her doing seem'd to justify the deed;
> Shee gave me of the Tree, and I did eat.     (*PL* X, 137–43)

The full measure of Adam's retreat from conviction of sin may be taken by observing that only his last words ("Shee gave me of the Tree, and I did eat") are both relevant and true, and even they are shot through with self-extenuation.

Samson, on the other hand, specifies his own guilt with uncanny accuracy; for whereas Adam has forgotten the antiextenuating descent of Raphael, *he* remembers the Woman of Timna:

> This well I knew, nor was at all surpris'd,
> But warn'd by oft experience: did not she
> Of *Timna* first betray me, and reveal
> The secret wrested from me in her height
> Of Nuptial Love profest, carrying it straight
> To them who had corrupted her, my Spies,
> And Rivals? In this other was there found
> More Faith: who also in her prime of love,
> Spousal embraces, vitiated with Gold,
> Though offer'd only, by the scent conceiv'd
> Her spurious first-born; Treason against me?     (*SA* 381–91)

The key to this passage is its opening words, which recall the charge given to Raphael in *Paradise Lost*. Just as, to render Adam inexcusable, the angel is commissioned to "warn him to beware / He swerve not too secure" (V, 237–38), "Lest wilfully transgressing, he pretend / Surprisal, unadmonisht, unforewarn'd" (244–45), so in *Samson Agonistes* the Woman of Timna is sent as the unwitting prevenient instrument of God's antiextenuating purposes. The memory of his sinless capitulation to the Timnite (he told her the solution to the secret riddle propounded in Judges xiv, 14) forces Samson to concede the absence of extenuating circumstances in his sinful capitulation to Dalila:[64] he "was [not] at all surpris'd" at his second wife's treachery; rather, in his first marriage, he had already been "warn'd by oft experience" not to trust Philistine women (Samson's *oft* is, incidentally, a telling hyperbole, conviction of sin leading him to exaggerate the Timnite's betrayal into a multitude of deception prototypes). More than adequately forewarned, Samson ought to have been more than cavalierly forearmed against Dalila's "impuden[t]" "importunity" and unsubtle "wiles" (397–402). He knew better; he should have been more wary. Admonished by the Timnite's treachery he ought, like Adam, to have "known thyself aright" (*PL* X, 156). Undeceived no less than our grand father, he was likewise "fondly overcome" (IX, 999) with "feminine assaults" (*SA* 403). Rendered thus inexcusable and thus overwhelmed with the profoundest conviction of guilt, Samson has no recourse except to say, "in sign / Of sorrow unfeign'd, and humiliation meek" (*PL* X, 1103–04), "Sorrie I am, my God, sorrie I am, / That my offences course it in a ring."[65] Thanks be to the Woman of Timna that he does. For like Raphael (and Eve) apropos of Adam, she is the preveniently arranged occasion of Samson's regeneration.

Has Samson benefited from the Timnite marriage? Assuredly, for how else are we to account for the virtual absence of extenuation in his unremitting examination of conscience? I can find only a single instance — and that a doubtful one — in which he retreats from full conviction (63–64); otherwise the hero manifests a proper guilt for heinous crimes inexcusably perpetrated.[66] His conviction of guilt, occasioned by the recollection of the Timnite's admonitory treachery, enables a contrite Samson to confess his crime, to expiate it, to depart from evil, and to convert to good — following the same regenerative path negotiated by Adam and Eve in *Paradise Lost*. After Manoa (420–47) quite brutally goads his son by animadverting upon the Philistine feast at which Dagon will be glorified and God blasphemed, Samson convicts himself of sin yet a fourth (pivotal) time, in what I take to be an incipient act of perfect contrition:

> Father [Manoa? God?], I do acknowledge and confess
> That I this honor, I this pomp have brought
> To *Dagon*, and advanc'd his praises high
> Among the Heathen round; to God have brought
> Dishonor, obloquy, and op't the mouths
> Of Idolists, and Atheists; have brought scandal
> To *Israel*, diffidence of God, and doubt
> In feeble hearts, propense enough before
> To waver, or fall off and join with Idols:
> Which is my chief affliction, shame and sorrow,
> The anguish of my Soul, that suffers not
> Mine eye to harbor sleep, or thoughts to rest.          (448–59)

There are no more memorable or more hopeful words than these in *Samson Agonistes*. Prodded by his nightmarish, antiextenuating recollection of the Woman of Timna, and jogged by the harsh accusations of a father whose reputation he has besmirched, Samson has, to cite Arnold Stein, "moved to a full facing of his crime and its consequences, which exceed the personal and so, it may seem, the personal power to expiate by punishment, or to have any human relation to, except that of a despairing recognition. The high point of moral advance, then, is the low point of psychological retreat. . . . Here we have the place marked, the point where the two lines cross. What shall we call these lines, or is there a name?"[67]

There is indeed a name — or rather two names — for this crucial conjunction of ethical progress and affective regression: Aristotle's anagnoresis (recognition or discovery) and peripeteia (reversal). The plot of *Samson Agonistes* is, as Milton's prefatory epistle puts it (echoing *Poetics* 10), "intricate" rather than "explicit"; in such plots the catastrophe is accompanied by (and ideally is effected by) either recognition ("a change from ignorance to knowledge") or reversal of fortune ("a change from one state of affairs to its opposite") or — even better, as in Sophocles' *Oedipus Tyrannos* — both (*Poetics* 11). Now Milton's tragedy outdoes its Hellenic predecessors by arranging for its catastrophic denouement to be the consequence of two anagnoresis-peripeteia complexes. The first — thanks be to the Woman of Timna — occurs early in this tragedy of regeneration when, in the fourth stage of a regenerative sequence, Samson recognizes *and confesses* the full hideousness of his offenses, including their farthest-reaching sinful implications.[68] His discovery is coextensive with and causes an immediate reversal of fortune, for conviction enables Samson to move beyond a purely despairing confession (of the sort that exulcerates Satan's tormented conscience in *Paradise Lost* IV, 13–113) to the faintly but genuinely felt hypothesis that he can sorrowfully atone for his transgressions.

Thus in a fifth admission of guilt (following hard upon its pivotal predecessor), Samson hopes (I use the term advisedly) to "pay on my punishment; / *And expiate, if possible, my crime*" (489–90; emphasis mine). This is admittedly only the subtlest, most tenuous hint of a brighter future — a secret joy, weakly clasped in the midmost heart of guilty grief — but it is decisive, and the advice Manoa now gives —"Be penitent and for thy fault contrite" (502) — has already been enacted: Thanks be to his Timnite bride, Samson's sixth confession (522–40) is preceded by the vital addition "[God's] pardon I implore" (521), a gesture that repeats fallen Adam's and Eve's restorative decision to "confess / Humbly our faults, and pardon beg, with tears" and "sighs" "sent from hearts contrite" (*PL* X, 1086–91). Although Samson's seventh (558–76) and eighth (999–1002) declarations of sin show signs of despair and disorientation, they are only minor reversals, the first brought on by the transient "sense of Heav'n's desertion" (632), the second a dramatic irony significant in the main for the matter-of-factness with which Samson can now allude succinctly to his offenses, contrite confession having largely neutralized conviction's "deadly stings" (623). Hence the ninth and last stage in the hero's exorcism of guilt and sorrow requires only the catalytic intervention of a male complement to the Woman of Timna. When Harapha of Gath taunts Samson (1156–67) by cruelly inventorying the punishments he has (unjustly) endured, Samson finds on the contrary that

> these evils I deserve and more,
> Acknowledge them from God inflicted on me
> Justly.                                        (1169–71)

But this is — dare I say it? — an almost trivial or at any rate a peremptory confession: it is as if Samson, having spread guilt thin by fully eight times rehearsing his known offense and God's own retributive justice, becomes impatient at reiterating a conviction by now self-evident (to everyone but Harapha). Anyway, regenerate Samson has more important things on his mind than crime and punishment:

> [I] despair not of [God's] final pardon
> Whose ear is ever open; and his eye
> Gracious to re-admit the suppliant.             (1171–73)

This hard-won insight, no labor of a Sabbath day, echoes and confirms regenerate Adam's conviction that "if we pray him, will [God's] ear / Be open, and his heart to pity incline" (*PL* X, 1060–61): both Samson and he are voicing an optimism altogether warranted, for both are (unwittingly) echoing God's promise in *Paradise Lost* III that

> To Prayer, repentance, and obedience due,
> Though but endeavor'd with sincere intent,
> *Mine ear shall not be slow, mine eye not shut.*
>                                 (191–93; emphasis mine)

At this juncture a fully revivified Samson has been readmitted to Naziriteship, and *Samson Agonistes* can proceed now rather more quickly than before to its climactic catastrophe. When Samson later declines to commit idolatry, a sin "which in [God's] jealousy / Shall never, *unrepented,* find forgiveness" (1375–76; emphasis mine), he knows whereof he speaks, for he has experienced, fully and deeply, the opposite process whereby *any* sin, however grievous, may become as if it were not. For the gift of sorrow unfeigned and humiliation meek that punctuates all nine of repentant Samson's laments, he owes thanks first to a loving God, whose prevenient grace descending has softened his stony heart, and second to the Woman of Timna, whom a provident God has sent to render him inexcusable:

> This well I knew, nor was at all surpris'd,
> But warn'd by oft experience: did not she
> Of *Timna* first betray me, and reveal
> The secret wrested from me in her height
> Of Nuptial Love profest, carrying it straight
> To them who had corrupted her, my Spies,
> And Rivals?

She did indeed, and no man ever owed more to a treacherous spouse: for her contribution to his first (*felix*) *culpa* Samson must therefore sing, *"Timnae gratias!"*

### III

I began this paper by citing epigraphically the concluding lines of *A Mask*, and I would like to return now to that point of departure. The poem contains Milton's first attempt to utilize the epic motif of celestial descent in anything like sustained fashion. The attendant Spirit who oversees its action descends from "the starry threshold of *Jove's* Court" (1) in order to protect the virtuous (12–15) — specifically a young Lady and her two Brothers — from the wicked enchantments of Comus. The descent is arranged and accomplished preveniently (78–82) in order to verify the heroine's conviction that

> the Supreme good, t' whom all things ill
> Are but as slavish officers of vengeance,
> Would send a glist'ring Guardian, if need were,
> To keep my life and honor unassail'd.                    (217–20)

The Lady's point is later reiterated by her Elder Brother (453–63), who complacently assures himself that his lost sister's virgin innocence will conduct her safely through the wild Wood into which she has wandered. The Brother imagines her safe conduct in terms of the motif of celestial descent:

> So dear to Heav'n is Saintly chastity,
> That when a soul is found sincerely so,
> A thousand liveried Angels lacky her,
> Driving far off each thing of sin and guilt.                    (453–56)

In any realistic reckoning these sentiments are pure hyperbole; and indeed by the time the Elder Brother, having learned that his sister is the captive of Comus, sets off on a search and rescue operation, reality's dark dream has shrunken his optimistic mathematics and transformed his facile confidence into the more modest entreaty "some good angel bear a shield before us" (658). But although he relies less now on supernature than on his drawn sword to protect the Lady, in the fantasy world of *A Mask* it is only the Brother's arithmetic that turns out to have been exaggerated: his prayer for a good angel has been answered before its utterance — in the person of the attendant Spirit disguised as the shepherd Thyrsis. After assorted complications (designed primarily to enhance the impact of the poem as spectacle) the Lady is duly rescued, safe, sound, and quite virginal. By way of conclusion the attendant Spirit "*Epiloguizes*," sententiously and magically, in propria persona:

> But now my task is smoothly done,
> I can fly, or I can run
> Quickly to the green earth's end,
> Where the bow'd welkin slow doth bend,
> And from thence can soar as soon
> To the corners of the Moon.                    (1012–17)

Consistent with the decorum of its genre, *A Mask* thus emphasizes the frankly contrived supernaturalism of its plot. Such is the firmly persuasive power of virtue in Milton's transcendental allegory that chastity can cause earthquakes (793–99), traverse the skies, and even summon God down to earth:

> Mortals that would follow me,
> Love virtue, she alone is free,
> She can teach ye how to climb
> Higher than the Sphery chime;
> Or if Virtue feeble were,
> Heav'n itself would stoop to her.              (1018–23)

In his anxiety to certify virtue's ability to venture Neoplatonistically beyond the primum mobile, the attendant Spirit speaks of celestial descent only hypothetically (for "Virtue" most emphatically is *not* "feeble"), but his apodosis may be taken indicatively and unconditionally, for the Spirit's own role in *A Mask* has been literally to stoop from Heaven in Heaven's stead virtue to defend.

The author of *Paradise Lost* knew, on the other hand, that in our world such dei ex machina as the attendant Spirit are hard to come by: that is why in his diffuse epic Milton reserves the notion of angelic descent for a time (*in illo tempore*) and a place (the fresh woods and pastures new of Paradise) in which such literal visitations might appear plausible. At the same time he immeasurably complicates the matter (compared to his practice in *A Mask*) by availing himself of certain motivational distinctions that he may have discovered in Vergil. Although

Mercury descends in the IVth *Aeneid* ostensibly to hasten Aeneas' departure from Carthage, Vergil is also concerned with the god's role as *psy-
chopompous*— guide to the underworld — a role that Hermes fulfills (for
example) in the XXIVth *Odyssey*. As Thomas Greene has pointed out,
"The chthonic associations of Mercury's staff [in the *Aeneid*] anticipate . . . the literal death of Dido, a death which his descent is to bring
about. Mercury's mission *is actually* to send a soul to the Lower World."[69]
We have seen that just this sort of distinction between apparent and
actual motives is needed to come to terms with the mission of Raphael
in *Paradise Lost*: allegedly conceived in pity but apparently executed
in legalistic self-righteousness, the angel's descent turns out *in the event*
actually to have been a restorative work of merciful supererogation. In
*Samson Agonistes* such motivational bifurcation is still more pronounced:
in the event (and only then) Samson's marriage to the Woman of Timna
is seen to have been designed by a loving God less to slaughter Philistines than to hasten the hero's regeneration — even if to his dying day Samson never comprehends this truth. But then why *should* the Danite perfectly fathom God's "uncontrollable intent" (1754)? Like everyone else
in the play, he frequently utters misspoken prophecies and essays erroneous projections of the divine will. To know more about why God urged
him to marry the Timnite obviously does not concern Samson (since he
no further knows); nor, more importantly, would such knowledge alter
his known offense.

　　*Samson Agonistes* of course returns us to the fallen world of *A Mask*;
moreover it is generically a tragedy, and if we may believe the prefatory
epistle, its author will have taken care in the "disposition of the fable"
to observe standards of "verisimilitude and decorum," standards derived
presumably from the Greek "Tragic Poets, the best rule to all who endeavor to write Tragedy." We can expect Milton assiduously to have avoided
any overt use of the celestial descent motif in his play, for it is probable
that he shared Aristotle's reservations about the appropriateness in tragedy of such a deus ex machina: "it is obvious that the unravelling of the
plot should arise from the circumstances of the plot itself, and not be
brought about ex machina. . . . The deus ex machina should be used only
for matters outside the play proper, either for things that happened before it and cannot be known by the human characters, or for things that
are yet to come and that require to be foretold prophetically—for we
allow to the gods the power to see all things. However, there should be
nothing inexplicable about what happens" (*Poetics* 15). In *Samson Agonistes* Milton is even more cautious than Aristotle about the deus ex machina: although God is everywhere present in the plot machinery, he and
his providential instruments come and go on viewless wings; any and all

miraculous celestial descents occur strictly offstage and are relegated to the distant past (23–29, 361). The poet is so concerned with exorcising the magical from his version of the Samson saga that he even demystifies the hero's hair, insisting that Samson's Herculean strength is circumfused throughout his body rather than somehow — God knows how — resident in his ample locks (1140–44).

But it is with regard to the Woman of Timna that Milton most skillfully makes a virtue of the verisimilitude enjoined upon him by the Aristotelian norms of tragic action. On the one hand, the regeneration of fallen Samson *must* proceed as a consequence of prevenient grace descending — Milton's theology demands as much. But on the other hand there can be no Raphael to descend ex machina in violation of tragic decorum. As Irene Samuel has said (albeit to quite different effect), "Milton's is so distinctively the ethic of the will and reason freely choosing that a deus ex machina resolution of plot would be repugnant to him on theological and moral no less than on artistic grounds."[70] I quite agree: Samson must oft be warned his sinful state by ordinary human means — so the extraordinary genius of Milton hits upon the quiet expedient of the Woman of Timna. Whereas a late redactor of Judges, embarrassed by the frankly sexual motivation of Samson's gentile marriage, added verse xiv, 4 (as a corrective scholium) to the preformed units between which it appears in the received text,[71] Milton goes the redactor one step better: in *Samson Agonistes* the Timnite becomes the indispensable *femina* ex machina when, in a master stroke of poetic compression, Milton calls upon her to do for Samson precisely what Raphael has done for Adam and Eve. In this way the poet can orchestrate the resolution of his tragedy's plot complications by relying on divine intervention (for only God can soften Samson's stony heart), but without forfeiting a scintilla of human probability (for there is no God but only a mere woman in the visible renovative machinery).

Moreover, the substitution of the Woman of Timna for Raphael has the additional convenience of anticipating Milton's kenotic Christology. The following parody of a stanza from *Ode on the Morning of Christ's Nativity* may serve to illustrate the point:

> That glorious Form, that angel affable,
> And that far-beaming blaze of Majesty,
> Wherewith God planned at Heav'n's high Council-Table,
> To help our father admit sin's gravity,
> He laid aside; and Samson thus to free,
> Forsook to call on Raphael that Day,
> But chose instead a Timnite bride, though made of
>     mortal Clay.

The decision to substitute the Woman of Timna for Raphael is as much Milton's as it is God's, of course; and how felicitously our poet has chosen! Mary Ann Radzinowicz has noted that in *Samson Agonistes* (and, I would add, in *Paradise Lost* as well) "predestination is adjusted to liberty so that from the human point of view it will always appear that God improvises after the event."[72] The Timnite episode seems to be such an improvisation, for Milton's God *appears* to have sent the Woman of Timna for the stated purpose of harrying Philistines and only post hoc — after Samson has succumbed to Dalila — to have devised a second strategy wherein she hastens Samson's regeneration by convicting him of sin. In reality, however, the whole scenario has been part of that predestination by which, thanks to his prescience, a loving God can providentially arrange for his creatures' regeneration before they have sinned.

In the prefatory epistle to *Samson Agonistes* Milton observes that "Tragedy, as it was anciently compos'd, hath ever been held the gravest, moralest, and most profitable of all other poems." Doubtless he has in mind chapter 26 of the *Poetics*, in which Aristotle compares epic and tragedy in order to document the aesthetic superiority of the latter:

> tragedy has everything that epic has. . . . Moreover, this form of imitation achieves its ends in shorter compass, and what is more compact gives more pleasure than what is extended over a long period. . . . Then there is less unity in the imitation of the epic poets, as is shown by the fact that any one work of this kind contains matter for several tragedies. . . . If, therefore, tragedy is superior to epic in all these respects, and also in fulfilling its artistic function, . . . then obviously, in achieving its ends better than epic, it must be the better form of art.

Although I hesitate to impose Aristotle's evaluative categories upon Milton's poetry — for as I have argued, *Paradise Lost* is an epic with a tragic center, and as I have implied, *Samson Agonistes* extends the boundaries of tragedy into epic — still I am tempted to conclude, from the solid intricacy packed into its Timnite episode, that Milton's closet drama outdoes even his Old Testament epic in the matter of poetic excellence.

The University of Texas, El Paso

### NOTES

I wish to thank the following individuals for helping me revise this paper: Eugene Cunnar, Louis Feldman, Mary Ann Radzinowicz, Irene Samuel, Camille Slights, Robert West, and Joseph Wittreich. I am especially grateful to James Simmonds, whose suggestions for condensation were particularly apt, and to my friend and colleague Larry Johnson, whose editorial wizardry continues to amaze me. The essay as a whole had its genesis in the reading of Milton proposed by my mentor John James Teunissen; for without contraries is no progression.

1. *Toward "Samson Agonistes": The Growth of Milton's Mind* (Princeton, 1978), p. xix.

2. All citations of Milton's poetry will be to *John Milton: Complete Poems and Major Prose*, ed. Merritt Y. Hughes (New York, 1957).

3. In my view, the definitive case for the traditional chronology has been made by Radzinowicz, among others. See *Toward "Samson Agonistes,"* Appendix E, "The Date of Composition of *Samson Agonistes,*" pp. 387–407.

4. Joseph Anthony Wittreich, Jr., *Visionary Poetics: Milton's Tradition and His Legacy* (San Marino, Calif., 1979), p. 191.

5. *Christian Doctrine* I, iv, in the *Complete Prose Works of John Milton*, ed. Don M. Wolfe et al. (New Haven, 1953–82), VI, p. 181. All citations of Milton's prose will be to this edition, hereafter cited as YP.

6. Edward Tayler, "Milton's *Samson*: The Form of a Christian Tragedy," *English Literary Renaissance*, III (1973), 317.

7. William Kerrigan, *The Prophetic Milton* (Charlottesville, Va., 1974), p. 203.

8. *The Blaze of Noon: A Reading of "Samson Agonistes"* (New York, 1974), p. 63.

9. "Calm Regained through Passion Spent: The Conclusions of the Miltonic Effort," in *The Prison and the Pinnacle*, ed. Balachandra Rajan (Toronto, 1973), pp. 13–16.

10. Rajan, "'To Which Is Added *Samson Agonistes*—'" in *The Prison and the Pinnacle*, ed. Rajan, p. 98; Radzinowicz, *Toward "Samson Agonistes,"* p. 284.

11. *Visionary Poetics*, pp. 208–09.

12. Ibid., p. 207.

13. Aristotle, *Poetics* 13, in *Classical Literary Criticism*, trans. T. S. Dorsch (Baltimore, 1965), p. 48.

14. But is Manoa right? See *Lycidas* 165–85, *PL* XII, 645–49, and Revelation vii, 17 and xxi, 4 for corroboration.

15. "*Samson Agonistes* as Tragedy," in *Calm of Mind: Tercentenary Essays on "Paradise Regained" and "Samson Agonistes,"* ed. Joseph Anthony Wittreich, Jr. (Cleveland, 1971), p. 239.

16. *The Reason of Church Government Urged Against Prelaty*, the introduction to Book II (*YP* I, 815); repeated thus in the prefatory epistle to *Samson Agonistes*: "Paraeus, commenting on the *Revelation*, divides the whole Book as a Tragedy, into Acts distinguisht each by a Chorus of Heavenly Harpings and Song between."

17. *Paradise Regained* more explicitly rejects Aristotle's sentimentalized definition of tragedy: according to Christ (*PR* IV, 310–12), the Greek tragedians are "Ignorant . . . / . . . how man fell / Degraded by himself" (the true Miltonic definition of tragic *hamartia*).

18. Of the thirty-four extant Greek tragedies only Sophocles' *Oedipus at Colonus* might genuinely be called a "tragedy of regeneration."

19. *Visionary Poetics*, p. 207.

20. Introduction to *Samson Agonistes*, in *The Poems of John Milton*, ed. John Carey and Alastair Fowler (London, 1968), pp. 335–43.

21. "Question and Answer in *Samson Agonistes,*" *The Critical Quarterly*, IX (1969), 263; "The 'true experience' of *Samson Agonistes,*" *MQ*, XIII (1979), 91–92; "'This Great Deliverer': *Samson Agonistes* as Parable," *MQ*, XIII (1979), 81–82.

22. *Toward "Samson Agonistes,"* p. 187.

23. Recent studies of the mission (that is, of *Paradise Lost* V, 219–450) have emphasized its biblical analogues, especially vis-à-vis the meal Adam and Eve serve Raphael. The work of her predecessors is conveniently summarized by Beverley Sherry, "Not by Bread Alone: The Communication of Adam and Raphael," *MQ,* XIII (1979), 111–14. The fullest treatment I know of the protocols of the visit is by Thomas Greene, whose work I cite in my next note.

24. Echoing, among others, *Iliad* II, 166–67 and *Aeneid* IV, 238–39. Many classical analogues to the descent of Raphael have been studied by Thomas Greene, *The Descent from Heaven: A Study in Epic Continuity* (New Haven, 1963).

25. *The Descent from Heaven,* p. 409.

26. Many allegedly impossible missions in *Paradise Lost* have been studied by Boyd M. Berry, who comments, in *Process of Speech: Puritan Religious Writings and "Paradise Lost"* (Baltimore, 1976), p. 179, "Milton's God repeatedly sends his creatures on missions which are strategically impossible and eventuate in no conclusion." He mentions Raphael's trip to Hell (VIII, 229–46) as "one such impossible mission."

27. In *"Paradise Lost" and the Classical Epic* (London, 1979), pp. 25–34, 47–48.

28. Greene, *The Descent from Heaven,* pp. 57–58, 99.

29. Ibid., p. 405.

30. "Structural and Doctrinal Pattern in Milton's Later Poems," in *Essays in English Literature from the Renaissance to the Victorian Age,* ed. Millar MacLure and F. W. Watt (Toronto, 1964), p. 187.

31. "Calm Regained through Passion Spent," in *The Prison and the Pinnacle,* ed. Rajan, pp. 12–13.

32. *Reading "Paradise Lost"* (Bloomington, Ind., 1980), p. 137.

33. *Visionary Poetics,* p. 34.

34. *The Descent from Heaven,* p. 409.

35. *Works and Days,* 83–89; in *Hesiod,* trans. Richmond Lattimore (Ann Arbor, Mich., 1959), pp. 27–29. All citations of Hesiod will be to this edition.

36. The same paraenetic purposes are operative in Hesiod's *Theogony,* 508–616, which recounts a slightly different version of the Promethean myth: there, emphasizing the punishment of the fire-stealer, Hesiod concludes: "So it is not possible to hide from the mind of Zeus, nor escape it; for not even the son of Iapetos, the gentle Prometheus, was able to elude that heavy anger, but, for all his numerous shifts, force and the mighty chain confine him" (613–16).

37. The identification of Pandora with Eve was a Renaissance commonplace. For example, see Henry Reynolds, *Mythomystes* (1632?), repr. in Edward Tayler, *Literary Criticism of Seventeenth-Century England* (New York, 1967), p. 256. That Milton censured Prometheus as a parody of Satan is implicit in his youthful poem *"In Inventorum Bombardae,"* in Prolusion II, "On the Harmony of the Spheres," in his *Defense of the English People* (YP IV, 1, 424–25), and in innumerable passages from *Paradise Lost.*

38. So Milton calls Adam in the *Doctrine and Discipline of Divorce* (YP II, 294).

39. I hasten to add that *Hesiod* does not view Zeus and Hermes in the pejorative light in which I have cast them; in the ancient world it took Aeschylus to do so — in the *Prometheus Bound.* Hesiod everywhere reveres Zeus, which confirms the view of Hugh Lloyd-Jones that the primordial "Greek notion of the divine . . . differed utterly from the Jewish or Christian notion," and that *"from a modern point of view"* the "gods are monstrously unjust. But for Homer, and for later poets also, they are perfectly within their rights" (*The Justice of Zeus* [Berkeley, Calif., 1971], pp. 3–4; emphasis mine).

40. Homer, *Odyssey* I, 28–43, trans. Albert Cook (New York, 1967), pp. 3–4.

41. On which see the learned commentary of M. L. West, ed., *Hesiod: "Theogony"* (Oxford, 1966), pp. 40–48.

42. *The Justice of Zeus*, p. 28.

43. In the *Christian Doctrine* I, xi, Milton catalogues the hideous litany of offenses included under the rubric of Original Sin (YP VI, 383–84).

44. For recent studies of this thesis see Philip J. Gallagher, "'Real or Allegoric': The Ontology of Sin and Death in *Paradise Lost*," *English Literary Renaissance*, VI (1976), 317–35, and "*Paradise Lost* and the Greek *Theogony*," *English Literary Renaissance*, IX (1979), 121–48.

45. I borrow the term from Desmond Hamlet, *One Greater Man: Justice and Damnation in "Paradise Lost"* (Lewisburg, Pa., 1976).

46. *The Shadow of Heaven: Matter and Stance in Milton's Poetry* (Ithaca, N.Y., 1968), p. 160.

47. For contrary readings, namely, that the regenerative processes of *Paradise Lost* proceed by quantum leaps and radical equivocations that are ultimately inexplicable in human terms, see Georgia Christopher, "The Verbal Gate to Paradise: Adam's 'Literary Experience' in Book X of *Paradise Lost*," *PMLA*, XC (1975), 69–77, and Boyd M. Berry, *Process of Speech*, pp. 254–67.

48. Because the announcement that prevenient grace has done its work is made ex post facto in Book XI, commentators have wrongly assumed the prevenient motions themselves to have begun only in Book X: Arthur Barker expresses this commonplace in his essay "*Paradise Lost:* The Relevance of Regeneration," in *"Paradise Lost": A Tercentenary Tribute*, ed. Balachandra Rajan (Toronto, 1967), pp. 65–67.

49. Justice does not require the descent of Raphael, for even without it Adam and Eve ought to have remembered the high injunction not to eat the Fruit; even without Raphael they were sufficiently forewarned. See X, 1–16, and Philip J. Gallagher, "'More Theirs by Being His': Teaching Milton to Undergraduates," *MQ*, XI (1977), 4–9.

50. *The Faerie Queene* II, viii, 1–2; in *Spenser: Poetical Works*, ed. J. C. Smith and E. De Sélincourt (1912; rpt. London, 1965), p. 106.

51. "The Regaining of Paradise," in *The Prison and the Pinnacle*, ed. Rajan, p. 116.

52. *Milton's Samson and the Christian Tradition* (Princeton, 1949), p. 89. Krouse waffles on the matter because he wants to see *Samson Agonistes* as an allegory and its hero as a type of Christ (pp. 119–33, especially 119–24).

53. "Structure and Style in Judges 13–16," *Journal of Biblical Literature*, LXXXII (1963), 65.

54. Ibid., p. 66.

55. Don Cameron Allen, "The Idea as Pattern: Despair and *Samson Agonistes*," in *The Harmonious Vision: Studies in Milton's Poetry* (1954; rpt. Baltimore, 1970), p. 83.

56. "*Samson Agonistes* and the Geneva Bible," in *Milton and This Pendant World* (Austin, Tex., 1958), pp. 201–22; "'The Lord's Battells': *Samson Agonistes* and the Puritan Revolution," in *Milton Studies*, IV, ed. James D. Simmonds (Pittsburgh, 1972), pp. 42, 48.

57. In 541–52. Milton may or may not have understood the word *misteh*. AV has "made there a feast" (xiv, 10), usage echoed in *SA* 1193–94.

58. Samson's decision to go with the Officer culminates a debate with the Chorus (1348–90) that anachronistically invokes distinctions found in Renaissance textbooks of moral theology. Camille Slights has studied the influence of these "cases of conscience" on Milton's play in "*Samson Agonistes* and Casuistry," *PMLA*, XC (1975), 395–413.

59. Slights, "*Samson Agonistes* and Casuistry," p. 398.

60. His ambivalence is perhaps the legacy of slavish adherence to the Mosaic law; on Milton's attitude to such adherence see Samuel S. Stollman, "Milton's Dichotomy of 'Judaism' and 'Hebraism,'" *PMLA*, LXXXIX (1974), 105–12. Alternatively, Manoa may be egotistically unable to approve Samson's "marriage choices," which *he* "approv'd . . . not" (420–24).

61. On the soundness of this Choral justification see Samuel S. Stollman, "Milton's Samson and the Jewish Tradition, in *Milton Studies*, III, ed. Simmonds (Pittsburgh, 1971), pp. 185–200, and especially Joan S. Bennett, "Liberty Under the Law: The Chorus and the Meaning of *Samson Agonistes*," in *Milton Studies*, XII, ed. Simmonds (Pittsburgh, 1978), pp. 150–53. (The Chorus is repeating distinctions articulated by Abdiel in *PL* V, 822–25; see also *SA* 322–24, which echo *PL* V, 826–31.)

62. Albert C. Labriola, "Divine Urgency as a Motive for Conduct in *Samson Agonistes*," *PQ*, L (1971), 102–03.

63. Quoting the felicitous language of Arnold Stein, *Heroic Knowledge* (Minneapolis, 1957), p. 146. Stein, however, concludes that Samson sins in marrying Dalila (pp. 145–46, 172) So do Anthony Low (*The Blaze of Noon*, p. 133) and (if somewhat equivocatingly) John S. Hill ("Vocation and Spiritual Renovation in *Samson Agonistes*," in *Milton Studies*, II ed. Simmonds [Pittsburgh, 1970], pp. 155–56) and (emphatically) Joan Bennett ("Liberty Under the Law," p. 153). Nevertheless I stand firmly with those critics who understand Samson's second marriage as sinless per se. See F. Michael Krouse, *Milton's Samson and the Christian Tradition*, pp. 96–97; John M. Steadman, "'Faithful Champion': The Theological Basis of Milton's Hero of Faith," *Anglia*, LXXVII (1959), 17; Samuel S. Stollman, "Milton's Samson and the Jewish Tradition," pp. 189–92; and (most persuasively) Camille W. Slights, "*Samson Agonistes* and Casuistry," p. 399.

64. Since Samson invented the riddle about honey coming out of the lion's mouth (*SA* 1016–17, 1064), it was within his jurisdiction to reveal it to whomever he pleased: hence, while he erred prudentially in telling it to the Timnite Woman, he did not sin thereby. The Nazirite secret was not his to tell, however; it was God's.

65. George Herbert, "Sinnes round," 1–2, *The Works of George Herbert*, ed. F. E. Hutchinson (Oxford, 1942), p. 122.

66. Georgia B. Christopher, "Homeopathic Physic and Natural Renovation in *Samson Agonistes*," *ELH*, XXXVII (1970), 361–73, argues however that Samson continues to extenuate until the apperance of Dalila, who stimulates his sense of conviction homeopathically.

67. *Heroic Knowledge*, p. 153.

68. The second occurs late in the play when, imitating *Oedipus*, Milton has a Public Officer summon Samson to the Dagonalia. "In *Oedipus* . . . the Messenger who came to cheer Oedipus and relieve him of his fear about his mother did the very opposite [peripeteia] by revealing to him who he was [anagnoresis]" (*Poetics* 11); in *Samson Agonistes* the Public Officer who comes to induce Samson to entertain the Philistines does the very opposite (occasions their destruction) by revealing to him what he can do (he can sinlessly disobey the second commandment).

69. *The Descent from Heaven*, p. 82; emphasis mine.

70. "*Samson Agonistes* as Tragedy," p. 242.

71. See *The Anchor Bible: Judges*, introduction, translation, and commentary by Robert G. Boling (Garden City, N.Y., 1975), pp. 229–30, n. 4.

72. Toward "*Samson Agonistes*," p. 47.